Ghost Images

Ghost Images

Cinema of the Afterlife

TOM RUFFLES

McFarland & Company, Inc., Publishers
Jefferson, North Carolina, and London

LIBRARY OF CONGRESS CATALOGUING-IN-PUBLICATION DATA

Ruffles, Tom, 1957–
    Ghost images : cinema of the afterlife / Tom Ruffles.
    p.   cm.
    Includes bibliographical references and index.

    ISBN 0-7864-2005-7 (softcover : 50# alkaline paper) ∞

    1. Ghosts in motion pictures.   I. Title.
PN1995.9.S8R84   2004
791.43'672—dc22   2004017522

British Library cataloguing data are available

©2004 Tom Ruffles. All rights reserved

No part of this book may be reproduced or transmitted in any form or by any means, electronic or mechanical, including photocopying or recording, or by any information storage and retrieval system, without permission in writing from the publisher.

Manufactured in the United States of America

On the cover: Drs. Venkman (Bill Murray), Spengler (Harold Ramis) and Stantz (Dan Aykroyd) are hi-tech *Ghostbusters* (1984)

McFarland & Company, Inc., Publishers
  Box 611, Jefferson, North Carolina 28640
    www.mcfarlandpub.com

For Karen

Acknowledgments

Thanks are owed to a number of people who gave valuable advice during the long gestation of this project: Charles Barr and Andrew Higson at The University of East Anglia; the librarians at UEA; the British Film Institute; The Society for Psychical Research and the Theatre Museum; Alan Wesencraft, past curator of the Harry Price Library, University of London; and the late Vernon Sewell, who generously shared memories of his films with me. Above all, thanks go to my wife, Karen, who gave me unflagging support and encouragement throughout.

An earlier version of part of the material on precursors to cinematic ghosts which appears in Chapter 3 was first published as Phantasmagoria Ghost Shows in *Udolpho* (Magazine of The Gothic Society), Volume 30, Autumn 1997, reprinted in the *Newsletter* of the Magic Lantern Society, No. 53, June 1998.

Table of Contents

Acknowledgments vii

Introduction 1

1. Visual Precursors to Cinematic Ghosts 11
2. Silent Ghosts 34
3. A Thematic Approach to Cinematic Ghosts 55
   Anatomy of Film Ghosts 55
   Representations of Ghosts 61
   Interactions with Matter 67
   Psychokinesis Versus Ghosts 70
   Ghosts of Those Who Cannot Rest 70
   The Expiation of Sins 75
   Consolation for the Living 77
   Ghosts Who Dispense Sage Advice 78
   Ghosts Who Return Because of Unfinished Business 82
   Ghosts of and for Children 87
   Ghost Lovers 89
   Ghost Lovers Who Return to Break the Bond 93
   AIDS-Related Ghosts 94
   "Hungry Ghosts" 95

Table of Contents

Ghosts Who Use the Living to Play Out a Drama from Their Own Lives	96
Possession	97
Meetings with the Ghost of Elvis	101
The Ghost in the Machine	101
Continuation Without Awareness of Death	103
The Haunted House	104
Ghosts of the Living	110
Ghosts That Appear to Be Phony but Are Real	111
The Parapsychologist	112
Mediumship	117
Near-Death Experiences	124
The Figure of Death	131
Depictions of Heaven and Purgatory	133
Angels	136
Summary	141
4. Ghost Films: Selected Case Studies	142
Dead of Night (1945)	142
A Matter of Life and Death (1946)	151
The Innocents (1961)	159
The Haunting (1963)	168
The Shining (1980)	180
Jacob's Ladder (1990)	191
5. Conclusion	199
Filmography	207
Chapter Notes	217
Bibliography	241
Index	257

Introduction

Ghosts pull us in two directions: they frighten us but at the same time console us, hinting that death might not be the end. Their ubiquity in both fiction and ostensibly non-fiction forms suggests a deep resonance in the psyche, a fascination with something that seems superficially to be frightening. At one level they are inscrutable; at another they are all too knowable, as we could be looking at our own futures reflected back to us. Fiction renders them palatable in a way that they might not be if we met them face to face.

But although the depiction of life after death on film has been a perennial topic in cinema, it is a little examined one. This is partly because of the ambivalence with which Western society regards death, and partly because of an association with what have been regarded as sub-literary and unwholesome forms—Gothic and horror literature, and subsequently horror films and comics. With increased critical interest in previously marginal fields, it is time to reappraise ghost cinema in the way that, for example, Gothic literature has been rehabilitated as a serious area of study. This is not to argue for any great aesthetic merit in the majority of ghost films, but to indicate that many, and particularly the best, address emotions that both attract and repel, and in so doing tell us something about ourselves.

Films do not exist in a vacuum, but are part of a discourse that incorporates books, magazine and newspaper articles, and television programs. Whether ostensibly fiction or non-fiction, these media, with their depiction of the paranormal as usually comprising extreme events, form a background against which reception of filmic ghosts should be judged. For example, William Evans has demonstrated that "there is a correlation between watching entertainment television and credulity,"[1] and that programs such as *The X-Files* help to create a climate in which it is assumed that the paranormal is normal. This entails suggesting that science is inadequate to the task of fully describing reality. Skepticism is usually a hindrance, often caused by scientists' being closed-minded.

Attempts to assess the likelihood of a given paranormal phenomenon is made even more difficult by those films which straddle fiction and (possibly) fact by dramatizing allegedly true stories, such as *The Search for Bridey Murphy*[2] or, more controversially, *The Amityville Horror*.[3] That it can be difficult for the viewer to make judgments about the verisimilitude of what is shown is indicated by the television production *Ghostwatch* (1992), modeled loosely on the Enfield Poltergeist case,[4] the resulting controversy showed that many viewers could not differentiate between special effects and something genuinely paranormal. There is thus a tripartite split in representations of the paranormal between what is presented as fiction, as alleged fact (the status of which might be unclear), and as an amalgam (prone to exaggeration for dramatic effect).

Some aspects of the supernatural are more amenable to treatment by cinema than others, which can easily create distortions of what has been discovered by parapsychologists. James McClenon portrays ostensibly paranormal occurrences in general as "wondrous events,"[5] but it is clear that some types of wonder are more photogenic than others. Apparitions, poltergeists, reincarnation and mediumship, for example, have become standard, albeit in a distorted form, because of their dramatic potential; card-guessing extra-sensory perception (ESP) experiments tend not to fare so well.[6] Poltergeists are portrayed as energetic manifestations of malevolence by a discarnate entity, whereas psychical researchers investigating a real-life case might look for a psychokinetic effect — the action of a living mind on matter at a distance — generated by one or more of the living personnel involved. Reincarnation is often reduced to a "body swap" comedy unknown in parapsychological literature.

While the post–Stoker vampire is usually aristocratic, and the zombie has a working-class ambience, the ghost achieves a kind of universality. Ghosts and hauntings exercise such a profound effect that Stephen King considers the ghost to be an archetype.[7] On the other hand Joseph Grixti stresses the extent to which ghost narratives are conditioned by cultural context.[8] Balancing these views, McClenon distinguishes between the "cultural source" and "experiential source" hypotheses.[9] The former states that supernatural narratives are culturally conditioned, from which one would conclude that they should differ from each other according to a particular tradition, the latter that they are constant across cultures, although colored by local conditions. He concludes, broadly in agreement with King, that a wide range of phenomena, including the ghost, are common across cultures, with only superficial variations.

Certainly, ghosts have a recorded history stretching back to antiquity.[10] This makes Mladen Dolar's assertion that ghosts "are something brought about by modernity itself,"[11] based on their coexistence with scientific rationality during the late eighteenth century, seem bizarre. Terry Castle sees a movement in the opposite direction, asking, "Why do we no longer believe in ghosts?"[12] Neither extreme is tenable. Attitudes towards the supernatural are not unitary, and ghosts considered to be genuine spirits coexist alongside fraud, misperception and mental instability. The analysis provided by Defoe's *Essay on the History and Reality of Apparitions* of 1727 which Castle sees as a transitional narrative, combining ghosts as objective with ghosts as mental constructs,[13] is still pertinent.

So what is it that makes ghosts as relevant to people today as in antiquity? They are reminders of mortality, but also invoke fear of what is *beyond* death, with its religious implications, a fascination that still exists in a largely secular society. A tension is set up between the desire for the survival of the personality, and fear of possible consequences. The fictional ghost is protean, but it is always relevant. Those on film have a variety of motives, benign and sinister, a confused response partly due to the distancing of Western society's relationship with the dead over the last two hundred years. Rendered safe by being marginalized from daily life, the memory of the deceased was celebrated and a kind of immortality assured. Films, and not just those showing ghosts, are a kind of extension of the *memento mori*.[14]

Genre Issues

Fictional ghost narratives are frequently part of the horror field ("Ghosts, ghoulies, and monsters have always been the staple of horror"[15]), and ghost is etymologically linked to "aghast" and "ghastly." But they stray into other genres, for example the war film, science fiction, melodrama and comedy, even the western.[16] Andrew Tudor's analysis found that about 20 percent of films in his database were on the edge of horror and adjacent genres.[17] This suggests flexibility both on the part of the ghost and audiences about the ways in which ghosts are considered. Tudor rank-orders various categories of "horror movie monsters" by incidence between 1931 and 1984.[18] Ghosts have the sixth greatest number of cases (77), representing 8 percent of the total, which makes it surprising that they have not been subject to intense scrutiny as a whole, unlike, say, vampire and zombie films.

Genres are fluid and imprecise, and the term "ghost story" can be applied to a variety of supernatural subjects. For example, Kim Newman claims to identify a "gentle-ghost sub-genre of screwball comedy."[19] He lists only *Topper, The Ghost and Mrs. Muir* and *Randall and Hopkirk (Deceased)* as examples, and the last two seem unfortunate choices, but this type of analysis is useful. Jeremy Dyson's discussion of the "supernatural horror film"[20] can only manage to define his field in terms of "the fantastic, the non-ordinary and the metaphysical," which is not exclusive to horror, even the black-and-white ones he favours. These films, it would seem, are more easily recognized than classified. Attempting to define the Gothic,[21] Lenora Ledwon says that "Any definition of genre is at best incomplete. There will always be exceptions, overlaps, and grey areas." Charles Derry tries to be specific, dividing horror films into three categories: horror of personality, of Armageddon, and of the Demonic.[22] The last covers supernatural films, but it is inadequate for ghost films. Julia Briggs feels that it is pointless to try to distinguish the subjects according to type, and sees the common denominator to be the "intention of inducing fear."[23] At this level the concept is evacuated of its power so that "ghost story" has no special meaning, and Briggs's book does cover more than just ghosts.

The ghost is worth demarcating from other inhabitants of the supernatural universe.[24] This book analyses those films that involve *the continuation of personality after bodily death*. There are difficulties, so limits are loosely drawn. James Robert Parish in his guide to Hollywood ghost and angel films[25] struggles with the issue and some of his choices are at variance with the criteria adopted here. For example, he includes fake hauntings on the grounds that the hero behaves as if confronting real phenomena, and discusses *Cabin in the Sky* (1943), which transpires to have been a dream. He excludes some films on the grounds that they deal not with deceased individuals but with non-specific extra-dimensional entities, but there is often an ambiguity about such films and they should not be excluded a priori. Most of his other omissions are reasonable — reincarnation, muses, gods on earth, zombies, invisibility, witches, self-delusion, science fiction supernatural beings — but whereas he excludes Hell, if the dead go there it seems reasonable to include it. Similarly the excluded "angels of death" and near-death experiences, if not hallucinations, suggest that personality continues after death.

Jörg Hienger locates horror stories within science fiction as long as reason is reinstated by the end, and only those stories without this "reactivated reason" fall outside S. F.'s purview.[26] This begs the question as to what reason's limits are, and since we do not know how ghosts might fit into a scientific schema they can rarely be absorbed into science fiction, except where they occur in an overtly S. F. context, for example *Solaris* (1972). Assumptions can be made, such as in terms of "energy vibrations," but these are arbitrary in the absence of information about their nature, so that to the extent that explanations are not offered, the vast majority of ghost narratives cannot be considered as S. F.[27] Difficulty defining postmortem personality has implications for a thematic analysis, for example when considering vampires, werewolves and zombies. Reanimated corpses are even more problematic, as are suspended-animation films. Even where evidence of consciousness is present, it is not always apparent that the motivating force of the action was a once-living but now-deceased individual, for example in poltergeist films where the agent could be alive and using PK, or never have lived as a human. Reincarnation films also present a problem in that memories may not be carried into a new incarnation. Sometimes it is a matter of interpretation, with no conclusion presented to the viewer.

Wider Considerations of Horror and Fantasy[28]

From the beginning, film was suited to the paranormal due to the ease of manipulation of the image, in particular double exposure. Many "Afterlife" films evoke emotions associated with horror,[29] and advances in special effects, along with a slackening of censorship, have increased the horror content. Some ghost films are psychological in intention, using suggestion rather than feelings of disgust, but Tudor has indicated how, since the Second World War, there has been a move from closed- to open-ended narrative structures, with a shift from a sense of security to one of paranoia. The increase in "body horror" is an expression of this trend, and it should not be expected that the traditional ghost story would remain untouched. Body horror and gore can be linked to earlier preoccupations with tombs and the physical aspects of decaying bodies. Revulsion occasioned by an exploding head is not so different from that caused by the thought of wandering alone in catacombs.

Robin Wood discusses "The Other" in terms of surplus sexual energy that is repressed and projected onto an external entity as a way of denying problems within society, but which returns as a threat to normality. Horror, including the ghost story, incorporates elements which society refuses to recognize, but which cannot remain repressed. Horror films "are our collective nightmares."[30] Freud's work, although influential in film studies, will not be discussed to any great extent here. It tends to involve concepts with little or no external validity and often resembles an appeal to authority rather than the application of theories arrived at by empirical research.[31] Barry Salt provides an apposite analysis of the shortcomings of Freudianism for film studies.[32]

Since the 1970s the expanding literature on horror has run parallel to an increasing interest in fantasy, but again it is a category more easily recognized than defined. It could be argued that fantasy does not constitute a genre but is a style that can penetrate genre. Films under consideration here could be subsumed under the term "fantasy," but it is difficult to assign a single label to them all, as they vary enormously in form and function. Mark Chorvinsky would like to try:

> Cinema realizes the fantastic, and in that sense it is intrinsically a fortean medium. Something that does not exist is made to exist, and legends may be given life, as may anomalous phenomena.[33]

Even within the sphere of fiction cinema, to which he is implicitly referring, some films fall into this category more readily than others. Portrayal on film is not sufficient to qualify as a depiction of the fantastic. Definitions may not be precisely defined but a ghost film in some sense has to be seen as more fantastic than a police procedural.[34] To identify the entire medium with the fantastic means that the term ceases to have explanatory power. James Donald suggests a negative definition, which he discards as inadequate, in which fantastic films are those which "depart from the rules of everyday reality,"[35] but this raises the difficulty of defining everyday reality.

Film as Communion with the Dead

That the medium (a phrase which sits comfortably in both areas) is suited to the portrayal of ghosts is summed up in the titles of such books as Paul Mayersberg's *Hollywood, the Haunted House* and Lotte H. Eisner's volume on German Expressionism, *The Haunted Screen*. Robert B. Ray connects the two strongly. After making the standard point that the film he is discussing (*Eureka* of c.1904) is a record of people now dead, he goes on to suggest that

> I am reminded that the Russian word for a film showing, *céanc*, not only sounds like the word *séance*, but also may be etymologically linked to it. Thus, viewers attending a showing of *Eureka* (or any other film, for that matter) are participating in a séance, a communion with the dead.[36]

Similarly, Paul Coates states

> If in some countries it is still customary to describe the screening of a film as a *séance*,[37] this surely reflects the degree to which the form is steeped in the ideology of nineteenth-century spiritualism: both film and the spiritualist materialize the dead....[38]

Chip Denman makes the link between cinema and Spiritualism:

> Hands are joined as the lights go out. The sitters drop their voices and wait anxiously for images to appear. A faint strain of music floats through the air. People sit as if their feet are glued to the floor. A modern séance.... Yup, a Friday night at the movies.[39]

The parallels are obvious. With both films and ghosts, the characters are there and not there. They are insubstantial, elusive, and rooted in the past. Indeed, powerful films can be said to "haunt us" long after the experience, suggesting that both activate similar emotional responses. We sit in the dark to watch films, and ghosts are associated with the dark. Paul Virilio quotes de Rochas who commented in 1900 that spirit communication allowed proponents "to move back in time or across space without too much effort."[40] The feeling can persist with newer technology. A character in the satire on television *Meet Mr. Lucifer* (1953) muses that if Gilbert Harding can enter his living room (while physically at "Ally Pally") then there is no reason why his dead father should not be able to—both would be equally mysterious. Perhaps the decline of Spiritualism in the twentieth century can be in part attributed to the growth of a rival means of moving back in time and across space more reliably, at the flick of a switch.

Structure of the Book

Both literary and visual sources have provided inspiration and motifs for ghost cinema. A consideration of literary influences, particularly stemming from the Gothic novel, but also from other sources such as Spiritualist and psychical research records, has been omitted as there is a large literature on the subject. On the other hand a discussion of visual influences is included as they have been accorded less attention by commentators. After this consideration of cinematic precursors, the focus moves to early cinema, where the gradual development of the ghost as a "personality" is seen as the form matures during the 1920s, so that by the time sound arrives, the lexicon of the filmic Afterlife has largely been established.

The longest chapter, Chapter 3, analyses English-language sound films that deal in some form with ghosts in an attempt to categorize them.

It is divided into some thirty sections that provide a schema into which ghost films can be accommodated. "Schema" is perhaps more appropriate than "taxonomy" or "classification." These terms suggest a scientific methodology, and as we have seen, the ghost is a slippery creature that gives problems of definition. In any case, a pseudo–Linnaean system would not be appropriate because the categories are not discrete but overlap, and most films could be placed into more than one (as will be seen by the reappearance of a number of titles in the chapter). As ghost films have not before received such an extensive treatment[41] it was felt worthwhile to try to include as many examples as possible.

As might be expected, many of the films dealt with are routine and their meanings easily exhausted. Some, though, are worthy of deeper analysis than a macroscopic presentation allows. Several have been taken as case studies in chapter five to exemplify the categories identified. A final chapter attempts to draw the threads together and reach some conclusions about the distinctiveness of films dealing with life after death.

Areas to Be Excluded

As the focus is the continuation of personality after death, there are areas that will be excluded. The most obvious are those where it cannot be assumed that it is an individual's consciousness that has survived, for example in films featuring poltergeists and demonic forays. There is a category in which an individual on the point of death is kept in suspended animation, such as the segment of *Tales of Terror* (1962) based on Edgar Allan Poe's *The Facts in the Case of M. Valdemar*. These films cannot be seen as dealing with post-mortem existence. Films that explore the survival of race memories in living individuals, exemplified by *Altered States* (1980), will not be discussed. The implication is that memory is somehow encoded in DNA, rather than positing the survival of a human personality. Inclusion of reincarnation films is problematic as persistence of memories does not presuppose the continuation of the full personality. Where these films are referred to, it is in the context of full survival.

Vampires are excluded partly on the pragmatic ground that it is a huge and well explored area of study, but also because it can be argued that these films focus on the "undead," not the dead. Zombies usually do not display much personality, and occasionally, especially when linked to Haitian voodoo, there is a suggestion that the victims are living but in a trance. On the other hand, zombies and vampires do share certain characteristics with ghosts. As Clive Leatherdale states in his discussion of vampire traditions, "the land of the dead seemed to be a place apart, governed by its own customs and laws of nature,"[42] and the same is true for filmmakers in this area. Some of their constructions can be difficult to classify, and like the type of werewolf that becomes a vampire upon death, often seem to float free of a strict taxonomy.[43]

It is worth mentioning the sub-species of Shakespearean apparition because of the large number of film treatments of Shakespeare's plays that feature ghosts. These include *Macbeth*, *Richard III*,[44] *Julius Cæsar* and over seventy versions of *Hamlet*. Space considerations preclude an analysis of the ways in which the ghosts in these films are depicted.

There are practical problems in including foreign language films, notably the quantity and availability. These have largely been omitted, though a number from non–English speaking countries have been included if notable or to make a point for which there is no English-language equivalent.

Borderline Cases

The ghost crosses genres so that there are borderline films only obliquely connected to the survival of personality. Examples would be mind transference, in which memories might survive but not the full personality; the revival of corpses; witchcraft; and demonic forces that imply but do not require explanations in terms of survival. A more recent development is the "ghost in the machine," riding on the popularity of the Internet and Virtual Reality. The example that brings survival of personality to the fore is *Ghost in the Machine* (1993), but a better known example, *The Lawnmower Man* (1992), is similar in that a previously corporeal individual is translated into electronic impulses that 'survive' in a computer network.

These films will be dealt with only insofar as they fall within the criterion of the continuation of personality. Often this will be a matter of degree. For example, reanimation films could be included if the corpse exhibited personality traits that indicated the continuation of a pre-mortem existence. The difficulty of drawing hard boundaries is indicated by *Chiller* (1985), in which a cryonically suspended man is revived but has lost his soul, turning him into a murderer.[45] In a sense he is enjoying a post-mortem existence, but it is hard to say whether his pre-mortem personality is intact, and nobody would claim that he was a ghost except in a metaphorical sense.

A category in the tradition set by Henry James's *The Turn of the Screw* (1898) leaves uncertainty in the viewer's mind as to whether the events have a paranormal or psychological explanation. In the absence of unambiguous evidence it may be necessary to assign a level of probability based on the evidence. Doubt can be caused by failure to distinguish between objective apparitions and internally generated images that are objectified for the benefit of the viewer. A good example is *The Three Godfathers* (1948). Using the rule of thumb that apparitions should be able to provide information that a living individual would not know, it has to be assumed that in this instance the figures are projections of the hero's mind. On the other hand, there is no reason why an apparition should supply information, so that it is feasible that the figures have an independent existence.[46]

Even where previously unknown information is supplied, there is still the difficulty of its being received from a living being by telepathy, or via clairvoyance from extant records. Hamlet's father does provide information — that he was murdered — whereas the apparition of Banquo in *Macbeth* does not. These differences would provide tentative evidence that the first was objective (though there is the possibility that the ghost externalises Hamlet's fears, which are coincidentally correct,[47]) whereas the second could be either objective in some sense, but seen only by Macbeth, or more probably an hallucinatory projection of a guilty conscience.

The Filmography

Several hundred English-language films can be regarded as dealing with post-mortem survival either in whole or in part, and the sheer number precludes a detailed examination of each one. No criterion of merit has been applied to determine worthiness for inclusion. Non-fiction programs have not been included, and neither have made-for-television films.[48] It does not pretend to be comprehensive, but it is hoped that enough are included to render the analysis authoritative. Films mentioned for comparison purposes, but that do not treat life after death, have not been included. Many of the silent films no longer exist and descriptions in secondary sources, identified in the text, have been used. Silent films have been included separately. Only foreign-language films referred to in the text have been included, and these comprize the third section. Film dates have been taken from the British Film Institute database SIFT where possible; otherwise the earliest recorded date noted has been adopted. The addition of director and country of origin should help to prevent confusion, especially where titles are similar.

1

Visual Precursors to Cinematic Ghosts

Influences from other popular traditions can be detected in early cinema, and the depiction of supernatural phenomena is no exception. As Charles Musser points out, "Early cinema ... evidenced a profound dependence on other cultural forms, including the theater, newspapers, popular songs, and fairy tales,"[1] and John L. Fell looks forward to the day when Victorian entertainments in particular will no longer be seen in isolation but as "braided strands in the skein of narrative storytelling."[2] Cinematic ghosts did not appear fully formed in the 1890s but were the latest in a long line of attempts to show what a particular age considered to represent a ghost. Ian Christie claims that:

> cinema might well be described as a temporary phase in the supernatural tradition which started as long ago as the seventeenth century and looks set to continue into the future with computer controlled virtual reality.[3]

Projection on film has a pre-history that stretches much further back than the seventeenth century. Catherine Haill traces theatrical ghosts to Classical writers, showing how supernatural characters originally commented upon the action,[4] but by the sixteenth century ghosts had become fully fledged characters. Antecedents to cinematic ghosts include mirror projection, the magic lantern, elaborate Phantasmagoria ghost shows, Pepper's Ghost, and influences from such diverse sources as spirit photography and the Dance of Death. This chapter traces these influences, showing how film makers were able to build on existing representations of ghosts, and examples of films that draw on these representations provide a link with subsequent chapters, which examine ghost cinema.

Skeletons and the Dance of Death

Early filmmakers, particularly Georges Méliès, tended to depict the post-mortem state in symbolic terms, drawing on the iconography of the enormously influential *Dance of Death*, dating from the 1370s.[5] Skeletons, increasingly accurate thanks to the researches of anatomists such as Vesalius and Leonardo, were depicted as emblematic of death, but in tension with notions of immortality in which the soul left the earthly body. Léonard P. Kurtz makes the point that the Dance of Death is a misnomer, since Death calls on the living, not the dead,[6] but it should be added that once the dance has begun, the precise status of the dancer is immaterial.

The figure of Death did not represent any particular individual but was a general personification, in the same way that nowadays, with the increasing reliance on technological intervention in dying, the state of death might be symbolized by a flat EEG. Its development can be seen as intertwined with that of the Black Death that began in Europe in the mid-fourteenth century. A good example is Holbein's influential *Der Totentanz* woodcuts, published in 1538, which showed a skeleton as the conductor of the dead, a tradition that had become popular in France in the fifteenth century. Bones would have been a familiar sight at the time not only because of the mortality rate, but also due to the practice of placing bones in ossuaries, often in aesthetic patterns.[7]

The intention of the Dance was allegorical, emphasizing the brevity of one's earthly term and satirizing human vanity and pretensions (*vanitas*). Every social station was targeted, including the clergy, all races and ages. It can be seen to offer retribution for sins committed during life, but would have also represented an invitation to repent sins and lead a better life while there was still time. As well as skeletons and draped figures, these pictures often included more realistic representations of the deceased with emaciated bodies, though often mutilated, a style that is particularly prominent in horror films. There was also an erotic component, as with the demon lover. The "victim" for example is sometimes a young woman, with a cadaver putting his hand up her dress. These images symbolized for its earliest audience the continuation of personality in the sense that it prefigured the Resurrection of the Dead and Day of Judgment, with the division of souls into saved and damned.

While the imagery of the Dance faded during the Enlightenment, the skeleton aspect has its own history, bridging the medieval depictions with filmic renditions. Athanasius Kircher's 1671 illustrations of the magic lantern in his *Ars Magna Lucis et Umbrae* included a skeleton with a scythe,[8] and the skeleton remained a potent symbol of death even after the Danse Macabre waned. It featured in popular entertainments such as the Phantasmagoria, and was associated with gothic literature, along with dungeons and ruined abbeys. In 1767 Franz Anton, Graf von Sporck, brought the Todtentanz up to date with illustrations of skeletal Death appearing in a contemporary setting,[9] as did Thomas Rowlandson, who produced a satirical series of seventy-two drawings entitled *The Dance of Death* (1816). Étienne-Gaspard Robertson's *Mémoires*, published in 1831, featured an engraving that included a sorcerer standing inside a circle, his wrist held by an accompanying skeleton in whose other hand is an hour glass, symbol of transience,[10] A booklet issued by the Musée National des Techniques[11] illustrates a number of 18th Century slides in the category "La Mort," featuring skeletons, including one sitting on a baby and another clutching a young woman. The link with the Dance as an expression of disaster was reaffirmed by its use in Germany after both world wars.

In the 1860s L. S. Beale invented the *Choreutoscope*, which comprised pictures of a skeleton in about a dozen positions either on a disc or in a strip, projected in conjunction with a simple shutter to give the impression of movement as the slide was pulled through the projector. Liesegang prints two of the strips, one originally painted on glass, the other made from metal,[12] The macabre subject matter is laced with humor as the skeletons leap, squat and lose their skulls,[13]

During the early days of moving pictures, films of X-rays became a popular entertainment, the two media having arrived almost simultaneously. Allen W. Grove argues that the discovery of X-rays legitimized the search for ghosts because it was now proved scientifically that the hitherto unseen could be made visible.[14] Not all sections of the population treated them with such seriousness, however. Albert A. Hopkins's influential 1897 manual, *Magic: Stage Illusions and Scientific Diversions Including Trick Photography*, includes a section on what could be loosely described as "fun with X-rays," termed "The Neoöccultism."[15] The gentleman in the accompanying illustration, given his likely exposure, could be expected to resemble the skeleton he is sitting opposite fairly soon. Nevertheless, the genuine human skeleton, as opposed to artists' renditions, became a familiar sight for the first time in centuries.

In so doing, it lost the impact that it had previously had in its close association with the grave, becoming a staple of early cinema in humorous as well as realistic forms, though this too had a venerable tradition— Kurtz refers to caricatures of the Dance of Death produced in the late eighteenth/early nineteenth centuries.[16] More so than print media of earlier ages, the cinema helped the process of removing the dead body from direct sight of the general public. The first-hand familiarity we once had with death was now provided at second hand. G. A. Smith's *X-Rays* (1897) has a professor turning his equipment on to a pair of lovers, showing their embracing skeletons. The following year Méliès made a film on the same theme, *A Novice at X-Rays* (*Les Rayons X*) in which a patient is X-rayed, causing his skeleton to appear separate from the rest of his body (using a double exposure), which promptly collapses in a heap. Reversing the switch restores body and skeleton.

Skeletons became a perennial favorite during the silent cinema. Hammond reproduces a row of Méliès's skeletons from *The Palace of the Arabian Nights* (*Le Palais des mille et une nuits*, 1905)[17] as well as Disney's *The Skeleton Dance* (1930) and a Choreutoscope slide.[18] Méliès also used a skeleton in the transformation film *The Vanishing Lady* (1896), one shocks a man in his night-shirt in Paul's *Undressing Extraordinary* (1901), and Pathé's *The Fairy of the Black Rocks* (1905) combines skeletons and shroud-like sheets. As well as affording comic possibilities, the skeleton, and especially the skull, signified death as sinister and even malevolent, as in *The Phantom of the Opera* (1925).

Not only the skeleton but the concept of the Dance itself survived. In *Metropolis* (1927), Lang inserted a sequence featuring Death and the Seven Deadly Sins to symbolize society's decadence. *The Seventh Seal* (1956) ends with Death leading his victims up the hillside, taking some but seemingly arbitrarily sparing others, in a moment of symbolic import:

> The players go off into light; the others into darkness. The Dance of Death reaffirms the black and light contrast of that part of the film's style....[19]

The Danse Macabre also moved back into print in the twentieth century, with the inclusion of skeletons and rotting corpses in comic books. David J. Skal compares a woodcut by Hans Holbein the Younger (1534) with the cover of an issue of *Tales from the Crypt* (1951) and the similarities are unmistakable. The satire of the originals is retained, but the difference is that whereas Holbein had conveyed a strong sense of judgment and retribution for sins, the modern version introduces personal revenge, thus, for Skal, "encouraging the reader to identify, rather gleefully, with Death as a sympathetic protagonist."[20] These elements of humor and revenge too have found their way into horror films. Stephen King has attested to the seminal influence of EC Comics's black comedy.[21]

Mirrors, Camera Obscura and the Magic Lantern

Hermann Hecht suggests that the projection of ghosts using mirrors goes back to antiquity, and was mainly utilized in temple worship.[22] Ptolemy in the second century A.D. discusses the properties of plane and concave mirrors, a theme adopted by Ann Joseph Eusèbe Baconnière-Salverte in his 1829 book *The Occult Sciences*, in which he suggests that classical accounts of appearances by gods could be explained by mirrors.[23] On the other hand the anonymous author of the 1851 SPCK book *The Wonders of Light and Shadow* thinks that "the apparitions of heathen gods"[24] were achieved by a form of magic lantern rather than mirrors because of the logistical difficulties of setting up the latter.[25] Milbourne Christopher also feels that mirrors were unlikely, and that the 'gods' were temple workers appearing from concealed niches under cover of smoke from the altar fires.[26] However accomplished, early descriptions of ghosts use such terms as "shadows," "vapor," "smoke" and "wind," and, while transparency is not usually implied, these descriptions suggest ethereal elements that serve as metaphors for the insubstantial status of the deceased, and provide a means of rendering projected ghosts plausible.

The use of mirrors, despite their drawbacks, may have continued — the historical Faust is supposed to have used them in a lecture on Homer at the University of Erfurt.[27] Another simple way of throwing images is the camera obscura. By 1600 it had been perfected, with a lens to sharpen the image and a concave mirror to re-invert it. Giovanni Battista della Porta describes a "Spectre and Magic Theatre" in his 1589 book on natural magic in which his "delighted, and often terrified audience, hardly knew whether what they saw was true or only an illusion."[28] This is a theme running throughout the history of image projection, by whatever means. When the technology is first introduced viewers have difficulty in establishing whether the image is real or illusory, and only once they become familiar with it do they become blasé. Even the advent of cinema in the 1890s caused some consternation in the audience. Itinerant entrepreneurs in the early seventeenth century traveled about with camera obscura ghost shows, telling audiences that the supernatural events they were witnessing were genuine:

> At a time when Europe was haunted by the remnants of the Inquisition people had vicarious pleasure in watching ghosts and spectres, pictures of hell and the devil projected in the dark and dismal fairground booths.[29]

By the sixteenth century Agrippa von Nettesheim is talking of projecting figures that spectators think are ghosts as if it were commonplace.[30] Hecht quotes Daniel Schwenter, writing in 1636 on the camera obscura and mirror projection: "One writes a great deal about magicians and witches who pretend to be able to make spectres and ghosts appear."[31] From the beginning, the projection of images was associated with fantastic elements, and the tendency became even more widespread with the popularity of the magic lantern.

The magic lantern, more flexible than the mirror and camera obscura, had been developed by the mid-seventeenth century. Unfortunately its origins are obscure, and as we have already seen with classical accounts, it is not always clear how a described effect was achieved. For example, Benvenuto Cellini's autobiography, begun in 1558, gives an account of a necromantic ceremony performed at the Coliseum in Rome; T. C. Hepworth describes the event.[32] There was a fire, perfumes and "drugs of fetid odour." Spectators were confined within a circle, each with a job to do. The figures appeared only after an hour and a half, which would have lowered the audience's attention threshold. Hepworth discounts the theory that a lantern was used to project images onto the smoke, assuming the use of confederates, while Sir David Brewster prefers the "optical apparatus" theory.[33] However accomplished, the technique prefigures Schröpfer's operation two hundred years later (see below).

What is clear is that supernatural elements were bound up in lantern shows from their earliest days just as they had been with the camera obscura:

> What were to become the main points of interest in literature for the following hundred, or a hundred and fifty years, are indicated by the titles of two French books: Abbé Pierre de Vallemont's "La physique occulte" (1693) and Jacques Ozanam's "Récréations mathématiques et physiques" (1694): magic lantern serving the occult on the one hand, and on the other, the lantern as an instrument of pleasure. Whilst most French authors ... describe the magic lantern as an instrument for amusing optical "recreation," there is a flourishing German magic lantern literature revealing a fascination with the occult.[34]

Lange-Fuchs adds that as time went by, the connection between "Natürliche Magie" and lantern projection became more tenuous. By the end of the eighteenth century, texts tended to discuss the issues of necromancy raised by secret lantern projection of ghosts, so that a technical note on the lantern might be lost in a wider philosophical discussion of the supernatural.

1. Visual Precursors to Cinematic Ghosts

Christiaan Huygens, possibly the inventor of magic lantern technology in the mid-seventeenth century, often referred to it as the "lanterne du peur,"[35] and the term was used in a letter written by Pierre Petit in 1662.[36] Kircher, another pioneer, utilized slides "consisting of rude figures of spectres, skeletons, heads, and hearts,"[37] and Liesegang illustrates two of these,[38] During the eighteenth century the technology became more sophisticated, and Johann Samuel Halle's 1792 book describes the principle of setting slides in the periphery of a geared wheel manipulated by a long rod,[39] He also provides two methods of projecting ghosts onto a churchyard wall, and shows how to make them appear to rise from graves. (Hecht accompanies this point with an illustration of Edmund Kelly engaged in necromantic practices taken from the anonymous *The Astrologer of the Nineteenth Century*,[40] although the original text makes no reference to projection.)

By a combination of a lantern and concave mirror it was even possible to make ghosts appear to float in the air. What would seem to be a foretaste of Pepper's Ghost involved a living person dressed as a ghost and "projected" by plane and concave mirrors, but using the lantern's lens system, unlike earlier efforts based solely on mirrors. Johann Carl Enslen used this system from about 1785; earlier he and his brother had inaugurated their *Philosophical Theater*, a nod to the French Enlightenment Philosophes, in which they exhibited "living ghosts." As well as the mirrors, Enslen used back-projection with a magic lantern that was movable and utilized a form of dissolve.[41]

The last three decades of the eighteenth century saw a bifurcation in France between science and the supernatural. Robert M. Isherwood describes the fascination with science and technology prevalent in Parisian society by the 1780s.[42] During the same period there was a revival of interest in the supernatural, emphasizing the bizarre and irrational aspects of Romanticism. A similar movement was also underway in Britain, most notably in the Gothic novel. It is in this context that the development in popularity of the magic lantern ghost show must be seen. More prosaically, improvements in lighting, notably the introduction of the Argand lamp,[43] meant that the magic lantern could be used in front of bigger audiences. The interpenetration between scientific and the non- (or perhaps pre-) scientific is a motif that can be seen today.

Johann Schröpfer (1730–1774)

Schröpfer's activities[44] can be located at one end of a trajectory that begins with a secretive ritualistic performance, purporting to be a genuine attempt to raise the spirits of the dead, and ends in supernatural elements in magic lantern shows as parlor entertainment for the middle classes. Like Robertson's Phantasmagoria some thirty years later, his performances were total theater, with atmosphere contributing significantly to the effect. Unlike the Phantasmagoria operators, however, who did make some attempt to tell their patrons that they were witnessing an illusion, Schröpfer posed as a genuine necromancer. Consequently it is only possible to infer the likely mechanisms of his apparatus through the second-hand descriptions of his 'séances'.

As described by Paul B. Thompson,[45] he had a special room draped in black, with an altar, candles and skulls, and reeking of incense. At his most famous performance, with Prince Charles of Saxony attempting to communicate with his uncle, the participants were also plied with wine, although the account of the affair was written by one of the abstainers, and Hecht adds that they fasted for three days beforehand,[46] which would hardly add to their ability to be objective. The experience was violent and noisy, and participants were obliged to remain within a circle, ostensibly for their protection, but perhaps because this would restrict their point of view, and prevent a close approach to the spirits. This was an early example of a mixed-media event, with confederates letting off pyrotechnic devices and creating sound effects by banging and yelling through pipes, and most importantly, using a magic lantern to back-project pictures (the face of Prince Charles's uncle for example), although this could have been used in conjunction with actors draped in robes. Schröpfer also projected onto smoke, a technique described by Edmé Gilles Guyot in 1770[47] and subsequently used by Phantasmagoria operators.[48]

The Phantasmagoria

The Phantasmagoria was a total theatrical experience that relied on the projection of mainly supernatural images, by means of a magic lantern, in a Gothic environment. Like its forebears, it played on anxieties regarding death and the Afterlife, in which sense it can be seen as the predecessor of the Spiritualistic séance; X. Theodore Barber argues that:

> Undoubtedly some Spiritualist mediums even used a magic lantern to summon ghosts, but their purpose was to deceive whereas the American Phantasmagoria showmen, like Philipsthal before them, stressed that their exhibition was rational and mechanically derived, a declaration in keeping with the growth of popular fascination with science. In fact, the Phantasmagoria represented a unique blend of both the irrational and the scientific, each of which was a prevalent interest among the general American public.[49]

Musser agrees broadly with Barber, stating that "Into the nineteenth century, mediums used projected images, concealed their source, and claimed these images were apparitions,"[50] and Erik Barnouw makes the more general claim that mediums used techniques developed by magicians that themselves owed a debt to the pioneering Phantasmagoria procedures.[51]

Although this strategy is possible in very limited circumstances, neither Barber nor Musser presents any evidence that Spiritualists did utilize magic lanterns in séances, but the fascination with both magic lantern ghost shows and Spiritualism, the latter appearing as the popularity of the former waned, suggests that the interest with both sprang from a similar source. Barber is probably overstating the case for the rational basis for the American Phantasmagoria, as it is unclear to what extent a contemporary audience would have appreciated the illusion, at least at the beginning of the form's popularity. There seems a willingness among modern commentators to give the Phantasmagoria operators the benefit of the doubt when attempting to uncover the extent to which they laid bare the mechanisms of their apparatus to audiences.

Phantasmagoria slides usually involved death and the supernatural, but not consistently. For example, Paul de Philipsthal claimed that his "Spectrology"—an effort at product differentiation—presented images of apparitions, but cunningly included portraits of living individuals under the rubric "Phantoms of the Absent." The poster for his appearances at London's Lyceum[52] perhaps hypocritically proclaimed that his aim was "to expose the Practices of artful Imposters ... and to open the Eyes of those who still foster an absurd belief in Ghosts or Disembodied Spirits." Yet the poster also shows a necromancer in a circle conjuring a shrouded spirit, an image surely calculated to have a greater impact than the text underneath, which states that he will exhibit "Optical Illusions and Mechanical Pieces of Art" (i.e. automata). Brewster describes a visit to one of de Philipsthal's shows at Edinburgh in 1802, in which spectators do not seem to have been disabused of the idea that they were witnessing an illusion.[53]

Jacob Philadelphia, active in the 1760s and 1770s, apparently announced that his show was an entertainment, according to Christopher:

> Philadelphia's masterpiece, the production of ghostly figures, was clearly labeled as his impression of an ancient necromancer. He was not, did not claim to be, a sorcerer....[54]

It is not clear to what extent Philadelphia made this clear, and if he did, to what extent he was believed. Christopher describes his show in dramatic terms as "surrounded ... with a heavy air of mysticism and pseudo-scientific mumbo-jumbo."[55] The ghost-show entrepreneurs, it would seem, were keen to have it both ways. To indicate the interest taken by intellectuals, Goethe saw Philadelphia's show in Weimar in 1777, and its impact can be gauged by Johann von Schiller's remark that Philadelphia "conjured with souls."[56]

Whatever the mode of presentation, Philadelphia's ghost projections onto smoke were banned in Vienna as being too terrifying.[57] Later in the lifecycle of the Phantasmagoria, mixed shows were common, sometimes even including comic routines, and the term itself came to cover any subject as long as it was projected in Robertson's style. That the fear of the pictures had dissipated is clear from the fact that Robertson's son, who toured the United States in the 1820s and 1830s, made a point of announcing that the images did not require total darkness, and that children were welcome (dire warnings had been given over the potentially dangerous effects of his father's show on children and pregnant women).[58]

Paul Philidor began magic lantern shows, posing as the genuine supernatural, in Berlin in 1789, but his ghosts were shown to be a fraud.[59] He went to Vienna (1790) and Paris (1792), where he seems to have had more success than Philadelphia. The latter was not the only magician to find that his ghost show was deemed too realistic. Andrew Oehler recounts in his 1811 autobiography how he had held a "séance" for the governor of Mexico in 1806, using a magic lantern. He was promptly arrested for sorcery and imprisoned, only being released when a Spanish marquis interceded on his behalf.[60]

Robertson (1763–1837),[61] who began his shows in March 1798, was — though not the first as he is sometimes credited — the most famous of these showmen, and he continued the preoccupation with the supernatural. As the Musée National des Techniques brochure puts it: "La mort constitue pour Robertson la principale source d'inspiration."[62] Robertson issued warnings that what the audience was about to see should not be taken literally, although couched in ambiguous terms that could leave the impression that the phenomena might be genuine; contemporary commentators frequently referred to his productions as "séances." His mise-en-scène recalls that of Schröpfer:

> ...a gloomy crypt shrouded with black draperies and pictured with the emblems of mortality. An antique lamp, suspended from the ceiling, emitted a flame of spectral blue.[63]

Blue had long been associated with the supernatural. In *Richard III* (1593?) Richard awakes from a dream and says that the lights burned blue, and the writer of *Haunted Hoxton* mentions lights of "a blue and spectral hue."⁶⁴ (By the release of *The Phantom of the Opera* (1925) and *Frankenstein* (1931), green had become "the color of fear,"⁶⁵ and Peter Wollen links the use of green in *Vertigo* (1958) with Alfred Hitchcock's memory of green associated with "ghosts and villains" when attending the theater at the age of five,⁶⁶ In Italy the color of fear is yellow, hence the "giallo" novels and films.) In addition to atmospheric lighting, heavy incense, incantations and sound effects (particularly Franklin's Harmonica) were used to increase the sense of unreality. Sound effects also helped to cover the noise made by stage assistants. The Republican anti-clericalism of the presentation was placed in tension with the associations of the venue, a redundant Capuchin convent to which Robertson moved after three years, "to create a mood of uneasy fear in the spectators...."⁶⁷

In his *Mémoires*, Robertson insists at length that he never intended to deceive, but to "arm his audience against irrational superstition."⁶⁸ It is hard to believe, given the mise-en-scène, that audiences thought that they were witnessing a frivolous show, and he admits that he often had to persuade people that he did not possess paranormal abilities, as people wanted him to provide them with information, look into the future, or contact the departed—attributes that would later characterize mediumship.

Hecht supplies an outline of Robertson's patent of 1799, but adds that Barnes had noted that this described an early version, and that it was improved over the years.⁶⁹ Robertson used rails fifteen to eighteen feet long in order to obtain a projection span of between five inches and eight feet, to create the illusion of movement (a small image would appear to be far away, a large one close to the spectators). The mechanism allowed manipulation of the light source for even illumination at different distances and had an adjustable lens to maintain focus. Back-projected figures appeared to advance on the audience, who would cry out as the images suddenly disappeared.⁷⁰

Robertson introduced black backgrounds to the images so that they stood out in the darkness, not having borders that would show them to be pictures. This also made it impossible to judge distances, upon which the illusion of the apparitions' approaching and receding depended. Earlier slides were transparent, and after a transitional phase in which black was used for the supernatural and clear for ordinary scenes, black was adopted as standard.⁷¹ Since the screen was not let down until after the house lights had dimmed,⁷² it was impossible for the audience to provide a frame of reference for the images, which seemed to float in the air.

The effect in the oft-reproduced plate of the Phantasmagoria audience being overflown by a demon and winged skull is presumably achieved by projecting the images onto smoke, although it could have been an overhead screen, as the necessary brazier cannot be seen in the picture. Recognizable deceased French luminaries were also presented, but the show ended with a skeleton complete with scythe, "the fate which is reserved for us all."[73] Dawes describes glass sliders being employed to give the illusion of mouth and eye movements.[74] Distortions could be introduced by the use of prisms.[75]

It is important to realize that Robertson was not merely presenting tableaux, and that contemporary engravings cannot do him justice. Robinson lists a number of the effects,[76] some of which were elaborate, including a potted *Macbeth*, *Young Burying His Step-daughter*, and a number of Biblical and classical stories, concluding that some scenarios, such as *The Death of Lord Littleton*, were so elaborate that they read like descriptions of early films. In addition to magic lantern slides, Robertson was able to project opaque objects, including living people and skeletons, using an adapted lantern called the *Mégascope*, and by using multiple lanterns created what he referred to as "ambulant phantoms," i.e. not always appearing in one position.

The Phantasmagoria was particularly popular in England. Sybil Rosenfeld describes a show at Sadler's Wells in 1816 that included a "living (sic) skeleton," presumably meaning that it was three-dimensional, and "death on a pale horse." The influence of the Gothic novel would account for the bleeding nun shown at the Whitechapel Pavilion in 1827, a show that according to Rosenfeld must have incorporated dissolving views.[77] Childe, who invented the dissolving view, gave a show in 1828 featuring the Castle Spectre inside a Gothic interior.[78]

The shows soon crossed the Atlantic, with Bologna and Tomlinson exhibiting in New York from November 1803. They made much of its rational basis, declaring in an advertisement in the *New York Evening Post* that

> This Spectrology professes to expose the practices of artful imposters, and to open the eyes of those who still foster an absurd belief in *Ghosts or Disembodied Spirits*[italics in original].[79]

As their show also incorporated elements that used front-projection, they possibly did have an educational effect on the audience by making clear the mechanism used.

Hecht stresses that Robertson's techniques were not original, even if he was the greatest showman of the group.[80] (Robinson slightly disagrees by stating that there appears to be no precedent for the use of two projectors simultaneously creating a superimposed image by means of front-

and back-projection.)[81] Robertson claimed that the Phantasmagoria grew out of his scientific preoccupations, thereby ignoring any debts to his predecessors. It had a tremendous impact on nineteenth century image projection, to the extent that in England magic lanterns were routinely referred to as "Phantasmagoria Lanterns."[82] To indicate how the two were linked, the author of a manual on the magic lantern published in 1865 used the pseudonym "A mere Phantom." In 1874, the editor of the new journal *The Magic Lantern* could sum up the transition, somewhat flamboyantly, in the first paragraph of the first issue:

> Some may think that we have taken up rather an antiquated subject, for as far back as the seventeenth century rude phantasms were thrown upon the screen to mystify and bewilder the Romans, by means of the first crude magic lantern. It was then used by wizards and necromancers to induce belief in their possession of supernatural powers. But now it is the means of affording amusement and instruction, and of demonstrating some of the most beautiful phenomena in science all over the world.[83]

As lanterns became more widespread, and the sense of mystery lost, the Phantasmagoria became passé, so that by the 1830s they were relegated to fairgrounds.[84] They lasted longer in Japan, and Lafcadio Hearn describes a show that he attended in the 1890s.[85] Musser's theory that "As belief in ghosts declined ... the apparent logic and effectiveness of projecting apparatus as instruments of mystical terror also diminished"[86] is ill-founded. Apart from lack of evidence as to what extent Phantasmagoria audiences were "mystically terrified," it is not true that belief in ghosts decreased during the nineteenth century, and so it could not have been the cause of the lantern's reduced fortunes. Cecil M. Hepworth reminisces in his autobiography about magic lantern shows he saw as a boy. It can be seen that the macabre elements of such presentations had not been totally domesticated in the late nineteenth century, as he remembered seeing Beale's *Choreutoscope* at the Royal Polytechnic Institution in the late 1870s. Hepworth reports that his father and John Henry Pepper were both on the Polytechnic's staff, and that the institution was a formative influence on himself.[87]

If it is true that a lantern was used to project a picture of the Virgin Mary and a pair of saints onto the church at Knock in 1879,[88] it would suggest that the technology could still possess the capacity to create a sense of wonder based, like the Phantasmagoria before it, on the audience's ignorance of the mechanism involved. The continuation of the genre by other means—including cinema—indicates that the ascendancy of scientific rationality is accompanied by unscientific urges that find fulfillment in a confrontation with the unknown. Alison Butler takes a view of the Phantasmagoria as more than merely one source among many for later exponents of the fantastic. She classifies it "as a rich metaphor for cinematic fantasy,"[89] and claims that seeing cinema in phantasmagoric terms "reminds us that the history of early film is really two histories: the history of a technology and the history of dreams."[90]

For Castle, the term "phantasmagoria" has evolved to mean something quite different from its original denotation. From being external to the viewer, it has come to stand for a psychological process. She sees the term phantasmagoria as a "kind of master trope in nineteenth-century romantic writing,"[91] and traces its use in what she terms "metaphoric displacement"[92] as an expression of the internalization of what had hitherto been external, so that what ancestors would have taken at face value was now seen as an illusion. This movement she attributes to developments in nineteenth-century science and philosophy and the increased interest in psychological as opposed to theological explanations, with the unforeseen effect that rather than being banished, ghosts were incorporated into a psychological perspective.[93]

This "haunting" ability of the mind helps to explain why there was a tension between those phantasmagoria operators who declared themselves to be educationalists and those who acted the parts of necromancers or magicians. It could also account for the movement from the position that ghosts were external agents to their being viewed as subjective hallucinations, although to extend the argument thus far, Castle would be unable to acknowledge that some spectres might originate outside consciousness. She traces the phantasmagoria's influence to Méliès, seeing him as a direct descendant of Robertson.[94] There would have been differences in their reception though, she continues, with earlier audiences tending to assume that what they were seeing was not a representation, whereas by the twentieth century the process of assimilation would have been complete, with no feelings of fear. That Castle overstates her case can be seen by the *frisson* of fear that frequently accompanies a ghost film.

Roger Sandell asserts that "the current image of ghosts as transparent figures seems to rest not on witness account [sic], but early cinema trick photography,"[95] This is claiming too much for cinema. Modern accounts by witnesses of the form alleged ghosts take do vary enormously, from solid to transparent, but the view that ghosts are transparent predates cinema. J. H. Brown, writing in 1863, states that witness accounts describe a ghost as "usually indistinct, and so transparent that objects are easily seen through it,"[96] Two magic lanterns were sometimes used in conjunction to create double images, but more importantly, by the 1860s spirit photography was well established, often using the same technique of double exposure, among others, as cinematic ghosts were to do over thirty years later.[97]

Spirit Photography

As well as theatrical ghost productions, photography provided another source of inspiration for early filmmakers who wished to portray the supernatural. Spirit photography has to be seen in the context of the Victorian photograph as memorial. Before the introduction of the technology on a large scale, the only way of remembering a deceased individual was through paintings, a method restricted to the better-off. For many people a photograph was the main means whereby an individual could be remembered by friends and relatives, and it was common for photographs to be taken of corpses as a reminder. It was a small step, in a flourishing climate of Spiritualism, for images of apparitions—"spirit extras"— invisible to the naked eye, to be found accompanying photographs of the living when developed. These were mostly of individuals known to be dead, assuming accuracy of identification, but there were also examples of living individuals appearing as extras, as well as objects and writing (the latter termed "psychographs").

Joe Nickell distinguishes between "photographing the paranormal" and "paranormal photographs," the former representing paranormal subjects such as ghosts, levitation and auras; the latter photographs allegedly obtained by paranormal means, which would include Thoughtography and religious images.[98] Spirit photographs fall into both these categories, but can be teased apart according to the circumstances. Spontaneous pictures ostensibly taken without the intention of capturing a supernatural image, but which have been found to contain a ghost upon examination, would be characterized as photographs of the paranormal. Paranormal photographs, on the other hand, would cover deliberate experiments, usually in a studio, where extras were found with the image of the sitter only after the pictures were developed.[99] These would sometimes, though often not, be known to the living subject. The spirit extra's appearance, however caused, is mediated by the equipment (not always a camera; sometimes sealed plates alone were used).[100]

Fred Gettings covers the history of spirit photography in both senses.[101] While acknowledging fraud he nevertheless assumes a large residue of photographs to be genuine, although not necessarily of the specific objects ostensibly depicted in them — all that can be said, in his opinion, is that some kind of discarnate agency must have been active. The capture of ghosts by photography seems to have been initiated by Mumler in Boston, Massachusetts, in 1861,[102] not long after Spiritualism's inauguration in 1848. It was also the start of the American Civil War, which perhaps gave the industry a momentum similar to that the First World War gave to Spiritualism (and Germany's Expressionist films) and the Second World War to film ghosts. Mumler set the style for many later practitioners by being charged with fraud, though he was acquitted for lack of evidence.

Helmut Gernsheim credits Brewster with the invention of spirit photography.[103] Brewster said he had devised it after seeing a photograph made in 1844 in which a boy had been seated while it was being taken, but had left before its completion, the lengthy exposures of the period giving him a transparent quality. This had given Brewster the idea of draping a person in a white sheet and then photographing them for only part of the exposure. Unfortunately, Brewster's account appeared in the *Scientific Review* in 1866, well after Mumler had inaugurated the craze.[104]

An examination of pictures produced in the latter half of the nineteenth century, the heyday of what can loosely be termed "experimental" spirit photography, indicates that a variety of methods was used.[105] Fodor cites unnamed experts as claiming that there were at least two hundred ways to produce extras non-paranormally.[106] Apart from séance room pictures of draped "ghosts," the most obvious, and a staple of filmic depictions later, was double exposure, underexposure giving the extra an ethereal quality. This approach could utilize pictures, perhaps, though not necessarily, of the sitter's departed loved ones, or living individuals. The two images could be superimposed, in which case the extra would appear to be transparent, or a mask could be used, the extra occupying a portion of the image. Pre-prepared plates could be substituted for the clients', should they have brought their own, or a transparency could be placed in front of the plate in the camera, under the hood.[107]

Other methods included drawing the extra onto the positive or, according to Gettings, painting the background behind the sitter with a fluorescent substance that was invisible to the naked eye but appeared on the print.[108] Simeon Edmunds mentions the use of a miniature electric lamp with a positive transparency mounted on it, or of a chemically treated rubber stamp, as ways of introducing extras.[109] In the séance room, photographs were taken of "spirits" that were paper cut-outs, three-dimensional models, or suitably draped assistants. Oddly for supposed denizens of a universal Afterlife, there seem to have been different dress codes for European and American apparitions. The former favored long flowing garments seemingly modeled on grave shrouds, whereas the latter tended towards everyday clothing of the sort they had worn pre-mortem.

The results seem very crude to the modern eye, but cameras only became widely available with the introduction of the Kodak in 1888, although at five guineas,[110] still out of the reach of much of the population; before then, photographs seemed inherently more mysterious. To those without knowledge of the processes involved, it might have seemed incredible that they could be faked. Only after wider exposure to amateur photography, and particularly after the publication of Hopkins's compendium of ways to manipulate the image in 1897, would it be fair to condemn believers in the grosser efforts as gullible. In 1898–99 an article entitled "Photographic Lies" was printed in *Harmsworth Magazine*.[111] It warned that fakery was easy, and illustrated the argument with, among other subjects, pictures of ghosts, with explanations of how they were made. Perhaps with the object of forestalling objections from photographers, the magazine continues:

> we doubt if photographers, amateur or otherwise, were ever guilty of using their knowledge of fakes for any purpose other than that of amusement....[112]

It should be added that spirit photography has its defenders. Eisenbud, for example, points to several factors that suggest the genuineness of at least some images: sometimes séance participants would sit incognito and acknowledge extras whom they recognized, and knew to be deceased; extras of people not known to have been photographed while alive would appear; as would recognizable images unlike extant photographs. These cases, he argues, render fraud less tenable as a catch-all explanation.[113]

Whatever opinion the general public had of spirit photographs at the end of the nineteenth century — some of the mystique lingered on, and the pictures definitely still had their proponents[114] — their production can be viewed as part of the repertoire available to the creators of film ghosts. Cinema readopted techniques already discarded by those with a serious interest in spirit photography:

> Most of the common tricks have been in use since the days of Mumler. The most common — double exposure — is so "old hat" that even before the end of the last century Henry Blackwell (who amassed more than 2,000 spirit photographs) complained that the famous French photographer Nadar should have known better than to produce a series of double exposures in order to show how Albert de Rochas might have been fooled, for the double exposure was a trick "known to most schoolboys."[115]

Any photograph preserves the memory of the subject, and a now-dead sitter and a spirit extra have a certain equivalence. André Bazin identifies this memorial function, where "the image helps us to remember the subject and to preserve him from a second spiritual death."[116] Unfortunately Bazin's fascination with the Platonic ideal of total cinema leads him to assert that "it is no longer a question of survival after death, but of a larger concept, the creation of an ideal world in the likeness of the real,"[117] as if the two would be contradictory; as far as any possible Afterlife is concerned, should one exist, it may be ideal, in the sense of being created in the mind, or have an independent status. The nature of the "real" is open to debate.

Bazin does mention the Surrealists' manipulations of photographs, but he downplays the extent to which photographs in general, and by extension film, can be altered, suggesting thereby that they correspond to objective reality. By insisting that photographs are more objective, and therefore more credible, than painting because there is less human interference, he is being naive. This line of argument ignores the prime examples of manipulation in photography and cinema that were available to him, spirit photographs and the work of Méliès respectively. The photographic image, whether still or moving, has never been a slice of unmediated life.

In addition to the role of spirit photography as a resource for filmmakers in putting ghosts on screen, the status of the extra nicely illustrates the difficulty of determining the veridicality of an apparition within a film's narrative. Castle, in discussing a picture by Buguet, who confessed to fraud in 1875, asks if the spirit could be taken to be projecting the sitter's thoughts.[118] Many of these pictures do strike the modern viewer as being akin to thought bubbles in cartoons, and they often bear a resemblance to inserts showing thought processes in early films.[119]

Theatrical Ghosts

Despite occasionally having actors dress up as ghosts, the Phantasmagoria and suchlike shows relied on slides, and of course these were not as convincing as a three-dimensional figure would have been. The Gothic had moved into the theater early on; for example, Matthew Lewis's *The Castle Spectre* had been mounted in 1797. As the Phantasmagoria and the Gothic novel both declined in the early nineteenth century, the vacuum was filled by supernatural-tinged melodrama that retained Gothic themes, and this too became an influence on film. Michael R. Booth claims that "The frequency with which ghosts appear in Gothic melodrama also distinguishes it from the rest of its class."[120]

Melodrama emphasized exciting visual qualities at the expense of characterization, with often oblique references in literary Gothic being made more explicit. They were plot-driven and relied on stereotypical stock characters. They were generally romantic and moralistic, with good triumphant: even dead heroes and heroines were often offered the consolation of heaven, a type of happy ending. Like film ghosts, they could be real or fake, and the real ones had a variety of functions, usually warning the living or gaining revenge on their murderers. There was also a strand of comic burlesque ghosts,[121] which could be seen as the ancestor of comedic ghost films. A well-known example of the increasing sophistication of the theatrical ghost was Dion Boucicault's 1852 play *The Corsican Brothers*, with "one of the last and most unearthly melodramatic ghosts."[122] Once again this relied on new technology, the appropriately titled "Corsican Trap," so that the deceased brother's ghost could make a gliding entrance,[123] a motion still frequently seen to characterize cinematic ghosts. Other attempts to evoke ghosts had to rely on costume, make-up and effects based on de Loutherberg's work from 1771 with filters, and gauze that was opaque when front-lit but transparent when back-lit.[124]

The Corsican Brothers was a late flowering of the supernatural, because by about 1840 naturalism had become dominant in theater. The ghost is of a transitional type in this play, because rather than appearing as a direct presence, he is seen as a vision, as is also the case with the earlier ghost of Marley in Charles Dickens's 1843 novel *A Christmas Carol* and later the unquiet ghost in *The Bells* (1871).[125] The presence of ghosts on stage did not disappear entirely, although to an extent the external threat they represented gradually gave way to psychological mechanisms, from "vengeful ghost to avenging conscience."[126]

Pepper's Ghost

However ingenious the presentation of *The Corsican Brothers*, it could not overcome the problem of showing a supposedly ethereal creature as all too solid on stage. Pepper's Ghost[127] was an attempt to rectify this as it used actors, out of sight of the audience, who were reflected by an angled sheet of glass, their reflections seeming to interact with the actors on the main stage. Unlike the Phantasmagoria shows, there was no attempt to persuade the audience that they were seeing anything other than an illusion: 'Professor' Pepper's advertising made a point of referring to "the wonders of optical science,"[128] and he was well known as an educationalist.[129] Even so, Pepper reports that he received many letters "treating it as a supernatural phenomenon, and not an effect from natural causes."[130]

On the whole, the domestication of the apparition, which the decline of the Phantasmagoria had begun, continued with "the Patent Ghost":

> Modern researches in spiritualism have led to one practical result — the discovery of a ghost. Not of an ordinary old-fashioned ghost, appearing in the midnight hour to people with a weak digestion, haunting graveyards and old country mansions, and inspiring romance-writers into the mischief of three-volume novels; but of a well-behaved, steady, regular, and respectable ghost, going through a prescribed round of duties, punctual to the minute — a Patent Ghost, in fact.[131]

The concept was formulated by Henry Dircks in 1858, and improved by Pepper, who added a hidden stage and used electric lighting — the original concept necessitated a small audience viewing the stage from a restricted vantage point that would have rendered shows uneconomic to stage.[132] Pepper's version was similar in effect to the "Living Phantasmagoria" — as distinguished from Robertson's version — presented earlier by Robin in France, and a dispute arose over priority, resulting in the failure of Dircks and Pepper to obtain royalties in that country.[133] Barnouw sees Dircks's and Robin's use of the term "Phantasmagoria" as transitional because it became associated with living people rather than slides.[134] To extend the point, film put apparitions back on the screen, but retained the people. These theatrical ghosts were closer to the spirit of cinema than were the magic lantern slides that more closely resembled the cinema in form.

Pepper's version necessitated the ghost actor standing beneath the stage,[135] with the glass angled about the horizontal axis; Hepworth, however, mentions the actor standing in the wings,[136] a much simpler procedure, which indicates that the glass would have to be angled about the vertical. Edmond H. Wilkie claims that R. C. Croft used this technique at the Polytechnic in 1874,[137] and Dawes also mentions this variant as a possibility, but does not indicate if it was used.[138] A bastardized Pepper's Ghost, the *Cabaret du Néant* (Tavern of the Dead) did use a vertically inclined pane, which in many respects harked back to the Phantasmagoria. The audience entered down a hall hung with black, the tables were formed from coffins and the waiters were in mourning dress. A member of the audience stood inside a coffin on the stage, an unseen sheet of glass was swung in front, and the subject appeared to turn into a skeleton in front of the audience, a reflection from a painted skeleton in the wings that was illuminated as the light on the coffin on the stage was turned down.[139] Hopkins also describes what is essentially a small-style Pepper's Ghost set-up, more suitable for a night-club than a large venue, indicating that the form carried on as a variety act long after it had ceased to be used seriously in theatrical performances.

The first full-blown Pepper's Ghost show was mounted in 1862, at the Royal Polytechnic. The "standard" ghost was still being formulated, as Pepper describes the first story put on at the Polytechnic, Edward George Bulwer-Lytton's *A Strange Story*, as involving "an apparition of a skeleton"[140] (this was a three-dimensional skeleton held by an assistant wearing black velvet). In a similarly confused manner, running concurrently with the well-known version of Dickens's *The Haunted Man*, actually a doppelgänger, was *Cupid and the Love Letter*, which involved "the ghost of a very pretty little boy dressed as Cupid...."[141]

Dircks lists a variety of possible subjects for his version.[142] Of these, only two, *The Haunted Man* and *The Returned Mariner*, in which the ghost of a sea farer returns to his loved ones, plus a phantom hand writing "Napoleon," could be classed as supernatural, despite Dircks's generic phrase "Spectre Drama." The term "Spectre" is clearly being used in the sense of "illusory," and need not apply just to the depiction of ghosts. The other descriptions read more like ideas for early trick films, and would have been difficult to stage, even without the constraints imposed by his method. Dircks felt bitter at the way in which Pepper's success had led to his own neglect, and his book grandly calls his own version "The Dircksian Phantasmagoria" to establish his link with a venerable tradition. He saw it as revolutionary, declaring it to be

> my invention for exhibiting optical illusions of a varied character hitherto unknown, except as inventions of romantic fiction, or as the result of some unhappy derangement of the optic nerve.[143]

That Dircks's descriptions of possible acts using his idea read like film descriptions is significant for Barnouw, because Dircks and Robertson were key figures in facilitating "the magician's persistent romance with ghouls,"[144] which later fed into the nascent cinema.

In June 1863, Dickens's *All the Year Round* carried an article, "Haunted Hoxton," about a visit to see a production that Hecht identifies as *The Widow and the Orphans!*[145] A reflected skeleton caused some derision, but the ghost of the widow herself impressed both audience and writer enormously, despite her being "a little foreshortened, a little out of the perpendicular...."[146] As with the Phantasmagoria, the novelty of Pepper's Ghost spawned a number of imitators. Price reproduces an advertisement for Gompertz's *Spectrescope* of 1867[147] that contains the usual blend of floating heads, haunted houses and Faustian temptation; *The Haunted House* is described as "the Laughable Spectral Farce."

Like the Phantasmagoria, however, the idea became stale, so that a newspaper correspondent who had witnessed its rise and fall could write:

> ...It was shown in "Faith, Hope and Charity," in which the villain is haunted by the spirit of his murdered victim. It caused such a sensation that again and again it was the feature of a play, until the novelty of the illusion was gone. Its last appearance at this theater [i.e. the Britannia, Hoxton] was in a pantomime in 1890.[148]

By the time of Pepper's death in 1900, an obituary could claim that his success was due only to an association with the interest shown in Spiritualism by the general public.[149]

Heard outlines the career of Randall Williams, who in the latter part of the nineteenth century ran a successful fairground show based on Pepper's Ghost before switching to film shows in 1896; other ghost shows at fairs were probably theatrical sketches with the 'ghost' as the draw, and including variety acts.[150] Heard sees this switch to film as part of a steady progression from the Phantasmagoria displays, begun with serious intent but later demoted to curiosities. Other showmen did not embrace the new medium, and Heard cites the ghost house and train, and, utilizing Pepper's Ghost-type effects, the Ghost Mansion, as heirs to the early ghost shows.[151]

Hepworth's autobiography describes a marriage of Pepper's Ghost with film.[152] Invented by Oskar Messter in about 1910 and christened variously *Alabastra*, *Tanagra*, and later — when demonstrated in London in 1912 — *Kinoplasticon*, this system used a film projector instead of a plain light source with a sheet in the opposite wing, invisible to the audience. The actors in the film wore white, had hands and faces whitened, and were photographed against a black velvet background, which was then processed for maximum contrast. When the film was projected onto the sheet, its image was reflected onto the stage where it appeared to be in the middle of the action. The image could be made to seem quite solid by increasing the intensity of the light, or more transparent by reducing it.

Hepworth reports that a number of such films were made, and were shown at the Scala Theater in London, but that there was little audience interest. Messter describes this effect in his 1936 book, but curiously the projector is placed in the pit, a style reminiscent of Pepper's original technique. According to Cassell's *Cyclopaedia* of 1911, the results were an improvement on Pepper's effect.[153] Messter is also credited by Paul Virilio as an early exponent of superimposition,[154] a staple also of spirit photography. According to Heard the technique, like Pepper's Ghost itself, was eventually consigned to a fairground side-show, harking back to the first itinerant cinema presenters.[155]

Conclusions

Barber points out the parallels between the magic lantern ghost shows of the nineteenth century and early cinema.[156] Images were manipulated to tell a story, there were sound effects and music, and a narrator. The effect of both was potentially overwhelming to an unsophisticated audience, to the extent that viewers could not distinguish between reality and fiction. With both, touring entrepreneurs hired halls on an ad hoc basis, continuity between portions of the show was minimal, and themes were copied if successful. Even practices were transferred, slides of heads becoming what Barber calls "precinematic close-ups." A contemporary account of Robertson's Phantasmagoria mentions that the performance lasted for ninety minutes, making it feature length:

> ...at the moment the display is to begin, the sudden extinction of the lights plunges them for one and a half hours into a darkness as dreadful as it is total....[157]

The two modes even coexisted. Paolo Cherchi Usai notes that Porter's *Parsifal* of 1904 utilized actors in the theatre, Wagnerian music played by an orchestra and magic lantern slides alternating with portions of the film.[158] Another way in which the magic lantern shows prefigured the cinema was in the development of a narrative structure. Simple transformations were performed, such as the sails on a windmill revolving, or the Three Graces turning into skeletons, but the story line could be much more sophisticated. Later developments in magic lantern projection, particularly when utilized by the Temperance Movement, often involved elaborate scripts read over a series of slides presented with a moral purpose.

It can be seen that during the eighteenth and nineteenth centuries the ways in which apparitions were portrayed changed. During the nineteenth, perhaps aided in part by the efforts of researchers to collect ghost stories from ordinary people, a consensus emerged, and the attributes of ghosts gradually became codified. By the time moving pictures came to be developed, there was already a rich tradition of depictions of the Afterlife on which to draw. The next chapter traces the development of ghosts on film through the silent period, showing how they were transformed from being the objects of trick films to full actors in their own dramas.

2

Silent Ghosts

The Beginning of the Cinema Age

The first filmmakers drew on the heterogeneous tradition bequeathed to them by stage shows. Adwin A. Dawes, discussing Étienne-Gaspard Robertson, finds common ground in the experiences of audiences of the Phantasmagoria and of the horror film:

> The formula of charging people good money to be, in many cases, frightened out of their wits is a sure and certain one, and Robertson may be regarded as the legitimate forerunner of all the Midnight Ghost Shows that gave vicarious thrills to cinema audiences in the USA during the nineteen-forties and -fifties.[1]

X. Theodore Barber is more concerned with the technological aspects used, and the effects that they can induce, but still stresses the continuity:

> It was the early trick films, however, that most clearly paralleled the Phantasmagoria, which in itself was part of the magic tradition. Many of these films included transformations, superimpositions, and rear projections, not to mention frequent appearances of ghosts, skeletons, and the like. With horror films later taking up these same techniques and motifs, the Phantasmagoria could be said to survive, but in a new form, to the present day.[2]

A. Nicholas Vardac finds it unsurprising that cinema was born at the end of the search in the theater, from David Garrick onwards, for ever-greater realism. This movement would account for the loss of popularity of ghost shows in the late nineteenth century, apart for a surge of interest in the 1860s. However, the interpenetration of the fantastic into realism could still be seen. Vardac describes a play mounted by Henry Irving in 1877, *The Dead Secret*, as "nothing more than a good old-fashioned ghost story."[3] From the description he supplies, it sounds like the sort of drawing-room séance that the Victorian medium D. D. Home gave, and Vardac counts this a "realistic presentation of the supernatural." He sees this sense of realism transferring to cinema, arguing that even Georges Méliès, despite the fantastic nature of many of his films, could see the realistic properties of cinema.[4]

Vardac's concentration on continuities between theater and cinema is at odds with Tom Gunning's *Cinema of Attractions*.[5] Gunning sees narrative complexity only beginning to make an impact on cinema after about 1906, before which films, of whatever kind, were "a series of views" with little emphasis on character development. They were merely one attraction among many available, and no more significant, often on variety bills with other brief acts. Filmmakers were not setting out to create a self-sufficient world, which accounts for the lack of psychological profundity. Gunning's analysis indicates why supernatural themes, which were popular in the first decade of cinema, declined in popularity thereafter until a resurgence in the 1930s. When films were brief sketches, a ghost or poltergeist made an interesting spectacle, but as the emphasis turned inwards, towards the portrayal of psychological depth, film was faced with the difficulty of making manifest something that by its nature is intangible. Charles Musser's general point about early cinema is particularly relevant to filmic ghosts:

> Here, if only for a moment, early cinema is worth defining negatively: its representational system could *not* present a complex, unfamiliar narrative capable of being readily understood irrespective of exhibition circumstances or the spectators' specific cultural knowledge.[6]

Once the psychological approach had been mastered and audience sophistication increased, the way was open for fantastic themes to return, but with greater depth. Whatever the reason, trick films made up a substantial proportion of early film production. Eileen Bowser provides figures that show how popular these were in the early years of the twentieth century, and how dramatic the decline was after 1903:[7]

Year	Percentage of Total Production
1900	26%
1901	20%
1902	21%
1903	10%

Trick films as a percentage of total film production, 1900–1903

She continues that after 1903, only four or five trick films a year were made in the United States. The percentages are very rough, but assuming that surviving films are representative of those made, they do suggest that trick films, of which those utilizing quasi-paranormal themes form a subsection, were a significant proportion of the total. The percentages were probably even greater for pre–1900 production. As trick films declined so did those with supernatural themes. It is also worth noting that production dropped off well before the 1906–07 date that Gunning gives as the heyday of the Cinema of Attractions, indicating that trick films outwore their welcome prior to longer, more realistic films' becoming the norm.[8]

Georges Méliès[9]

The specific link between filmic representations of the supernatural and their visual precursors was the type of trick film pioneered by Méliès, whose films can be seen as part of the stage-magic tradition. He was influenced by magicians, in particular John Nevil Maskelyne and George Cooke. Maskelyne, like Harry Houdini later on, disliked bogus mediumship, and had exposed fraudulent mediums the Davenport Brothers.[10] Méliès made a film in 1902, *The Cabinet Trick of the Davenport Brothers* (*L'Armoire des Frères Davenport*), in tribute to Maskelyne. Georges Sadoul emphasizes Méliès's familiarity with Albert A. Hopkins's 1897 compendium of stage illusions, the second chapter of which concerns "Optical tricks," but Hammond points out that by the time it was published, Méliès would have been aware of the types of act discussed, indeed was already using some of the principles in his stage work.[11]

Méliès began mounting stage illusions from 1888, an intermittent career that ran alongside his film work, emphasizing the link still further. An 1889 act, *The Fairy of the Flowers, or Cagliostro's Mirror* (*La Fée des Fleurs ou le Miroir de Cagliostro*) is based on Pepper's Ghost, but without the supernatural element. It is also a foretaste of his later transformation films. The audience see themselves, as if a mirror is in front of them. The lighting shifts and they turn into a bed of flowers in the center of which is a bouquet, which opens to reveal a woman's head.[12] A later stage show, *American Spiritualistic Mediums, or the Recalcitrant Decapitated Man* (*American Spiritualistic Mediums ou le Décapité récalcitrant*, 1891), satirizes a medium who will not stop talking even when his head has been removed, and features a skeleton carrying the medium's head pursued by its owner's body. His last stage illusion, *Spirit Phenomena* (*Les Phenomènes du Spiritisme*, 1907) has a medium visited by a ghost that proceeds to undress him, but is trapped between the pages of a prayer book. Although the techniques available to the filmmaker were more flexible than when designing stage shows, Méliès's films pursued similar themes.

Méliès was not the only filmmaker working in a non-realistic style, but he was the most significant, to the extent that Frazer quotes Carlos Clarens's statement that "Ghoulies, ghosties, all things that go bump on the screen, are forever in his debt."[13] Frazer qualifies this by pointing out that Méliès's ghosts are never frightening (and although we cannot determine exactly what an early audience felt, this seems reasonable). They were simply a variety element: "Transparent beings are one species among a number of high-flying entertainers."[14] Hammond compares him favorably to the Lumières, suggesting that the difference can be summed up in the image of a bourgeois having his portrait taken. In one, he stares at some distant horizon, in the other:

> The same man poses in the same manner, except that a ghost looks over his shoulder: one image calls the other into question[15]

Many Méliès films that have titles suggestive of a supernatural element have been lost, but enough remain to be able to determine his approach. His repertoire was wider than trick films, and of these there were very few that included ghosts—The Devil and demon-like creatures are much more frequent. He did make films with moving furniture and other props that could suggest poltergeist activity, but no cues are provided to indicate that the movement is caused by a discarnate agency.

The Bewitched Inn (*L'Auberge ensorcelée*, 1897) features an unruly hotel room in which objects move or disappear, the effects being created by stop-substitution and wires, but as the title suggests, this could be accounted for by magical rather than supernatural means. According to Frazer, this film and the later more elaborate but otherwise similar *The Inn Where No Man Rests* (*L'Auberge du bon repos*, 1903) may have been influenced by a scene set in a haunted house in a play first presented in 1839, called *The Devil's Pills*.[16] These two films highlight the problem filmmakers had in distinguishing internal from external states: the guest at *The Bewitched Inn* is apparently sober, in which case the events might be seen as objective, whereas the one at *The Inn Where No Man Rests* is drunk, and the events could be regarded as hallucinations. Nothing within either film provides this information, which has to be inferred by the viewer. The English title might be regarded as evidence, because it suggests that nobody gets any rest, drunk or sober, but the ironic French title does not carry such an implication. The poltergeist style was satirized by Max Linder's *Entente Cordiale* (1912) which has pictures and furniture dancing around with Max and his friends.

Even when apparitions appear, it is often in a diabolic context. *The Haunted Castle* (*Le Manoir du Diable*, 1896) features Mephistopheles conjuring up phantoms and skeletons from a magic cauldron.[17] *The Cave of the Demons* (*La Caverne Maudite*, 1898) has a number of double-exposed transparent ghosts through which the walls of the cave can be seen. Patrick Robertson asserts that this was the first use of such a technique,[18] but Rachael Low, Roger Manvell and Denis Gifford claim precedence for G. A. Smith's *The Corsican Brothers* of the same year (Smith is discussed below).[19] *The Devil in a Convent* (*Le Diable au couvent*, 1899), as described by Sadoul,[20] has the ghosts of nuns appear to drive off a number of imps accompanying Satan. By 1903, Méliès was combining effects with panache. *The Apparition, or Mr. Jones' Experience With a Ghost* (*Le Revenant*), combines poltergeist-style activity with a double-exposure apparition, once again set in an inn. Objects move and harass a guest, and then a lady appears who turns into a demon, an effect accomplished by double exposure. Hammond mentions some of the effects, quoting from the Star Film Catalogue's description:

> A traveler, suffering from hallucinations, sees a phantom grow indistinct then clear (focus), become transparent then opaque (exposure), and 'enter into the most marvelous vibrations, horizontal and vertical.[21]

The Infernal Cauldron (*Le Chaudron infernal*, 1903) features veiled spirits rising from a cauldron and hanging in mid-air, kicking their feet, before vanishing. In *Alcofrisbas, The Master Magician* (*L'Enchanteur Alcofrisbas*), also made in 1903, Méliès's young rival is threatened by five sheet-clad apparitions dancing in the air. A prince is menaced by the spirits of the dead in *The Witch* (*La Fée carabosse ou le Poignard fatal*, 1906). In *The Knight of the Snows* (*Le Chevalier des neiges*, 1912), his penultimate film, the hero is given a rose by a good spirit, and at the end the villain is claimed by Mephistopheles, to whom he has sold his soul.

These characters tend to be generalized symbols, as are the demons that populate his manichean universe, rather than post-mortem personalities. It could be argued that the last example does show a specific individual who has survived death, even though it entails his eternal damnation, but his name is Hugh the Cruel, known as the Black Knight, to counterbalance the Knight of the Snows. He is an idea rather than a person. Katherine Singer Kovács[22] locates this dualism in the influence on Méliès of the Féerie tradition, a form born shortly after the French Revolution, making it almost contemporaneous with the Phantasmagoria. Productions in the Féerie style comprised a struggle between good and evil, with a supernatural component incarnated in gnomes and witches, and featuring numerous sudden transformations.

Skeletons are present from time to time in Méliès's work, possibly influenced by *The Light and Dark Séance* show that he saw at the Egyptian Hall in London, put on by Maskelyne and Cooke, which featured a skeleton with rattling jaws and a detachable head.[23] The *Vanishing Lady* (*Escamotage d'une dame chez Robert-Houdin*, 1896) is turned temporarily into a skeleton, but this is an instance of a general tendency to compose stop-motion transformations. *Whimsical Illusions* (*Les Illusions fantaisistes*, 1910) also features a skeleton, which moves around as part of a series of effects. *A Spiritualist Photographer* (*Le Portrait spirite*, 1903) is another metamorphosis, using a dissolve, on a white rather than a black ground, and not a double exposure as the title might suggest.[24] The title in either language is misleading, as there is no attempt at producing the familiar type of spiritualist photograph. The film concerns the transformation of a woman into a painting, but it is not clear whether the title was designed to act as a lure or to mislead.

For Méliès himself, differentiating between types of effect would perhaps seem pointless. Frazer quotes Méliès's declaration in the catalogue accompanying the *Exposition Commemorative du Centenaire de Georges Méliès*:[25]

> It is the intelligent use of trick work which enables us to make visible the supernatural, the imaginary, even the impossible.

This suggests that he regarded "trick work" as the common denominator underpinning his effects, whatever category they could be deemed to fall into, and that a "spirit" was no different from, say, a vanishing lady or an impish-looking and distinctly unthreatening demon.[26] The binding thread was that rationality was undermined, and aetiology was unimportant.

Stan Brakhage hints at this:

> Thus George became the first man to recognize motion pictures as medium of both super-nature and under-world — an instrument for unveiling the natural through reflection ... and also the gateway for an alien world underneath the surface of our natural visual ability.[27]

Other Early Filmmakers

As well as Méliès, other filmmakers were making trick films in the first decade of the medium's history, some obviously inspired by Méliès, but others taking an original stance. Stuart Blackton and Albert E. Smith had made a Vitagraph film exploiting interest in the supernatural as early as 1899 in their *A Visit to the Spiritualist*, which featured a skeleton conjured up during a séance, made unconvincing by showing the person in the skeleton suit not against a black background, but instead against a flat representing a brick wall, resulting in maximum contrast.[28]

Many early films contained depictions of what would in real life be hazardous if not fatal activities, such as chases, but these were generally treated in knockabout fashion — the policeman in Robert Paul's *The ? Motorist* (1906) who is run over is able to reconstruct his body. Death and its possible aftermath are not considered. One film that could be construed as ending with the death of the protagonist is Cecil Hepworth's *How It Feels to Be Run Over* (1900). The car 'crashes' into the camera, and the screen goes black, a representation of death used by Laurence Sterne in *Tristram Shandy*, who uses a black page.[29]

Cinema was still in the process of constructing a viable representation of what life after death would be like. Rather than showing an apparition arising from the wreckage, Hepworth mixes a literary device for suggesting death, but which later comes to represent mere loss of consciousness, and the implication that the camera has come off worst, the blank screen indicating that the camera has stopped functioning. The words scratched directly onto the emulsion, "Oh dear, mother will be pleased," suggest both that the filmmaker has been reduced to animating the film given the catastrophe that has befallen the equipment, and the possibly dying words, or even post-mortem words—coinciding as they do with the blackness—of the accident victim. Hepworth would later depict a ghost, in *Dr. Trimball's Verdict* (1913), in which the doctor murders his rival and later buys a skeleton, which it transpires is his victim's. The ghost appears on the bones, frightening the doctor to death.[30]

Frazer suggests that the idea for Blackton's *The Haunted Hotel* (1907), the forerunner of animation in which objects moved around without the aid of wires by means of single-frame exposure, came from the same sources that inspired Méliès, if not from him directly.[31] It is certainly derivative: a man is in bed, the room shakes violently, and he turns through 360° several times. Then a coffee pot pours coffee unassisted, a sugar bowl puts in sugar and a spoon stirs it. The milk jug, though, has trouble, and suddenly an imp jumps out and helps it. This can only be classed as a haunting in the generalized way that Méliès used the term. Blackton made a number of trick films, usually involving his "lightning sketches," and *The Haunted Hotel* has to be seen in the context of these manipulations: the events would not have been taken as a serious representation of a haunting, or even a poltergeist, which the film is closer to in spirit than it is to depicting a haunted room.

The haunted hotel was clearly a favorite device for filmmakers who wanted to display their trick effects. As well as the Méliès and Blackton efforts, Thomas Edison made two films on the theme, *Strange Adventures of a New York Drummer* (1899) and in 1900, *Uncle Josh in a Spooky Hotel*, one of three "Uncle Josh" films released as tie-ins with Edison sound recordings.[32] The Drummer is a traveling salesman who puts up in a typical poltergeist-ridden hotel room in which, via stop-motion, he finds his clothes changing and objects appearing and disappearing. In 1904 Hepworth's *The Bewitched Traveller* (a title presumably intended to allude to Méliès's 1897 *The Bewitched Inn*) sees the table in an inn disappear and reappear on the opposite of the room; outside his transport disappears, and finally he vanishes himself.[33]

Another Méliès-style film was Biograph's 1902 *A Mystic Reincarnation*. The term reincarnation is used loosely, as the film features a magician assembling a woman from parts. The language of psychical research was available to filmmakers, but it was used in a debased form to suggest something sensational, rather than as an attempt to describe accurately the contents of the film.[34] The word "mystic" was also popular as a peg upon which to hang anti-realistic events. Before *A Mystic Reincarnation*, Edison had brought out *The Mystic Swing* (1900), in which a girl on a swing disappears and is replaced by a skeleton, as at the end of Méliès's influential *The Vanishing Lady* (1896). The use of skeletons and the word "mystic" is a direct bridge with contemporaneous stage shows that used the same underpinnings for magic illusions.

The use of esoteric-seeming terminology to indicate the nature of the filmic contents, even when these had no relation to any depiction of the supernatural, is seen in other films of the period that borrow the language of psychical research. For example, in 1904 Lewin Fitzhamon directed a comedy called *The Haunted Oak*, in which a boy hides inside a hollow oak as a prank. Also in 1904, W. R. Booth made a film for Paul called *The Haunted Scene Painter*, in which theater properties, including a ghost as well as a dragon and moon, become animated. Even Méliès was not averse to trading on extra-filmic associations: in 1898 he made *Illusions Fantasmagoriques*, a standard stop-substitution treatment of a stage illusion, *The Box Trick*.

After Méliès, the best-known of the pioneers working in the trick/quasi-supernatural proto-genre was G. A. Smith (the two were in correspondence during the early years[35]). Smith made several films with a supernatural flavor, in a more realistic style than Méliès and Blackton. This is contrary to David Shipman's assertion that he "was a follower of Méliès,"[36] although he did film the highly Mélièsian subject of *Faust and Mephistopheles* in 1898. His interest in supernatural subjects perhaps stemmed from his intense involvement in the early Society for Psychical Research, for which he assisted in telepathy experiments.[37]

He made a version of Boucicault's *The Corsican Brothers*, also in 1898, pioneering superimposition, a device for which Smith had been granted a British patent the year before.[38] The ghostly brother was achieved by filming the actor for a second time using black velvet, a technique previously used in spirit photography. A later vision, showing a duel in a vignette, used the same technique, but superimposed the image onto a black part of the background so that no detail showed through, making it seem solid.[39] This inset technique was influential in suggesting internal processes and was adopted by Zecca and Porter, either using a film insert or a second stage behind the main set. The same year Smith made another film linking back to spirit photography double exposures, *Photographing a Ghost*. The subject, having been carried into the studio in a large box labeled "Ghost," refuses to keep still, disappearing and reappearing until the frustrated photographer attacks him, whereupon the apparition sinks through the floor; "A clean, sharp, and perfect film" as Smith's catalogue modestly describes it.[40] In *The Gambler's Wife* (1899), the gambler is persuaded not to commit suicide by his wife's ghost.[41] Double exposure was used to show Mary's ghost in *Mary Jane's Mishap* (1903).

At about the same time, Billy Bitzer was complaining that Biograph was at a disadvantage when making trick films because its cameras perforated the film strip as it was exposed, which made rewinding the film inside the camera to obtain double exposures impracticable.[42] This had not prevented the company from reassembling old footage in 1900 to make a series of 'new' films using superimposition, including *Neptune's Daughters*, combining a ship, ghosts and dancers, and *The Ghost Train*, with a train and moon scene.[43]

Another early example of a trick film that invokes the supernatural is Paul's *The Haunted Curiosity Shop* (1901). It has much in common, in subject and method, with Méliès's *The Vanishing Lady*, as a floating head joins the torso of a woman, then the bottom half enters, they join up, and become a whole woman. Paul also showed that he was able to tackle a serious subject with *Scrooge; or, Marley's Ghost* (1901), though in 1906 J. H. Martin directed the comic *The Medium Exposed* for him.[44] The other pioneer who owed a debt to Méliès was Booth, whose *The Magic Sword* (1907) features a ghost on castle battlements, perhaps inspired by *Hamlet*, except that Booth includes a giant. Earlier, in 1899, Booth had made a serious drama, *The Miser's Doom*, in which a miser's victim returns to haunt him, whereupon he dies of shock.[45]

Erik Barnouw examines early "supernatural" films as part of his discussion of the role played by stage magicians in pioneering cinema techniques. The problem was that when these transitions from one medium to another were successful, they carried the means of their own destruction because of their proliferation, including that nineteenth century magic staple, the apparition.[46] The magic went out of magic through mass-production, so that the novelty wore off. This coincided with the increasing length of feature films and a greater complexity of narrative structure. Early trick films, including those featuring ghosts, came to be regarded as unsatisfactory.[47] Cinematic ghosts were largely de-centered as subjects, making appearances as peripheral elements in other types of film, notably melodramas. The situation was evident as early as 1902, with the first version of the Maria Marten story, *Maria Martin [sic], or the Murder in the Red Barn*, in which Maria's ghost appears to a condemned William Corder.[48]

This marginalization only changed in the 1930s, when ghosts were again allowed to take center stage. There were ghosts in the intervening period, for example Biograph's *The Ghost* (1911), released the same year as their *Won Through a Medium*, which features a séance but nothing paranormal. The ghost in *The Ghost* is merely the backdrop to a robbery caper in which the burglars attempt to impersonate the ghost, which is so familiar to the residents that they ignore it.[49] Méliès was in decline by now, and ceased production in 1912, but those films which dealt with ghosts in this period, with the notable exception of D. W. Griffith's, still tended to be made outside the United States.

Ghosts Take on Personality

A serious attempt at depicting life after death is to be found in the Russian *The Mermaid* (1910), one of a number of Russian films of the period in which a ghost lures the hero to his fate.[50] A prince spurns a miller's daughter who drowns herself. He marries, but Banquo-like, she appears at the feast. Only the prince can see her, causing one to wonder about her veridicality. Eight years later, the prince, having fallen out of love with his wife, goes riding. An intertitle proclaims: "Some strange force ... drags me against my will to these sad banks." Nymphs, of whom the daughter is one, have congregated at the miller's ruined house, and they inveigle the prince into the water. After an intertitle "At the bottom of the river Dnepr," a tableau shows the dead prince with the miller's daughter, accompanied by the other nymphs. This apotheosis scene appears to have been influenced by Méliès, and the producer commented that it was particularly popular with its early audiences.[51] The Russian title is *Rusalka*, which would have made the subject matter clear to its original audience. A *rusalka* in Russian folklore can, among other features, be the ghost of a drowned maiden who haunts the location at which she met her end, or be a water-spirit, analogous to Western European elves and fairies. They often inhabit beautiful underwater palaces.[52]

The narrative complexity is a long way from earlier films that utilize perceptions of what might constitute supernatural phenomena as a peg for displays of tricks. The morality seems confused — the prince, the cause of suffering by both the miller and his daughter, is reconciled to his first love, hardly a punishment, at the expense of his blameless wife who, it is suggested, still loves him — but the apparition, unlike most of her filmic predecessors, motivates the story by suggesting that the prince regrets abandoning her, and is literally "haunted" by her death. When she appears at the wedding there is a possibility that the prince, overcome by remorse, is producing her to punish himself, which might mean that he commits suicide at the spot where she had died. The concluding underwater scene, however, suggests that she has an objective existence, that her earlier appearances were veridical, and that he has willingly responded to her call so that they might be rejoined.

As might be expected, the First World War inspired a number of meditations on life after death by film-makers. A transitional type of ghost film — and unusual in that it takes a left-wing perspective — is *The Spirit of the Conqueror* (1914) which, as well as the ghosts of famous deceased Americans, also features The Spirit of Re-Incarnation.[53] This Spirit joins a Messenger from Earth to give a baby newly born into a family of rich industrialists the soul of Napoleon. As an adult he initially supports his father, but by challenging injustice is disinherited and becomes a strike leader. He dies in the class struggle just as Labor wins the dispute, and his soul is welcomed back to Heaven.

Griffith made two films of particular relevance to ghost cinema. His most significant exploration of life after death, *The Greatest Question* (1919), examined below, bookends the war, at least for European countries, with another of his feature-length films that contains supernatural happenings, *The Avenging Conscience* (1914).[54] As the plot of the latter, concerning a man killing his uncle, transpires to have been a bad dream brought on by reading Poe, the ghost of the uncle is clearly an hallucination, which as Pauline Kael and Edward Wagenknecht both indicate,[55] prefigures German psychological dramas of the 1920s. But as the audience along with the protagonist discovers only this at the end of the film, the appearance of the uncle, Jesus, and even a group of demons, reaching what Lindsay called "a higher demoniacal plane,"[56] are all accorded the status of objective events.

There is no reason to doubt that they are real as the plot unfolds, yet as Roberta E. Pearson points out,[57] there is a discrepancy in acting styles and camera position between the vision of Jesus and the scene of the interrogation by the detective. The supposed remorseful murderer is seen groveling in an histrionic manner in long shot in a style, Pearson suggests, of a Biograph film of 1908,[58] that is, it is retarded for the period in which it was made, whereas the interrogation contains more close-ups and realistic (given the assumption of guilt) acting, a mode in keeping with the norm for the period. The visions would have seemed stylized to their first audience, hinting at their subjective nature.

The uncle's ghost, a double-exposure, makes its first appearance, when the nephew is talking to his girlfriend, from the wall behind which his body has been placed. Unfortunately Griffith misjudged the distances when photographing the uncle, with the result that he looks larger than the couple (or perhaps his size is symbolic, representing vengeance). They do not see him, but he points accusingly, then melodramatically mimics being strangled. Suddenly the young man looks serious and feels his throat. The uncle fades. Neither of the living sees the uncle, but he is able to affect his nephew. The second appearance is when the young man is in bed. This time the nephew can see the ghost, which again points before approaching and crouching menacingly before slowly fading away. Later, Jesus appears to the nephew, first vignetted in a corner of the scene, then on the cross superimposed against clouds. The nephew is looking somewhat deranged, but then four demons appear amidst smoke. The uncle intervenes to drive them towards the camera, at which sparks fly up. Although not stated, this is presumably part of the guilty conscience, with a conventional view of Hell, likely to be his destination except for his uncle's intervention.

During the interview with the detective, he has a vision of himself with a semi-dressed skeleton, which harks back to the trick films in which skeletons and ghosts function as tokens of supernatural occurrences. The uncle rises up between the nephew and the detective, again somewhat overlarge in the frame. The nephew can see him and looks aghast, but the detective is confused. Dream-logic overwhelms the narrative as the nephew leaps at his uncle, but stands back as his own double-exposed self takes his place in a fight with the shade, trying to strangle him as the nephew strangled him in life. To the detective, whose point of view we now see, the man merely seems to be twitching his hands feebly before we see him jump back into the fray, clutching the air as the double and the uncle disappear. Needless to say, by this stage the game is up.

The paucity of examples suggests that films dealing with the Afterlife in a *developed* manner were uncommon during the early period. This hiatus surprisingly includes the First World War, when it might be expected that supernatural elements would be on filmmakers' minds, as they were to a certain extent during the Second World War. As Low puts it in her discussion of the first war:

> Nor, for that matter, did the British film go through an early phase of morbid thrills comparable to the "Gothic" tales of the early nineteenth century. It is true that vampire stories from abroad had a short vogue during 1916, but weird and exotic British films were few and for the most part mild....[59]

Great War film ghosts were rarities, although there are several examples from 1919, suggesting a delayed reaction to the stresses of conflict. A consolatory example from the 1914–18 period itself is *The Man That Might Have Been* (1914) in which a man dreams of his dead wife and child until he is reunited with them by his own death. In 1917 *The Ghost of Old Morro* shows a revenge action going wrong and leading to the death of the instigator who then becomes a ghost, without the opportunity to expiate past sins.[60] This reduction in the quantity of ghost films during the war was matched by the decline of the written ghost short story. Julia Briggs contends that the war, and Sigmund Freud, inhibited the writing of such stories, heralding the decline of the form in the 1920s.[61] Whatever the cause, the effect was not confined to cinema.

One of the post-war efforts is Griffith's *The Greatest Question* (1919), which is about whether there is life after death. The theme is answered in the affirmative, but is overshadowed by the melodrama centering on Lillian Gish, her adoptive family and the villains who employ her. The ostensible subject-matter is signaled by the first intertitle: "However light or frivolous we may be, all of us rebel at the thought that our high dreams, hopes and loves shall only end in the bitter dust of death," and the second: "If only one that we have known, who has gone before could return to give a word of hope! For behind the strongest faith, there is a Great Question." The supernatural element, despite its brevity, was a clear indication to the bereaved that they would be reunited with loved ones, although in fact the son's appearance could be attributed to telepathy, and need not presuppose his survival.

Prior to his departure for the war, John's mother has a premonition

2. Silent Ghosts 47

that she will not see him again, to which he replies that there is something between them that no bullet can kill. The life-after-death theme is reinforced by the family retainer, Zeke, telling the children a ghost story, after which they are frightened at the cemetery ("lodgings made safe by superstitious fears" an intertitle calls it) by seeing a fugitive in a white sheet that they mistake for a ghost.[62] Wagenknecht and Slide reproduce an advertisement that *First National Exhibitors Circuit* ran in January 1920 suggesting that cinemas showing the film should collaborate with the local newspaper to offer a reward, on a sliding scale according to gender and color, to anyone willing to stay alone, chained to a bed, in a graveyard, and recount his or her experiences with ghosts to the newspaper the following day.[63]

John is killed when his submarine dives while he is on deck. An intertitle quoting John 8:51, "Verily, I say unto you if a man keep my saying he shall never see death," is shown, followed by a shot of the mother reading the Bible, and cuts between the mother and John as the submarine dives link the pair. The next scene shows John entering the house during a storm, and he embraces his mother by the open door, significantly while the father has turned away, so that it is not clear whether he too would have seen his son had he been looking. The scene is tinted blue, the traditional theatrical color of the supernatural, but after the embrace it turns brown, perhaps suggesting warmth transcending the coldness of death. John is then seen to have vanished, but later the family receives a telegram announcing his death, at the very time that he had appeared. Technically then, he was a crisis apparition of the kind familiar in psychical research, but his appearance could have been the result of a telepathic transmission from a dying man to a loved one. In either event, the mother is comforted, and still feels her son's presence.[64]

The father is a skeptic, and when the family is in financial trouble the mother exhorts her son to prove his existence to his scoffing father. The son appears, and both parents see him, though again the mother is the key to John's return. The father changes his attitude, and whereas before he had railed against Providence, now he is reconciled. An intertitle allows John to speak the line: "Farewell, until our tomorrow," hinting that he will not appear again, but that he and his loved ones will still be reunited when their time comes. Wagenknecht suggests that Griffith, with his very profound religious beliefs, was not merely capitalizing on the interest in psychic matters following the war; but whatever his motives, the fact that the subject of life after death did not capture the public's attention is attested to by Gish's recollection that the film was a financial failure.[65]

Another major cinematic representation of ghosts in this period was

Gance's *J'Accuse* (1919). Dead soldiers rise up from the places where they had fallen and begin to march in a weary column, looking as they did in life, with torn clothing and ragged bandages, carrying those unable to walk. Their purpose is to find out whether they died in vain. Only a few shots are double exposures, and their absence gives the dead a solid and implacable look. A witness, Jean Diaz, runs to calm terrified villagers in their path, before berating them for complacency. Because the villagers can see the soldiers, it is clear that they are not figments of Diaz's imagination. The residents cower as the soldiers enter the village and look through the windows, the thin glass symbolizing the fragile barrier between life and death that can be so easily shattered. The dead find that they did not die in vain, but the effort of acting as an intermediary, a surrogate national conscience, drives Diaz insane, after which he dies: "For Diaz's sacrifice has brought back the dead to the audience of 1919."[66] In Gance's 1938 version, another war approaching, Diaz calls on the dead to arise, whereupon they get up and march on the village. Diaz tells the villagers that they have betrayed those who sacrificed their lives, but this time the living are shown to be unworthy of the dead, and they burn Diaz. The dead arrive in time to lift his body from the pyre.

The scarcity of filmic portrayals of the Afterlife immediately after the Armistice is in contrast to the boom that mediumship enjoyed during the same period, with the bereaved using mediums to contact friends and relatives killed in battle. Shipman refers to *The Man That Might Have Been* as a novelty item, suggesting that such films were indeed rare.[67] *The Phantom Honeymoon* (1919) has a pair of ghosts wronged in life chase the villain, himself now also a ghost.[68] This triangle containing one or more ghosts was to become a common motif, but is probably unique in having the couple go on the titular honeymoon, though it is not clear who married them, before settling down to haunting. The same year's *The Market of Souls* has a ghost in a somewhat tangled set of relationships provide information, that he lied to his brother when alive, thereby resolving the plot. The *Exhibitor's Trade Review* said of the film:

> At the present time spiritualism has a decided vogue.... [I]t follows as a matter of course that the screen should dip into the spirit world for inspiration. It is a timely departure from the beaten path, and, whether you believe in phantoms or not, possesses undeniable fascination.[69]

The phrase "dip into" suggests a trickle rather than a flood. One reason for this discrepancy might be the late entry of the United States into the war, which meant that its losses were relatively light compared to other combatants. The distance between home and the war, both geographically and psychologically, might have militated against an engagement with the possibility of an afterlife. An explanation in terms of the lack of development of narrative structure in film is less plausible, as by this stage narrative technique had achieved a high level of sophistication that could have incorporated supernatural elements should filmmakers have wished to use them. Furthermore, the United States already exercised an increasing hegemony over the international film industry that meant it was likely to exert a damping-down effect on filmmakers in other countries, closer to the action, who might have contemplated producing films on the subject.

In Germany, by contrast, supernatural themes were extremely popular into the 1920s. Lotte Eisner's *The Haunted Screen*[70] ascribes this to a combination of innate German characteristics, such as pessimism and romanticism, and the psychological impact of defeat in the war, with the economic difficulties that followed. Reductionist explanations in terms of national characteristics are never satisfactory, but perhaps the trauma of defeat did provide a general stimulus for the displacement of despair into cinema and art, whereas in the victorious countries grief remained at a personal level, and found its outlet in religious or quasi-religious observance. German expressionist cinema produced fewer ghosts than might be expected from a style that dealt so heavily with the supernatural, but an exception was *Dr. Mabuse, der Spieler* (1922), in which Mabuse is haunted by the apparitions of his victims, though as Mabuse is insane the status of the ghosts is problematic.

Nobel Prize-winner Selma Lagerlöf wrote stories with a paranormal theme that were adapted by Mauritz Stiller (*Sir Arne's Treasure*, 1919) and Victor Sjöström (*The Phantom Chariot*, 1920). *Sir Arne's Treasure* features the ghost of the heroine's sister, murdered by one of the thieves who stole the treasure and who later courts the heroine, Elsalill. The ghost is depicted by means of superimposition, which looks forward to Sjöström's film. Her objectivity, though undermined by her appearances in Elsalill's dreams, is established by the information on her suitor that she provides, and which is verified by eavesdropping on the murderer confessing his crime. Maureen Turim overstates the case when she claims that

> here the supernatural apparition the dream thought, and the memory flashback have become merged — the border between the psyche and the fantastic is thoroughly ambiguous and it is possible to interpret all the flashbacks and apparitions in the film either as products of Erselille's [sic] unconscious or as visions produced from a power beyond the grave.[71]

This is possible but unlikely. The apparition evades the ambiguity ascribed to it by Turim because Elsalill would not have known, when her sister escorted her to the guildhall in her dream, that if she went there the following day she would hear the confession. It could be argued that Elsalill was using precognition presented by her own subconscious in the form of a visit from her dead sister, but the film is couched in terms of life after death, and it is more plausible that Elsalill discovers her lover's perfidy through the intercession of her sister than via super–ESP.

Sjöström's *The Phantom Chariot*[72] is a member of the class of films that appear to be objective events but transpire to have been a dream (a venerable device already seen in *The Avenging Conscience*) and of supernatural happenings that are revealed to have been hallucinations—not always as clear cut as in this case, in which there is no doubt as to the lack of veridicality of the events. The story is based on the Breton folk-tale of the Ankou, the "King of the Dead," in which the ghost of the last person to die on New Year's Eve is obliged to drive the phantom carriage for the next year.[73] The ghostly driver of the eponymous *Phantom Chariot* is seen in a double exposure to collect the ghosts of two individuals, a suicide and drowning victim, each of whom separates from the corpse in a superimposed image.

The main character, Holm, is seen lying on the pavement but sits up, a double exposure while his "body" is still prone, as the carriage approaches him. Walking with the driver through the wall, he is shown his destitute wife about to kill herself and their children, a scene that causes him to repent. He wakes up on the pavement and rushes back in time to prevent his wife from committing the act. Although Holm was supposed to have died, which would have accorded the story the status of an objective event, he was in fact unconscious, and the preceding story was the product of his fevered imagination. This does not though explain Holm's knowledge of his wife's intention, except by weak appeals to telepathy or to intuition based on intimate knowledge of her psychology.

For Turim, "Memory of the past links the supernatural, the morality tale, and the dream state in a way that recalls Charles Dickens's *The Christmas Books* (1843–48), said to have been an influence on Lagerlöf," a technique that Turim claims also harks back to Méliès.[74] The influence is in fact quite explicit—the novel upon which *The Phantom Carriage* was based is called *My Christmas Carol*. Like Scrooge, Holm, by being allowed to eavesdrop on a scene that works on his conscience, is allowed a second chance, and rather than withdrawing from the world is enabled to intervene with a good act, so redeeming his soul. Ingmar Bergman was probably influenced by the image of Death in the film, with scythe and cowled hood, when making *The Seventh Seal* (1956),[75] and the chance to review one's life can be seen in *Wild Strawberries* (1957).[76] The Dickensian Christmas also features in *Fanny and Alexander* (1982).

Earthbound (1920) has a murdered philanderer unable to move on because he did not believe in God or an afterlife. Once he has enabled his murderer to escape punishment, received forgiveness from his wife and reconciled his lover and her husband, his killer, he is able to move on. According to the *New York Times*, although there had been ghosts in films before, this was the first in which one was present for so much of the duration, "and in which were so illustrated the subtleties of its presence, its growing faint to the vanishing point and strong almost to materialization according to the perception of those on this side of death and the dramatic significance of the action."[77] It is not clear how this effect was achieved, although a *Harrison's Reports* review mentioned an effective use of double exposure.[78] It is clear from the remark about this being the first film in which the ghost was present for so much of the running time that the *New York Times* journalist had not been watching European cinema.[79]

An unusual ghost film, in that it was based on a real case, was the Australian *The Guyra Ghost Mystery* (1921, the year of the events), in which a family alleged to have been subject to psychic phenomena played themselves in a reconstruction, albeit with "comedy relief."[80] This type of semifictional documentary is an ancestor more of the television reconstruction than cinema representations, although there are hybrids in both media, for example *Ghostwatch* (1992) and the first Amityville film (1979). Putting the phenomena center stage contrasts with *Beyond* (1921). A dead mother appears to her daughter, Avis, to hold her to a promise Avis had made on her mother's deathbed — to take responsibility for her feckless brother.[81] The ghost here is a device to ensure that the daughter goes to New Zealand to make him reform, and can be shipwrecked on her return, allowing melodramatic complications to ensue.

Nineteen twenty-two saw a film in which the spirit is not only the motivating force of the narrative, but provides an instance of possession.[82] *One Glorious Day* features mild-mannered professor Botts who becomes transformed, rather like Jerry Lewis's *The Nutty Professor* (1963), though as a result of being taken over by an aggressive spirit, "Ek," at a séance rather than by chemical means. Botts is played by Will Rogers, a popular light comedian, undermining the gravity normally to be expected of a professor. Unfortunately it is not clear how Ek takes over Botts, nor precisely how the spirit is depicted (although *Variety* refers to "The old device of the double exposure"[83]) and Ek is played by another character. Like *The Nutty Professor*, the professor changes personality, loses his previous shyness, and overcomes his enemies.

Once the spirit has left Botts's body he does not remember what has happened, but his life has changed irrevocably. Ek, a name perhaps intended to evoke some form of ancient entity, but more likely the Indian guides so beloved of mediums and channellers, is clearly not the focus of the film, but the possession aspect is unusual, and ahead of its time. It links to later examples, usually within the horror rather than comedy genres, but there is a significant difference: Botts is easily released from Ek's power, the spirit leaving when it could most easily have retained control: when Botts is exhausted. This is unlike the 1970s examples following *The Exorcist* (1973), in which the controlling entity is evicted only after arduous effort and an appeal to religious faith.

An interesting aspect about Botts is that although it is not clear precisely what he is a professor of, he presumably holds some form of college post yet is at the same time chairman of the spiritualist society, suggesting a rapprochement between Spiritualism/ psychical research and academic life. On the other hand, the possession seems to be an unintended result of an experiment, as Botts had announced at the séance that he was going to project astrally so that he would appear in spirit form among the sitters. Ek was able to occupy Botts's soulless body while this was occurring, which could be seen as a general danger of mediumship. Perhaps too there is a covert warning, despite the film's happy ending, that even academic qualifications, signifying expertise, are no protection when one is meddling in the spirit world. This too is a theme taken up later in horror films in which scientists, for all their rationalism, show themselves to be incapable of understanding, let alone overcoming, the phenomena with which they are confronted.

René Clair, director of *The Ghost Goes West* (1935), made another ghost film in 1924, again with a light-hearted phantom, called *The Ghost of the Moulin Rouge*. The same year, DeMille made *Feet of Clay*[84] which looks forward to the failed suicide (with life-affirming consequences) of *Between Two Worlds* (1944), and is an early example of a Heavenly judge assigning the destination of souls according to the life led, also something that occurs in *Between Two Worlds*. A husband's sister-in-law, Bertha, attempts to seduce him but is accidentally killed hiding from her own husband. As a result of the scandal, husband and wife decide to kill themselves with gas, but as they pass over they meet Bertha who urges them to go back. This they manage to do, to their relief. These types of ghostly representation have a kind of solidity missing from those in early cinema, but the ghost could still function as a deus ex machina, as in 1924's *Unseen Hands*, in which a ghost materializes and his murderer dies of a heart attack at the end of the film.[85]

The ending of *The Mermaid* is echoed by a 1926 Rex Ingram film, *Mare Nostrum*. Ulysses, a Spanish sea captain, falls in love with an Austrian spy, Freya, during the First World War. Under her influence he transports German sailors to a submarine that later sinks the British vessel on which Ulysses's son is traveling. Ulysses is distraught, but cannot overcome his feelings for the spy when they meet again. His son's ghost appears and shakes his head sorrowfully. Ulysses prepares his ship, Mare Nostrum, for service with the French, while Freya is arrested and shot. At sea, the submarine torpedoes the Mare Nostrum, which hits the submarine as it sinks. Death, a skeleton in a robe, chalks the name of the ship from a blackboard, as the U-boat captain had crossed off the Mare Nostrum from Lloyds' list.

In a final sequence, Ulysses sinks through the water of the Mediterranean, "Mare Nostrum," and is met by the spirit of his lost love floating up to embrace him, despite the fact that she was not killed at sea. Like the prince in The Mermaid, Ulysses both assuages his guilt and is reconciled with his true love — who happens not to be his wife — underwater, and is seen with her in the final moments of the film, providing a satisfactory resolution. The presence of water is perhaps intended to suggest purification, as in baptism, as well as symbolizing a spiritual journey, a "crossing" again made explicit in Between Two Worlds (1944).

Also in 1926 appeared a version of the 1871 play The Bells.[86] A burgomaster, Mathias, is to bestow an enormous dowry upon his daughter, using money stolen from a Jew he murdered fifteen years before. He hears a jangling sound that comes from bells round a horse's neck, the horse pulling a sled upon which is the murdered man. The sound of bells pursues Mathias until his mind is threatened, and the sound of the horse's bells becomes confused with his daughter's wedding bells, the threat of the past impinging on the happiness of the present. He is found out when he re-enacts the crime under hypnosis. Once again internal and external states are elided until it is not clear what status the events have, whether guilt renders Mathias insane, or whether the victim is haunting his murderer, either for revenge, to make him confess, or both. Revenge for past wrongs, at least perceived, is seen in Mizoguchi's The Passion of a Woman Teacher (Japan, 1926). A spurned woman commits suicide because her lover prefers her student, whereupon she returns to haunt them literally to death in revenge.

A more positive view of the motivation of the dead is provided at the end of the silent period when Fairbanks plays D'Artagnan in The Iron Mask (1929). He is killed by being stabbed in the back during the climactic sword fight, and staggers into the garden where he dies. His pre-deceased colleagues can be seen standing above him in double exposure, gesturing, laughing and calling to him to join them. He leaps up and stands with them, while in the garden his body is lying on the ground. The four musketeers stride away arm in arm, off and up into the distance.[87]

It can be seen that by the end of the silent period all the elements of the mature ghost film are in place, even those, such as possession, more associated with the post–Second World War horror film. Ghosts have a range of motivations, degrees of influence on their environments and level of visibility. By the time Lewis Seiler could declare that *The Ghost Talks* (1929) they had become full-fledged protagonists in their own stories rather than excuses for trick film effects.[88] The ghost had achieved a degree of autonomy that could be developed in later decades with even greater thematic variety. The ghost often remained mute in sound films, but rather than stay a peripheral onlooker of the living's activities, frequently moved center stage.

3

A Thematic Approach to Cinematic Ghosts

Anatomy of Film Ghosts

A comprehensive anatomy of filmic ghosts is difficult to establish. They are used in a wide variety of ways, unlike for example vampires and zombies, the film ghost's closest unliving relatives, whose repertoires are relatively impoverished. The bulk of this chapter is devoted to teasing out categories, often overlapping, into which ghosts on film can be assigned.

To begin with, it is worth taking a high-level view of the attributes that condense those categories and delineate ghosts' general characteristics. These overlap with but are not identical to the characteristics that have been identified in the psychical research literature.[1] Sometimes the designation is difficult to determine, and not every category is applicable to a particular film. The depiction might even involve the possibility that more than one applies, from which arises the dramatic tension, but every cinematic depiction can be seen to a greater or lesser extent to fall in one or more of the following categories. Together they form a series of decisions that have to be taken to assess the status of an alleged ghost in a given situation:

1	Veridical (objective)	Hallucination (subjective)
2	Crisis	Non-crisis
3	Genuine haunting	Fake haunting
4	Place-centered	Mobile
5	Seen by all present	Seen selectively

6	Consciousness present	Consciousness absent
7	Supplying information	Supplying no/problematic information
8	Purposeful	Purposeless
9	Hostile	Benign
10	Transparent	Solid
11	Interacting with the environment	Ignoring environment/ unable to interact
12	Speaking	Non-speaking
13	Communicating directly	Communicating via a medium

High-Level Overview of Attributes of Filmic Ghosts

These categories examine different aspects of the phenomenon, looking both ways, from the ghost outwards and the spectator inwards. Together they supply an "ecology" that can be applied to ghost films in order to analyze the role of the apparition. Working through the table, the most important is the status of the ghost (No.1), whether or not it enjoys an existence independent of the percipient's mind — it could be subjective, and therefore not a ghost, or objective.[2] If the former, the ghostly existence could be caused by a crisis, or be a natural progression after death (No. 2). If the latter, it could be a genuine ghost or a fake (No. 3). A film might try to balance these possibilities so that it is not clear if phenomena are objective or subjective — *The Innocents* (1961) is the best-known example.[3]

If genuine, a ghost can be place-centered, existing in a single location throughout the tenures of different sets of living individuals, or mobile, unrestricted to the point where death occurred or places of major significance while alive (No. 4). The ghost might appear to a variety of people, or to one (no. 5). The more people who see it, the more likely is its reality to be accepted. In some cases, only one person might see the ghost while other people are present, which can make persuasion difficult, as a selective appearance in the absence of other evidence would hint strongly at mental disturbance.

The film ghost usually has some form of personality, but it would be possible for the apparition to be merely a kind of energy imprint, so consciousness cannot be taken for granted (No. 6). The major means of establishing genuineness is the supply of information, leaving aside the difficulties of GESP[4] as a counter-explanation — not a significant issue in ghost films except for the evaluation of mediumistic communication (No. 7). Lack of information does not rule out a ghost's genuineness; it may exist independently of the percipient but not provide the means to allow a determination of its existence to be made.

Assuming that a ghost does have an external existence, the next elements in the table focus on its intentions, and presuppose a guiding consciousness. The ghost may have work still to do on the earth plane, or it may be trapped or reluctant to leave, leading an aimless existence (No. 8). It may be friendly, even an ersatz guardian angel, or it may pose a threat to the living (No. 9). The level of opaqueness tends to correlate with the amount of interaction with the environment,[5] although some ghosts vary the strength of their solidity, being solid and transparent at different times (Nos. 10/11). The ghost might be mute or be able to communicate, a differentiation that bears on whether information is supplied (No. 12). Those who do not speak tend to be the most menacing, as communication can be a means of reassurance. Silence hampers the ability to gauge intentions. Even if it can speak, the ghost might not appear, but instead rely on a medium, which introduces the problem of a kind of supernatural Chinese Whispers, with possible distortions of the message (No. 13).

To return to the first and most important item in the above table, the problem of determining the reality of ghosts is tied up with the problem of delineating subjective states and objective external events, however confused by the witness's cognitive processes. Mark Sanderson defines ghosts as being entirely subjective when he refers to them as "memories that materialize: guests that are both wanted and unwanted,"[6] like the "ghosts" that haunt the denizens of the space station in *Solaris* (1972). In some cases that is undoubtedly true. For example, out-of-body and near-death experiences, night terrors, the feeling that one has been abducted by aliens from bed, these can all seem to have the status of external events even when they are hallucinations. The majority of survey respondents who are asked,[7] though, feel that ghosts represent an external deceased individual who is identifiable, at least in theory, as opposed to being an internally generated image. Unfortunately the cinema viewer, limited to a surface view, has to make an inference based on the behavior of both the apparition and its witnesses.

A number of writers have tried to plot the fortunes of the ghost film, sometimes attempting to tie its progress to social and economic factors, but frequently in simplistic terms. For example, Andrew Tudor notes the coexistence of the rise of the ghost during the 1940s with the decline of the vampire.[8] The interest in life after death was also found in the "mad scientist" films of the period, which tended to involve the continuation of the personality after death and the restoration of life.[9] Tudor sees little in common between the ghost and haunted house films made in this period except a natural interest in the Afterlife created by the war, although he does later characterize ghost films of the 1930s and 1940s, along with those dealing with vampires, as portrayals of invasion by the forces of nature.[10] Peter L. Valenti[11] sees these two decades differently, coining the expression "film blanc" to cover some of the ghost film production of the period, sentimental films he contrasts with film noir as providing reassurance that the sacrifice was worthwhile. Of course these propaganda elements were not confined to ghost films, nor to the Second World War—for example, *I Want You* (1951) played a similar, non-paranormal, role for the Korean conflict.

Similarly, James Robert Parish briefly examines the evolution of ghost films in the context of technological and societal changes.[12] He sees these changes leading to greater cynicism and a loss of that innocence that made romantic ghost films so popular before the Second World War, and meant an increasing disengagement with succeeding manifestations of that type of story. Filmmakers, according to this view, turned to special effects to win audiences back, leading to a backlash that produced *Ghost* (1990), and possibly auguring well for such similarly-themed but venerable properties as *Smilin' Through*. Parish may be over-optimistic about the paranormal melodramatic love story—*Ghost* did not have a notable success in re-establishing a romantic tradition.

Bryan Senn and John Johns also give a "potted history" of the sound ghost film.[13] They begin in the 1930s with comedy ghost films such as *Topper* (1937),[14] but note a darkening after the Second World War with *Dead of Night* and *The Uninvited*,[15] followed by low budget efforts in the 1950s, for example by William Castle. An explosion followed in the 1960s, which include two of their "Big Three" (alongside *The Uninvited*)—*The Innocents* and *The Haunting*. The 1970s saw a decline in production to less than half the 1960s number of ghost films, but then a resurgence in the 1980s, and they calculate that about 40 percent of ghost films up to the time of publication were made between 1980 and 1989,[16] including a revival of the comedy ghost alongside the standard horror. The success of *Ghost* (1990) is mentioned as auguring well for the future of the form.

Fowkes also attempts a high-level overview of the ghost film's post–Second World War development, which she ties to economic and gender issues. The more recent spate of remakes of 1930s and 1940s films (as well as the renewal of film noir) can be regarded in terms of the scrutiny of gender roles in both periods.[17] She sees a hiatus in ghost films in the 1950s and '60s, perhaps caused by a lessening of interest in romantic love and an emphasis on a "gritty version of reality" inimical to ghost films, followed by a resurgence in the late 1970s and '80s, when first social debate over a "legitimacy crisis" in public life (Vietnam, Watergate), followed by the spread of AIDS, caused a reevaluation of sex, and the "companionate" attitude of the 1930s screwball comedies reemerged.[18]

All these neat schemata, with their divisions into decades fairly distinct from each other, do not do justice to the complexity of the ways ghosts are portrayed on screen. For example, how is one to account for the massive explosion in ghost films in the period 1988–90? John Lyttle, in one of the reflections on the matter common in the wake of *Ghost*'s success, notes that the last time the studios had had such an interest in the Afterlife, excluding horror films, was during the Second World War.[19] But the two periods are very different, and whereas films from the earlier period could be regarded as expressions of grief in an uncertain world, the recent films for Lyttle are no more than New Age (i.e. non-denominational) responses to yuppie angst. Ultimately, the ghost refuses to be pinned down to specific social and economic conditions.

As with any type of film there are cycles, and there has been a trend, along with horror in general, to more graphic depictions of ghosts, with a greater preponderance of the sorts of Gothic-style malicious ghosts that would not have been welcome under Production Code restrictions. Frieda Grafe distinguishes between non-sound and sound ghosts, the former being labeled objective, the latter subjective.[20] While there was a tendency towards subjectivity, no clear-cut division can be discerned, and the two have co-existed — there are many objective ghost portrayals in the sound period to prove Grafe wrong. The biggest change came much earlier, with the increasing sophistication of narrative structures before the First World War, and no significant modification occurred as a result of the transition to sound — there was certainly no wholesale move towards subjectivity, although hallucinatory ghosts did become more common after the Second World War, in line with an increasing emphasis in cinema generally on the portrayal of internal states.

It is not clear to what extent war is a stimulus to the ghost film. Leslie Halliwell feels that the Second World War did bring an increasing awareness of the supernatural,[21] but it is just as likely that for every person wanting the consolation that death is not the end, there was another not wanting to face the possibility of death, however positive the portrayal of what might come afterwards. The prediction in *Harrison's Reports* that 1944's *Between Two Worlds* would not be commercially successful because "those who seek to be entertained by pictures do not relish seeing pictures in which the characters are dead people,"[22] was possibly caused by the U.S. casualty rates, as pre-war ghost films, notably *Topper* (1937) had had no such negative effect. Similarly, Sue Harper, discussing *Latin Quarter* (1945), argues that this film, along with such other supernatural efforts as *The Halfway House* (1944) and *Dead of Night* (1945), was unsuccessful due to a general antipathy towards occult elements as well as violence and male neurosis.[23]

John Kobal talks of a "revival of mystical themes" in the theater after the First War (*Smilin' Through, Death Takes a Holiday, Liliom, The Return of Peter Grimm*), all plays that were eventually filmed, and suggesting that the experience of war does have an influence, though sometimes delayed, on cinema.[24] Kobal also sees a contrast between pre–Second World War supernatural films, with their emphasis on Victorian romance and attitudes, and what might be characterized as a muscular approach more relevant to those mourning the loss of loved ones after it.[25]

The situation is made more complex by the attitude of the British Board of Film Censorship (BBFC) to films dealing with life after death in the United Kingdom. According to Gary Don Rhodes, *Outward Bound* (1930) was denied a certificate on the grounds that the Board's rules did not allow life after death to be shown,[26] although the destruction of the BBFC's pre-war records makes it impossible to arrive at a definitive reason for its ban. *Outward Bound* was subsequently passed for exhibition by the London, Middlesex and Surrey county councils as long as no under-sixteens were present.[27] Prima facie evidence for official hostility can be illustrated by the rarity of British films of the inter-war period dealing with the Afterlife: *At the Villa Rose* (1920), in which supernatural elements are marginal, *The Medium* (1934) and *The Ghost Goes West* (1935). European countries were similarly reticent. Marcia Landy ascribes the paucity of 1930s British horror not only to official censorship but also to self-censorship caused by "cultural taboos," as well as "the unadventurous technical nature of many films of the era."[28] Only in the United States, with its relatively minor involvement in the First World War, insulation from the horrors of mass bereavement and more advanced film industry, did the cinematic ghost flourish.

Tudor draws up a three-way scale for the analysis of horror.[29] The binary oppositions he identifies are "Supernatural/Secular," "External/Internal" and "Autonomous/Dependent." He defines "spirits" as lying within the Supernatural/Internal/Autonomous area. The second element of the triad might seem surprising, as ghosts have their origin external to humanity, but Tudor defines the term in relation to the threat's locus, which in this case is internal to the percipient. The third element defines the origin of the threat, which is external to the percipient. On the other hand, when discussing Supernatural/External/Autonomous films,[30] he refers to "demonic intercession" films: *The Omen* (1976) and sequels and

The Amityville Horror (1979), the latter film having an internal/secular element with the supernaturally induced father's insanity grafted on. Tudor also talks in terms of "cross-fertilization between sub-genres which is crucial to several eighties developments,"[31] by which time the complexity of his approach betrays a lack of precision in his methodology.

The ghost is not as easily compartmentalized as Senn and Johns or Tudor would wish, and trends are as difficult to grasp as ectoplasm. Despite a number of cases that are hard to interpret, the current filmic ghost is still usually an objective person, with will power and often an agenda. Earlier ghosts, however, do not have this unambiguous status. When motivation is provided, and the ghost is not merely the peg for a piece of trick work, it is not always clear whether the ghost depicted is objective or subjective. Perhaps unintentionally, these early attempts captured contemporary debates within the psychical research community on the status of ghosts, whether they were objective spirits or dependent on the percipient's telepathic ability, or were perhaps nothing more than the result of "a piece of undigested potato."

Representations of Ghosts

Ghosts, in real life and on film, contradict our expectations of the reliability of the world.[32] To see something, we perceive photons reflected from the surface of a solid object, and it is difficult to comprehend how a non-entity can reflect photons. Our notions of epistemology are undermined by the ghost's presence because the gaze of the viewer, already problematic,[33] is further complicated by the fact that something is reflected back even though no physical object is there. Film ghosts also highlight a perennial concern of psychical research, but usually only grappled with at an academic level: the problem of something's being able to communicate in the absence not only of sensory organs, but more crucially, of a brain. Ghosts, whether cinematic or otherwise, entail mind/body dualism, whereby the former can operate independently of the latter.

To complicate the issue, the viewer suspends disbelief because the object (the actor) really is there but has usually been rendered invisible within the context of the film, possibly to certain actors but not others, a device at least as old as the play of *Macbeth*. This might have been accomplished by an optical process or costume and make-up, or alternatively the audience is expected to assent to the opacity of a ghost and its ability to interact with the environment, to the extent that the living characters might not realize the true status of the dead ones. Veridical sightings that occur under such selective conditions might be regarded as hallucinations on the part of percipients, but in a film context there is frequently independent evidence to attest to their reality, sometimes to the extent that to a third party what is seen could be attributed to a poltergeist rather than a ghost.

The supernatural status of ghosts can be shown in a symbolic way to make them both close and distant at the same time. For example, in *All That Money Can Buy* (1941) the ghostly jurors are solid, but with a mist covering their faces to suggest a remoteness both from the living and, as traitors, from the American Way. In *Beetlejuice* (1988) the house's deceased occupants try to scare new owners away by covering themselves in sheets, a style reminiscent of Victorian spirit photographs. They are taken to be practical jokers, until it is realized that they have no legs. A representation that might have been convincing in the nineteenth century is now nothing more than a childish game.

As well as the difficulty over the seeming contravention of physical laws simply by existing, the ghost can also often flout physical laws in more dramatic ways. They can fly (*Alice*, 1990), drive while invisible (*Topper*, 1937), fade in and out (*The Canterville Ghost*, 1944), appear as smoke (*The Ghost Goes West*, 1935), walk through walls, and become visible or disappear at will (various).[34] They have attributes in common with shamans, but whereas the latter achieve their alleged abilities through a rigorous apprenticeship, for the ghost it is a natural state, in which it can perform magic without any education or apparatus.

For Zygmunt Bauman, death is impossible to define because it stands for non-existence; perception is intentional, i.e. it requires an object to which to anchor itself, and thus perception cannot perceive the absence of perception — "death is the archetypal *contradiction in terms*."[35] It is only possible to perceive the death of others, as this is an event in the world of objects. We infer our own death by proxy, through observing the deaths of others, or by analogy, for example comparing it to sleep. In a strong sense, we see death in metaphorical terms, just as *Peter Ibbetson* (1935), about to be reunited in death with his beloved who has just passed on, does not see her as herself but as a beam of light that represents her newly acquired ethereal nature.[36]

There is thus a paradox in portraying something on screen that represents the absence of life. When in *Sunset Boulevard* (1950) we discover that the narrator is dead, and the narrative is a flashback covering his last weeks and the events leading up to his death, it raises the question of how an individual can be so organized to be able to project a coherent personality, with memories, desires and regrets, in the absence of bodily organization. What is it exactly that constitutes Joe Gillis, so that an entire

3. A Thematic Approach to Cinematic Ghosts 63

person can be inferred from a voice-over? *Sunset Boulevard* is an interesting case too in that we do not see a ghost, or even the effects of a ghost on the environment. The question of survival is dependent on the viewer's attitude to the status of the flashback. If film can jump around in time, then perhaps so can the narrator, so that Gillis is always in the present, just as the narrative in one sense is always a depiction of the present. The problem with this interpretation is that Gillis's voice is able to co-exist with the image of his corpse floating in the swimming pool. He cannot be alive and dead at the same time, so his existence becomes problematical.

A similar device opens *Shallow Grave* (1994). A voice-over, which it transpires belongs to David, is heard over the image of his face, showing him as he is, dead, at the end of the film. The difference between this and *Sunset Boulevard* is that at the beginning of *Shallow Grave* we do not know that David is dead (it could be a still or him lying unblinking) nor whose voice it is. We are not cued to regard the film as a flashback, as happens when we see the clearly dead Joe Gillis in the pool. The form may be the same, but the effect in the earlier film is that, throughout, Gillis is regarded as doomed, and his voice-over is a sign of omniscience that depends on the continuation of life after death. *Shallow Grave*, on the other hand, wastes the opportunity, and the voice seems to be more an objective narrator's viewpoint than David's.

A further variation on the technique is in *Casino* (1995). There is a voice-over from a character we see get into his car, which then explodes. He even refers to a time "before I got blown up," and the film has a flashback structure. We assume that, like Gillis, the narrator is dead, except that at the end we return to the car bomb and discover that he survived the assassination attempt. Surprisingly we realize that the narration has been provided by somebody who is alive — to underline this, another character also provides a narration, and this is cut off as we see him killed.

The difficulty in disentangling hallucination from veridical apparition is the fact that they can be represented in the same way. The conventions are not clear-cut, so that a double exposure could mean a hallucination or the presence of spirits. Sensory modalities other than sight, such as hearing — nocturnal sounds for instance — or smells — such as the scent of mimosa in *The Uninvited* (1944) — are even less reliable than vision, as it is more difficult to rule out ordinary explanations. Often the only clue is provided by the context, or even, as in the John Ford version of *The Three Godfathers* (1948), by the probability that a particular interpretation is the most likely, in this case that the companions are hallucinations caused by privation and the desire to deliver the baby to safety.

Ambiguity is also provided in *Zone 39* (1993) when the image of a murdered woman is repeatedly seen by her husband, himself dying. She tells him that she is a hallucination caused by the tranquilizers he has been taking, although she acts like her pre-mortem self. Her status is made more complex by the fact that when she died she was pregnant, and in some scenes is carrying a baby. Despite her protestations, she may be veridical, although her husband could probably have worked out the information she provides for himself. Reinforcing the subjectivity, at the end, a man he has been working with cannot see the wife although he can, thus there is a selective point of view that hints at a hallucination. On the other hand, we see all three descend the stairs,[37] which raises the issue of whose point of view we now assume.

The pioneers of psychical research considered the possibility that telepathy might play a role in perceiving ghosts,[38] but this aspect of the paranormal has not fed through to film to any great extent. In *Beyond Bedlam* (1993) an experimental drug is being used on a psychotic mass murderer, but an unforeseen side effect is that he is able to manipulate people's minds, concretizing subconscious fears. A dead wife reappears, cosily domestic except for the bullet hole in her chest that suggests her subjective origin, remembered as she was at the time of death. But she may still have an independent existence, brought into being by the murderer's tapping into memories and creating a concretized thought form that possesses all the mental attributes she had before death. Looking at the outside is not enough. If the returnee behaves precisely as when alive, that might be a tribute to the strength of the memories rather than a positive indication that consciousness has continued. Even the disappearance of the "ghost" after the murderer's death does not necessarily mean that she had no objective existence. Possibly his projections were necessary to provide the energy needed for her to remain on the earth plane.

Kipps (1942) has a moment when Kipps is day dreaming romantically about his teacher, Miss Walsingham, and he imagines himself approaching her and declaring his love, to which "she" responds positively. First Kipps is seen as a double exposure leaving his body and walking away, then the same happens to Miss Walsingham, and the two hold a conversation that in reality exists only in Kipps's head. In a different context, though, the double could have been interpreted as an astral projection or a ghost leaving a corpse: if Kipps had had his eyes shut or was apparently unconscious, the possibility might have arisen that he had died, and the uncertainty would be resolved only by more information. As he is awake, and had been staring at the object of his affection, it is clear that the double is a depiction of his fantasy, and not an element projected by his consciousness. This inference is confirmed when Miss Walsingham's double leaves her body in a similar fashion and talks to Kipps's double.

This is a clear-cut case, but more often the only way to disentangle the two possible scenarios, subjective versus objective, is if the entity provides verifiable information that the percipient could not have received by normal means, or if it is seen by, or able to interact with the environment in the presence of, a third party. This third party can include the viewer. A sea captain in *Barnacle Bill* (1958) comes from a long line of sailors but suffers from seasickness. At the moment he is faced with a crisis they appear to him as double exposures.[39] They could be a hallucination, as their earlier appearances had been in the form of a flashback while the captain was describing his lineage, but after he leaves the room they remain, with no other witnesses, and dance with joy as he engages the enemy at sea (the Neanderthal ancestor interacts with the radar screen). Their objectivity is more convincing for their detachment from the living captain.

A complicated example is in *Photographing Fairies* (1997). Charles eats a flower that apparently allows access to the Afterlife. He hallucinates that he is making love to his wife, who died on the first day of their honeymoon, so that the scene seems to be a wish fulfilment. Then she says, "This is not a dream," which implies that he has pierced the veil. But her saying that could also be part of the dream state. All we are left with is the unlikelihood that a dream subject would say that it is not a dream subject.

Ghosts can be rendered differently, and their subjectivity emphasized, by point of view, which can make them seem subjective even when there is evidence that they are objective. This was seen as early as 1910, in *The Mermaid*, when the miller's daughter appears to the prince, although the wedding guests cannot see her.[40] A similar technique was used in Hepworth's version of *Hamlet* (1913). When the ghost of Hamlet's father first enters, he is seen by everybody present, which gives him credibility that he would have lacked if it had been to only one person. Yet later he appears to Hamlet when he is with Gertrude, and although Hamlet can see him, his mother cannot, and she fears for his sanity. Later such effects were used in a comic manner, as for example when the person who cannot see the ghost attempts to talk to it, and the ghost moves off, leaving the speaker addressing empty air. Spectators of scenes where the ghost is selectively visible experience a kind of gestalt because the ghost is simultaneously there and not there, and they can see both versions simultaneously, according to whose point-of-view they adopt.

Ghost (1990) provides an interesting example of the point of view difficulty. Sam cannot be seen or heard by the people around him, including his lover Molly, although the medium Oda Mae can hear but not see him. The audience can see and hear him, as well as other ghosts also invisible to the living around them. Towards the end of the film Oda Mae allows Sam to occupy her so that he can kiss Molly. Sam and Molly are then seen to be embracing, although as Oda Mae's body is being used, she should have kissed Molly. This, with the added complication of racial difference, would have been counter to the heterosexuality preceding it, but the only point of view from which Sam kissing Molly is feasible is Molly's imaginary one of what it would be like if Sam were physically present. A single point of view is hard to establish in a world where characters either have full perception of that world (the ghosts, the audience), partial perception (Oda Mae's clairaudience) or strictly limited perception (the living characters), and the cheat of Sam instead of Oda Mae kissing Molly highlights that difficulty.

There is a unique ghost in *Portrait of Jennie* (1948) who, normal in every other way, grows up at incredible speed. She also talks about past events as if they were contemporary, so that to begin with it might be possible that the artist, Adams, whom she meets in the park, is wandering intermittently into a time slip. This possibility is soon ruled out by the buildings visible at the edge of the park as they walk, although the canvas-like special effect brings to mind Miss Moberley's account of her first visit to the Petit Trianon in *An Adventure* where she refers to the landscape seeming *"like a wood worked in tapestry."*[41] The mechanism of Jennie's maturation is never explained, but points to the inadequacy of linear time, a theme made popular by the theories of J. W. Dunne.

The reason for the connection between the two main characters is never specified, but Adams had been painting near the spot where Jennie had drowned. The link through the lighthouse alludes to a deeper bond than either can understand. Martha Wolfenstein and Nathan Leites argue that Jennie lives a portion of her life over again so that she can meet the right man for her, who has been born at a later date.[42] Leaving aside Adams's greater age (explainable in terms of the Hollywood convention regarding the male/female leads' age discrepancy), there is no reason why Jennie should experience accelerated growth; why is she not either at the optimum age, or the age she was when she died?

It is proposed to Adams that he had created her as a source of inspiration, and it is true that at one point he can see her walking away while his companion cannot, supporting a subjective basis, but the history she recounts is verified so that her reality has to be accepted. GESP is still a possibility, as in many ghost films, but never proffered as a possibility, and effectively ruled out by the mise en scène. Indeed, the ending is effectively a twist, because after the repeated assertion that love conquers death, it is a great surprise to find that Adams has survived the climactic storm. Instead of joining Jennie in death, the expected conclusion, he goes on to paint far better pictures than before, happy that her personality continues. It is unexpected because the usual formula is for lovers to be reunited — Wolfenstein and Leites are correct when they say that it "denies the deprivational impact of death,"[43] but it is an exception.

The cinematic ghost is usually that of an identifiable individual, and it is clear that some form of consciousness has survived. In *Lifeforce* (1985), however, life after death does occur, but not the survival of the individual personality. Instead of separate post-mortem entities, the undifferentiated "lifeforce" of the dead is collected and beamed up to a spacecraft as energy for the "space vampires." This is life after death shorn of any theological trappings. Ironically, in this film the souls of the departed do go upwards as in a film with a religious element, but instead of going to Heaven, they are used as a food source by aliens.

The "divine spark" leaving at the moment of death has been widely discussed in theology and represented in religious paintings. Its existence is implicit in discussions of out-of-body and near-death experiences, as is the Hindu/Buddhist astral body that is also in Spiritualist doctrine, with the addition of a silver cord linking it to its corporeal form. The divine spark concept has not been incorporated into films to any great extent, but exceptions are *The Asphyx* (1972), *The Breakthrough* (1993), *Fluke* (1995) and *Photographing Fairies* (1997). The term "asphyx" refers to the soul, and that film concerns the attempts of a Victorian scientist to capture it at the moment of death, ensuring immortality. The analysis of the soul was a nineteenth century interest, and as well as weighing dying patients to see if they lost weight just after death, the difference being the weight of the soul,[44] attempts were made to photograph the "vital spark" leaving the body.[45] The scientist in *The Asphyx* is successful, but it is debatable whether this classifies as life after death as in effect death is postponed by the capture of the asphyx. *The Breakthrough* (1993) treads similar ground, albeit with more sophisticated technology and the complication of CIA engagement similar to the military's involvement in *Brainstorm* (1983). Again the soul is able to exist separately from the body, but capture torments it, and the equipment is destroyed. In *Photographing Fairies* the vicar's "breath of life" leaves as he dies.

Interactions with Matter

Ghosts exhibit a variety of degrees of interaction with their environment, ranging from inability to interact to such a mastery of their environment that it is difficult to ascertain that they are dead (such as the nanny in *Kiss of the Beast* (1990); this type of ghost has a long lineage: the literary revenant, for example, was notably corporeal). This may be relevant to the effect—for example, if the ghostly status is supposed to be a surprise, after audience and characters have assumed that the ghost is alive.[46] The degree of interaction may be arbitrary, subject to plot exigencies, such as the ghost in *Heart Condition* (1990) interacting only with the policeman who has been given his heart. The ghost of a small boy in *The Changeling* (1979) is able to interact with matter to an amazing degree, from depressing a piano key and moving a small wheelchair, to engineering traffic accidents and finally setting fire to a house, all as the plot demands.[47] *The Ghosts of Berkeley Square* (1947) begin death as double exposures, and have to learn how to materialize from a manual they are given, after which they are able to mingle with the living on equal terms.

A rule of thumb is that the more opaque the ghost, the more able it is to 'pass as alive.' This is not always the case, however. *Casper* (1995) is able to interact with matter, despite protestations to the contrary, and even to feel pain, while looking like a large soap bubble.[48] While this form is designed to maintain consistency with Casper's previous image, it is interesting that he looks nothing like the 12-year-old boy he is briefly incarnated into as a reward for his good deed. This is unusual, as ghosts tend to look like their pre-mortem counterparts, though there is no reason why they should, not being constrained by the same physical laws as flesh and blood.

Some ghosts who seem to be alive betray their ghostliness by certain attributes, such as *The Extraordinary Seaman* (1969)'s self-filling whisky bottle, or the aunt in *Phantoms* (1990) who looks normal except when she has a knife protruding from her stomach and the wife in *Beyond Bedlam* who bears bullet holes. Sometimes logic dictates that something must be awry: the grandfather in *The Last Winter* (1990) is suddenly in good health after suffering what appears to be a heart attack, holding a horse that it has been established is also a ghost, so it comes as no surprise that he has died. Ghostliness can be conveyed by some indefinable aspect of a person's manner, a certain feyness. Ernest Thesiger, who played the ghostly doctor in *A Place of One's Own* (1945) said of his performance:

> I looked at a distant object without focus and put a faraway tone in the voice—these are the secrets of being a ghost.[49]

The degree of interaction can be arbitrary. If ghosts do not have to obey human physical constraints, they should not have to adhere to any

David Niven plays *The Extraordinary Seaman*, Cmdr. Finchhaven, RN (1969).

consistent physical requirements at all. In *Lady in White* (1988), the little girl is able to play with toys while invisible, float, and be either transparent or solid. She communicates and seems to possess free will. Yet later the hero witnesses a replay of her murder during which she is carried as she was then, floating in the air because this time the murderer is invisible, thus preserving the climax when his identity is unmasked. This sequence is similar to the type of story in which an apparition goes through stereotyped motions, with no evidence of personality. Another example is the ghost in *Topper Returns* (1941) who is alternately visible and invisible as the plot demands, and has varying degrees of solidity, at one point getting dressed.

  Some ghosts are restricted by the rules that govern their particular filmic world, with no opportunities for personal growth. In *Ghost*, on the other hand, it is possible, with practice, to affect the environment. In this instance it is convenient for the plot, because if early on Sam had been able to interact, he would have been able to warn Mollie of the danger she was in, which would have curtailed the narrative. By the end of the film he has learned enough to be able to engage in a fight. Similarly in *The Man in the Trunk* (1942) the ghost begins as a trainee, unable even to walk through walls. By the end he has been promoted to Ghost First Class after learning to bang on the inside of the trunk (inside which his skeleton was found) to catch his murderer, yet still has to accompany it when it is removed.

Psychokinesis Versus Ghosts

A continuum can be drawn at one end: psychokinesis by a living agent as the cause of supernatural phenomena, and at the other an influence on objects by discarnate entities. The former is exemplified by *Carrie* (1976), the latter by *Poltergeist* (1982). At the mid-point is an area where it is not clear whether phenomena are caused by a living or dead agent. These are unlikely to be pure instances, as the viewer will be tipped in one direction, but there are cases in which there is always doubt. In *The Haunting* (1963) it is possible, however unlikely, that Eleanor is causing the events. On the other hand it could be the spirits of the house's previous occupants. The viewer has to weigh up the probability of each possible explanation. In cinema, the default assumption is still that if a poltergeist label is attached to an occurrence, the agent is deceased.

The rest of the chapter is devoted to a breakdown of the sorts of situations cinema ghosts can be found in, and the ways intimations of immortality impinge upon the living. Examples are given to support the divisions, but they are not exhaustive. Overlaps within individual films must be borne in mind; categories are not self-contained.

Ghosts of Those Who Cannot Rest

When given a motive at all, a common reason for a ghost to haunt is because he or she cannot rest in peace, and must prevail upon the living to do something, typically rebury their bones or right a wrong. *The Return of Peter Grimm* (1935)[50] has Peter's ghost obtaining information not available to him when alive, and engineering justice for his ward. The only person who can see him is a sickly child to whom he had given a home, and at the end the child asks to go with him. His spirit rises up to join Peter in a manner more in keeping with the romantic films in which the loved one who has died is able to join the lover's ghost.[51]

The Ghosts of Berkeley Square (1947) are confined to their house as penance for accidentally dying in an attempt to imprison the Duke of Marlborough to prevent what they wrongly anticipated would be defeat at the Battle of Malplaquet.[52] They are to remain in situ until a reigning monarch visits, which only happens when Queen Mary comes to inspect the damage after the house is destroyed in a zeppelin raid. As in *Beetlejuice* and *High Spirits* they are provided with a manual, in this instance the suitably military *Eternal Regulations*, although as it is dated with the year it is presumably updated annually; they also have a newspaper, the *Daily Spectre*. In *A Nightmare on Elm Street 3: Dream Warriors* (1987) we learn from his mother that the only way Freddy Krueger can be stopped is for his bones to be buried in consecrated soil. This is done, but to no effect. The conquistador who haunts Charlie in *Charlie's Ghost Story* (1994) had been walled up alive by Indians. His bones on display at a museum consign him to purgatory, which can be alleviated by burial. This type of haunting, a ghost seeking appropriate burial rites, was typical of accounts of the early mediaeval period,[53] so that the conquistador is acting in a manner befitting the beliefs of an even earlier period.

Other ghosts cannot rest because of an injustice. *The Man in the Trunk* (1945) appears when said trunk is found with his bones inside, and can only rest once his murderer has been captured. Herman accidentally frightens the countess to death in *The Queen of Spades* (1948) while trying to wrest the winning formula for faro from her. She returns as a ghost and gives him the wrong one, after which he sees her face on the right card (the Queen of Spades). A model murdered as the foundation for a sculpture in *Crucible of Terror* (1971) haunts the sculptor responsible. The heroine of *Warlock Moon* (1973) is helped to avoid the unwanted attentions of a group of cannibals by the ghost of their first victim. *Ghost Writer* (1989) has a ghost use a living woman writer to find out how she died, just as the following year's *The Forgotten One* features a male writer fascinated with a ghostly woman who had been murdered. The hit-man in *Cold Sweat* (1993) is followed about by the accidental victim of a previous job, until he sees the error of his ways and apologizes to her.[54] Sometimes the ghosts are symbols of a guilty conscience, as when those he ruined return to haunt *Citizen Cohn* (1992) on his death bed, or the victims look on as their murderer goes to the execution chamber in *Dead Man Walking* (1995).

Family ties frequently play a role. In *House of Darkness* (1947), a man is haunted by the ghost of his brother, whom he had murdered. Captain Elwood in the *Jack the Ripper Quartette* (1958) murders his wife, and her presence, demonstrated by the repeatedly overturned table, echoing an action she had taken when alive, leads him to confess. The result is his own death, as the only ship he can secure is a "rust bucket," and when it sinks he is the only one lost, implying divine retribution. Similarly, in *The Corpse* (1969), a ghost haunts his family, who were responsible for his death. *The Haunting of M* (1979) prefigures *Candyman* (1992) in that the ghost is the lower-class lover of a woman whose relatives had him murdered and who comes back for revenge.

In *The Dead Can't Lie* (1988), a ghost tries to retrieve jewels buried with her but dug up by her husband. She is an example of the type of ghost who passes for human to the extent that the investigator assigned to protect the husband cannot at first tell that she is dead, despite a physical relationship. Clearly there are no attributes, such as coldness, which might alert her lover — part of the early interest revolves around her status, whether she is dead or pretending to be as part of a fraud. Later she commits acts, such as throwing herself from a building or vanishing from a boat, which leave little doubt. At one point she is found submerged in a bath.[55] The title *The Dead Can't Lie* proposes an addition to the mythology when the husband asserts that ghosts cannot directly tell lies, although they can delude the living. This theory is exploded as preposterous by a Russian Orthodox priest who says that lies are their business. He takes the opportunity though to add some myths of his own, such as the inability of ghosts to walk on consecrated ground and the "folk tale" that if one sleeps with a revenant, one dies — a fate the detective escapes. This severe interpretation of the post-mortem state makes the ghost closer to the vampire than is normal for ghost films, even when they are cast in succubus terms.

The ghost ship emerges from *The Fog* (1979).

The Fog (1979) involves the return of shipwreck victims to gain revenge on the descendants of wreckers who lured their vessel onto rocks a century before. They have a ghost ship that moves in a mysterious fog, and psychokinetic capabilities on a scale not normally seen in a ghost film. Their relationship to the fog is not clear. Early scenes, with the fog invading the town, imply that they need it to move around, but when they enter the church they are able to do without it. By the end six townsfolk have died, one for each conspirator a century before, though not always a descendant. Symmetry is achieved at the expense of justice. John Houseman as the old sea dog sets the scene at the beginning, telling ghost stories to children — standing in for the audience[56] — around a fire on the beach. This links back to *Jaws* (1975), which also begins with a group sitting around a fire on a beach, and forward to *Ghost Story* (1981), Houseman again sitting by a fire, this time in an upper-middle-class study, swapping ghost stories with fellow members of the chowder club, formed to try to expiate guilt over their complicity in the death of a woman when they were young. *The Fog* and *Ghost Story* deal in the return of repressed emotions, and both emphasize the oral and literary antecedents of the traditional ghost story while at the same time moving beyond them into a more visceral form.

A derivative film, *The Supernaturals* (1986), which could be described as *The Fog* meets *Southern Comfort* (1981), reduces the encounter between the revenants and the soldiers to revenge for a past war crime on one side and pure survival on the other. The resemblance between one of the living soldiers and the dead husband is confirmed by means of a photograph, as the resemblance between the living writer and dead lover is established in the later *The Forgotten One* (1990). Another probable source for *The Supernaturals* is the early splatter film *Two Thousand Maniacs* (1964). A Confederate 'ghost town' destroyed by General Grant's army in the American Civil War is reconstituted, to the cost of a careful of Yankees passing through.

A link is often made in ghost films between ghosts — representing the past, something lost — and memories and regrets. Rarely is this made as specific as it is in *Field of Dreams* (1989),[57] about a farmer, Ray Kinsella, who hears a mysterious voice[58] and as a result builds a baseball stadium despite financial problems. The ghostly baseball players who arrive to play are a projection of the desire to build the diamond implanted in Ray by the voice, thereby carrying the weight of the film's message, one that has been seen as illiberal and patriarchal.[59] The uncertain status of the ghosts, their underdescribed aetiology and relationship to reality, leads Caroline M. Cooper three times to describe the visitors as being reincarnated.[60] Arguing against some form of reincarnation is the fact that their souls have not been transplanted into others' bodies, either as babies or in a body swap, but instead they have kept their own bodies from a time when they were at peak fitness, a Summerland optimum.[61] Also, although they interact with the other characters (albeit only the pure in heart, which makes one wonder how perception is regulated), they possess a certain insubstantiality as they melt into the boundary of the field whenever they depart to an unspecified place — perhaps a kind of limbo, self-actualization only occurring during baseball.

Traffic between past and present is two-way. The ghosts are in the present, but the living are also allowed the opportunity to reach into the past to redeem regrets and mistakes. They exist in a symbiotic relationship, without which each is spiritually poorer. Robinson was interested in the ability "to reach into the past and right old wrongs and heal wounds that should be healed."[62] Baseball becomes a New Age religion whereby the Black Sox are allowed a second chance, Dr. Graham is given an opportunity to carry on where he left off to pursue medicine, disillusioned ex-radical Terence Mann loses his cynicism, and Ray can meet his father, whom he had spurned in his youth. But at the same time, rapprochement between past and present does not obviate the need for sacrifice, as Doc Graham's saving Ray's daughter at the expense of his second chance shows. There is a benign circularity in that Doc Graham is able to bring Ray's child back to life, just as Ray brought him to life.

The players are only one manifestation of an overarching spiritual force operating throughout the film, which validates the Kinsellas' 1960s idealism. The sentimental lesson is that Paradise is on earth for those who can see it: "Is this Heaven?," to which the reply is "No, it's Iowa." Eventually Ray concludes that perhaps it *is* Heaven, not a separate region, rather found within. But it is not a state of grace for everyone. Only those in tune with the Kinsellas' spiritual values can see what is happening on the baseball diamond, so that Ray's greedy brother-in-law is not vouchsafed knowledge of the presence of the Black Sox players until he has given up his land-grabbing ways and achieved his own redemption. The words spoken by the mysterious voice to Ray, "If you build it, they will come," have been adapted in both *Wayne's World 2* (1993) and in *The Haunting of Seacliff Inn* (1994), to suggest a ghostly presence and the sense of intervention from Beyond in the lives of ordinary people, even though in the latter case, the words are spoken even before the couple move into the haunted inn. A miraculous intervention in people's lives hovers in the phrase, so that if the characters follow some kind of Divine Plan, their destiny will be worked out.

The major point made in *Casper* (1995) is also that it is not only ghosts, the "living impaired," who have unfinished business. Kat's father has uncompleted business caused by the death of his wife, despite working as a therapist helping ghosts to move on. His wife finally arrives and is able to help him become reconciled to his loss, and makes the point that his desires are actually keeping her back from spiritual progress.[63] An unusual ghost story, in that it reverses the usual format of ghosts helping the living to come to a decision or complete a task, is *Ghost Town* (1988). A deputy sheriff assists a town of ghosts, literally a "ghost town" that, like the scenario in which outlaws torment innocent townsfolk, is being persecuted by a gang. This time rather than ghosts frightening the living, it is the other way around. Finally the town is destroyed (purified) by fire, and all receive their just desserts.

The Expiation of Sins

A sub-category of ghosts who cannot find rest are those who still feel guilt over some misdeed performed in life. In *The Scoundrel* (1935), Noel Coward is a Lothario who accidentally drowns. His unquiet ghost returns, dripping and festooned with seaweed,[64] to ask forgiveness of those he has wronged, unable to ascend to Heaven unless he can find somebody who will cry for him within a month. This he manages to do by considering somebody else for the first time.[65] *The Ghost in the Invisible Bikini* (1966) was an attempt to fuse the haunted-house and beach-film genres. A ghost has to perform a specified good deed within a day in order to go to Heaven, where he will also become young again. He succeeds, but finds that he has become three years old. Max in *The Devil and Max Devlin* (1981) is Hell-bound until he strikes a deal with "Satin" that if he can get three innocent people to sign their souls over, he will be saved. This he manages, but protests when he learns that their souls will be taken immediately rather than at the end of their lives, and volunteers to go in their stead.[66] This enables him to be restored to life as he is patently unsuited to Hell.

Liliom (1930/1933), based on Molnar's 1909 play and first filmed as *A Trip to Paradise* in 1921 (comprising a happy ending with the trip to Heaven a hallucination), later enjoyed success as *Carousel* (Broadway play 1945, film 1956), making it a success after both world wars. Liliom wants to do penance for letting down his daughter by embracing a life of crime, so he is allowed to return after ten years in Purgatory to see her for a day and perform one good act. *That's the Spirit* (1945) is similar in that a woman, the Angel of Death, arrives to escort a man to Heaven. Afraid that her presence could have been misconstrued by his wife, he seeks permission to visit Earth to explain, but is denied. Eighteen years later, though, he is allowed back to help his daughter escape his tyrannical father-in-law. His wife is finally visited by the Angel of Death and is reunited with her husband.

Evildoers are often cursed, sometimes in a witchcraft context. *Blackbeard's Ghost* (1967) is obliged to do a good deed before progressing to a higher sphere, not through guilt or divine intervention but because of a curse put on him by his wife, who had been a witch. Although usually tied in with witchcraft, curses can be used in a non-witchcraft context, as in

And Now the Screaming Starts (1973). A decadent baronet rapes a servant's bride and cuts the servant's hand off, causing him to curse his employer. The fulfillment of the curse is visited upon the nobleman's grandson whose wife is in turn raped by the husband's ghost and in a Lamarckian manner gives birth to a one-handed baby.

Subsumed within the category of expiation is the notion of family honor. The ghosts in *The Ghost Goes West* (1935), *The Canterville Ghost* (1944) and *The Extraordinary Seaman* (1969) are all in their predicament thanks to besmirching the family name, each sentenced to exist on earth until he has redeemed himself. The punishment is an expression of patriarchal authority, in the first two for cowardice, in the latter for incompetence. Murdoch's father in *The Ghost Goes West* is a hypocrite in that he dies a drunkard yet, allowed into Heaven, lectures his son, consigned to Limbo, on honor. Sir Simon de Canterville is actually murdered by his family for disgracing his father, whereas Murdoch was killed by accident.[67] Unlike Murdoch, though, Sir Simon's brave deed must be done by a descendant.

Scrooge is a character who expiates his sins, with a little encouragement. There have been numerous renderings of *A Christmas Carol* (1843). Silent versions include one as early as 1901 (*Scrooge; or, Marley's Ghost*, by W. R. Booth), and others followed in 1908, 1910 (twice, one by Edison the same year they made *Frankenstein*), 1912, 1913, 1914, 1916 (called *The Right to Be Happy*) and 1923. It was still popular in the sound era, with productions in 1935, 1938, 1951, 1954, 1970 (a musical), 1979, 1988 and 1997. There have also been numerous television versions, live action, puppet and animation. While still using Charles Dickens's basic characters, not all have retained the Victorian trappings. The 1979 version is set in 1930s America, but the most audacious attempt, *Scrooged* (1988), is set in a television company. Like the versions in 1938, 1951 and 1979, it contains a deprived childhood,[68] watering down the message because Scrooge is not redeemed from wickedness but reminded that he is capable of being good. In all of them he has had a wasted life, which is Dickens's message, and why Pauline Kael feels that the film has never been a great success,[69] an odd opinion given the number of times it has been remade.

The adoption of the term "Scrooge" into the language demonstrates that *A Christmas Carol* conveys a level of meaning that transcends its melodramatic boundaries. For Geoffrey Rowell, it is a story of conversion and release, the smog-filled streets haunted by ghosts "suffused on Christmas Day with the light of heaven."[70] Scrooge himself reaches mythological proportions, and his redemption gives him nobility, aided in those versions referring to his neglected childhood, which renders him incapable of affection. If his flaw is due to circumstances beyond his control, then it is hard to blame him — he is a victim of Fate and should be pitied. With help, Scrooge is able to overcome his nature, showing first that character is not immutable but can be changed if cajoled sufficiently, and second that the individual is responsible for the well being of others, not the state or other impersonal institutions.

The tours that Scrooge is taken on can be likened to the life reviews that sometimes accompany NDEs (although not in cinematic representations, which tend to simplify the experience). The ghosts themselves are atypical, being more similar to Méliès's apparitions, who are less like the spirits of precise individuals than generalized allegorical types. Of the 1951 version, Keyser reasonably claims that:

> Hurst's death figure forcefully combines Dickens's ghost, Leech's [illustrator of the first edition of the book] spirits, Bergman's allegory [in The Seventh Seal], and horror film conventions in a chilling amalgam.[71]

Consolation for the Living

The most basic aspect of ghosts, whether good or bad, is that they show to other characters within the films, and suggest to the audience, that there is life after death. That may be the extent of a filmmaker's intentions, but even with transition to an incorporeal state, ghosts can still take an interest in the living. This may be especially true in wartime, when those left behind have to come to terms with the loss of loved ones, often in horrific circumstances.

The Human Comedy (1943)[72] encapsulates a number of themes that touch on loss. The dead narrator, Matthew, remains to look over his family, but is not a distressed earthbound spirit. When his wife tells her eldest son that his father still lives on in their thoughts and talk, the audience can see Matthew, although she cannot. The message is conveyed that although we may speak comfortingly of somebody dead being present, when we remember them, it is possible that they really are there. When the eldest son is killed, he and Matthew can be seen together on the porch as double exposures. They follow the others into the house, to signify the strength and continuity of the family (an image reinforced by the fact that the middle son is played by Mickey Rooney in his Andy Hardy persona, with all of its resonances of small-town virtue and homely wisdom).

The same year that MGM released The Human Comedy, Twentieth Century Fox made the similarly themed Happy Land, also set in small-town America. Lew's son Rusty has been killed in action and Lew is inconsolable, until *his* grandfather arrives to help him. The crux of Lew's bitterness is that Rusty never had a chance to live, but Lew and his grandfather are transported back in time and witness scenes from Rusty's life. Lew realizes that it did have meaning and richness, despite its brevity, and is consoled. The propagandistic element is more forthright than in *The Human Comedy* because Lew had fought in the First World War and his grandfather was an American Civil War veteran, so fighting for one's country is something with which every generation has to come to terms. Also, by showing that Rusty had had a good life, the implication is that Lew had one too, and owes his country a debt, to be repaid by carrying on with life. Both *The Human Comedy* and *Happy Land* end with a comrade of the dead son, neither one with a family, arriving to offer condolences and being welcomed. Although members can be lost, the country can act as a surrogate family.

Even in peacetime ghosts can still want the best for their loved ones, though one might think that, having learned that life is only a prelude to a potentially greater experience, ghosts would find the concerns of those left behind of little consequence. Some on the contrary take a great interest in earthly matters. In *Sentimental Journey* (1946) and its remake *The Gift of Love* (1958) a woman about to die adopts a girl to look after her husband. After she has died, she still guides the girl in her efforts to overcome the husband's resistance. There is an increase in the supernatural quotient in the two, the later version being more explicit about the wife's influence.

A ghost's reason for appearing to the living can be less clear-cut. The patriarch of *The House of the Spirits* (1994) has a sister with (unconsummated) lesbian tendencies. He sends her away when he finds her asleep in bed with his wife, but one day she walks in to the house, kisses the wife and turns away. The wife, who is mildly clairvoyant, knows that she is dead, which they find is the case. Later the wife, now also dead, visits her daughter in prison to strengthen her resolve, and later still visits the patriarch as he is dying. These episodes, which seem to be tacked on to retain the Magic Realism credentials of Isabel Allende's novel, do not move the narrative forward, apart from indicating regret by the deceased.

Ghosts Who Dispense Sage Advice

Ghosts who help the living often have a family connection. *The Ghost of Frankenstein* (1942) visits his son, who is contemplating destroying the creature, and advises that the diseased brain be replaced with a sound one; the simple country boy in the second story of the *Creepshow* (1982) anthology is told by his father's spirit not to put water on the "meteorite" he has found — in vain; in *Betsy's Wedding* (1990) Eddie still takes counsel from his deceased father, who does not play a role in the action; the same is true for The Phantom's father in *The Phantom* (1996), and the village's oldest inhabitant in *The Milagro Beanfield War* (1988) talks to his dead friend; Darkly's parents in *The Passion of Darkly Noon* (1996), with bullet holes, sit in a tree; the spirits in *Gildersleeve's Ghost* (1940) helping Gildersleeve's political ambitions are ancestors attempting to atone for their own past misdeeds.

Often the ghosts are not related to their clients, and advice is given for no other reason than that the ghost has a rapport and wants to guide a person to make a correct choice. Jacob Marley in the numerous versions of *A Christmas Carol* recommends that Scrooge mend his ways to prevent him from making the same mistakes that Marley himself had. In *Blue in the Face* (1995) the tobacco shop's owner, Vinnie, is thinking of selling. After the locals have been discussing the Brooklyn Dodgers, deceased baseball star Jackie Robinson visits Vinnie and makes him reconsider. Robinson had no vested interest in the continuation of the shop, but helps Vinnie come to the right moral, if not financial, decision.

The ghosts in *The Halfway House* (1944) give advice, or at least cause the visitors to their hotel to examine their consciences. Superficially like the living, they exhibit subtle differences, such as not casting a shadow (except for one probably inadvertent occasion when the daughter casts a faint shadow on a wall) nor reflecting in mirrors, which might in another context have marked them out as vampiric. A number of statements, such as replying that he got "a message" when the owner, Rhys, is asked if he had received a telegram, imply divine involvement. The time element is left unexplained: the father says that they and the guests are both inhabiting their own time but does not elaborate on this cryptic statement. Charles Barr sees the film as metaphorically playing on time, mirroring in its own temporal shifts the experience of the audience that is watching images from the past.[73]

It is possible that the living guests have entered a timeslip, and gone back to 1942, but more likely that the hotel is still existing in a kind of limbo in 1943, forever repeating the raid; if the latter, it is still unclear how the spectral hotel, which springs back into existence as one character searches for it with binoculars, actually operates, whether it is called into being on an ad-hoc basis by the perceived spiritual needs of travelers, whether it springs into existence Brigadoon-like at set intervals, or if this is a one-off. The logic may be unclear, but the functions of the situation are as obvious as the film's title, delineating various circumstances with

A variety of characters, including William Oakley (Alfred Drayton, left) and Jill French (Valerie White, right), arrive at *The Halfway House* where the hosts, Gwyneth (Glynis Johns, standing) and Rhys (Mervyn Johns), offer some life lessons (1944).

which the audience might have to contend. *The Halfway House* portrays people halfway between desolation and positive living, the latter concomitant with the values of society as a whole. Some decide to reform (the cashiered officer, the black marketer) or commit (the hitherto disengaged Irish diplomat), others find a renewed fulfillment in previously desolate lives, showing that the individual is as important as the collective (the dying pianist, the old couple, the young separated husband and wife brought back together by their daughter). Even the inn's owners are still able to express themselves individually by helping the living to see life in a new perspective.

The title of *The Halfway House* is evoked by 1944's *Between Two Worlds*. The passengers on the ship in the latter are between life and whatever fate awaits the dead, whereas guests at the Halfway House are at an individual point in terms of having to make a personal decision. For example, the elderly couple who have lost their only son — and she, being French, her country — react in different but equally dysfunctional ways. The grieving wife's attempts at Spiritualistic communication are derided by her husband, made bitter by war but still caring in his blunt way. Ironically, she is unable to make contact by means of a séance while staying in a hotel containing ghosts. That they never enable her to receive a message from her son suggests that the knowledge that life after death continues has to be enough, and that proof is not necessary. By putting her grief in perspective, and seeking to understand her husband, himself grieving for the loss of his son and his own naval career, she is able to live fully again.

It Happened Tomorrow (1944) must have been timely, when many people would have been wondering when the war would finish. The ghostly newspaperman, Pop, who seems to be alive, gives the following day's newspaper to Larry, but bald facts are capable of misinterpretation; not knowing can be better, avoiding the hubristic belief that one can control the future. Pop, though he does not seem to be one, acts like a plain-clothes angel. He need not go through the charade of showing Larry the paper, because presumably he could explain precisely what the descriptions signify, but the lesson is that experience is better than an explanation. The same year's *Heavenly Days* has Fibber advised by the ghost of his American Revolution ancestor to go to Washington to give the politicians the benefit of his insights, which he does, with mixed results. The experience is again a learning process—Fibber learns that even if one is average, it is still possible to make a difference. In *The Ghost Goes Wild* (1947) a ghost is inadvertently 'called up' by a pair studying the paranormal in order for one of them to masquerade as a ghost. The ghost is able to provide information that enables the plot to be wound up satisfactorily.

There is always the possibility that ghosts who offer advice might actually be projections of an individual's conscience. A disillusioned journalist fleeing further engagement with the political situation in Europe takes refuge as a lighthouse keeper in *Thunder Rock* (1942) then peoples his domain with the victims of a shipwreck from the previous century. Through a dialogue with them, understanding the reasons why they too fled Europe, he comes to the conclusion that he is running away when engagement with events is vital.[74] It is not clear whether they are figments of his imagination, generated to help him resolve his internal conflicts, or are supposed to be shades called up by the keeper in his anguish, but the effect is the same.[75]

Eddie, who visits the titular *Alice* (1990), is the first in a series of people from her past who tell the truth about her. As a result of these meetings, in conjunction with information obtained while invisible, Alice abandons her shallow marriage for a more fulfilling life. It is possible that Eddie and the other advisors are a means whereby Alice can legitimize her feelings of guilt by attributing them to an external agency and giving her confidence that she is doing the right thing. Eddie has varying degrees of solidity and is able to fly them over Manhattan to a club that had been destroyed ten years before but is now intact,[76] with a spotlight that seems to operate itself. He may be real, but the cumulative effect is of an imaginary fantasy world.

Similarly, *Deadly Advice* (1993) has murderers who advise the antiheroine Jodie on how to remove people who might thwart her. These are probably subjective, and the fact that they are from an earlier age of criminals on whom there is a vast literature, and the setting is Hay-on-Wye,[77] reinforces that supposition. What they tell her could be a projection of her own musings, their bickering a reflection of her indecision. Nevertheless despite the evidence for their subjective origin, their solidity hints at an independent existence. It is debatable, however, whether their advice would constitute a successful long-term strategy. Similarly, Sigmund Freud is not particularly effective in *Lovesick* (1983) when he arrives to guide the erring psychoanalyst, Dr. Benjamin, though even he expresses disquiet at the way his ideas have burgeoned into an industry. Freud is probably a projection of Dr. Benjamin's guilt complex: when Benjamin breaks into his patient's flat Freud smokes a cigar but she does not remark upon it. Yet at the end he says that he is going to Oaxaca to continue his research, implying objectivity.

Ghosts Who Return Because of Unfinished Business

A traditional motif is the person who dies having left a task unfinished and returning to see its completion through another. It is an important element in a large number of ghost films, providing a convenient motivation for the plot. This often involves provision for the deceased's family. In *The Cockeyed Miracle* (1946), for example, Sam dies and is fetched by his father, but asks to stay to oversee completion of a business deal that has ramifications for his family's future. When his erstwhile partner decides to keep the money, Sam's father kills him with a lightning bolt, having stressed to Sam that limitations in terms of power are a matter of attitude. Despite father and son being a murderer and accomplice respectively, they leave with the victim, presumably for Heaven. Part of the comedy hinges on the father, who died when young, being younger than his son when the two are ghosts.

Other examples of films which have a ghost enlist the help of the living are *The Remarkable Andrew* (1942), in which a man wrongly accused of embezzlement is able to establish his innocence and expose municipal

3. A Thematic Approach to Cinematic Ghosts

corruption with help from the ghosts of famous Americans, and *Wonder Man* (1945), with Danny Kaye playing twins, including the ghost of one of them (a similar scenario to *The Corsican Brothers*). The ghost, Buster, persuades his reluctant bookworm brother Edwin to impersonate him, assisting him by possessing his body — until Buster runs out of ectoplasm — in order to deliver information to the D. A. to convict the criminals who had had him killed. Wolfenstein and Leites see it as an example of a "comic reversal of mourning:" "Where the dead live on in this fashion, they stimulate the living to a fuller life."[78] They also mention *Topper* as another film with ghosts more alive than the living.'

The Time of Their Lives (1946) has two rebels in the American Revolution mistakenly shot as traitors, and they have to remain at the scene until they can locate a letter that will attest to their allegiance. In the twentieth century, a psychic housekeeper makes contact and the letter is found in the museum. The film contains a gag unknown to psychical research: Costello runs through his fellow ghost and ends up wearing her clothes.[79] In the 1940 version of *Earthbound* a ghost helps his widow to expose his murderer. *The Headless Ghost* (1959) is a comedy about a ghost who is

Nick Desborough (Warner Baxter) and his widow Ellen (Andrea Leeds) join forces to bring his killer to justice in *Earthbound* (1940).

helped by three students, to recover an executed ancestor's head and the apparently evil ghosts in *Ghosts of Hanley House* (1968) merely want the help of the investigators in achieving burial for their bodies.

In *Hearts and Souls* (1993), four ghosts have been linked with an unpleasant businessman, Thomas, since he was a baby because he happened to be nearby when they died. Faced with removal on a ghost bus, their souls required for future lives, they coerce him, partly by possessing his body, to assist them in completing a last unfinished act each. He agrees, each completion allowing the ghost to board the 'bus, except the last, a woman whose regret had been putting off her boyfriend who had wanted to marry her. The bus driver is impatient, and Thomas pleads "stall Him," an implicit reference to God. But the boyfriend is dead, and the ghost realizes that her job was to tell Thomas, who had been afraid of commitment, that he should not waste his own opportunity. The bus leaves, and as Thomas and his girlfriend kiss, the camera cranes up from them to the sky where four stars can be seen shining brightly.

Sometimes ghosts are allowed to return because they find themselves in a predicament not of their choosing and intervention from above is exercised on their behalf, albeit grudgingly. *Here Comes Mr. Jordan* (1941) and its remake *Heaven Can Wait* (1978) show the divine powers allowing Joe to continue his earthly business despite having to find him a makeshift body, because of the worryingly common 'clerical error' to which the heavenly authorities are prone. *A Matter of Life and Death* (1946) necessitates a trial to prove that extra responsibilities have accrued as a result of the error.

Revenge on malefactors is a common motivation for a ghost's return. *Strangler of the Swamp* (1945) has the ghost of a man wrongfully hanged for murder return for vengeance on the granddaughter of the man who not only accused him but was himself the murderer. She and her boyfriend take sanctuary in a church which the ghost cannot enter, and eventually she offers herself to save her boyfriend and his father. His power broken by the gesture, the ghost vanishes—a harsh end given the wrong done to him originally. James Robert Parish notes that the message that vengeance should be left to God, and that peace should be made with Him, was highly appropriate for the time.[80] In *House of Darkness* (1947), a murdered man returns for revenge against his stepbrother who had killed him; in *The Nesting* (1981) the ghosts need revenge on those who murdered them before they can be at peace. The protagonist of *The Wraith* (1986) also returns, with a supernatural car, to kill the gang responsible for his death.

In *High Plains Drifter* (1973) a mysterious cowboy defends a town from three gunslingers, but at a cost (he literally paints it red and rechristens it "Hell"). This is possibly a revenge film, although it is never made explicit whether the stranger is a ghost. David H. Smith quotes three possibilities: he is the murdered marshal, another ghost, or a live stranger passing through.[81] These are all feasible, but Smith considers the interpretation to be weighted towards the first: when he rides into town he jerks when he hears the sound of a whip, recalling the manner of the marshal's death. Bullets fired into his bathtub have no effect (but it is conceivable that the water would slow their velocity). The dead marshal's grave has no marker, and it is postulated that without one a person cannot rest. At the climax, the stranger too wields a whip. Although the stranger as embodiment of the dead lawman is the strongest candidate, there are others. Smith quotes Neil Sinyard's theory that the film is the dwarf's fantasy, giving him heroic stature,[82] and Clint Eastwood's assertion that the stranger is the marshal's brother.[83] While these are weak alternatives, it is still not clear whether the stranger is the marshal or another vengeful ghost. Smith floats the possibility that the marshal's spirit entered the stranger as he rode through the graveyard[84] (which ties in with the idea that without a marker it would not find peace), but when the dwarf says that he did not know the stranger's name, the reply is "Yes you do," which can only mean that he is the marshal; if he were somebody else the dwarf really would not know.

A companion item by Eastwood to *High Plains Drifter* is *Pale Rider* (1985), although whereas in the earlier film the stranger is a kind of avenging angel, the later film is gentler and the characterization more selfless. The supernatural elements are more restrained too, the main cue, apart from the film's title, being his appearance, on a pale grey horse, following a girl's prayer for help over her dead dog, and as she is reading from the Bible about Death on a pale horse. The sheriff thinks that he recognizes the stranger, believing him to have died, but this is poor evidence. The major support for the paranormal theory is provided by five bullet scars on his back, which look as if they would have been fatal, but like the bullets fired into the bath water in the earlier film that fail to kill him, there is still a possibility that a normal explanation exists.

There is a vengeful ghost in a voodoo context in *Mark of the Devil* (1984). The protagonist murders a voodoo-practicing tattooist for his money but during the struggle the murderer is pricked by a knife and from the wound a tattoo begins that eventually covers his whole body. As in *The Illustrated Man* (1969) the tattoos tell a story, in this instance of his crime, and eventually, of his fate. When told by another adept that he must return to the murder scene where he will be purified, her speech is ambiguous. She tells him he must "go down," and that his tattoo will never be seen again, which he interprets as meaning that he will have to enter a cellar, and that the tattoos will disappear, but downwards also has connotations of descending to Hell, and the disappearance of the tattoos could involve his disappearance too. He returns to the parlor, whereupon the ghost of the tattooist leaps from a mirror and strangles him. Like the changelings who transform back to their original selves upon death, the tattoos vanish.

Sometimes revenge is domestic. A man inadvertently kills his spurned lover when she falls from a lighthouse in *Tormented* (1960). She haunts him, her presence announced by traces of seaweed, wet footprints and a drop in temperature. Her revenge takes the form of attempting to destroy his happiness until he too falls from the lighthouse. A wife killed in a burglary in *She's Back* (1989) returns as a revenant to nag her husband into killing the attackers, using the threat that if he fails to, she would not only haunt him while alive but also through eternity. He does as commanded, making the film more *Death Wish* than *Ghost*, but although he is killed she continues to nag him.

The unfinished business need not be a specific act, but perhaps simply an inability to come to terms with the new situation. The dead residents of *Our Town* (1940) are as vigorous a community as their living counterparts. When Emily dies in childbirth she is advised to forget her life, but she wants to go back to relive a day and chooses her sixteenth birthday. She is able to realize the importance of life and how the living take it for granted. Thornton Wilder's play, with its downbeat ending, was changed so that Emily wakes up to find that the experience was caused by the traumas of labor so that the film technically does not deal with life after death (perhaps an atypical NDE) but the ending does not diminish Wilder's lesson, to make the most of life, that it is important even when it seems to be humdrum (Parker Tyler is more scathing, declaring the spirit life to be a display of "unimaginative conservatism"[85]). The sense of bereavement felt by those on both sides of death is undiminished.

Sometimes dead people do not return to complete a specific job but merely because they have to prove that they are worthy to go to Heaven — angels particularly often have to "earn their wings." In *Topper* (1937), the Kerbys who have been killed in a car crash haunt dull Cosmo Topper in order to make him a more outgoing individual. *Topper Takes a Trip* (1939) does not have Mr. Kerby, who has ascended, but Mrs. Kerby is still earthbound,[86] until she helps Topper through his (naturally aborted) divorce. This theme of earning a promotion has been jettisoned by the final sequel, *Topper Returns* (1941), which is a straightforward murder mystery of the

Cosmo Topper (Roland Young) is caught between a ghost (Joan Blondell), who wants his help to solve her murder, and his wife Clara (Billie Burke) in *Topper Returns* (1941).

old "dark house" variety, with Topper as the reluctant investigator pestered by the ghost of the murdered woman.

Ghosts of and for Children

Children are often credited as being more perceptive than adults. This plays on the idea that psychic ability is something that children possess, losing it as they become hardened by age. It is a child in *Lady in White* (1988) who is able to see a replay of the murder and ascertain who carried it out. Adult ghosts can build a strong rapport with children, and when included in a children's film can assume a parental role.[87] They have achieved wisdom through having had a long existence (the Canterville Ghost being an exception) and are able to help children who may have social difficulties. This is a way of maintaining a safe distance between children and adults—the adult ghost in these films is usually male—desexualizing the ghost while enabling him to act as a role model, perhaps in return for a service from the child. The child ghost too can be seen as rendering safe any possible impropriety by putting the child beyond the bounds of sexual contact when non-family from an older generation is involved. The occurrence of child ghosts also plays on the fear of parents over the vulnerability of their children, and the poignancy of death.

Parents who lose a child may feel guilty that they did not prevent the catastrophe, and the ghost could represent a wish fulfillment fantasy. John Baxter in *Don't Look Now* (1973) dies because he is fascinated by the physical similarity between his dead daughter's coat and that worn by a murderous dwarf. John seems to be the one better able to come to terms with the loss, though the vehemence of his anger when he thinks that his wife has fallen under the spell of the sisters ("My daughter is dead, Laura. She doesn't come peeping back at me with messages from beyond the fucking grave. She's dead dead dead") shows that the suppression of his feelings is not as complete as he would like to think. At the moment of his death his ESP breaks down, and any hope that the figure in red is his daughter is cruelly removed.[88] Julia in *Full Circle* (1976) is murdered by a rare example of an evil child ghost after failing to save her own daughter. At the climax, Julia reassures Olivia, as in *Don't Look Now* John reassures the figure in red, and each is promptly killed. Julia's death, though, is ambiguous. Her guilt in a sense causes her to haunt herself,[89] leading one to wonder if Olivia, the evil child, is real, or if Julia has been driven mad by grief. Her death could have been due to murder by Olivia, Olivia could have forced her to kill herself by strength of will, or Julia could have committed suicide to avoid the unbearable burden she carries.

Ghost films made especially for children, for example *Emily's Ghost* (1991), *My Friend Walter* (1992), *Casper* (1995), *Little Ghost* (1996) and *The Legend of Cryin' Ryan* (1998), as well as *Charlie's Ghost Story*, introduce the concept of death through a safe, domesticated view. When the ghost is also of a child, the young viewer can begin to familiarize itself with what it might be like to be dead. Ghosts, as well as angels, can often only be seen by children in films—one needs purity of heart and a certain openness and innocence untainted by doubt to see them. Throughout *The Last Winter* (1990), the son is repeatedly encouraged by his grandfather to use his imagination, and is the only one to see a ghost horse. When the grandfather dies and appears with the horse, the boy is able to talk to him and be comforted.

The most significant of these films dealing with the relationship between a living child and an adult ghost is *The Curse of the Cat People* (1944). The focus on the child, Amy, is so strong that the film is frequently described in terms of being a "poetic study of childhood loneliness." The ghost, Irena, is tangential to the story, although she does play a role in terms of the effect her memory has on her husband Oliver, remarried to

Amy's mother.[90] J. P. Telotte points to this haunting's being metaphorical as well as literal: "In effect, it is Oliver who conjures up Irena's specter, who maintains the ghosts that haunt him and his family."[91] Instead of a threat to Amy from Irena, it comes from the living, either overtly or as a by-product of incomprehension. Irena herself only appears after Amy has made a wish and seen her photograph, so there is always the possibility that she is subjective, an imaginary friend, although the moment when Amy's ball is returned from the bushes hints at objectivity, and her reality is given weight by *Cat People* (1942).[92] Kim Newman argues that the shot of Irena alone after the Reeds have gone into the house signifies her objectivity. Whatever her status, Irena's effect is minimal, and even at the end Amy is saved because she confuses the person menacing her, Barbara, with Irena, thus disarming Barbara. Yet Irena's presence hovers over the film to such an extent that both Peter Nicholls and Butler assume that she is Amy's mother[93]

At the end, in an apparent effort at empathy, Oliver tells Amy that he can see Irena in the garden, as she and the audience can. As he is not looking into the garden his motives are unclear — he is either taking Amy seriously for the first time or is being patronizingly insincere.[94] Presumably if he had seen Irena he would have made more of it, as it would have had implications for his second marriage (of the sort treated comically in *Blithe Spirit*). Oliver, though probably lying, has finally realized that a compromise must be made when dealing with children, between being truthful and helping them.[95] Irena, whether veridical or not, is able to fade away because she is no longer needed.[96] The problem here, as with other films dealing with living children and ghosts, is that the latter are never adequate substitutes for positive relationships with the living.

Ghost Lovers

The ghost lover has a long history in literature, related to the notion of the Demon Lover. The ghost lover can be truly demonic, vampiric — literally or metaphorically — or merely a sinister ghost. In cinema it is more often tender, relationships changed but not terminated by death.[97] The filmic nexus continues a trend apparent in pictorial art:

> During the nineteenth century, an erotic aesthetic emerged in which young dead bodies were celebrated as objects of desire, crossing the age-old prohibition against representing love between the living and dead.[98]

Sexual relations can be disagreeable, the dead exercising power over the living.[99] The prime example is *The Entity* (1982), but the medium in

The Legend of Hell House (1972) gives herself to what she believes is a lost soul in the mistaken belief that physical love will provide him with peace.[100] If the stranger in *High Plains Drifter* (1973) is a ghost, his rape of the townswoman would fall into this category. These are dead males menacing living females. By the same token, female ghosts threaten patriarchal values and the established sexual order. They can be subversive, especially when they have the strength to overpower or terrify living males, or even to seduce them.

At the other extreme, *The Ghost and Mrs. Muir* (1947) was considered a "women's picture" when released, and the description might be used of other ghost films with a romantic attachment in which the dominant patriarchy is not threatened, and physical expression is made difficult if not impossible. *Peter Ibbetson* (1921/1935) has a couple who fell in love as children, separated later by prison but reunited in death, linked in the interim by a dream life that amounts to a psi connection. More recently, in *Ghost Fever* (1985) two policemen find a pair of ladies in period costume in an old house. The officers realize that the women are ghosts, nevertheless the four fall in love. The solution to the conundrum of how to proceed is solved when the living partners are killed, enabling the couples to remain together.

Another example of romantic love surviving death is provided by *Smilin' Through* (1922 and 1932[101]). It shows how a ghost can assist the living to come to terms with grief at a loss that can blight the survivor's life. John is full of bitterness because his beloved Moonyean was murdered by a rejected suitor moments before she was to wed John. In the 1932 version, John talks to Moonyean, who can be seen only by the audience in double exposure.[102] She tells him that they will one day be together, and he seems to sense her presence. Eventually he dies, his double rises from his body and he sees Moonyean. Young again, he says that there is nothing to dying, and everything. Surrounded by ghostly well-wishers, they climb into a wedding carriage to complete the ceremony cut short by her death. The vehicle is superimposed over the garden, and this, plus John leaving his body, are similar to images in *The Phantom Chariot* (1920). True love transcends death, but the implication too is of a wasted life caught up in bitter memories that preclude earthly progress. The poignant realization is that he needed to die to achieve happiness. A sex-reversed musical version of *Smilin' Through* is provided by *Maytime* (1937), in which a man is murdered, leaving his beloved to mourn for the rest of her life. She dies and is reunited in young form with her double exposure lover.

The Ghost and Mrs. Muir (1947) traces a love between a living woman and dead man that is only requited at her death when both are reunited.

3. A Thematic Approach to Cinematic Ghosts

A widow, Lucy Muir (Gene Tierney) falls in love with the ghost of a seaman, Captain Gregg (Rex Harrison), in *The Ghost and Mrs. Muir* (1947).

She had rejected him in life because he could not satisfy all of her needs, and he utilizes the unusual ghostly attribute of being able to induce amnesia so that she might forget him. By giving him up she loses those comforts his presence might have afforded, and even more ironically the passage of time is signified by pounding surf that elsewhere might connote sexual rapture. The two are reunited by her eventual death in old age, but when her superimposed spirit rises up from the corpse it has taken the conventionally filmic form of her as a young woman, when Captain Gregg first met her. Frieda Grafe, influenced by the point in the novel when Mrs. Muir talks of hearing Captain Gregg's voice internally,[103] builds an argument that he is subjective, his portrait used as a prop for her imagination, the knowledge needed to write her book gleaned from her father's library as a child.[104] This approach foregrounds the problem of making inferences about a film based on the back story and the likely psychology of the characters. It also highlights the difficulty in distinguishing between the survival hypothesis and other possible explanations, such as Super-ESP or cryptomnesia.

That the Captain is not seen by Mrs. Muir's relatives does not make him subjective; the selectively witnessed ghost is common in both fiction and psychical research literature. The spirit that rises from her dead body at the end of the film could have no meaning in terms of her point of view, only the audience's, suggesting that it is objective, and that Captain Gregg also exists. Her claim that she dreamed the book is reasonable given her amnesia of the Captain's dictation. Would it be reasonable to suppose that as a child she had access to her father's racier books? Grafe too is a little hazy on the attributes of ghosts. She asks rhetorically "Who ever heard of a cowardly ghost?"[105] forgetting *The Canterville Ghost*. She continues "He casts a clean, sharp shadow on the wall, something that ghosts, as we know, don't do."[106] Ghosts on the contrary come in all shapes, sizes and degrees of clarity, some of whom it is difficult to tell apart from the living. Captain Gregg as a by-product of Mrs. Muir's imagination is less likely than his objective presence, and about as likely as the film's being a portrayal of schizophrenia.

Love between living and dead can range from such romantic attachment through to more earthy activities, and *High Spirits* (1988) provides a picture of the latter. Director Neil Jordan describes the film as a "necrophilic romance" in the introduction to his script,[107] and the centuries prove not to be a barrier to sexual fulfillment. The hauntings cover a wide variety of types. To begin with, the master of the castle does not even know it is haunted, although his mother does. Only when financial ruin is imminent do the ancestral ghosts show themselves. The main ghosts initially appear as the type of haunting which has the same scene replayed every night, although with more detail than is normally associated with this kind of apparition, and with such realism that they are initially taken to be actors. When actions by the living cause the dead to be released from their replays, they are able to interact with the living. Information on how to proceed is provided by a handbook, *The Book of High Spirits*. Perpetual relationships are only possible when the living woman dies, becoming a ghost herself, and the previously dead woman takes over the newly dead wife's body, although with her own features. Symmetry is retained although the partners have swapped.

This category would not be complete without a mention of the Hong Kong genre that unites ghosts, soft-core eroticism, and sometimes martial arts. Hong Kong supernatural films tend to be hybrids, ghosts mixed with wizards and magic, demons, vampires, zombies and love interest bordering on necrophilia. They are frequently explicit enough to warrant a "Category 3" certificate, intended for films with "adult" content, although others are played as comedies. Such fare as the *Erotic Ghost Story* series, *Ghostly Love*, *Ghostly Vixen*, *Seeding of a Ghost*, *Spiritual Love*, *Rouge*, and

Tale of a Female Ghost run the gamut of sexual and emotional feelings between the living and dead.

Ghost Lovers Who Return to Break the Bond[108]

Rather than return to be with a living partner, sometimes ghost lovers have to return to try to wean loved ones away from them in order to allow them to begin new lives (thus making these types of films a subset of those dealing with unfinished business). A potential problem is determining the ghost's veridicality, as there is the possibility that we could be witnessing a wish fulfillment. This type of ghostly activity is fairly recent, with few instances before the 1980s. Why this should be is unclear. Perhaps in an age when divorce was a relative rarity there was a premium on the continuation of a relationship at all costs, whereas in an age in which relationships are more flexible, death can be seen as a kind of quasi-divorce, albeit a friendly one, and the prospect of serial monogamy more acceptable.

Of these early ones, *A Guy Named Joe* (1943) has a dead pilot become a guardian angel to his replacement. He helps the young man become a hero, and is reconciled to the relationship with the dead pilot's girlfriend. The action is updated to the present in the loose remake *Always* (1989), the emphasis more on the romantic triangle, although the re-creation of the milieu (the pilots are aerial fire-fighters) and camaraderie are similar to the original. In both, the dead pilot needs to let go, as does the partner left behind. The difference between the two films is that the original, like other wartime dramas on a similar theme, aimed to comfort those who might die, and their relatives. By 1989 that was not a general problem, and critics at the time of *Always*'s release felt a sense of redundancy.[109]

In *Miracle in the Rain* (1956), also a Second World War story, a dead soldier returns to give his girlfriend the will to live. He does this by declaring his love and leaving a coin she had given him, though until the moment it is found in her hand it had been possible to attribute the ghost to a hallucination. The consolation theme would have fitted in with the sorts of ghost films made during the war, notably *Happy Land* and *The Human Comedy*, and its similarity could possibly be a delayed reaction to the Korean War, which had been over for three years. *Truly, Madly, Deeply* (1990) and *Kiss Me Goodbye* (1982)[110] both revolve around the attempts of widows to carve lives with new partners. There is an honest approach to the effect death has on the survivor, particularly in the former, with its unsentimental evocation of bereavement, the honesty of which has been compared to *Ghost*, usually to the Hollywood product's detriment.[111] Jamie offers more commitment to Nina in death than he had in life, and learning Spanish means either post-mortem intellectual and perhaps spiritual growth, or an ESP component to the relationship (Nina is a translator, a kind of medium, of Spanish). Possible subjectivity is undermined, though not ruled out, by the correlation of the absence of vermin, and the presence of Jamie and his ghostly friends.

Even *Kiss Me Goodbye* (1982), though more superficial than *Truly, Madly, Deeply*, refers to the anger that Kay felt when Jolly died that he had deserted her. One wonders why Jolly waited three years to return to persuade Kay that she should get on with her life, precisely at the point at which she has come to terms with his loss and decided to remarry. If veridical, he could be acting through jealousy of her potential life with a new mate. In a sense, her mourning (like Nina's for Jamie in *Truly, Madly, Deeply*) would have been a means of keeping him alive, and remarriage might consign him to the loss of even the consolation of living through memory. Kay is unable to decide which she wants, the fun-loving but dead Jolly, or staid but living Rupert. The names set up the predicament cheaply, and jokes about Rupert's Egyptology emphasize his dullness compared to Jolly's profession of choreographer. Jolly could easily be seen as an externalization of Kay's unreadiness to commit herself to a new relationship and fear of betrayal of the dead spouse, except that Jolly provides a piece of information relating to Rupert that Kay would not have known, to prove his existence. Despite this, the fact that Jolly can only be seen by Kay, and is never visible when she is absent, suggests a subjective element, and he acknowledges that he is a mental, not a physical, image.

AIDS-Related Ghosts[112]

There is a group of films focusing on AIDS, often including a ghost who urges his dead lover to move on rather than either mourn excessively or withdraw from emotional life. In *Zero Patience* (1993), Zero appears as a ghost to a still-living Sir Richard Burton[113] in order to correct the erroneous folklore that has grown up since his death, and which Burton is perpetuating in an exhibition on Zero and AIDS. The difference in their status does not prevent the pair from having an affair, with Burton seeing his error.

Disease is less important in *To Die For* (1993) than the lifestyle of the surviving partner, Simon. The film, as most reviewers noted, has echoes of *Truly, Madly, Deeply*, but whereas in that film the dead partner returns to help the living to move on, Mark in *To Die For* wants Simon to see that his hedonistic lifestyle is destructive. The style also harks back to *Randall and Hopkirk (Deceased)* (1969), not least because of Mark's white clothes and the familiar selective point-of-view shots whereby Simon can see Mark, but nobody else can. The major difference is that not only can Mark affect matter, but he can be affected too; on one occasion Simon shoves him, and he flies through the air, and on another a neighbor pulls a stool he has been sitting on, and we and Simon, although not the neighbor, see him shoot across the room. It is these interactions that indicate he is objective, rather than being a subjective product of Simon's guilt and confusion. The finale, where the two kiss, Simon having realized how much he did love Mark, nods to *Ghost*, as Mark, mission accomplished, ascends to Heaven. As in *Ghost*, Mark is trapped until he can resolve his business with the living, and when the loved one is healed, he has to leave.

The ghost in *Jeffrey* (1995) is much less central to the plot. Jeffrey is frightened to have a relationship, given the extent of AIDS. A friend, Darius, who has the disease, dies, and Jeffrey meets Darius's partner Sterling at the hospital. The two argue over Jeffrey's reluctance to pursue a relationship when suddenly Jeffrey sees Darius. The design conforms to descriptions of NDEs, with white clothes, strong back-lighting, and a group of Darius's deceased relatives who have come to escort him to the Afterlife. Darius urges Jeffrey not to be afraid to have sex. The ghost might be seen as an extension of Jeffrey, allowing him to give himself permission to take a risk for the sake of leading a full life, except that Sterling sees Darius too, judging by the reaction shot of him smiling.

"Hungry Ghosts"

Folkloric "Hungry Ghosts" are spirits trapped on the lower planes after death through an inability to renounce desire and evil. Individuality is retained with its unpleasant characteristics, preying on those who wish to communicate with the dead, and attempting to entice the newly deceased to their mode of existence. Some might not realize that they are not alive, and be confused that the living people they speak to ignore them.[114] In film terms, ghosts who return for revenge might be included, and there is not a definite line between such hungry ghosts and Hellish demons. Both can threaten the living, souls as well as lives, and can be sexually voracious. The wish to return can be motivated by a desire for revenge, or it can be displaced onto someone innocent who happens to live in the house where the injustice occurred, or who has a personal problem that renders him or her vulnerable to psychic attack.

For James B. Twitchell, "The destructive woman is one of humankind's oldest images of terror, but she first became vampiric in romanticism."[115] The preponderance of female ghosts, benign or sinister, is in contrast to slasher films where females are menaced by a male with seemingly supernatural powers, punishing their transgressive sexuality. Both forms may spring from the same fear of women by men.[116] The female ghost can be alluring or threatening, the former type made safe for male consumption, the latter reinforcing male fears of female autonomy.

The dangerous female hungry ghost who returns to menace those left behind can be seen in *Ghost Story* (1981) and *The Dead Can't Lie* (1988).[117] Two Poe-inspired examples are Morella in *Tales of Terror* (1962), who discovers that her mother's body has been kept by her father, and is possessed by her, and Ligeia in *The Tomb of Ligeia* (1965), who dies but comes back to possess the hero's second wife, Rowena. The element of incest in the former is diverted by the fire that kills all three protagonists. The past returns to claim the future with an evil intention in both cases, in *Ligeia* signaled by the respectively dark and blonde hair of dead and living wives, both of whom are played by the same person. The presence of a black cat too suggests that the dead woman has tapped occult forces through witchcraft. The interchangeability of the two women makes the final conflagration ambiguous. Ligeia is supposed to have been destroyed, but the possibility remains that Rowena has died, sparing Ligeia.

The Forgotten One (1990) contains a spirit who essentially becomes a hungry ghost by attempting to murder her living lover, Bob, so that he can be with her. The menace is signaled early on when the camera takes what transpires to be her point of view, complete with heavy breathing, in a style redolent of slasher films. There is a reincarnation element in that she believes Bob to be the man over whom her husband had murdered her, and indeed Bob does look like him. Bob is also psychically linked to the house, and obtains the story of the tragedy through his dreams. From being a pathetic lost soul she becomes increasingly powerful until her obsession with Bob appears to be a mental imbalance. He falls in love with her, but is understandably frightened by her attempts on his life, until in an unmotivated change of heart he decides to drown to be with her.

Ghosts Who Use the Living to Play Out a Drama from Their Own Lives

Some ghosts are caught in a drama that they are condemned to perpetuate, using the living as surrogates. One of the living is frequently caught up and drags others in unwillingly, and often the current domestic situation mirrors the historical one. The films are distinguishable from those in which the dead use the living through possession to carry out their wishes, although there is an overlap.

An example of this theme is the "comic" *The Spirit Is Willing* (1967). A cheated wife kills her husband and his mistress but he in turn stabs her to death. There is an established triangle that is disturbed by the living. The ghosts' resentment causes various disasters to befall the newcomers, all blamed by the family on an adolescent boy, until one of the living is killed. The wife can pair with him, and order be restored. Another triangle is found in *The House Where Evil Dwells* (1982), which taps into a Japanese tradition of revenge ghosts,[118] using the living to continue unfinished business. In this instance, the characters become influenced to carry out these actions, the 1840 sexual entanglement being reflected in the contemporary situation. The difference between the two periods though is that the ghosts are not just playing out the drama through the people living in their house, but obtain a kind of solidarity through plotting the destruction of the living. In Japanese folklore violent death causes a spirit to become vengeful, an *onyro*, able to possess the living, an aspect of the Afterlife dealt with in the following section.

There is another triangle from the past that has repercussions for the present in *The Haunting of Seacliff Inn* (1994). Mark and Susan purchase a hotel. After experiencing low-level ghostly activity, they discover that the deceased builder, Hastings, had a mistress and murdered his wife. The mistress arrives, seemingly alive, and attempts to seduce Mark, driving a wedge between him and Susan. When Hastings arrives and begins to undress her, she is only brought to reality by Mark's voice. She resists until Hastings's wife appears and the ghostly pair go up in flames from knocked-over candles. As in *The Amityville Horror* (1979), another film in which it seems history will be replayed, money problems are a key element at Seacliff Inn. Strife is created by exacerbating the financial crisis, for example by causing a flood. Perhaps emotional worries of the living provide a kind of handhold for a ghost, allowing it to participate in the present.

Possession

Possession films fall into two broad categories, those with a living person occupied by another identifiable, but dead, individual, and later films, mainly post–*The Exorcist* (1973), which feature possession by an evil spirit that may never have been alive.[119] There may be an awareness that there is another consciousness co-existing with the victim's own, or the host's consciousness may be suppressed, perhaps emerging precariously and weakly (Regan's embossed "Help Me" in *The Exorcist*, for example).

The common thread is the ability of the deceased to impose his/her/its will on another, with one of four main outcomes: the controlling entity leaves when its mission is accomplished; external agents such as an exorcist drive the spirit away; the possessed one dies; or, rarely, the possessor happily continues to occupy its new home indefinitely.

The idea of possession blurs into mediumship, where a medium invites communication, but it is not clear how far control is exercised over the spirits. In *The Uninvited* (1944), for instance, a séance is held at which one of the participants begins speaking Spanish. She is channeling her mother, who has benevolent motives, but such an act could be construed as possession. That condition is generally indicative of an evil intent on the part of an occupier, forcing a superior will on that of the host, best exemplified by the variations on the *Donovan's Brain* theme. The relationship need not be a malign one, nor long-lasting: Sam is allowed to occupy Oda Mae's body to kiss Mollie goodbye in *Ghost* (1990).[120]

Sometimes artistic types possess surrogates in order to continue careers cut short by death. Maxie Malone, in *Maxie* (1985), is a silent-film actress who possesses an inhibited woman of the 1980s in order to pursue her acting aspirations. In this instance the possessed gains from the experience, being transformed into somebody more outgoing, like the possessing spirit. Possession here is more akin to collaboration. In *Shadow Dancing* (1988), a modern-day ballerina is possessed by a dancer who died half a century before. A more ambiguous example is *The Legend of Lylah Clare* (1968), in which Lylah may or may not be possessing the actress, Elsa, who is impersonating her. It seems to be saying that actors masquerading as other people are all possessed by some element of those they imitate, so that it is hard to determine whether Elsa is controlled by Lylah or merely consumed by the role.[121]

Possession can be linked with revenge. In *Supernatural* (1933) a murderess occupies the body of a woman to exact revenge on the man who had informed on her, himself a fake medium. In *Ruby* (1977) a gangster murdered by his gang takes revenge after having been called back by his daughter. He possesses her, but the murders themselves are not carried out by her directly, rather by using poltergeist-like effects. The gangster's lover sees him regularly, as he was after he was shot. She finally gives herself to him by drowning in the lake into which he had fallen after being killed, and is embraced by his skeleton, sinews remarkably preserved. A similar revenge-through-possession approach is taken in *Retribution* (1988), in which a man occupies the body of a suicidal artist in order to be revenged on his killers. In *Last Gasp* (1995), an avaricious property developer murders a Mexican Indian who threatens to thwart his ambitions. He is possessed by the dead man who destroys him in turn. That contacting the wrong sort of dead person can be hazardous is shown in *The Phantom Speaks* (1945). The spirit of an executed murderer controls the mind of the psychical researcher who communicated with him and forces him to commit murders for revenge. The scientist in turn is caught and condemned to death — once again paying the penalty of meddling with Things Best Left Alone.

There is frequently a racial, class or gender twist. *The Possession of Joel Delaney* (1971) makes the possession a class issue, as the possessed is upper-class and the possessor a poor Puerto Rican. Additionally, Tonio's spirit moves into Joel's sister at the end as he is gunned down. Charles Derry compares the film to *The Exorcist*, as an exorcism fails because of the non-belief of the sister, just as the priest in *The Exorcist* fails because of Regan's mother's atheism.[122] The difference is that Regan in the latter is possessed by a demon, while Joel Delaney is possessed by a spirit that was once living. *Heart Condition* (1990) uses the theme of a heart transplant to portray benign possession, with a racial twist, the original black owner haunting its white recipient until (and perhaps after) his death has been explained. There is no loss of consciousness by the possessed, and the two bodies do not coincide, but the organ acts as a kind of connective tissue between the two. It is a symbiotic relationship with control exerted by means of first irritation and then friendship. The twist is also legal in *J.D.'s Revenge* (1976), as the spirit of a 1930s gangster possesses a law student in order to pursue a vendetta.

Occupation might be caused either by familial proximity or by chance. The extrovert Buster possesses his introverted twin Edwin in *Wonder Man* (1945) so strongly that when Edwin drinks alcohol, Buster gets drunk as well. Ligeia, in *The Tomb of Ligeia* (1965), possesses her husband's second wife, in *Back From the Dead* (1957), a woman is possessed by the spirit of her husband's first wife, who had been a Satanist. On the other hand, the lawyer in *All of Me* (1984) is occupied by his deceased client in error, an exercise in metempsychosis becoming possession, and is unusual in that the two personalities inhabit the body on equal terms at the same time, rather than the new one displacing the old, a situation made more complicated by the fact that the incomer is a woman. The doctor in *Nomads* (1986) suffers overshadowing after being bitten by a patient who was to become a revenant (at which point, his soul gone, she is free). Sometimes predestination is involved: Annette in *A Place of One's Own* (1945) says when she is hired as companion that she felt compelled to come, and afterwards is possessed by the spirit of the woman who had lived in the house.

Ghosts Can't Do It (1990) features a form of permanent possession in which a dead man occupies the body of a younger individual to be with the possessed's wife. There are clearly links with reincarnation, or at least metempsychosis. *Here Comes Mr. Jordan* (1941) and *Heaven Can Wait* (1978) also featured this type of occupation, but *Ghosts Can't Do It* differs, in that the original's consciousness continues whereas in the two earlier films it is lost. This is ironic given that Mr. Jordan himself, and the personality transferences themselves, attest to the continuation of consciousness after death.

Possession often ties in with witchcraft, black magicians of both sexes managing to return to continue their evil deeds through their descendants. In *Back from the Dead* (1957) a woman becomes possessed by the spirit of her husband's first wife, who was a Satanist. A warlock burned at the stake in *The Haunted Palace* (1963) occupies a descendant, and in *The Mephisto Waltz* (1971) a musician transfers his soul into a younger man, who then possesses his abilities. His wife dies, but she has transferred her own soul into the musician's daughter, with whom he was having an incestuous affair. In *Beyond Evil* (1980) a dead woman who had dabbled in occult practices during her lifetime remains in her house, to which a young couple move. She attempts to evict them while unsuccessfully trying to possess the wife.

Another type of possession unknown in the psychical research literature is that of otherwise inanimate objects, usually dolls. The most famous of these, for extra-cinematic reasons, is that of Chucky in the *Child's Play* series, but precursors can be found in *Dead of Night* (1945), *Ghost Story* (1974), *Cathy's Curse* (1976) and *Magic* (1978). A malign form of possession can only be dealt with by exorcism, to force the entities out by religious ritual.[123] The cinema's first exorcism occurred in the Yiddish film *The Dybbuk* (1937).[124] A young man who has asked for Satanic aid to help him win the object of his affection dies. He possesses his lover as she is about to marry another, and has to be exorcised. The effort is unsuccessful, but the dybbuk takes pity and leaves. Naturally more restrained than *The Exorcist*, the exercise does look forward to the later film's mode of operation, although in *The Dybbuk* the occupying entity is a ghost rather than a demon, and leaves through compassion rather than force.

Film ghosts as opposed to demons tend not to have to suffer exorcisms; usually they either go voluntarily or a medium moves them into the light. An exception is in *Kiss Me Goodbye* (1982), in which an ex-priest attempts to remove the spirit of the dead husband who is threatening to ruin a newly-remarried wife's happiness. Demon possession is satirized by having the exorcist think that the husband's spirit is in the dog. As this is a romantic comedy, the types of extreme behavior depicted in *The Exorcist* are avoided. An unusual ghost film featuring exorcism is *Beetlejuice* (1988). Betelgeuse is a "Bio- Exorcist," who claims to be able to get rid of the living from properties that the dead still inhabit. The dead too can be exorcised, characterized as "Death for the Dead." Unfortunately Betelgeuse becomes just as much of a threat to the ghosts as to the living, and after he has been subdued the dead reach an accommodation with the living to share the house.

Meetings with the Ghost of Elvis

Paranormal phenomena can in some circumstances reflect prevailing cultural and media interests.[125] For example, there are several films that feature the ghost of Elvis Presley, reflecting his continuing importance in the American psyche, and paralleling tabloid stories that the real Elvis did not die in 1977 but either still alive, or died after that date.[126] In *Mystery Train* (1989), a film saturated in references is to The King, a widow escorting her husband's remains to Rome is stranded in Memphis. Lying in bed at her hotel she stares at Elvis's picture (every room has one), and he materializes in his gold lamé suit in front of her. This could be regarded as a hypnagogic experience stimulated by her exposure to the Elvis cult, but he looks confused, says he must be in the wrong place, apologizes, and fades away.

Presley is a running motif throughout *True Romance* (1993). He is in two crucial scenes. In the first, Clarence is contemplating shooting his wife's ex-pimp, and Elvis exhorts him to carry out his intention. The second time is during a drugs deal, when Elvis tells him how well he handled the situation. On neither occasion is he seen full-face (something that could have been done by using an impersonator à la *Mystery Train* or *Honeymoon in Vegas*) but is rather suggested by glimpses of costume, fuzzily in a mirror, and crucially by his voice. Elvis is thus literally a ghostly presence, and although he can be seen by Clarence and by the audience, the fact that he appears with Clarence alone in the bathroom, and is not seen completely, raises the possibility that he is a wish fulfillment. He tells Clarence things he wants to believe — it is easy to get away with murder, he is an accomplished drug dealer. Neither of these is true, so if Elvis is not a figment of Clarence's imagination, he is an extremely unreliable confederate.

The Ghost in the Machine[127]

That ghost films do not form a watertight compartment can be seen in those where ghosts exist within electrical and computer networks. These do not presuppose the dualism of the non-corporeal type, as a physical structure is available to accommodate them. Examples are *The Horror Show* (1989), *The Lawnmower Man* (1992) and *The Ghost in the Machine* (1993). These electronic denizens are able to communicate, and even to interact with the world. What sets them apart from more conventional ghost films is that there is no sign that a soul as well as a personality has been retained. In the second two the computer inhabitants display psychotic tendencies, possibly caused by the lack of a soul, which tends to equate to a moral sense. The difference between the two is that The Lawnmower Man undergoes a personality change as a result of his cyber-experiences, whereas in *Ghost in the Machine* the victim of the electrical accident is a serial killer who is still able to conduct precisely the same campaign he intended to before his metamorphosis.[128] *The Shocker* (1989) also has a dead serial killer roaming the power system to strike his victims. A hybrid example of a discarnate entity occupying a machine is provided by *And You Thought Your Parents Were Weird* (1992) in which the inventors' father uses their robot to interact with the world, but had been summoned by the use of a Ouija board. Unlike the psychotic examples above, though, the father has become a more mature person since death.

An example of memories being transferred from one brain to another is provided by *Brainwaves* (1983). Here the transference is given a neurological rationale, in that a coma victim is subjected to a procedure using the brain patterns of a deceased person in order to stimulate the damaged regions of her own brain. This film is different from depictions of individuals having some form of essence downloaded into a computer in that the dead girl's personality has been lost, giving the memories a synthetic quality more in common with those possessed by the replicants in *Bladerunner* (1982) than with other films discussed here.

Machinery and electronic equipment can assist high-tech necromancers in summoning up spirits. Dr. Blair in *The Devil Commands* (1941) attempts to communicate with his dead wife. He explains that communication is analogous to radio, a model popular at the time, influenced by the title of Upton Sinclair's account of ESP tests, *Mental Radio* (1930). Although Blair's colleagues had scoffed, he is not gullible, quickly exposing a medium with whom he is working as a charlatan (the ectoplasmic presence that appears is closely modeled on the extras typically found in spirit photographs from the previous century).

Blair succeeds in reaching his wife, but only when their daughter is close by. Blair hooks her to the machine, as her waves are almost identical to her mother's, suggesting a genetic component. Just as a mob is breaking down the door, the equipment explodes and the roof crashes down, killing Blair. All his efforts translate into a few squiggles on paper and the whispering of his name by his wife. He becomes an example of the unthinking scientist who, although a good person, disregards the consequences of his actions in the pursuit of knowledge. In 1941 that was a point with wider ramifications than attempts to contact the dead. He is not a cold-blooded unemotional monster but rather a victim of desire. Emotion and intellect can be a dangerous combination, is the lesson, but searching for knowledge is preferable to the mindless reactions of those who seek to destroy what they do not understand. Blair becomes a tragic hero, selfless in his devotion to the quest, but manipulated by the scheming medium, and undone by shutting out love for the living, represented by the daughter whom he ignores.

Continuation Without Awareness of Death

There are films in which a person has died but does not realize it, and neither does the audience until the climax. Examples include the three Amicus anthologies: In *Dr. Terror's House of Horrors* (1964) five travelers on a train discover at the end of their journey that they are dead; that realization strikes five tourists who have wandered into catacombs in *Tales from the Crypt* (1972); and the same befalls the five who find themselves in the cemetery crypt in *Vault of Horror* (1973). Other examples are *The Survivor* (1981)—a pilot persuaded to investigate an airplane crash by the ghosts of its victims discovers that he himself is a ghost; *Siesta* (1987)—a woman realizes that she has been murdered by her lover's fiancée; *Carnival of Souls* (1962) and possibly *Jacob's Ladder* (1990).[129]

Mary in *Carnival of Souls* has lost the part of her that makes her an empathic human, and the scenes in which she becomes invisible to those around her hint that she is shifting in and out of everyday reality. In a key scene, one that looks forward to *The Nightmare on Elm Street* series, Mary falls asleep in her car while it is being repaired. She opens her eyes when she hears footsteps, and goes to see the doctor. When he turns to face her, however, she finds that it is the ghoul who has been haunting her, and then she suddenly wakes up back in her car. The scene is ambiguous, it not being made clear whether she was dreaming or somehow projecting, her astral self solid in a shadowy world.[130] This depiction of a subjective experience seems real enough to the audience, which throws doubt upon the entire narrative's reliability. Whatever the explanation, her predicament seems to be caused by resistance to her fate, encapsulated by her vain attempt to leave town.

Death can be a state of mind that has to be accepted. Similarly, in *Por-*

trait of Jennie (1948), a painter becomes enamored of a young girl he realizes eventually is a ghost, although she thinks that she is still alive. This lack of awareness is different from the situation in *Universal Soldier* (1992), in which dead soldiers have been revivified and their consciousnesses suppressed by chemical means. *Universal Soldier* follows the pattern of *Revolt of the Zombies* (1936) in which a regiment of dead Indochinese soldiers are brought back to life and utilized by the French in the First World War.

The Haunted House[131]

The haunted dwelling links the horror genre throughout its various forms and periods, and is a major sub-type within the ghost film. It has a history older than that of film, and was common in the fairgrounds that were also the initial home of cinema. The haunted house stands for the unknown, for ignorance that threatens the safety of the occupants. Roger Corman said of *The Fall of the House of Usher* (1960) that "The House is the monster."[132] It provides the claustrophobia useful for escalating tension both between the on-screen characters and in the audience. Two variants need to be distinguished, although demarcation is not always easy.[133] The first encompasses those in which the house itself somehow participates, with a distinct character over and above individuals that once inhabited it (*The Haunting, The Shining*). In the second the house is merely a venue for the action (*The Changeling, The Forgotten One*). *The Legend of Hell House* straddles the divide in that the creator of the building is still important after death (responsible for the energy that keeps it active) though the house has become a protagonist in its own right.

The house that is normally a place of safety is subverted by a ghost's intrusions. It also embodies memory, with a longevity denied to humans, so that it can be a battleground upon which to play out ancient struggles.[134] Noël Carroll stresses the haunted house as involving "a narrative of renewal, predicated upon restaging an altogether

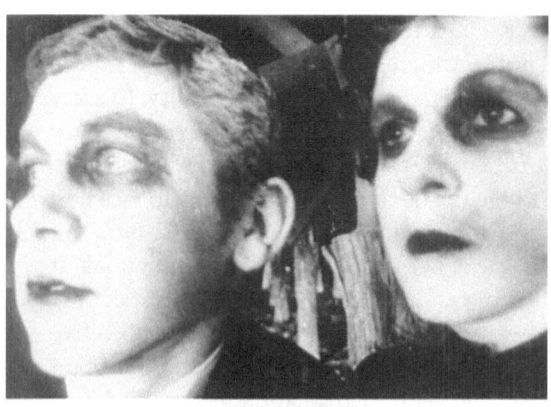

A young woman who has apparently survived a car accident is menaced by mysterious ghouls in *Carnival of Souls* (1962).

unsavory past."¹³⁵ Memory playing itself out suggests passivity and a lack of renewal, but *Céline et Julie Vont en Bateau* (1974) shows the possibility of altering the narrative structure, as well as making the point that sterility and lack of progress within the house can be contrasted with the potential for development outside it.¹³⁶

A refinement to the atmosphere inherited from the Gothic novel is the emphasis on mood and disorienting angles seen in Expressionist film — a distillation of which can be found in *The Haunting* (1963). Stephen King regards the haunted house as a place of authoritarianism and imprisonment,¹³⁷ the "archetype of the Bad Place."¹³⁸ Sometimes there is a bad place within the Bad Place, the room into which nobody wants to go, with a sinister atmosphere or far colder than the rest of the building. The cold spot outside the nursery in *The Haunting* is an example, as is the cold studio in *The Uninvited* (1944). Ghosts tend to be referred to as "place-centered," linked to one location, but *The Ghost Goes West* (1935) provides a different slant because the castle is removed from its original location, so that Murdoch could either remain where he is haunting, now presumably a bare patch of earth, or he could follow the building, even when no longer recognizable as it is packed in crates.¹³⁹ He chooses the latter course.

The haunted house can be seen to have its filmic origin in the trick films of Méliès and his contemporaries.¹⁴⁰ Even at this early stage, the haunting, although bearing connotations of some residue of a deceased individual, incorporated generalized paranormal manifestations with no attempt to define their origin in human consciousness. Early films used the trappings of poltergeist effects but the emotional arousal of fear was lacking. Technique was foregrounded and they took place in the light, more variety show than haunted house. In this tradition, although debased, William Castle's *13 Ghosts* (1960) is a haunted house film notable for its *Illusion-O* gimmick, red/blue filters that enable the audience to see the ghosts.

A key feature of early films featuring allegedly haunted houses was the emphasis on thriller and detective mysteries, often tied to comedy rather than horror. They rode on the back of the similar popularity of stage versions, such as *The Bat* (1920) and *The Cat and the Canary* (1922), although these melodramas were so clichéd by the mid–1920s that they had become the subject of satirical films such as *The Monster* (1925) and *The Haunted House* (1925).¹⁴¹ Despite this lack of respect, a new tranche of haunted-house thrillers, sound versions of silent films, was produced from 1928, but audiences had again become tired of them by 1930.¹⁴² The genre has fluctuated ever since, but haunted-house thrillers and comedies, like their horror counterpart, have continued to the present day.

In Abel Gance's spoof haunted house film, *Au Secours!* (1923), Max Linder bets that he will remain until midnight, and is menaced by a variety of creatures and objects. Despite an assault on his girlfriend, contemporary audiences would have associated him with his dandyish persona, undermining any menace. Later efforts that attempted to generate fear owe a debt to Paul Leni's *The Cat and the Canary* (1927). Clarens says of Leni that he had "updated *The Castle of Otranto* without disturbing the cobwebs."[143] Leni's achievement was to popularize the style of the haunted house: a large country pile, made sinister by use of chiaroscuro, Expressionist angles and, later, music, becomes the site of intangible menace against which it is unclear whether there is a defense. Even when many of the haunted house trappings had been dropped, such as manipulable pictures, panels and beds, an ensemble cast (one of whom might be a murderer) plus sinister butler and comic relief, the visual style remained, and not only influenced ghost films but also body-horror films in which the house represents invaded domesticity. A mixed case occurs in *The Ghosts of Berkeley Square* (1947), where the house has a deserved reputation for being haunted and is marketed as a tourist attraction, though with fake phenomena supplied courtesy of the showman — until the outraged ghosts protest, and are signed up to do magic tricks.

Ghosts can act as a *deus ex machina* to bring retribution on the wicked or a happy ending to the good. In these instances the function of the house itself is neutral. One of the sections of *Twice Told Tales* (1963) is a loose adaptation of Hawthorne's 1851 novel *The House of the Seven Gables*. A murderer searching a house for treasure meets the ghost of a man who had been burned as a witch by an ancestor, who brings about his destruction. In *The Ghost Catchers* (1944), two entertainers help a Southern colonel and his daughters remove ghosts from their house.[144] Eventually the ghosts assist the protagonists to rid the house of living villains. This is similar to the same year's *Don't Take It to Heart*, in which a lawyer and the daughter of a castle's owner, assisted by the resident ghost, combat an avaricious landowner. Similarly, in *Twice Dead* (1988), a family inherits a mansion haunted by its previous owner and used by a gang as their headquarters. When the new occupants are threatened by the thugs, the ghost takes their side and eradicates the gang members.

Newman argues that the haunted house film is unique in horror in that its appeal is not cyclical but rather holds a perennial interest, so that when instances occur, they cannot be seen to be responsible for imitations in the way that other genre films tend to be.[145] This is due to the respectability of the form in a field where excess is the norm. Charles Derry asserts that the haunted-house film was the "dominant element (in terms of number of films released) in the supernatural horror" between *Les Diaboliques* (1955) and *Psycho* (1960), although he notes that they were in the tradition of the haunted-house B-pictures of the previous decade.[146] This temporal limitation does not give the haunted house the credit it deserves. Derry also implies that by subverting old-dark-house conventions, *Psycho* undermined them, reducing their effectiveness. It could be argued that they would have declined temporarily in any case, considering that, as Derry points out himself, in the 1950s they were largely the province of the likes of AIP and Castle. Perhaps, as with the horror cycle of the 1930s and early 1940s, the haunted house film would have withered thanks to an abundance of shoddiness, if not for Hitchcock's intervention. Either way, *The Haunting* was released only three years after *Psycho*, to be followed by a steady stream of haunted house films that comprise a respectable proportion of supernatural horror films.

As well as a place of threat, the mature haunted house is a study in timelessness, especially true when characters enter a "time bubble" where they see a house as it was at some point in the past rather than as it now is—*Return to Glennascaul* (1951) and *Haunted* (1995) are examples. The house may be subjugated to the will of a deceased individual, or be the abode of some undifferentiated entity, but its major facet is the contrast with the progress outside. The haunted house tends to be old and with its original furnishings and fixtures intact. Visitors must agree to its terms. They are in alien territory, with its own rules. There is no middle ground in this static world, and the living and dead do not (except in *Beetlejuice*) accommodate each other. Those too weak to retain their own identity become its victims. As Thomas Allen Nelson says of *The Shining*, but with wider application, "Jack Torrance forgets that in a contingent universe an obsession with timelessness becomes tantamount to a love affair with death."[147] The haunted house is partly a metaphor for progress, with the insecurities that engenders. If an individual cannot move forward, death results.

Some ghosts do break out of their timeless prison, notably those who manage to complete business left over from when they were alive. A haunted location where a deceased individual manages to move forward is in *The Legend of Hell House* (1972).[148] A parapsychologist, his wife and two mediums, one physical and one mental,[149] have a week to prove life after death. The parapsychologist comes equipped with an impressive array of equipment including a machine that works on the assumption that the house has absorbed electro-magnetic radiation from humans and is acting like a giant battery. His solution is to reverse the polarity of the atmosphere, as he puts it, and dissipate the energy. Unfortunately the person responsible for the phenomena has shielded his sanctuary with lead which makes it impervious to the machine.

There are echoes of *The Haunting*: the title (Jackson's novel is called *The Haunting of Hill House*); a mixed group of investigators, supposedly with complementary abilities; a house with a mysterious past; the leadership of a parapsychologist who is from another field — in this case a physicist; unusual camera angles; the seeming use of a woman as a tool by the house, or whatever is in it; a focal point of the power — the nursery in *The Haunting*, the chapel here; vague sounds and cries conveying that the building is in torment. But whereas the events at Hill House are mostly suggested, and no definitive explanation offered, at Hell House the Aleister Crowley-like Belasco is responsible for everything that happens, and the body count is much higher. What appeared to be a mixed haunting, with remarkable poltergeist and auditory effects, possession and an unseen phantom lover, had been created by Belasco as a means of misdirection. Unusually, parapsychologist and medium are both partly right in trying to explain what is happening, although the former and the mental medium die, and the battle with Belasco is won by the physical medium.

Houses where quasi-demonic activities occur, such as *Poltergeist* or the *Amityville* cycle, undermine one's confidence in a refuge immune from external interference.[150] When an attack occurs inside the bedroom or bathroom, with associations of forbidden desire and helplessness respectively, the threat feels all the greater. One exception to this type of scenario is *Beetlejuice* (1988), in which the ghosts rather than the living are the victims. This inversion is summed up in the ghosts' efforts to seek an exorcism to get rid of the live intruders. Eventually both sets of residents are reconciled and the boundary between living and dead is overcome in the name of domesticity, with the Maitlands happy to remain earthbound. The contrariness to the laws governing ghost-film conventions is neatly summed up at the beginning of the film when the then-living Maitlands are driving into town. A dog rather than the proper black cat runs across their path, and it is the dog which, on the return journey, will be inadvertently responsible for their deaths.

The *Amityville* films crystallize the elements of the haunted house genre, involving adolescent rage, the impotence of religion, implausible poltergeist phenomena (given that the film was supposed to be based on a true story[151]), unlocked repression, and the high cost of real estate.[152] The evil that terrorizes the family does not have a precise cause, though it is clearly intelligent. As with *The Shining*, possibly the house itself is causing the male of the family to go insane; as in *Poltergeist*, it is built on an Indian burial ground, suggesting the rape of the land.[153] Other factors come into play, such as stress-related PK, a reference to an eighteenth-century Satanist who had lived there, even the Devil (referred to obliquely by the flies). Non-supernatural explanations—intruders for some of the events, even faulty plumbing- are not considered.

The Amityville Horror spawned seven sequels, none with any pretension to historical accuracy. *Amityville II: The Possession* (1982) is a prequel, dealing with the DeFeo killings that occurred the year before the original's events. The free-floating malevolence of its predecessor is given a solid form in the shape(lessness) of something slimy in the basement that gives the young son instructions via his personal stereo.[154] As in the first film, there is a priest, this time made of sterner stuff than before, who tackles the entity. By the third film, *Amityville 3D* (1983), the clergy have been replaced by parapsychologists, who fail just as badly. Later films too move away from the haunted house format to focus on a haunted object somehow imbued with the evil of the original house (the penultimate one to date, *Amityville: A New Generation* (1993) uses a mirror taken from the house that forces the inhabitants of its new home to become murderous[155]).

The most significant of the more recent haunted house stories is *The Shining* (1980), which Newman refers to as "a love story between Jack and the Overlook."[156] The film is examined in more detail in the next chapter. There is also a sub-type of haunted-prison film, such as *Slaughterhouse Rock* (1987) and *Prison* (1987). In the latter, the ghost of a wrongly executed prisoner wreaks havoc on the prison where he died, finally, in a moment of poetic justice, electrocuting the warden responsible for the miscarriage. The action is episodic, the ghost a variant on the mass murderer typical of the conventional stalk-and-slash film. A related cycle is the haunted school, with teens in danger from the murderous ghost, such as the eponymous heroine of *Hello Mary Lou, Prom Night 2* (1987). She returns in *Prom Night 3: The Last Kiss* (1989) to murder all those she feels stand in the way of her passion for a living student. Also from 1987, clearly a peak year, is *The Newlydeads*, with a slasher element (the ghost of a murdered transvestite comes back fifteen years later, as his murderer is getting married, and proceeds to dispose of the guests).

Equal to the haunted house, and often co-existent with it in terms of manipulation of expectation, is the influence of shadows. Darkness, with a spooky atmosphere, now a cliché of the horror film, can be seen clearly in Gothic novels and it is also associated with underground passages and vaults, the domain of the dead. Light and dark can be seen as analogues of life and death, and shadows suggest how easy it can be for light/life to be snuffed out. Fear of ghosts, unlike that of the slasher whose power is clear, is bound up with a lack of knowledge of their powers and intentions, how much of a threat they might pose to the percipient's physical and mental safety.[157] S. L. Varnado cites Henry James to the effect that if "ghosts are only frightening ... the air of mystery is lost,"[158] yet cinema ghosts that are frightening can also be mysterious. The shadow symbolizes this effect, both shadow and ghost obscuring the observer from what lies beyond. "Shadow" and "shade" are etymologically linked, indicating that throughout the history of ghosts they have been linked with the darkness, connecting to myths linking death to the underworld.

Ghosts of the Living

While not uncommon in the psychical research literature,[159] apparitions of the living, apart from doppelgängers, have made almost no impact in films. The doppelgänger, seen most notably in the 1913, 1926 and 1936 versions of *The Student of Prague*, combines Ernst Hoffmann and Edgar Allan Poe in a literary mix removed from those instances when a double appears to others, who do not realize that they are not looking at the original but at a facsimile. Only three examples of the latter realistic type have come to light during this research, and one is a minor aspect of the film in which it occurs. At the climax of *The Changeling* (1979) an aged senator, the changeling of the title, is transported back to the time of the murder from which he benefited, at the house where it happened. In the present he experiences a heart attack at home that proves fatal, but not, if the sequence of shots is temporally linear, until after his image has been seen at the murder house. As he is not dead this must be an instance of bilocation. Also, the fact that he does expire classifies it as a crisis apparition.

A more substantial example is in *The Veil* (1958), starring Boris Karloff. In one section, he plays a rural Italian doctor whose newly qualified son, with no interest in country medicine, returns home. The son goes to an emergency while his father is on a call, but the family is unwilling to allow him to perform surgery, asking for his father. He sends his car to fetch his father, who later enters, and although he does not speak his presence relieves the family, the son operates and the patient is saved. The family acknowledges him as a real doctor. He tells his father to go back in the car, but while returning finds that the car has broken down, and his father had never been collected. Reaching home, he finds his father in an armchair. The audience is primed for the old man to have died and his spirit to have visited the cottage, which would account for his odd behavior, but he wakes up and is fine, though with no memory of his "journey." The son changes his mind about rural medicine. No explanation is given to account for the episode; indeed it is a tenet of this film and its companion *Jack the Ripper* portmanteau (1958) that some things are unexplainable.

The final example is in *The Haunting of Lisa* (1995). Nine year-old Lisa sees the apparition of a dead child's mother, though she is not dead, but is in a persistent vegetative state. Her apparition is the age she was when her child was murdered, not as she is during the course of the film, now an old woman. She dies when the case is solved. A double does not automatically entail life after death, but does suggest the possibility. If the living apparition can exist independently of the original person, and seemingly interact with the environment, then the case for the double's continued existence after the original's death is stronger.

Ghosts That Appear to Be Phony But Are Real

Sometimes ghosts are fakes, perhaps involved in a financial fraud. Occasionally at the end seeming fakes are found to be genuine, or if not, there is still a real ghost mixed up in the trickery. *The Ghost Breaker* (*The Ghost Breakers* in the 1940 version) was a popular play that was filmed five times, the first in 1914, again in 1922[160] and 1940, the last two times as *Scared Stiff* (1945/1953). Jeremy Dyson describes the 1940 version as "basically a remount *The Cat and the Canary* (1939)"[161] — Bob Hope is in both — forgetting that the first version of that film was only released in 1927, and that *The Ghost Breaker* is therefore the older of the two stories; both owe a debt to the Ann Radcliffe school of Gothic, though in the 1940 version a real ghost appears at the end.

In similar vein, *Spook Chasers* (1957) too is nominally a spoof ghost film with the arbitrary insertion of a real ghost among the fakes. *Ghost of Dragstrip Hollow* (1959) has a real ghost residing in a haunted house that has been the venue for a fake ghost's shenanigans, but it would be crediting the film with too much cohesion to characterize it as a spoof ghost film, as it also encompasses hot rods, a pajama party and rock 'n' roll. In *Night of the Ghouls* (1959), Dr. Acula has been posing as a medium to obtain money from the bereaved, using some paraphernalia associated with the profession, but some, such as skulls on the séance table and skeletons sitting around it, which are not. The sound effects and floating trumpet, staples of the nineteenth-century sitting, are manufactured artificially, as is the electronically produced voice of the "dead" body that sits up from a coffin. The white ghost haunting the grounds is an accomplice to scare unwelcome visitors, but the black malevolent ghost is genuine.

The Parapsychologist

Paranormal events can be accepted as being beyond comprehension, or professionals can be introduced to explain them, although their failure to do so can serve to reinforce incomprehensibility. The latter category often involves experienced parapsychologists with high-tech equipment but usually little understanding. Their rationality may actually count against them when confronted by irrationality, and there is frequently a discrepancy between their expectations and the reality of the situation. One of the scientists in *Poltergeist* (1982) talks excitedly about small movements of objects in a previous investigation to a family that has suffered a major upheaval. Sometimes they refuse to accept the blatantly paranormal phenomena with which they are surrounded, such as Holden in *Night of the Demon* (1956), whose refusal nearly costs him his life; only when he accepts the existence of a supernatural force is he able to combat it. In *Poltergeist 3* (1988) Dr. Seaton dies because of her disbelief. Scepticism can be justified, though, when phenomena are kept from them — in *The Haunting* (1963) and *Ghost Story* (1974), investigators are teased by entities that stage major events outside their purview.

There is an early depiction of a psychical researcher in *The Ghost Goes West* (1935), when a member of the "Society of Psychic Researchers" [162] is invited to the climactic dinner. She does not bring any equipment to record what occurs. A parapsychologist makes an appearance in *The Haunting* (1963), examined in more detail in the next section. Here the major equipment utilized is a notebook and pen, and the surviving occupants have to admit defeat in their efforts to understand the dynamics of the phenomena. Later investigators arrive better prepared. Those in *The Legend of Hell House* (1972), *Poltergeist* and most notably *Ghostbusters* (1984) feature instrumentation rarely seen in the real world of psychical research.

In *High Spirits* (1988) a skeptical parapsychologist comes to investigate the allegedly haunted castle, equipped with measuring equipment (notably an "ectoplasmeter"), albeit modest by the standards of parapsychologists in some other films. Unlike most depictions of researchers, his character is rounded out. He is initially domineering and narrow-minded, but is perceptive, quickly seeing through an apparition faked using a mirror, and is redeemed by his recommendation to the rest of the party to ignore the activity, which would have been successful had it not been for the sexual activity occurring between living and dead. Scepticism need not be all-embracing. The parapsychologist in *The Legend of Hell House* (1972), for example, is convinced that paranormal phenomena need not be explained in terms of life after death, but is happy to talk in terms of

3. A Thematic Approach to Cinematic Ghosts 113

"psychic energy" and ectoplasm as externalized thought. These parapsychologists go out into the field, but in *The Entity* (1982) the incubus comes into the laboratory, which contains a specially built mock-up of its victim's house, coalescing domestic and scientific.[163]

Vernon Sewell has produced a small body of ghost films that are notable for returning to the same theme over a long period, combining the supernatural, thriller and melodrama. David Pirie's pioneering discussion of Sewell likens his fascination with the format to Howard Hawks's return to the elements of *Rio Bravo*,[164] and it could be argued that Sewell does conform to the definition of an *auteur*. In Sewell's case his 'standard plot' was inspired by *L'Angoisse* by Pierre Mills and C. de Vylars, first used in *The Medium* (1934), utilizing haunted premises and a psychical researcher calling in a medium who is able to recount the story of the haunting. Sexual jealousy often provides the trigger for the action.[165] Sewell's devotion to this theme is noteworthy and his efforts are worth examination.

Sewell's first effort after *The Medium* was *Latin Quarter* (1945). Charles, an artist, is in love with Christine, the wife of a sculptor, Minetti, who is becoming unhinged. On the point of running away with Charles, Christine vanishes. Minetti is arrested for murder, but the body is that of his mistress. He subsequently dies. Charles takes over the studio, and falls into a depression that not even his model Lucille, who is in love with him, can alleviate. The police are unhappy with the unresolved situation, so Dr. Krasner, a friend of Charles and Christine, investigates.[166] When supernatural events occur — a broken organ plays itself, an oil lamp flickers at 11 p.m. — the initially skeptical Krasner calls in a professional medium. She is unable to cope with the intensity of the evil and flees, but Lucille is a natural medium and is able to channel Christine, who tells of her last hours with Minetti and where he had hidden her body — inside a sculpture of her.[167]

In *Ghost Ship* (1952) the theme is more integrated into the narrative. Guy and Margaret are interested in a steam vessel. They are told that it had been found drifting with its passengers missing, and that since then it never stays long with one owner. They buy it, but soon people are mentioning cigar smoke, and engineers quit. Guy is skeptical but Margaret tends to believe the stories, and becomes scared. Money is an issue, as it would be later in *The Amityville Horror*, Guy pointing out that they have sunk their savings into the ship, which makes him reluctant to leave. They receive a mysterious call from the bridge and investigate. She sees smoke, but by the time she has pointed it out to Guy it has gone, and he remains unconvinced. Then he sees a man in the engine room who is smoking, an encounter filmed in a manner later to be used in the schoolroom scene in *The Innocents* (1961): there is a cut from Miss Jessell to the governess, then a cut back to where Miss Jessell was standing, but now she is gone, even though she would have been in the governess's sight all the time. Similarly in *Ghost Ship* we see the smoker, there is a cut to Guy and a cut back to the now empty spot where the man was standing. Guy does not seem to know what has happened, although he would have had the intruder in view all the time.

As a result of these experiences, they call in a member of the *Institute for Investigation of Psychic Phenomena*, an SPR-style organization. The film plays on the stereotype of the psychical researcher as an eccentric character. When the couple go to meet the man from the IIPP they at first assume that he is the elderly gentleman with the cloak and flowing locks, whereas he is the young(ish) man with a briefcase and business suit. He charges the not inconsiderable sum, for the time, of £10 for his services. His explanation for the phenomena, and for the different sensitivities of Guy and Margaret, involves tuning forks as a metaphor for vibrations that exist in nature, vibrations that can be stored and received, according to the conditions. Everybody is psychic to an extent, he says, but to different degrees. Hence Margaret smelled smoke but Guy did not because she has "clairolfactory perception." He saw the apparition because of the heat in the engine room, which is conducive to sightings, as witness the amount of psychic phenomena in hot countries.

In order to solve the mystery the psychical researcher calls in a medium. He uses a tuning fork in front of her as she goes into a trance, in order to allow her to attune herself to the required vibrations. The story is told in flashback. The owner, Martineau, killed his wife and her lover as they were plotting to kill him, put their bodies in a disused shipboard water tank and jumped over the side — and the details turn out to be true, although the medium cannot remember what she has said once out of her trance. They realize that Martineau has been on the boat as their hired hand, and once found out he kills himself. His presence enables Guy to try to rationalize the experience by wondering if Martineau was the figure he saw in the engine room, although the audience knows from the flashback it was that of the lover.

House of Mystery (1961) covers similar ground, but with a more complex flashback structure. A couple viewing a cottage are greeted by a woman they assume is the housekeeper, who tells them why the price is low.... A young couple living there experience strange events, then the woman sees what she thinks is an intruder, though there is no trace of him. His face later appears on the television screen. They contact a psychical

A house-hunting couple (Colette Wilde and Ronald Hines) are told a disturbing story by Jane Hylton in *House of Mystery* (1961).

researcher who determines that the man was the previous owner, found dead in his workshop six months after his wife and best friend vanished. The researcher describes the ghost in terms of electrical impulses generated by violent emotion that are picked up by the brain, an explanation in keeping with the electrical theme of the film. He calls in a medium and there is a further flashback during which she tells what happened. The owner, an electronics expert with a weak heart, had overheard his wife and friend plot to kill him and had narrowly escaped death after they tampered with the bathroom heater. He wires up the living room, trapping them, and tells them that if they can escape by midnight, they will be free to leave, otherwise they will die. The lover is killed in the attempt, and presumably the wife is as well. The lover is found buried under the workshop. When the prospective purchasers ask if the wife was found, the 'housekeeper' says that it is believed that the body is hidden behind a wall, then she gradually dissolves into one.

These parapsychologists are on the whole sympathetic to the paranormal, but the psychical researcher who investigates the house in *The Ghosts of Berkeley Square* (1947) is possibly the most skeptical in cinema.[168] Despite incontrovertible evidence that the haunting is genuine, being a victim of the ghosts' magic show, this member of the "Psychical Research Society" refuses to endorse its validity, on the grounds that to do so would mean to label himself as either a liar or a fool, and to bring the society, whose sole function is a debunking one, into disrepute. He declares the haunting to be a hoax.

By the time of the *Ghostbusters* films (1984, 1989), cinema parapsychologists had become hi-tech, to the extent that the film's pseudoscience has had a strong impact on the public's perception of what psychical research entails and has even influenced the presentation of certain investigative groups.[169] The humor also assisted its influence, as did the range of personality types that characterized the ghosts, from naturalistic apparitions of individuals, through *Casper*-style caricature to undifferentiated entities that may or may not be the ghosts of individuals rather than manifestations of general evil. The films combine the supernatural ghost story with a science-fiction reliance on hardware. There is no need to rely on the uncertain assistance of a medium to act as a conduit when ghosts can materialize, be very powerful, and leave behind unambiguous evidence of their existence (despite which the premise of *Ghostbusters II* is that the authorities think that the Ghostbusters are frauds). Confronted with the most momentous opportunity to study life after death ever afforded to science, the team are in effect glorified vermin catchers.

The Frighteners (1996) has a ghosthunter, Frank, working with a trio of ghosts who infest premises that he then clears. Unlike other charlatans, Frank really is psychic. This too is a comedic treatment, with an unpleasant aspect in the form of a spectre, masquerading as Death, which mur-

Drs. Venkman (**Bill Murray**), Spengler (**Harold Ramis**) and Stantz (**Dan Aykroyd**) are hi-tech *Ghostbusters* (1984).

ders citizens by squeezing their hearts. Frank has been bereaved and, like Kat's father in *Casper* (1995), buries himself in his paranormal work, but here ethically dubious, as a coping mechanism. The common mixed haunting, with apparitions and poltergeist effects combined, is played on by means of point of view.[170] The ghostbuster can see the ghosts, but the clients cannot, and consequently they only see objects floating around. It is unusual for the psychical researcher also to be psychic, because the traditional film stance is to oppose scientific rationalism to the medium's superior intuition. The use of the term "Recurrent Spontaneous Psychokinesis" to describe the effects delineates the expert, although it implies that the aetiology lies in one of the living occupants. The expert for once really does know what is behind the activity because he has set it up. An attempt to induce an NDE, to put the investigator on the same plane as the killer, involves using a deep freeze, a ploy used in a *Randall and Hopkirk* episode, "Vendetta for a Dead Man" (1970).

Mediumship

There has been an ambivalent attitude to mediums in cinema. They have usually been regarded as fakes, even by themselves, but often find that they do indeed possess the ability to communicate with the departed (Oda Mae in *Ghost* (1990) being a good example). Others have been sincere but deluded. Both mental and materialization mediums have figured in film, but the lengthy processes involved in running a séance have always been heavily truncated. Apart from the trance state, means of communication include the Ouija board — for example in *Blithe Spirit* (1945), *The Oracle* (1986), *And You Thought Your Parents Were Weird* (1992), *Witchboard* (1986) and *Witchboard III: The Possession* (1995) — and automatic writing, in *The Changeling* (1979).

In 1911 Biograph produced *Won through a Medium*, in which a séance is used as a mechanism for removing a love rival.[171] This is done by having the beloved, Harry, hide in the séance room and provide answers to questions posed by the medium, the girl's aunt. The rival, Clarence, is terrified and makes a speedy exit. This film can be seen as pivotal in the changing attitude of filmmakers and presumably their audiences to the depiction of the supernatural. Previously, films that portrayed what could be construed as paranormal events, either by the action or by the title, had had a jovial air, with no chance that a percipient, or the audience, might find the experience a frightening one. Now a character is disturbed enough to quit the house, despite the inducement to stay of being his potential mother-in-law's favorite.

The action may be intended to be comic, but it draws on concerns that communication with the dead frequently arouse. Although Clarence is terrified, articulating feelings that audience members might have had in similar circumstances, it can be seen that he is duped, and that his flight is absurd. There is no suggestion that the aunt really can achieve communication, and the setting merely provides an excuse to mount the triangle in which the unworthy rival is vanquished. The film simultaneously projects both a sense that films are taking the paranormal seriously, and a comic approach to the same subject. In later years this split widened, to give comic portrayals of ghosts on one hand and fear-inducing portrayals on the other.

By 1920, filmic séances had attained the level of mysteriousness and desire that characterized their real-life counterparts. In *At the Villa Rose* (1920), based on A. E. W Mason's novel, a socialite obsessed with the Afterlife is strangled during one. The light level is extremely low, although she can be seen to be staring fixedly at a crystal ball and talking animatedly, presumably relaying messages from a Spirit. Before he produces the rope, the murderer caresses her face, at which she smiles—perhaps believing that she has managed to materialize an entity.[172] A mystery is provided by her companion, who is supposed to be a materialization medium. Just before the séance she had been bound by conspirators to prevent her participation, and later suspicion for the murder is thrown onto her and she herself is threatened by the gang, before being rescued. She is thus placed in a positive light, but from a flashback it seems that her performances are fraudulent. The mistress is sincere in her efforts to see Beyond, so it is unclear whether she is unaware of fraud by her companion, or whether the scenario assumes that this is how séances are conducted.[173]

Other examples of fake séances are in *Supernatural* (1933) and *You'll Find Out* (1940), which has an approximation of a Victorian séance, except that larger numbers, including a full band, are present. Objects float above the sitters, and ghosts materialize. At a second one, after the tricks have been uncovered and the charlatans unmasked, the strange electronic voice heard during both is found to be caused by the sort of false voice box used by throat cancer sufferers. The fake medium in the Boston Blackie vehicle *The Phantom Thief* (1946) dresses as a swami and claims to be providing a social service for the bereaved and neurotic. The most outrageous portrayal is in *London Belongs to Me* (1948), mercilessly satirizing the profession. Squales is a fake medium with a silly high-pitched voice and a lama called "Payam" as a control. The organizer of the sitting tells a skeptic that Squales had "materialized a pseudopod at Brighton," but the skeptic learns that Squales had faked a spirit photograph there. Despite being further uncovered during a murder trial, he is last seen at another séance, still using his high-pitched voice, his control now called "Mocking Bear."[174]

Morgan, the hero in Tod Browning's final film, *Miracles for Sale* (1939), is clearly based on Houdini. A professional magician and inventor of illusions, one of which, a water tank, is similar to Houdini's own escape trick, he is a debunker of mediums. He is tolerant, inveighing only against frauds, and acknowledging that there is an area of experience that cannot be explained. The medium, Mme Rapport, believes herself to be genuine. The plot hinges on a séance she agrees to give to the murder suspects at which she will attempt to contact the victim, Sabat. The result is the closest film has come to reproducing Victorian spirit photographs. Mme Rapport goes into a trance, her chest becomes pale in color, and a cloud of ectoplasmic-like substance rises from her, its 'tail' streaming back towards her as it rises. The shape elongates and the face of Sabat appears. A conversation is conducted by means of yes/no raps until Mme Rapport comes out of her trance and screams, and the ectoplasm vanishes. Morgan confesses that the proceedings had been faked by him to force the murderer's hand, but that Mme Rapport knew nothing of the deceit. She is sincere if misguided, having been convinced by Sabat that she had genuine powers, and is treated with respect, even by the crusading Morgan. Lighting is used to emphasize her unblinking gaze, high cheek bones and aristocratic demeanor, leaving the impression that she might be genuine after all.[175] Browning gives the impression that although Spiritualistic procedures can be duplicated by stage magic, it does not follow that all such demonstrations are phoney.[176]

Examples of direct voice mediumship, that is, the medium uses his/her vocal chords while in trance, but the words are purportedly those of the deceased, can be seen in *Spellbound* (1941) in which the hero's dead fiancée is first heard and later materializes in double exposure,[177] *Latin Quarter* (1945), when Lucille recounts Christine's fate; *Night of the Demon* (1956), where Meek speaks in the dead Professor Harrington's voice; *Family Plot* (1976), in which Blanche speaks in the voice of her control; and *Witchboard* (1986), when a supposed ten-year-old boy speaks through a medium, though later he is revealed to be a warlock who possesses her. Another instance is in *Rashomon* (1950), which examines an incident from four different viewpoints, one through a direct-voice medium. This communication appears to be genuine, although no more trustworthy than those of the others involved (no definitive verdict can be reached from the conflicting stories). However, the murdered man's narrative is not equivalent to the others, because the medium cannot be assumed to be a straightforward carrier. Other possible explanations must be ruled out before it can be assumed that the testimony, untainted by transmission, is emanating from a deceased being.

Similar ambiguities surround the medium Meek in *Night of the Demon* (1956) and the blind Scottish sister, Heather, ostensibly gifted with second sight, in *Don't Look Now* (1973). We only ever have her word that the dead daughter Christine is with the Baxters. The brief shot of Christine running that accompanies Heather's assertion that she is happy could be confirmatory, but it follows a flashback of the family leaving home in England shown while John is sitting on his own, so the image of Christine could also be John's memory of her, as the flashbacks during his death throes are clearly his memories.[178] Still, as we also see Heather's eyes during the sequence that includes Christine, the possibility exists that the images could be hers, acquired either telepathically from John or clairvoyantly from the original scene.[179]

Utilizing his ability to sense his daughter's danger, John rushes out to the pond in the film's opening sequence, albeit too late to save her. That and his premonitions suggest that he possesses clairvoyance and precognition, even though he chooses to ignore their warnings (in this he is like a filmic parapsychologist who refuses to acknowledge the reality of paranormal events).[180] But even if, in Kristi Wilson's words "His inability to perceive what is behind the "fragile geometry." ...is the key to his self-propelled downfall,"[181] one still wonders why he has been marked out. It is ironic that his disavowed psychic abilities cause his death; if he had not had the premonition of the funeral cortège while Laura was in England, he would not have set in motion the train of events that lead to the self-fulfillment of the vision.[182] James Gifford sees John as "the consumate Man of Reason who turns this gift into a curse by refusing to accept it or its implications...."[183] For John, seeing is *not* believing.

Possibly Heather possesses a form of telepathy that is able to draw details from the grieving couple that are then dressed up. Alternatively she could be extremely intuitive, though this is less likely, particularly as she would not have the ability to read body language, a highly useful talent when performing a cold reading (interestingly, when Laura recounts Heather's description of Christine, she mentions the red coat though Heather had not spoken about it, a mechanism typical of cold readings).[184] Despite the apparent hits when describing Christine, niggling doubts about her genuineness remain. Certainly, although she is correct when she claims that John is psychic, when she tells Laura that there is no need to be sad, she is wrong, because the death of Laura's husband is to follow.[185] Her warning that the Baxters should leave Venice because their lives are in danger, though, turns out to be largely correct, although like many premonitions it is maddeningly vague — why could she not tell John to beware small figures in red coats?. As Mark Sanderson argues, the fact that Laura, the weaker partner, believes the sisters' claim, is not by itself a strong endorsement.[186]

The audience is placed in John's position in being unable to take anything on trust. One of the major themes of reviews of the film is the search for clues, and the necessity of sorting what is relevant from what we later learn is not.[187] Even the shot of the weird sisters laughing is problematical: Gomez, discussing the difficulty of distinguishing the significant from the trivial in the images that make up the film (a problem that John himself has to confront), makes the point that as no context is provided for the shot, it cannot be assumed that it occurs at the same time as John and Laura's conversation about them. However, the facts that we see the sisters while they are being spoken about, and that there is evidence that Heather possesses ESP, suggest that somehow the sisters can hear what is being said, and are therefore laughing at the Baxters' expense.[188] On the other hand, the sex scene shows different actions in the same place, so there is no reason why the sisters' laughing while John and Laura are discussing them should be simultaneous actions in different places. Nicolas Roeg is exhibiting a form of the Kuleshov Effect: the viewer is teased into making connections that may or may not be valid.

Mediumship is dealt with intelligently in *The Legend of Hell House* (1972) which features both a mental and a physical medium, even if the mental medium, Tanner, acts like a physical medium and the physical medium, Fisher, like a mental medium. At a séance, ectoplasm emanates from Tanner's fingertips and the parapsychologist asks for a sample to be dropped into a jar for analysis. The ectoplasm then withdraws quickly into Tanner. This causes shock, as Spiritualists would predict. When analyzed the ectoplasm turns out to be mostly from the medium herself, as an externalization of thought. She is later possessed by the deceased owner of the house, Belasco, masquerading as his own son. Fisher at the end of the film is able to pronounce the house to be clear, but Belasco has shielded the chamber his corpse is in with lead, which suggests that a medium's abilities are akin to X-Rays.[189]

The medium in *The Changeling* (1979) is recommended by the university "Psychic Research" Department, and she first engages in automatic writing, supplying accurate information. She holds a séance and objects move, climaxing in glass smashing. When the musicologist who is investigating the strange events in his rented home plays back the tape, he hears the voice of the murdered boy answering questions, in counterpoint to the medium, thereby demonstrating that she is tuned to his level, hearing what the other living people in the room cannot, except with electrical instruments. It is never made clear whether the death of his wife and child, which opens the film, is connected to the events in the house, whether he is made more receptive by his loss. The renting of the building seems to be arbitrary, yet he finds there the score of a composition he had written, and therefore considered original, suggesting a psychic link.

There are a few comedic portrayals of mediumship (the satirical treatment in *London Belongs to Me* is too sharp for Squales to be considered humorous). In *Man Alive* (1945), a husband who is pretending to be dead appears, when his wife holds a séance, in the guise of a ghost. Unfortunately his ruse backfires when the family doctor persuades his wife that all she has experienced is a wish fulfillment. *Blithe Spirit* (1945) also has a comedic portrayal of a medium, brought in after the inadvertent recall of a writer's deceased first wife caused by ignorant use of a Ouija board.[190] The Bowery Boys' brushes with the paranormal usually involve exposing fakery, and in their *Ghost Chasers* (1951) bogus mediums prey on the vulnerable. The Boys investigate Madam Zola, who charges $100 to contact the son of their neighbor. Zola works as part of a ring run by another fake,

The ghostly appearance by the first wife of Charles Condomine (Rex Harrison), Elvira (Kay Hammond, standing), strains the marriage to his second wife Ruth (Constance Cummings) in *Blithe Spirit* (1945).

Margo the Medium. Margo hypnotizes them, but they are saved from drowning by a 300-year-old ghost and expose the villainy.

A depiction of a professional medium that does not indicate genuine communication, but does suggest that mediumship might involve pathological states, is *Seance on a Wet Afternoon* (1964). Myra is fuelled by grief at the death of her young son Arthur, with whom she claims to be in contact as her control, and is able, at least until her demands become monstrous, to manipulate her weak husband. She tells him that she did a party piece as a child, presumably involving mediumship, and that she never had to make up her messages, suggesting that she is sincere. As she tells him the story a child's laugh, perhaps her own as a kind of auditory flashback, is heard on the soundtrack, electronically distorted, perhaps suggesting that Myra is living in a fantasy world, that she has never grown up.

She feels that whatever she does is right, and that merely holding weekly small-scale séances is not enough to do her gift justice. The plot to kidnap a little girl so that she can demonstrate her psychic abilities to a wider audience amounts to pious fraud in her eyes. Her scheme, however, escalates into a desire to kill the child as a companion for Arthur. Claiming that he is telling her what to do in effect abrogates responsibil-

Myra Savage (Kim Stanley, top center) presides at a *Seance on a Wet Afternoon* (1964).

ity. The séances are drab suburban affairs, but the attendees are genuine in their pursuit of knowledge — even the policeman, whom one would assume to be a tough-minded empiricist, has an interest in the subject. Myra though is shallow in her pronouncements. During a session with the girl's mother present, the child in the next room moans while in a fever, and her mother reacts, though she cannot hear the sounds themselves; the parental bond is stronger than the complacent medium's self-proclaimed link to the hereafter.

The difficulty of disentangling surviving personalities' communications from ESP is illustrated in *Black Rainbow* (1989). Martha is a platform medium who initially gives out standard descriptions of Summerland, fishes for information and alters the nature of the message in accordance with the feedback she gets. Suddenly the messages start to become evidential, with visions of violent deaths that are far more convincing than anything that has gone before. Far from impressing people, they start to see her as having witch-like abilities. She herself thinks that the accuracy of the information proves the existence of life after death, but the source is not revealed, and it could be some form of super–ESP.

A hitman sent to kill her because of the accuracy of her messages shoots at her, but the bullets go through her and kill her father. The suggestion that Martha can suddenly astrally project is emphasized by her Blithe Spirit–style stage costume. She then seems to disappear. The film is told in flashback, with a journalist investigating the case tracking Martha to the shack where she has been residing. She refuses to talk to him. To frame the story he decides at the end of the film to talk to her again, but he finds the house abandoned, and the local shopkeeper under the impression that she had died, as nobody had seen her for years. This revelation that Martha was possibly dead during at least some of the events of the film changes the tone of the film retrospectively. Superficially the film bears a resemblance in tone to *Carnival of Souls* (1962) but *Black Rainbow*'s ending is tacked-on and contrived, rather than challenging assumptions about what has gone before.

Near-Death Experiences

Interest in near-death experiences (NDEs) grew after the publication of Raymond A. Moody's book *Life after Life*, in 1975, and an industry has developed around the idea that they can provide a glimpse of the Afterlife, by extrapolation from NDE survivors' reports. Opinion is divided on the phenomenology.[191] It might be expected that NDEs would be linked to films dealing with high-tech communication with the dead, as reports in the psychical research literature usually come from those suffering from such severe trauma that they need to be resuscitated by sophisticated equipment. Technology is involved in a number of these films, but even when it is not, the imagery associated with the NDE has become such a cliché that the viewer will understand the elements as shorthand for the experiences, either objective or subjective, of a dying character, even though that person might not be revived to report them.

Moody's influence can perhaps be gauged by reference to *Don't Look Now* (1973). As John lies dying, instead of an NDE he experiences a series of flashbacks over his life, or at least that part of it dealt with by the film. A past-life review can also be part of the NDE, but before the 1970s these types of flashbacks were considered to be typical of the death experience, effectively a form of self-judgment.[192] In *Somewhere in Time* (1980) the camera has become subjective, used to represent the dying protagonist's ascending soul, and by implication his point of view, by craning up while looking down at him. *Resurrection* of the same year included bright lights, a meeting with friends and family and increased spiritual awareness afterwards, all classic NDE components. The healing abilities that develop as a result, though, are not typical in the literature, and the insistence in the film that they have a secular basis, based on love rather than religion, goes against the common but fallacious conclusion that the NDE, positive evidence of life after death, in turn entails the existence of God.

A similarly secular view of the NDE is taken in *Map of the Human Heart* (1993), where disjointed reality can be explained readily in terms of failing brain function: Avik is lying on an ice floe near death, and his hallucination takes the form of shifting points of view (he sees himself and his girlfriend in a balloon, then he sees himself looking down from the balloon on his body lying on the ice, then back to himself lying on the ice looking up at the balloon). These viewpoints are undermined by the impossibility of Avik's being in both places at once — the camera becomes complicit with Avik's state as he struggles to make sense of his ebbing life.[193]

In the psychical research literature it is not clear to what extent NDEs can be seen as precursors to a post-mortem existence. There is no reason why the state reported by survivors should be identical to that pertaining after death. Films though see NDEs, or some form of representation that can be inferred to suggest them, as evidence for an Afterlife. The depiction might be in traditional NDE terms, the subject feeling transformed into some form of immaterial substance immune to the laws governing the physical body, or it might be in terms of an extended hallucination, individuals feeling the same as before but external reality having altered, and possibly not realizing that the separation has occurred.

The couple in *Between Two Worlds* (1944), for example, only gradually realize that they are on a ship of the dead, and they, and the audience, assume that they have died. The twist is that they recover consciousness when the window of their gas-filled room is broken, making the experience strictly speaking an NDE, although having a joint experience suggests veridicality. Whatever form it takes, the NDE suggests dualism of soul and body, with the former not dependent on the latter, suggesting that the soul could survive after the dissolution of its fleshly home.

The boundary provided by water, related to the sort of journey from the known to the unknown seen in *Between Two Worlds*, though not necessarily involving an NDE, provides a regular motif. In *The Mermaid* (1910) the prince and the miller's daughter join at the bottom of the river, while in *Mare Nostrum* (1926) Ulysses sinks through the Mediterranean to be met by his dead love. Showing the longevity of the idea, at the end of *The Forgotten One* (1990) Bob and his ghostly admirer embrace in a lake as he drowns. *Intersection* (1994) consists of the main character's life flashing before his eyes during a car accident, and in one of these hallucinations he is seen swimming through water in a way reminiscent of Ulysses in *Mare Nostrum*. Similarly, in *An Awfully Big Adventure* (1994), as a character is drowning, he sees an image of the woman he had once had a relationship with holding her baby, a child who had grown up to be the sixteen-year-old with whom he had inadvertently had an incestuous affair.[194] Water is also involved in the deaths of characters in such disparate films as *Carnival of Souls* (1962), *The Reincarnation of Peter Proud* (1974), *Ruby* (1977), *Made in Heaven* (1987), *Beetlejuice* (1988), *Ghost Dad* (1990) and *Switch* (1991). In all of these, the overriding, though not the only, theme is that the drowning, by entering a domain inimical to the living, are on a voyage of self-discovery as well as across the threshold of death.

The difficulty of drawing a line between an NDE as evidence for a transcendent experience and a hallucination is provided by *The Wizard of Oz* (1939). This has certain characteristics that can be seen as suggestive of an NDE translated into fantasy terms. Dorothy thinks that she is under threat from the tornado, and NDEs can be induced simply by the perception of danger. She has been hit on the head, and although the injury is light, as evidenced by her recovery, it is indicated as the cause of her hallucination. During it she meets two classes of witches, good and bad, which are analogous to angels and demons; the good Witch of the North even comes and goes in a ball of light, which might elsewhere be seen as a divine conveyance. Finally, as in many NDE accounts, Dorothy is faced with a choice, whether to go back to Kansas or to stay. Here she parts company with those who have experienced NDEs, because typically they want to stay but are told by those who meet them that it is not time. In this instance, it is Dorothy who wants to go back, while her companions want her to stay in the Emerald City.

A similar problem of interpretation is involved in one of the dance routines in *Ziegfeld Follies* (1945). A "Chinaman" (Fred Astaire), attracted to a woman who had wanted a fan in a shop window, is shot during a riot. As he lies unconscious there is a section that is meant to represent a threatening subjective state, featuring the fan fluttering away of its own volition out of his grasp like the society woman, after which he is menaced by figures with enormous heads before the mood lightens and he is able to dance with the woman of his dreams. After this vision, the camera resumes its objective pose, with him on a couch. That he briefly recovers, with no medical intervention, long enough to see the woman toss away the now disheveled fan before he dies suggests that he was not close enough to death for the experience to be labeled an NDE, rather being the type of hallucination that cinema often associates with a feverish state.

Brainstorm (1983)[195] does not particularly relate to communication with the dead, as the scientific project within the film deals with what is called 'telepathic engineering.' This is an early exploration of Virtual Reality, a method of recording emotions and experiences to be played back by others, who will reexperience the sensations. One of the scientists, Reynolds, manages to record her dying moments, and a colleague, Brace, wants to explore the tape's promise of illustrating what happens after death. He sees a light show of flashbacks, perhaps a life review, but weighted towards Reynolds's time at the Institute, and pleasant imagery contained in bubbles suggesting the possibility of a Heavenly Afterlife, the banality of which is hinted at in descriptions in reviews of "what appear to be bits of undulating silvery tinsel looking like angels"[196] and "Heaven, or God, is represented by a glowing white light surrounded by lots of flapping pillow cases."[197]

These images are supposed to represent the transitional state between life and death. The inference is that even if she had been resuscitated the images would have been identical, suggesting that an NDE is truly the first stage of whatever follows death. Unfortunately, apart from the dramatic problem of not being able to convey the accompanying emotion when the audience sees the machine's output, making the images seem sentimental, its exploration as an aid to psychical research is flawed within the terms of the film. Brace does not consider the possibility that the images were a wish fulfillment fantasy generated by an anoxic brain; as there is no time-index correlating the scenes with the state of Reynolds's mentation, it cannot be assumed that the images represent some objective dimension experienced after cortical activity had ceased. It is just as likely that they correlate with physiological changes that might occur in the brain between cardiopulmonary arrest and the cessation of mental activity as the blood supply exhausts its oxygen store.

If the recording is of a pre-death hallucination, it would have the same status as factual accounts of near death experiences, in that the patient has not suffered a complete dissolution of neural function. NDE accounts can only *imply* what will happen after that dissolution. The strength of Brace's response suggests a different order than typical NDEs, but the machine itself could be the cause, as NDE accounts are reported afterwards, when their impact has been vitiated, whereas experienced directly they could retain their power. It is possible that Douglas Trumbull intended the event to be ambiguous, although no doubt is ever expressed that the tape might contain a hallucination. The first image is of Reynolds having an out-of-body experience. She seems to be dead already, and the implication is that her soul is leaving her, although as some people experience an OBE while not in a life-threatening situation, a subjective origin is the most likely explanation. Merely because she appears to be dead does not mean that brain function has ceased, and it would be surprising if it had so short a time after her heart attack.

The following images are also typical of NDEs. The scenes from her life might be an abbreviated past life review, and she also enters a tunnel of light, although this description bears more of a resemblance to the Stargate sequence of *2001* (on which Trumbull was special effects director) than to reported NDEs. As tunnel images are frequently described by survivors, it is possible that most persons near death have them, and they therefore need bear no relationship to the death state itself. The angels too suggest a dying brain trying to construct a stable environment for itself. Knowing she was dying, Reynolds might think of angels with big wings, which despite the reviews is what they are intended to be. The only counter-argument to the subjective state theory is that the tape lasts longer than Reynolds's dying appears to take, but the hallucination could have continued after motor function had been lost and she appeared to be dead. It is quite common for NDE experiments to find that their outlook has changed, and they become much more serene. Brace assumes that he has had some kind of transcendent experience as a result of his NDE by proxy, leading to a reconciliation with his wife, when actually he might have been misled into thinking that Reynolds's recording had some validity external to her dying brain.

In earlier films NDEs resulted from external trauma, but the focus of *Flatliners* (1990) is the attempt to induce them artificially, working on the assumption that the experience can be extrapolated to the post-death state. According to Brosnan,[198] Rubin disliked the film because he felt that it depicted the Afterlife in negative terms, which he regarded as irresponsible. This might be a surprising verdict given his involvement in *Jacob's Ladder*, which also has negative aspects. The origin of *Flatliners* could lie in *Omni* magazine. In a 1982 issue, various readers responded to an article by Michael Sabom, another NDE authority. One expressed the concern that information on the subject could prompt the impressionable young searching for novel experiences to attempt to induce NDEs even though they did not know how to return. Another in similar vein wondered about the feasibility of "going to the other side of life for a look around. The electrical-shock method should be able to work. Any ideas?."[199]

The young medics in *Flatliners* certainly possess knowledge, but the subtext of addiction is underscored by (literally) bad trips and guilt-driven flashbacks. It is saved from the flaw in *Brainstorm* because the protagonists ensure that their experiences coincide with a flat EEG, eliminating the possibility that brain activity could account for what they report. It does raise the question of where the experiences are being processed, but suggests that they are veridical. The experience, given that it supports dualism, acts as evidence for the Afterlife within the film. Experiences can be negative as well as positive, and the participants are punished for real or perceived misdeeds. Further, they can spill over into waking life, even though the brain processes involved would be completely different. The lesson is that the experients are obliged to confront their failings and past traumas, so that flatlining becomes a kind of extreme therapy.

A film which suggests that an NDE is the same as experienced by those who pass over is provided in the human-into-dog reincarnation film *Fluke* (1995). A motorist crashes into a tree and the screen apparently switches to his point of view, a tunnel and a bright white light, before returning to an objective viewpoint, showing a puppy that, we later discover, is the same person as the driver. It is possible that the tunnel is induced by anoxia, as, like *Brainstorm*, no index correlating physiological and psychological states is provided. It is less likely, though, as the accident is sudden, and given the speed of the car as it hits the tree, death would probably be instantaneous. The tunnel here is an integral part of the death process, both literally and metaphorically providing a passage between this existence and the next — not as in some cases, including *Brainstorm*, from this world to Heaven, but into another earthly incarnation.

The NDE can be a means of increasing spiritual awareness, but *Hideaway* (1995) gives its experients psychic powers. Hatch is given an experimental drug after drowning and finds himself linked telepathically to another NDE survivor, a psychopathic serial killer, who also had the drug. More interesting is the treatment of the NDE in each case. Due to the time between apparent death and revival, the depiction should be seen in terms of the death process itself rather than *near* death, with the two brought back from beyond death using a "very special resuscitative medicine program." It is analogous to the flat EEG of *Flatliners* used as a criterion for death, though here the state lasts for much longer than the minutes the medical students allow themselves (two hours for Hatch).

There are similar characteristics between Hatch's and the psychopath's deaths, but there are distinctions indicating that one was "good" whereas the other was "bad." The psychopath at first ascends the tunnel towards a white light but sees his mother, whom he murdered, at which point the experience turns negative, and he rushes down a tunnel now predominantly red, with figures trying to push out of the membranous walls, like souls in torment. He hits some kind of mesh and his "body" disintegrates. The following year, *The Frighteners* (1996) utilizes a similar representation of the tunnel: Frank's NDE involves a tunnel of light, which he enters with two serial killers, one dead, the other alive. The tunnel goes up in the conventional manner but it turns red, with snake-like projections coming from the wall, and the two evil ones plummet downwards, the tunnel finally turning into a snake that has "swallowed" them. Frank continues up and meets dead loved ones, including his wife, who tell him that it is not yet time and send him back

Hatch's death by contrast to the psychopath's is more peaceful, although the blue tunnel flecked with red is perhaps the sign of a *mostly* good life. He meets his dead daughter, but is pulled back the way he came until the light at the end of the tunnel becomes the light above the operating table upon which he is revived, a technique also used in *Jacob's Ladder* (1990). This meeting is different from typical NDE accounts, as Hatch's daughter is welcoming, whereas in NDEs the greeter usually tells the experient to return. Perhaps this is meant to suggest that Hatch is supposed to go with her, although she reappears at the climax to do battle with the psychopath's evil force, and her beatific smile does not reveal any feeling that Hatch should not now be among the living. The battle, involving the participants wreathed in their emblematic red and blue, is seen by all, reinforcing the objectivity of the revival experience. By this stage, the elements of the NDE, building on the pre–NDE life review, have progressed from the ethereal experience in *Somewhere in Time*, where the death of the character brings closure to the film in an epiphany, to a plot element warning, as with *Flatliners*, that modern science, meddling with things it does not understand, can bring ruin on the perpetrator's head.

The Figure of Death

Death personified is common in the cinema, sometimes taken from the type of skeletal figure familiar from the *Dance of Death*, but more often full-bodied, a figure familiar since at least the mystery plays.[200] His role too can vary, sometimes hovering over the action, as in *Mare Nostrum* (1926) and *Metropolis* (1927), on other occasions a direct participant, for example in *The Phantom Carriage* (1920), *The Seventh Seal* (1956), and most notably perhaps, *Death Takes a Holiday* (1933). He suggests the omnipresence of an inescapable destiny, the scythe he frequently carries symbolizing his role as "Reaper of Souls." His existence entails postmortem survival even when the consequences of his presence are not shown directly. One difference from cinematic Death's forbears is that whereas in cinema the figure of Death is generally male, this is not so in a number of folklore tales, in which Death is portrayed as a woman.[201]

The first of the depictions of Death as an individual, the German *The Sea's Shadow* (*Das Schatten des Meeres*, 1912), produced by Oskar Messter, features Death attempting to persuade a woman to commit suicide.[202] *Without a Soul* (1916) was the first of a series of "restoration" films (though with an obvious debt to *Frankenstein*, itself filmed in 1910 by Edison). A woman killed in a car crash is brought back to life by her scientific father. As he is reviving her, Death, a gaunt-looking man in monastic costume carrying a scythe, hovers by, vainly attempting to claim her. He is filmed in double exposure, and unlike the implacability possessed by other versions of Death, this one is powerless to affect the tangible world when confronted with the father's advanced apparatus. Yet the seeming victory of science is ambiguous. The woman has lost her soul, making her cruel, and when she dies once more her father destroys his machine. The message is that meddling in the province of the Divine brings unanticipated repercussions, and that although death/Death can be cheated, the cost may be too high. This is an example of what became a popular genre of resuscitation films, but although death may have intervened, they differ from ghost films in their restoration of the victim to a body, either his/hers or another's, as opposed to an incorporeal existence.

Fritz Lang made *Tired Death* (*Der Müde Tod*) in 1921, featuring an active Death who bargains with a woman for her husband's return after his death. She refuses Death's offer to exchange her husband for the life of a child, and when eventually she herself is killed the two are reunited, triumphant in defeat. Sometimes Death's intervention can be seen as evil, a kind of Satanic stand-in, but usually, when personalized at all, he is a dispassionate messenger, as much a victim of a Greater Will as those he seeks to convey. The action can occur due to Death's inaction as much as his direct intervention. *Death Takes a Holiday* has people wanting to die, rather than typically fearing Death's arrival, when he takes a break.[203]

As well as tragedy, death is frequently played out as a joke. There is a group of comedies that spoof Death, based upon contrasting his grim seriousness with the undermining of his dignity. It is as much this deriding the sense of an implacable mission in *Bill and Ted's Bogus Journey* (1991) as the direct reference to *The Seventh Seal* that is the basis for the humor. Even in Ingmar Bergman's film itself, in which Block has lost his faith, the personification of Death was created to be like a combined skull and clown's makeup,[204] making clear Block's ambivalence. Other humorous examples are contained in *Love and Death* (1975) and *Last Action Hero* (1993), again both based on *The Seventh Seal*, and Monty Python's *The Meaning of Life* (1983). (A direct quotation from *The Seventh Seal* in *The Meaning of Life* is Death's expectation that the guests will form a line to dance up the hillside with him, but he is thwarted when they climb into their cars to make the journey, which themselves become "ghosts" via double exposure.)

Death in *The Seventh Seal* is willing to negotiate with mortals about the time of death, but not by their pleading; Block is able to defer it by offering the intellectual challenge of chess. He is given special treatment, perhaps because although he has come to doubt his faith, at least he is willing to debate with himself honestly. It is agreed by the two that the game can only postpone the inevitable — although Death can be fooled, as Block does by knocking over the chess board and allowing Jof and Mia to ride off— and Death does not feel compelled to observe a code of honor during the game. At the end of the film, Death scoops up the group in Block's castle and leads them up the hill. That the individuals in the *Dance* are not the same as those in the castle has led Andrew Sarris[205] to tie himself in knots attempting to reconcile the discrepancy, which he tries to do in terms of Jof's subjectivity. A more pragmatic answer is that the shot was made on the spur of the moment at the end of the day when some of the actors had left, necessitating stand-ins.[206] In any case, Sarris has miscounted, because although it is difficult to determine which character is which, in silhouette as they are, only Block's wife seems to be missing, not the dumb girl as well, as he maintains.

Whatever Bergman's personal religious views, ultimately the knight's fears come to nothing, as the dancers are described as having their cheeks washed of tears by the rain. Whatever Block's motive in praying just before his death, whether he has regained his faith or is pleading with God, the outcome is the same. Death is an objective force, not a projection of Block's doubts. Jof's wife may not be able to see Death and the dancers, but the fact that Jof and Block have done so indicates Death's ability to become personalized. The message given by the dance is that the Afterlife is a more positive state than fear of it suggests it will be.

Death as a positive force, however inscrutable his motivation, is rare in cinema. A more typical depiction is provided by Death's role in the fate of mortals in *The Masque of the Red Death* (1960). Death is portrayed as a cowled monk who remains aloof from the debaucheries of Prospero's castle, his role enigmatic, as the pestilence bloodily kills the revellers. Nor need he be invincible. In *On Borrowed Time* (1939) Death is a helpless figure, stranded up a tree from which he cannot descend until invited. Finally, Death in *The Frighteners* (1996) is not Death at all, but the spirit of a serial killer acting in the guise of the Reaper.

Depictions of Heaven and Purgatory

Heaven tends not to be dwelt on in detail, and is often sketchily depicted. In *Things to Do in Denver When You're Dead* (1995), after the crew's deaths there is an overexposed shot of them on a boat having drinks, "boat drinks" being a toast they had when alive to their idea of "Heaven," suggesting that they have made it to their own personal Paradise. Nor need Heaven be unambiguously objective. A more elaborate rendering, that of *A Matter of Life and Death* (1946), is possibly a delusional construct. Taking Heaven further inward still, in *Made in Heaven* (1987) things can be brought into existence, or people into one's presence, by thinking of them, and in *What Dreams May Come* (1998) whole environments can be created from the mind (it is possible to move into those of others, but director Vincent Ward wanted to portray the protagonist's first glimpse of Paradise as "a hell of aloneness"[207]).

Often Heaven is suggested by a character's looking upwards, or by references to stars. In *Lady in White* (1988), after the murderer falls over a cliff, the ghost of the mother and her murdered daughter fly towards the stars.[208] *And You Thought Your Parents Were Weird* (1992) ends with a shot of stars, again suggesting that the dead father has gone to Heaven, mission accomplished.[209] A number of codes can cue the spectator, such as clouds seen from the ground, heavenly choirs and even a minor key in the music. Heaven in *Intolerance* (1916) is manifested by the descent of a Heavenly host, bathed in light, causing the soldiers to cease fighting. Light is also used to immerse Antonia's dead mother in a divine brilliance in *The Tales of Hoffman* (1951).

Heaven usually adheres to a Christian code, even when non–Christians are included, as with the Sikhs in *A Matter of Life and Death*

(AMOLAD). Heaven as an erotic fantasy, common in non–Christian images,[210] is absent (flirting in *AMOLAD* notwithstanding). Instead, inhabitants rise above previous earthly desires. White decor, minimalist furnishings and dry ice in *The Horn Blows at Midnight* (1945) have been influential in depictions of Heaven, and bureaucracy surfaced again the following year in *AMOLAD*. The Afterlife in *The Horn Blows at Midnight* is Jack Benny's subjective state, and there is no confusion between this and filmic reality, something Powell and Pressburger achieve, as it is clearly a dream. A similar depiction from the same year — this time not a hallucination, since the character in question, Ziegfeld, was undoubtedly dead, but an unquestionably stylized presentation — is to be found in *Ziegfeld Follies*. He resides in a large room full of furniture but open to the sky, making it clear that earth is below, and God above.

The dead may be judged,[211] often in the context of reincarnation, notably in *Defending Your Life* (1991). *Made in Heaven* (1987) is also a reincarnation film, although people can also be born in Heaven.[212] As in *Here Comes Mr. Jordan* (1941), a person dead before his time wangles his way back to earth, but, like *Defending Your Life*, because of an attachment made in the Afterlife. Sometimes the Afterlife's status is not clear. It could be a form of Purgatory or merely a way station (the latter's interim location is often shown by "clouds" at camera level)— the eventual destination being either up or down. The temporary halt is commonly found in reincarnation films: the airfield in *Here Comes Mr. Jordan* (1941) and *Heaven Can Wait* (1978), the cloudy way station in *Chances Are* (1989), the forest in *Always* (1989).

The residents in *Wings of Fame* (1990) are assigned quarters in an hotel on the basis of residual fame among the living. As their earthly reputations wax and wane, their accommodation is changed accordingly. The background is not sketched in, so for example it is not clear why the celebrities are all twentieth-century.[213] Even how fame is calculated is vague, the lack of a mention in an encyclopedia being used as a rough-and-ready measure in one instance. Once fame on earth has evaporated, the person is cast out and the staff deny that they were ever there, leaving to hang the problem of what would happen in the event of a reputation being rehabilitated. The question is asked whether they are in purgatory or perhaps hell. Hell is a possibility, the inhabitants waiting for the day when, as the hotel manager tells them, the end of time will spell the end of earth and therefore their own extinction. Purgatory suggests a more positive place to do penance in before moving to a celestial realm, and the way off the island would be loss of earthly reputation. The only exception is to win a lottery, which one character does. He and his companion go back to earth, in the present time, but the question is then begged — they cannot be themselves as they have been dead for almost a quarter of a century, so how can they live? Perhaps that is a subtle twist on what might constitute purgatory.

Purgatory has not been clearly defined theologically,[214] as Heaven and Hell have. On film it may have to be inferred from prior actions; in *The Adding Machine* (1969) a clerk who murders his boss when made redundant by a calculator, after execution finds himself operating an adding machine, a punishment to fit the crime but one that does not seem to be Hellish. Where Purgatory does exist, it can be in terms of self-judgment. A spirit has to be ready to move on, which means an ability to let go of earthly concerns, as in *Carnival of Souls* (1962), *Always* (1989), *Jacob's Ladder* (1990) and *Ghost* (1990). Until that stage in spiritual growth has been achieved, the spirit might not even realize that death has occurred. Reincarnation films might suggest purgatory, as individuals traverse repeated lives towards enlightenment, but the inference has not been drawn in cinema, where the focus tends to be on a single iteration.

In *Defending Your Life* (1991) the dead have to justify their existence during an examination at Judgment City, a municipality run by a large staff. The successful proceed to their eternal home, but those who cannot throw off the trappings of earthly existence have to go back to earth in a new body with no memory of previous incarnations (although there is a screening in Judgment City that illustrates some of these). Purgatory in *Beetlejuice* (1988) is also a bureaucracy[215] whose civil servants are those who have committed suicide (as has the steward in *Between Two Worlds* (1944)[216]). It is governed by regulations, and the deceased, who retain the visual signs of cause of death, are assigned a caseworker. Unlike the Spiritualist version of the Afterlife, these denizens are not transformed into an idealized version of their living selves. Newly arrived inhabitants are provided with a manual, the *Handbook for the Recently Deceased*,[217] which tells them that most of the living will not, rather than cannot, see ghosts, and it is fortunate for them that a young Goth who moves in is on their spiritual wavelength.

Three business partners in *Beyond Tomorrow* (1940) suffer different fates after an airplane accident. One goes to Heaven, another to Hell for no reason other than he was a cynical workaholic. The third remains on earth in order to bring a young couple back together. This contravenes the rules, and he has to fight, even facing the prospect of staying on earth forever, to finish the job. This is a reversal of the typical situation in which somebody is kept out of Heaven until a good deed is accomplished. This done, he ascends, only to meet the colleague who had been sent to Hell. He had had a surprisingly rapid change of heart and is now in a better mood than hitherto. Like the later *Jacob's Ladder* (1990), one's fate in the Afterlife is tied to one's frame of mind, and repentance can secure release.

The Afterlife can be tailored to the individual, as in *Defending Your Life* (1991), in which the architecture is designed to be familiar to those passing through. In *Ghost of a Chance* (1987) the dead black jazz pianist walks through a dry-ice Heaven accompanied by an angel, also black and wearing a white dinner suit. He sees Louis Armstrong, Billie Holiday and Duke Ellington, and finds himself in a version of the Cotton Club. This is his paradise. When he sees Hell, it is full of rednecks playing country and western music and taking an interest in him. Heaven in *Meaning of Life* (1983) is also a nightclub, although the pleasures are more ambiguous: every day is Christmas and Tony Bennett does the floor show. Chris in *What Dreams May Come* (1998) inhabits a Heaven that resembles one of his wife's garish paintings. Oddly, although the general impression is one of New Age self-actualization (even reincarnation is an option, if one desires), his wife is punished with Hell for her suicide (under extreme provocation) in an extremely reactionary Roman Catholic manner. Chris has to travel there to rescue her, although as it is possible to move anywhere by the power of thought, the trip is redundant.[218]

The journey as a metaphor is a powerful one when used as shorthand for defining the pre-mortem and post-mortem span. Joseph Campbell saw it as an archetypal myth, a cultural constant.[219] It is noteworthy that transport of all kinds features in so many Afterlife films. This journey may have to be put aside until a task has been accomplished, or be one that the deceased is unable to begin until helped by the living. The destination can either be overtly specified, perhaps to Heaven or Hell, or left undefined, to an undiscovered country. Sometimes the journey is the entire story of the film, perhaps with the destination only implied, as with *Outward Bound* (1930) and *Between Two Worlds* (1944), both based on Sutton Vane's 1923 play *Outward Bound*.[220] There has been some confusion about the settings for these films. Philip Strick[221] asserts that they are both set on spaceships, whereas each is set on board a ship. Paul Virilio[222] thinks that the first is set on an airplane, which he sees as premonitory of Leslie Howard's fate in 1943.[223] Also revolving around transport, in *The Heavenly Kid* (1985) Purgatory is a subway train that must be ridden until the dead Bobby is given an assignment, in order to move from "midtown" to "uptown."

Angels

Angels in a film demonstrate that Heaven exists, placing them within an Afterlife framework. They come in two main forms: in plain clothes, when they are usually guardian angels giving advice, or in stereotypically Heavenly garb, with wings, sometimes cumbersome, more recently streamlined. This guise need not preclude them from advice-giving.[224] A smaller category features them as symbolic of the Afterlife, as shown on the tape in *Brainstorm* (1983). Angels either have never been human, or more commonly are deceased individuals (the latter is in contradiction to the Bible, but not to lay Christian opinion). Also unbiblical is the fact that film angels are almost always gendered. An exception is *The Prophecy* (1994) which concerns angels fighting each other. One is destroyed, and upon autopsy is found to be hermaphrodite. This is not in keeping with scripture, in which angels are deemed to be sexless, and those in *The Prophecy* appear to be male when dressed. Angels can even fall in love with mortals, as in *Wings of Desire* (1987) and *City of Angels* (1998). The difficulty in portraying God's own sexlessness is grappled with in *Switch* (1991). Here the Supreme Being speaks with both male and female voices, separately and in unison. Yet when Steve/Amanda is accepted into Heaven s/he has the choice of being either a male or female angel, though being able to take eternity to choose suggests that there could be a third way.

Wings have changed their function since their popularization by medieval artists. From a convention authenticating the reality of angels to the church congregation, they have become a token of subjectivity to the cinema audience. The number of wings has been fixed at two, although the seraphim are described in Isaiah 6:2 as possessing six. Wings appear as early as 1910 in Biograph's *Paradise Lost*, in which a drunk is fooled into believing that he is in Heaven to make him reform. They also appear in *The Kid* (1921), when Chaplin dreams about the absent Jackie Coogan. These wings were unwieldy looking, but by 1925 D. W. Griffith in *The Sorrows of Satan* had streamlined them to look more like those of mediaeval angels, and this has tended to be the standard, with exceptions, ever since.

Ziegfeld Follies (1945) depicts angels without wings. One sketch is about a couple of men who meet briefly over a long period, the final time at St. Peter's Gates. Dressed as elderly men about town, they possess small harps but, despite singing that they have them, no wings. They are wearing a style of dress that would not be out of place in an angelic mission to earth, where wings are not obligatory. The explanation is probably that large wings would hamper the dancing of Fred Astaire and Gene Kelly. Similarly, the angels in *A Matter of Life and Death* (1946) do not possess wings, although new arrivals are given enormous impractical pairs, lending support to the interpretation that Heaven is a complex hallucination consequent upon brain injury.[225]

Angels can sometimes be seen to represent a hallucinatory idealized image of Heaven rather than a plausible depiction. They can also be seen as comical, perhaps out of touch with everyday concerns of mortals. In Laurel and Hardy's *The Flying Deuces* (1939) deceased Ollie ascends to Heaven wearing an absurdly small pair of wings, making him look more like a cherub than an angel. Heaven is not a permanent state in this film, however, because he is reincarnated as a horse. The wings stamp the proceedings as fantasy, but attain a certain consistency within the comic universe created. Another comic angel, the product of a trumpet player's dream inspired by an advertisement for "Paradise Coffee," is the Heavenly messenger in *The Horn Blows at Midnight* (1945) ordered to an earth deemed out of control. He is to blow the last trump, but fails, due in part to the machinations of "fallen angels," sent on a mission but who failed to return. He wears mufti on earth, but Heavenly attire is the traditional long white robe. Part of the humor of the angels' visits to earth is their naiveté, which is counterposed to the superior knowledge expected of them. *Date with an Angel* (1987) also has an inept angel, sent to escort a man to Heaven, though for the bulk of the film he is obliged to look after her. She falls in love with him, and not only does she get a leave of absence for herself but finally obtains permission for him to remain on earth.

To Die For (1993) has a climax that includes the unearthly light familiar from such films as *Jacob's Ladder* and *Ghost*, but the terminally ill Mark is not only met by a phalanx of angels, but they are covered in gold paint, and the senior one has large feathery wings. It is possible that the transition is a subjective one as Mark had been a female impersonator, and his vision of the Afterlife might involve gold paint and feathers. Alternatively the depiction could be intended as objective (his partner Simon is present, but we have no means of knowing whose point of view — Mark's, or Simon's and the viewer's — is authoritative) and meant as a "camp" climax. Hudsucker in *The Hudsucker Proxy* (1994) has to be seen in a non-naturalistic context, in that time itself has been stopped by the expedient of thrusting a broom into the building clock's gears, saving Norville from falling forty-four floors.[226] Time is frozen, but snowflakes are *not* "frozen." Norville is suspended in mid-air when Hudsucker, wearing a long costume with big furry wings and playing a ukulele, descends to where he is hanging. Unlike earlier angels,' Hudsucker's wings are articulated like a bird's, so that they flap gently. His illuminated halo resembles the hula-hoop that Norville has invented, and he jokes that all the angels are wearing them — though they are only a fad.

Some angels display more of the qualities of social workers than divine messengers. Clarence in *It's a Wonderful Life* (1946) has the task, in order to earn his wings, of persuading George that his life has had a purpose, and that things would have been worse if he had never existed.[227] In *Angels* (1994),[228] a remake of *Angels in the Outfield* (1951), a boy, Roger, can see angels who respond to his plea that his baseball team, the (California) Angels, win the series.[229] The angels, gendered and multi-racial, are robed in traditional white, with halos and feathery but slim wings, trail an iridescent sparkle[230] and are able to travel at speed. They can be seen only by the boy, but their poltergeist-style effects are obvious to all as they help the team. The chief angel is different, as he is not dressed like the other angels, appearing in a white shirt and able to morph into, for example, the liquid in the bottom of a coffee cup or a bubble.[231] In keeping with theology, the angels do not need to do things directly for their influence to be felt. At the climax of the game, the pitcher is spurred to victory thinking that they are helping him. The message is that belief is necessary to achievement, and that the angelic spirit is within all of us if we only acknowledge it. The overarching moral universe, guided by divine providence, is reinforced by repeated shots of clouds and the stars, suggesting the reality of Heaven.

Other films that have angels whose mission is to help mortals achieve self-realization include *The Bishop's Wife* (1947) and its remake *The Preacher's Wife* (1996). A novice angel, Dudley, comes to earth to enable a clergyman to realize how much his wife loves him, although not before the angel himself has been attracted to her. Dudley is more catalyst than manipulator, able with his social skills to create harmony. In *Charlie and the Angel* (1973) an angel comes for Charlie who has had three near-fatal accidents. He is told that he must make amends for neglecting his family, which he does and is spared. In this type of scenario the Heavenly messengers lack the knowledge one would expect from them. *The Heavenly Kid* (1985) shows that being an angel/guardian can involve passing on a baton. Bobby is killed and helped by an angel, and later helps his own son to avoid the same mistakes, in the process being redeemed by proving that he loves somebody more than himself. Of the more recent batch, *Dad, the Angel and Me* (1995) has a female angel helping a girl and her estranged father bond[232]; *Michael* (1996) is a befeathered angel who, while indulging definitely earthly appetites, raises a dog from the dead and enables two lovers to achieve union; and *A Life Less Ordinary* (1997) sees a pair of angels manipulate an earth-bound love story in order to secure their own future in Heaven.[233]

The sexual component of angels seen in *Michael* can also be seen in *Forever Darling* (1956) in which an angel arrives to help a couple whose marriage has lost its sparkle. A level of intertextuality is provided by the wife's asking the angel (played by James Mason) why he looks like James

Mason, to be told that he looks the way she wants him to look. The wife's father assures her that she should not worry because angels have frequently visited the family in the past, which suggests that angels bond to certain individuals rather than helping people on a random or deserving basis.

Angels appearing in human form has a Biblical precedent (Hebrews 13:2). The angel in mufti is exemplified by *For Heaven's Sake* (1950), which also includes the souls of unborn babies growing up as if they were alive, leading ghostly lives unseen by their prospective parents. Considering the references to Heaven (the angel masquerading as a Texan says he is from "God's Country"), where one would expect God to be omniscient, the drama revolves around whether or not a career couple will have a baby. As it seems unlikely, the angels have been sent to retrieve their child/not child, but one angel becomes flesh and after a period of temptation reconciles the couple, who duly become parents.[234] The film proposes an explanation for child prodigies — they had to wait a long time to be born, with more opportunity to absorb skills they will later use — but at the same time amnesia sets in with birth, so that the waiting period is forgotten. Rather than assisting ordinary individuals, the Depression fantasy *Gabriel over the White House* (1933) has a philandering U.S. president injured in a car crash and possibly visited by Gabriel, who is not seen, only suggested by fluttering curtains. After the president's recovery he becomes a much better person. The fact that the claim to have been visited by an angel came after a head injury is evidence that the experience might have been subjective, but like NDEs, it has life-affirming consequences whether hallucinatory or veridical.

Angels in whatever form, even surrogates such as Mr. Jordan, can be used as troubleshooters. In *Heaven Only Knows* (1947), a western crossover, an "accounting error" means that a man who was supposed to be good has been bad, and the archangel Michael helps him to redeem himself. If a person's destiny is determined by Heavenly powers, it is not clear whether there is free will, or a divinely ordained, if unreliable, fate over which there is no control. *Two of a Kind* (1983) has God, depicted as a male-voiced Being of light, decide that Earth is too wicked to save, propose to destroy it and send its occupants to Heaven. Four angels beg Him to spare Earth and agree that if they can find two randomly chosen people who, will make a great sacrifice for each other, the planet will be spared. God capriciously chooses two unpleasant people, who with help from the angels, and ironically from "Mr. Beazley" who realizes that God's plan would deny him souls for hell, are suitably redeemed, saving the planet.

These angels are all resolutely Christian, but *The Angel Levine* (1970) has a Jewish context. A tailor with numerous personal problems chides God and is sent a black angel, Levine, who is on probation, his mission to convince the tailor that he is genuine. When the tailor's faith waivers, Levine goes. The tailor's doubts are reasonable, as he knows that Levine in life was a petty crook, and had been killed leaving the scene of a crime, but skepticism still causes his undoing, the lesson being that faith is necessary even if the evidence is less than sound.

Summary

The foregoing has tried to give an idea of the extent of the Afterlife on film in all its diversity. As in life, dead individuals vary in motivation and character. They can be good or malign, helpful or unhelpful, can take center stage or be consigned to the periphery of the drama. Appropriately, the role they play can be transparent or opaque. This chapter has attempted to sketch out this diversity, and the next one takes a number of the most interesting films and subjects them to more detailed analysis.

4

Ghost Films: Selected Case Studies

In any genre, certain films stand out by reason of story, acting or technique, or because they resonate in some way with the zeitgeist. The following films have been chosen for greater analysis because of their richness, and because they deal in different, but hopefully representative, ways with the issue of life after death as portrayed in the cinema.

Something they have in common to a greater or lesser degree is ambiguity, an uncertainty as to whether events are objective or the products of a disordered mind. The audience hesitates between competing explanations, and the resulting enigma is a source of pleasure. This is not the only valid approach — other interesting films are unambiguous in their presentation of the paranormal — but these are more profound than most and repay greater study than could be afforded in the previous thematic examination. All are post-war, two from the 1940s, two from the 1960s and one each from the 1980s and 1990s, and are English-language. It is coincidental that five were made in England (although two of these are set in the United States, with American directors), and the sixth has an English director. They attest to the strength of the roots of the ghost film in the English heritage of supernatural literature.

Dead of Night (1945)

SYNOPSIS: An architect, Walter Craig, visits a house to discuss alterations, and meets the members of a soirée in progress. He feels that he has been there before in a recurring dream, and met those present, though the feeling is not reciprocated. He does not recall how the dream ends. His certainty prompts the guests in turn to tell him about strange experiences they have had (five in all). A racing driver, Hugh, tells of a symbolic precognitive dream he had in the hospital in which he sees a hearse with a driver who enigmatically says "Just room for one inside, sir." Upon release, he is about to board a bus and realizes that the conductor is the hearse driver. He even uses the same words, so Hugh declines to board, and just afterwards he sees the bus crash. Next, Sally tells of a party she went to in which, playing hide and seek, she goes upstairs and finds a small boy crying. Only later does she discover that he had lived in the house long before, and been murdered by his older sister. The third story concerns a mirror that Joan buys for her fiancé Peter. He can intermittently see another room through the mirror, though Joan cannot, and gradually he becomes aggressive and jealous. Joan discovers that the mirror had once belonged to a man who had murdered his wife in front of it. Peter finally attempts to strangle Joan, at which point she too sees the other room in the mirror, and by smashing it frees Peter from its influence. The next story concerns two golfers who vie for the affections of a young lady and decide to play golf for her. The loser drowns himself, then discovers that his partner cheated, whereupon he returns to haunt him. He cannot remember the actions he must perform to disappear, and in experimenting on the wedding night, his living rival vanishes, whereupon the ghost is free to enter the bedroom. The final story is narrated by a psychiatrist. He tells of a ventriloquist who is terrified his dummy wants to leave him for another performer. In a paranoid rage he shoots his rival, and in his cell destroys the dummy, thereafter, totally mad, speaks in the dummy's high-pitched voice. The stories ended, Craig and the psychiatrist are left alone. Craig becomes confused, the stories he has heard jumbled in his mind, with him present in each, and he feels compelled to strangle his companion. He finds himself at home in bed, having woken from a bad dream. He receives a telephone call inviting him to visit a farmhouse in a professional capacity, and as the film ends he drives up to the house he had seen in his dream, the closing shots echoing those at the beginning of the story.

Dead of Night has a solid reputation. Hutchings describes it as "arguably the most famous ghost story ever produced within British cinema," "an intense and obsessive meditation on issues arising from the transition from a wartime to a post-war society."[1] Charles Barr states that it "remains one of the key films of the whole [Ealing] output, most notably for the section directed by Robert Hamer [the mirror story]."[2] Alex Cox, in his introduction to a screening in the BBC 'Moviedrome' season called it a "classic British horror film — indeed *the* classic horror film of all time," and, placing it in a wider context than the British industry,

George Perry declares it to be "one of the best films ever made about the supernatural."[3]

Dead of Night is usually described as a compendium of ghost stories, but in fact only two of the segments, the second and fourth (Sally's and the golfing sketch) can definitely be characterized in this way. The first story concerns a precognitive vision, the third the absorption of an evil influence by a mirror, and the last the power of a puppet over its owner. The stories, however, are not easily labeled. It *could* be argued that the mirror is controlled by its original owner's ghost, and Francis, the "ghost" described by Sally, has a solidity that could hint at a time-slip, of the sort alleged to have occurred to C. A. E. Moberly and E. F. Jourdain at Versailles.[4] Of the five stories, critical interest has centered on the mirror and dummy segments. The others, particularly the golfing anecdote, have been largely dismissed. In both of the major sections, a male is threatened with the loss of personal identity. In the first the man is rescued by his wife, in the other he fails and loses his own, frail, personality.

Mark Jancovich quotes Robin Wood's argument that *Psycho* marked a turning point for the horror film.[5] For Wood, prior to 1960, monsters had been externalized, solid figures representing a threat to society, whereas *Psycho* had the threat proceeding from inside, from the family. Jancovich criticizes this position as simplistic, and argues that Alfred Hitchcock's concerns were part of a wider movement exploring relations between horror, madness and the family.[6] It can be seen that the mirror and dummy stories too center on monsters from the id, leaving aside the possibility of evil's being objectified in mirror and dummy to the extent that each is able to control its ostensible owner. In this sense, Wood is correct in stressing the return of the repressed, unleashed upon the world.

The Frame Story

Hutchings draws attention to the distinction between public and private in the film.[7] Craig has been asked to design new bedrooms, and the bedroom is a private area that contrasts with the more public rooms downstairs. It is also "the site of dreams." Films during the war had concentrated on portraying the collective life of the community, in which individual desires, including sexuality, were submerged for the greater good, but this requirement had now passed, and individuals' needs could reassert themselves. This too is a major theme of *A Matter of Life and Death* (hereafter *AMOLAD*).

Hutchings elaborates this distinction. Multiple narrative structures were familiar by 1945, and were associated with an emphasis on collectivity, which symbolized national unity during the war. *Dead of Night* subverts this expectation, however. Whereas its predecessors stressed the move from the home to the collective, *Dead of Night* moves in the opposite direction, reflecting post-war society. The stories told by its inhabitants are examples of extreme subjectivity that cannot be validated. Further, far from portraying a homogeneous community, the characters form a disparate group of individuals whose relationships to each other are sketchily drawn.

Craig is invited to the house for his professional services rather than by virtue of being from the same social class as the rest of the house party. He is not even to be put up in the house, but in the barn, 'outside.' The slightly patronizing way in which he is treated reveals that the others are aware of this discrepancy in his status. He and van Straaten[8] are both outsiders in this milieu. Another distinguishing factor is Craig's Welshness. Coming from the "Celtic fringe," the stereotype is that he is more in tune with the supernatural, as would be the case with the women, possessing a more developed sense of intuition than the men. Mervyn Johns would also have been familiar to the audience from the previous year's *The Halfway House*, in which he played a ghost.

The van Straaten character indicates confusion between psychiatry and psychoanalysis. He tells Craig that to understand the latter's problems he would have to psychoanalyze him, then later says that he is a psychiatrist, and it is clear that he is when he interviews Frere. Just prior to his murder, he tells Craig that it is his job to listen and Craig's to talk, bringing to mind the psychoanalytic method. This confusion may simply reflect the filmmakers' ignorance rather than subtlety. His continental name summarizes a clichéd depiction of the analyst. On one level, he can be seen as a straw man, his function to play the "trick cyclist" who cannot explain life's deeper mysteries and therefore attempts to explain them away. But his role is more significant than this. Barr has likened the telling of the stories to an Ealing brainstorming session[9]; they could also be seen as a form of talking cure. Each character gains relief from recounting a disturbing episode, even van Straaten.

The process is most intense for Craig, and by the time he has told his story a situation of "negative transference" has been established, which he cannot control. The final strangulation echoes its usage in the second and third stories— Craig has become a character in his own plot. The final mixing together of elements, which Carlos Clarens unfairly characterizes as a "farandole which redundantly mixed all the stories together,"[10] foregrounds the nightmarish, illogical nature of the experience, and also collapses time. None of the narratives is allowed to have priority over the others. They exist in a timeless universe.[11]

The Racing Driver's Story

This segment is based on a story supposedly involving the First Marquis of Dufferin and Ava.[12] For Hutchings, obsessed by the notion of symbolic castration, the racing injury that Hugh suffers symbolizes the trauma inflicted on men in general as a result of the war.[13] Seen in this way, Hugh is reduced to a state of helplessness, mothered by the capable nurse whom we discover later he has married. His reaction to the sight of the conductor from his hallucination is one of passivity, and he can only watch helplessly as the bus crashes—his sole recourse is to close his eyes.

This is plausible, but perhaps overstates the case. The transition from war to peace would have affected people in different ways. Despite the majority's heaving a collective sigh of relief, there would have been individuals for whom the cessation of hostilities would have been an anticlimax. Hugh's background is not filled in, but he can be seen as a man of action, unable to settle down, for whom driving is an attempt to recapture the adrenaline buzz of combat. Rather than traumatized, he is dissatisfied, and certainly not damaged enough to fail to win the nurse. The final shot of Hugh could be viewed as stoicism rather than helplessness.

Sally's Story

Sally's story concerns a party she had attended. She had been the oldest child present, and her status, as child or young woman, is ambiguous. The theme of public versus private is strongly drawn in this section. Evading the young host's unwanted attention, she climbs from the noisy, boisterous domain downstairs into the mysterious sphere of the upper rooms. The ground floor is palatial, whereas upstairs consists of dusty attics full of rubbish, passages and claustrophobic rooms, one of which hides a dark secret. Her movement might be considered analogous to a shift from the conscious to the hidden and cluttered unconscious.

After hearing a child crying, then having found and comforted the ghost Francis,[14] Sally is identified as a surrogate sister by him, which sets up a polarity between her as the good sister, and Francis's blood sibling as the bad one: the two girls are mirror images, just as in the following story the "good" and the "bad" rooms are mirror images. It emerges that Francis's half-sister first strangled him, then cut his throat. For Hutchings[15] the latter act is important, because the cutting of the body is often taken as a writing of sexual difference on the body, usually female, i.e. a display of male power.[16] Here the situation is reversed, and the male is subject to a symbolic castration. He links this with Sally's rejection of the youth who is holding the party and who makes a pass at her.

In fact the story had been inspired by the case of four-year-old Francis Kent, who was killed in similar circumstances, except that he was smothered rather than strangled, by his sixteen-year-old half-sister Constance in 1860. An analysis of the case is provided by Bernard Taylor.[17] Unfortunately for Hutchings and Creed, Taylor suggests that the boy's *father* cut the throat of the already dead child in an unsuccessful attempt to throw suspicion onto the perpetrators of several murders in the neighborhood in which the victims' throats had been cut, and away from his daughter.

The Mirror

The most celebrated section takes up themes from earlier in the film and prefigures others. For example, the mirror's original owner cut his throat after strangling his wife, a fate — throat slitting followed by strangulation — echoing that which befell the young Francis in the preceding story. The triads that have been linked previously — Hugh, Peggy (for whom Hugh calls in his delirium) and Joyce; and Sally, Francis and his sister — now become more pronounced. In the present story there is a third male, Guy, again not shown, who acts as a catalyst for the jealous rage that brings events to head. In the last two stories the three-way form of the drama is made explicit.

Hutchings has stressed the role of the gaze in *Dead of Night*: "...men seem to spend most of their time staring anxiously into space (and, implicitly, into their own minds)."[18] Gaze is central to this story, to the extent that the mirror becomes the central protagonist. The plot is an exercise in narcissism, not just in the sense of self-absorption, but in the wider sense of a loss of ability to distinguish between the boundary of the self and the outside world. Peter so loses touch with the 1940s that he eventually becomes merged with the domain behind the mirror.[19] It is a window onto another world, as the film is for the audience, with the Dionysian attempting to break through into Peter's sterile Apollonian world. For Pirie and Barr, the sumptuous bedroom comes to symbolize contemporary sexual repression in which feelings are sublimated and spontaneity suppressed. Tensions become too much to bear, but rather than arrive at a creative solution the mirror is smashed, and disturbing energies for which it has acted as a generator are once more suppressed.

Peter is passive and introspective, Joan strong and capable, a reversal of the usual expectation. In his introduction to *Dead of Night* in BBC2's

"Moviedrome" season, Alex Cox (mis)quotes Peter's words "What shall we do tonight — dress up and spend a lot of money?" as an example of stilted dialogue. He fails to realize that the words do not convey any superficiality in the *film* but rather the emptiness of Peter's character (his profession, accountancy, would later become a byword for dullness). Dyson describes the style as "Terence Rattigan drawing-room,"[20] the disjunction with the action rendering the events all the more disturbing. They signify a reversal in the expectation of the roles of the two characters: the stereotype is that the woman would utter such words.

Peter can see the nineteenth century image, whereas she cannot, which at first could be interpreted that he possesses a stronger imagination. As he comes under the mirror's control, however, it has to be seen rather as indicating the relative weakness of his mind. She as a stronger person is immune from its influence. When the mirror is smashed, Peter has no recollection and is surprised to find that he is hurt. His cut echoes the event behind the mirror, in muted form. Twisted though his character was, at least the mirror's original owner possessed an energy that Peter does not. That there is a residual appreciation that something has been lost is perhaps contained in his dismay at the mirror's destruction.

The apparitional room, contrasting with that on the other side of the mirror, echoes Gainsborough melodramas and looks forward to Hammer horror films, both with their sumptuous Regency/Victorian settings.[21] As Pauline Kael pointed out, it is the fact that the locus is contemporary that renders the supernatural element "more shocking than if the characters were Gothic or Transylvanian."[22] It is this discrepancy that is unsettling. As in the previous stories (the Victoriana of the hearse in the present, Sally's meeting a dead child), past and present elide momentarily to create a sense of the uncanny.

The Golf Story

This story has been universally dismissed as the weakest section, and it does sit oddly, its major function being to allow a breathing space between the emotional intensity of the mirror and puppet stories. It is also different in tone from the other segments and the responses of the characters jar. Given acceptance of such matters as precognition and apparitions, the portrayal of events has a realistic underpinning. With the golf story, the narrative is more clearly fantasy, and psychologically implausible. The other stories directly concerned one of the people present but the golfers' duel is reported second-hand, which alters its status. It is apparent early on that it is being played for comedy, and Radford and Wayne would be familiar as comic characters.

Unlike other women in the film, the female at the center of the dispute is passive, and allows her suitors to decide her fate. She is disengaged, and does not care which she marries. She agrees that the competition for her is the perfect solution. If not quite going as far as to say that a woman cannot be satisfied by only one man, there is at least a hint that two are better than one.[23] This links to the preceding story, in which Guy's role is left in doubt. To the golfers, the woman destroys the bond between them, which is based on what they do for a living. The greater sacrifice is not to give up the woman but to give up golf. The golf club becomes a phallic symbol of independence and self-confidence, the loss of which would amount to emasculation.

The Ventriloquist's Dummy

We are given the tensions of a (stereotypical) gay love triangle in a way that would not have been acceptable if one of the participants had not been a dummy. In addition, Hugo might be seen as a detachable phallus, symbolic of Frere's insecurity. By destroying Hugo he is reduced to speaking in the high-pitched tones of a castrato—he has mutilated himself. Women play a peripheral role. The night-club owner in Paris is capable and independent, all the more striking in that she is black. The two women in the London hotel bar are more sketchily drawn, and rely on Harry to stand up for them, with much persuasion. Women are able to get what they want, either by their own efforts, or by manipulation of males. This story summarizes the gender crisis exhibited in the preceding sections.

The audience is teased by the thought that Hugo might have a will of his own as opposed to being a secondary personality of Frere's that has been concretized in the puppet. The depersonalization of Frere at the end, to the extent that he speaks in Hugo's voice, is repeated by Hitchcock in *Psycho*, at the end of which Norman adopts his mother's voice.[24] A resolution has occurred in van Straaten's narrative, but it is not certain whether Hugo has managed to obliterate Frere's personality with his stronger one, or whether Frere has allowed his secondary personality to become the primary one as an escape from reality.

The examination of perception in *AMOLAD* is well known, but it is also an issue in *Dead of Night*. There is a tension between what Peter and Hugh see (mirror, hearse), things that might not be there in the film's terms but are there in the audience's. The two of them accept as real what could be subjective. This works with the film as a whole. When it becomes clear that the ending is repeating the beginning, the audience no longer knows what is supposed to be real and what is the dream that has been the ostensible subject of the film. Both characters and audience are in a vicious circle, with no reassuring closure.

A related issue is that of free will versus pre-ordination of events. The circularity, if it be so, implies that the characters have no free will but are condemned to endless repetitions of the same actions (James Agee in a contemporary review suggested that the ending would have been improved if "The End" had not been superimposed upon it. He also felt that it should have ended with the first full close-up of Craig, where he is seen staring at the house with a puzzled look on his face).[25] Further, there is reflexivity here in that the viewer knows that the characters have no free will — they are actors with scripts — and also in the sense that, once captured on film, the characters will go through the same actions whenever the film is projected. There are larger forces at work that neither the characters, nor the audience, understand.

Dyson argues that the question of whether events in the film are supernatural or the result of insanity is answered during the final montage: they are supernatural. This is a false dichotomy, and only really relates to the last story, which Dyson prioritizes by saying that the issue of whether Frere is mad or Hugo possessed "neatly encapsulates the whole thrust of the film."[26] No cues have been given in the earlier stories to suggest that they are other than veridical, so there is no reason to wonder whether there is some dialectic that needs resolution. Only at the end of the film do we hesitate, when we wonder if Craig has had a precognitive dream (and after all, we have already accepted Hugh's experience of the future) or whether it was all in his mind.

Taking the opposite stance to Dyson's, Pirie feels that "the whole action is finally revealed to be a nightmare which is about to come true," and Hutchings quotes Metz to the same end — "For Metz, the dreamer waking demarcates real from false."[27] It might seem that there is no reason why the unfolding of events during the film should be privileged over those that can be assumed to occur afterwards. If the film has been a *recurrent* dream, it would be arbitrary to assume that the final shots represent a qualitatively different state, being in some sense real, whereas what went before, being a dream, was not; though unless Craig is in a never-ending solipsistic state, it is reasonable that the dream will end after one of its iterations. Why not the one we have just witnessed?

Butler convincingly strengthens the "end of dream" position by pointing to the shot of Foley on the telephone to Craig.[28] Hitherto events have been seen from Craig's viewpoint, Butler concludes, so that even when he has been told a story by another character we have seen what has been told to him. The shot of Foley changes that because Craig has not yet met him, destroying the sense of circularity. After this visit Craig will not wake up. It is an ingenious argument, though a heavy freight for a single shot to bear. The only counter-argument is the feeling that we are in a realm where appearances are deceptive, and that if Craig is capable of having such an accurate precognitive dream, he is capable of "seeing" Foley clairvoyantly — assuming of course that he is not still asleep, in which case Foley would have the same status as the house guests, as parts of Craig's dream.

Dead of Night can be seen as representing a post-war failure of nerve by the middle classes. The hostilities had thrown up a fierce debate about social justice, and the need for a more equitable society after its end. British films during the conflict had gradually scaled down the importance of the officer class, and concomitantly scaled up those of working-class characters, as a reflection of the mood of national rapprochement that prevailed.[29] Old class-based notions of gentlemanliness were deemed inadequate (and it is noteworthy that Churchill's Conservative Party was defeated in 1945), particularly in light of the awareness of the changing balance of power in the world. The stories overall allude to the stresses caused by the social upheaval of the previous six years, and Craig's prognostication seems gloomy.

A Matter of Life and Death (1946)

SYNOPSIS: RAF pilot Peter Carter bails out of a burning airplane without a parachute, but instead of dying is washed up on the English coast. He meets June, the American radio operator to whom he had been talking before he jumped, who happens to be passing, and they fall in love. Unfortunately, the records section in Heaven, which is monochrome, as opposed to Earth's Technicolor, is in a flap because Peter's escort, Conductor 71, missed him in fog over the Channel. Conductor 71 is sent down to Earth to rectify the matter, but David argues that he should not have to go as, thanks to Conductor 71's negligence, he now has responsibilities (June) that have accrued since his landing. A trial is set in Heaven to adjudicate, but Peter cannot decide on defense counsel. At the same time, June's friend Dr. Reeves, a brilliant neurologist, diagnoses a brain tumor and a date is set for an operation. Peter is worried that he will not be able to find someone suitable to defend him against the formidable prosecutor, anti–British Abraham Farlan. Just before the operation, however, Dr. Reeves is killed and is able to act as Peter's defense. The trial is successful, as is the operation, and Peter and June can look forward to a long life together.

A Matter of Life and Death (*AMOLAD*) is in that tradition which implies that the story can be seen either as objective representation or as the subjective experience of one of the characters. This split does not have to be completely coherent for hesitation to occur. The bulk of the evidence can be on one side, but minor discrepancies can supply a counter-argument, however weak. In *AMOLAD*, the bulk of the evidence is for the hallucination hypothesis—Powell stressed that material for the hallucinations was culled from medical textbooks[30]—but this is undermined in several instances, so that the reality of "the other world" is left as an uncertainty. The relationship of the two worlds has certainly exercised critics since the film's release.

Although the film can be examined in the context of life after death, it covers other issues as well. It is concerned with themes of national identity and the relationship between Britain and the United States, the transition from war-time to peace-time societies, the place of the individual in a society that no longer needs to stress the unity of the nation, sexuality and the nature of desire. An anonymous Soviet reviewer saw the "matter of life and death" to be the creation of a British/American bloc against the Soviet Union.[31] All these elements are interlinked, making it difficult to treat the depiction of the Afterlife in isolation.

The titles at the beginning of the film state clearly that this is the story of two worlds, the one we know, and the one in the mind of a young airman. That this dichotomy is not specific to Peter is suggested by the manner of presentation of the titles: we see "This is a story of/two Worlds/the one we know/and another/which exists only/in the mind," after which they begin scrolling, to make the specific reference: "of a young airman...." Powell reiterates this subjectivity in his autobiography: "Peter is living in two worlds at once: the world we know and an imaginary one which is created by his vivid imagination."[32] Dr. Reeves also takes this line, and his "diagnosis" and the operation seem to bear it out. But this is constantly undercut, suggesting that Heaven has an objective reality. The film can be considered to be a detective story for the viewer, who has to consider the evidence just as the celestial jury has to weigh Peter's own situation.[33]

Peter's survival is the first intimation that the decision will not be an easy one. There have been cases of people falling large distances without parachutes and living—examples that may have inspired *AMOLAD* occurred in 1941 when John North's parachute failed to open and he broke both legs landing in a field, and in 1944 when Nicholas Alkemade jumped from a burning Lancaster, his fall broken by a fir tree and snow drifts—but a doubt is left. It is as hard to believe that this happened to Peter, with the added escape of not drowning, as it is to believe that Conductor 71 missed him in the fog. Other possibilities, such as ditching the aircraft, are not raised (Peter's cut head in the burning airplane is a red herring, because the injury that caused the medical problem had already been sustained). Later, when the jury's foreman at the trial states that they would like to interview Peter and June, the camera pulls away from the auditorium, and it can be seen that this is part of the Milky Way, a concrete location for Heaven, although it could be argued that Peter's imagination had placed it there.

The revelation that the judge is the same person as the surgeon might be seen to undercut the assumption that the Other World is real; Peter's fevered mind has transferred the image of an authority figure from one context to another. Unfortunately for this reading Peter had not met the surgeon. Other pieces of evidence that "Heaven" is an hallucination are provided in the airplane. Peter asks June if she believes in ghosts, and then talks about the next world, mentioning the sorts of characters—Plato, Aristotle, Jesus—who will be discussed later with Conductor 71. He also wonders whether he will be given wings or a propeller. When he regains consciousness on the beach, he is looking up at the clouds, beyond which Heaven would be, and—perhaps by Divine intervention—he is near June's digs and able to intercept her on her way home.

Subsequent events can be seen as an elaboration of these initial musings, implying that they are the product of brain damage. New entrants to Heaven are given wings, large impractical ones, but of a piece with the hallucinations of an airman who had previously obtained his "wings" upon completion of RAF training. Conductor 71's "Peter, come back" turns into June's voice saying the same thing, Peter could have overheard the doctor in the ambulance telling June of Reeves's death. There is no information that Peter possesses which he could not have obtained by normal, as opposed to paranormal, means. As Reeves says, "he never steps outside the limits of his own imagination." A history graduate, Peter would be familiar with the historical facts discussed during the trial. June is called to give evidence, yet does not mention it at the film's conclusion, again suggesting that it occurred in Peter's mind. One piece of evidence for Heaven's existence would be if June died at the age of 97, as Conductor 71 said she would.

The film does not specify the relationship between the outcome of the operation and the appeal. They can be seen as intertwined, with Heaven as subjective, created by a fevered mind that has undergone considerable trauma and is fighting for its survival, as Dr. Reeves diagnoses. Or they can be seen as separate, making Heaven a real place, and Peter's injury and survival coincidental. As both were successful, there is no necessity to

From left: Conductor 71 (Marius Goring), Peter Carter (David Niven), Dr. Reeves (Roger Livesey and Bob (Robert Coote, right) examine June (Kim Hunter) for evidence that will help Peter's case in *A Matter of Life and Death* (1946).

make a decision about whether Heaven has or has not an independent status. But if the operation had failed, and the appeal still been successful, would David have effectively been allowed to return from the dead?

On the other hand, if the operation had succeeded, but the appeal been disallowed, how would he have been recalled to Heaven? For the Soviet reviewer the medical prognosis is causally dependant on the outcome of the trial. If it is positive, he will recover.[34] The film itself does not support this contention so unambiguously, and it could as easily be argued that the trial is dependent on the operation. Only if the injury is repaired will he win in Heaven. Either reading is valid, and the happy ending closes off other outcomes, the failure of the operation and/or the loss of the appeal, which do not have to be considered as prospects.

John Ellis too draws attention to the problematic status of the Other World.[35] To him, each world represents a different type of narrative discourse, fiction and documentary, the clash of which caused so much disquiet to the film's first critics. The opening commentary, redolent of a school science film, avers the operation of natural law, and it is this that will later be challenged. Humans are puny in the grand scheme, not even unique in the universe, which makes Peter's victory all the more admirable. The documentary feel undercuts the stated subjectivity of the experience; there are no distorted or exaggerated elements. Normally, Ellis argues, if more than one mode of discourse is utilized, one will be anchored in the other. In *AMOLAD* each has equal status, and the narrative consists of the playing out of the tension created. It is part of this tension that the audience is unable to decide whether the monochrome sequences represent an hallucination or have an objective basis.

The earthly romance and the Other World, whatever its status, are heavily contrasted. The former vibrates with color and the monochrome sections have a pearly quality. Black and white was associated with the documentary movement and lush color with melodrama, but historically where the two types were combined in a single film no fixed convention can be discerned.[36] If an association with documentary is inferred, that would support the reality of those scenes. Or it could convey a neurological problem, as Peter's ailment did involve his optic nerve, so that his hallucinations were perforce in black and white. The association of Conductor 71 with fried onions also points to a neurological origin.

The difficulty in pinning down the reality or otherwise of the Other World is summed up by the vanishing chess book[37] (something that worries Patricia King Hanson, who also notes the difficulty in fitting Peter's survival sans parachute into a non-paranormal framework[38]). Peter alleges that it has been stolen after meeting Conductor 71 in Reeves's study. It is a big book, and it would surely have been found before June discovers it in Peter's jacket after the operation, when the jacket was being packed, for instance. This is evidence that it really was missing. In the meantime Conductor 71 has returned the book to Reeves, yet it is Conductor 71 himself who throws it back[39] (in Erich Warman's novelization of the film Reeves throws it). This could be a continuity lapse, but the thrust is firstly that the Other World exists, which is why the book is not discovered earlier in the jacket, but then that the events are all in Peter's mind, the subjectivity of which would not balk at allowing Conductor 71 to throw back a book that he no longer had.

In his autobiography, Powell is adamant that the "Other World," as he calls it, was not Heaven: "Throughout the film, we were careful not to use that mighty word."[40] This is surprising, given the preponderance of religious imagery. The incoming airmen receive wings that conform to the stereotypical image in religious paintings, although these are not seen in use, just as well given their bulk. The chief receptionist in one shot stands with her head directly in front of the clock, which frames her like a halo (she also wears a white uniform, an angelic non-color). Later she tells Bob not to use the phrase "holy smoke," because "there's no smoke without fire, and we don't call smoke holy," presumably meaning that fire is the preserve of Another Place. She also says, after hearing the comment "It's heaven, isn't it?," which could be taken literally or metaphorically, that "there are millions of people on earth who would think it heaven to be a clerk." At the end of the trial, the judge quotes Sir Walter Scott — "For love is heaven, and heaven is love."[41] The fact that to get to the Other World requires ascent supports the notion that it is Heaven. It is even possible that the lingering of the camera on the harmonica player's shadow is a pun, the monochrome world as the preserve of shades.

Heaven, by whatever name it is called, is a curious place. It is authoritarian, based on The Law (even checking the invoice to ascertain that a mistake has been made is against regulations), and it takes Peter's case to establish that love, at least on earth, is a more potent force, although one would have expected the heavenly hierarchy to know this already. It is bureaucratic, as the vast records office indicates. The amount of information collected on individuals, without their knowledge, would do justice to a police state. The American airmen are told when registering that all are equal, but are asked for name *and* rank. No families are seen, only professional groups, subdivided along ethnic lines.

Ellis cites Raymond Durgnat's criticism of earlier commentators who saw parallels with Nazi Germany.[42] Durgnat argues that the Other World was only "coldly efficient," rather than "malicious." It brought to mind certain epithets—"planned, bureaucratic, idealistic, totalitarian, colorless, theoretic [sic]—all these are words Tories like to use of Socialism." For Durgnat, the Other World is a version of the Welfare State, and in these terms, Peter's individualistic struggle can be seen as an affirmation of the rights of the individual over those of centralized control (even during the trial Farlan has a number of assistants, whereas Reeves has only the unofficial help of Conductor 71). This is a limited autonomy, as despite the fact that Reeves and Farlan reach an agreement, they do not seek to preserve the rights of the individual per se. They are concerned with the uncommon, rather than the common, man. Exceptions can be made, but when the head of the records section is worried that the appeal might set a precedent, it is clear that Peter's case is the exception and that central control based on a legalistic interpretation will be maintained. Perhaps Powell was propounding autonomy for an elite, but not for the entire population.

Desires have not been banished entirely in Heaven. Despite the segregation at the trial sexual interest still exists, as indicated by the attention displayed by Bob towards the receptionist, and later exhibited between the airmen and the nurses at the appeal. Even Coca Cola is available. One can carry on the kinds of activities that interested one in life, play chess, monitor events "down below." Ellis argues that sexuality is peripheral to the documentary element of *AMOLAD*, that it is the province of the romantic fictional form. This is true to an extent, and can be seen as related to Peter's internal struggle — the Other World symbolizes his repressed desires, and the need to express an individuality stifled by the exigencies of wartime.

The choice of David Niven for the role of Peter is an interesting one because there are several connections between *A Matter of Life and Death* and *The First of the Few* (1943) in which Niven is the narrator of the story of Spitfire designer R. J. Mitchell. It begins, like *AMOLAD*, with a view of the Earth from space, accompanied by a solemn male voice-over. Niven's character is a test pilot who rejoins the RAF and after a crash is seen lying in bed with a bandage round his head. The film ends with Mitchell dead from overwork but the Spitfire, with Niven at the lead, fighting the Battle of Britain against enormous odds. In three years (although Peter is now a bomber rather than a fighter pilot) the emphasis has switched from personal sacrifice in the interests of the State to the rights of the individual against the State, whether national or celestial.

The relationship between the three main characters in *AMOLAD* evolves, so that to begin with, after the quasi-love scene played out over the radio, Reeves and June compete for Peter. Reeves uses his professional knowledge to establish a feeling of intimacy with Peter. During the initial examination, June is excluded by the discussion of Peter's medical history, and by Reeves's knowledge that he is a poet. While playing table-tennis, Reeves tells June only so much, and then refuses to go further. When Peter faces his medical crisis, Reeves exercises total control, to the extent that June refers to him as "Doctor" rather than "Frank" when he gives her orders.

Gradually June gains the ascendancy so that she moves from being an object of desire to a subject, and her victory is completed with Reeves's death. The rival is removed from the sphere in which sexuality predominates to that in which it is marginalized, and he can find a new role as a purely paternal figure. By the conclusion of the film, Peter is able to acknowledge the partnership by telling June "we won," an upgrading of her from "I ... won ... my case" in the novelization. Defining who "we" are is not that simple, as Peter had moments before been calling for Frank. It could be that Frank's replacement by June is not complete, but the closing image is of heterosexual love triumphant and on equal terms.

Reeves's uncertain status is perhaps recognized by the novel, in which he is firmly described as a widower in his early forties, and the most eligible bachelor in the neighborhood (the book is apparently based on an earlier version of the final script. Powell in his autobiography mentions that Conductor 71's line was originally "One is starved for color up there," and this line is in the novel.[43] Reeves also quotes from *A Midsummer Night's Dream* in the book: "My cherry lips have often kiss'd thy stones,"[44] which renders his sexuality even more problematic, but this speech is absent from the finished film). We learn that Peter's father died before he was born, and that he has two sisters. If he was brought up in a predominantly female household, with no male role model, his attitude to Reeves could be read as a belated desire for a father.

The love story is part of a wider examination of the place of love in the cosmic scheme of order based upon law. This debate provides the resolution of the film and the reconciliation of the two narrative structures. The disjunction that results from their clash is elaborated by a variety of demonstrations of perception, and its relationship to cinema, constituting what Barr terms "meta-cinema."[45] Ellis gives numerous examples, such as the reference to Technicolor, Peter's point of view on the operating table from inside his head,[46] Reeves's camera obscura, the voyeurism that he practices, mirroring the cinema audience's, the two sequences in which Reeves and June play table tennis, the first with a moving, the second with a static, camera, and so on. Conductor 71's comment on stopping time that "it is only a trick" might be added. Looking through windows and doorways becomes a recurring motif, symbolizing the distinction between the boundaries of one world and another: Peter sitting in the bomber's hatch, June framed in the doorway of Reeves's workroom, or looking through the window into the operating theater, Reeves walking down the corridor to the theater, the camera looking through the library window into the covered porch. Reeves is even killed at the hospital gates.

A Matter of Life and Death is grappling with a new type of society, with a dramatic shift in perceptions of sexuality. It and *Dead of Night* are concerned with the transition from war- to peace-time societies (despite the fact that *Dead of Night* never refers to the war, and is full of able-bodied men who do not appear to have served in the military). In both, gender is of crucial importance, as are related issues of desire and the relationship of the individual to the collective. They address these issues in different ways, one optimistic, allowing progress, the other restricted to a replaying of past events. Hutchings sees them as films that address the problem of portraying desire in a medium from which it had hitherto been banished:

> ...both *Dead of Night* and *A Matter of Life and Death* produce a sense of desire as something which is difficult or impossible in two connected ways: first, via a problematisation of the film image itself (in *Life and Death* the hero is never quite sure whether his 'visions' of Heaven are real or hallucinations) and second, through a questioning of male vision and sanity.[47]

As the film's initial titles conveyed to its 1946 audience, it is not just Peter Carter's mind that has been shaped by war, but everybody's. The spiritual message is that, in a sense, whatever the status of the Afterlife, we make our own Heaven and Hell.

The Innocents (1961)

> SYNOPSIS: A sheltered young woman, Miss Giddens, is appointed governess to two orphaned children, Flora and Miles, by their uncle who wants nothing to do with them. The children are currently in the care of the housekeeper, Mrs. Grose, though Miles is away at school. Initially charmed by Flora, Miss Giddens is disturbed when Miles is sent home for being a bad influence on his school fellows. She also learns that her predecessor, Miss Jessel, had had an unwholesome relationship with the valet, Quint, and killed herself when he died. She starts to feel that there are others present in the house, and then to see the two ghosts. The children also act mysteriously, as if they have a great secret, and seem to possess knowledge beyond their years. Eventually Miss Giddens decides that the children are being used by the ghosts to continue their unsavory activities. She tries to make Flora acknowledge Miss Jessel's presence, but the child becomes hysterical, and Miss Giddens tells the now-alienated Mrs. Grose to remove her to the uncle's. Miss Giddens is left with Miles, and at the climax, as she tries to neutralize Quint's evil influence, the boy collapses and apparently dies.

The Innocents (1961) is an attempt to translate Henry James's verbal ambiguities in *The Turn of the Screw* (1898/1984) into visual terms.[48] The film attempts to replicate the problem of distinguishing between whether the ghosts are real or a figment of the governess's imagination, and following on from the novel is probably the most often cited example of a film that attempts to balance subjective and objective interpretations. The novel can be seen in terms of Todorov's hesitation. Whether the film can also be seen in the same way is more difficult to answer, although Alain Silver and James Ursini reply in the affirmative.[49] They do not tackle the problem that seeing the ghosts is not on the same level as reading somebody's account of them. The ghosts possess a solidity on screen that confers a greater weight than in the print version. But the ways the things Miss Giddens sees—or thinks she sees, to put it neutrally—are depicted do leave their status in doubt.

The book's influence on commentators on the film has been significant, causing *The Innocents* to be regarded in the same light. This balance between objective and subjective has been the focus of a number of critics, although judging by the contemporary reviews that Kael quotes to show how they have missed the essence of the film ("...new developments in Jamesian scholarship" as she dryly puts it),[50] "hesitation" as used by Todorov may be another term for confusion. So George E. Haggerty, talking of the novel, says that the governess, Miss Giddens, "is beset with an ontological crisis that results in the fusion of objective and subjective states in the tale."[51] This is wrong for two reasons. Firstly the objective and subjective do not fuse, the tension comes from the gap between the two. Secondly, the governess is not beset with an ontological crisis because she is convinced for the bulk of the story that the ghosts are real (only at the end of the book does she have any doubts, and none in the film).

Clearly differences between novel and film have to be taken into account when attempting to establish what is being presented. The book is filtered through the governess (it is after all her account, however unreliable it is), whereas point of view in the film is more complex.[52] But although the events in the latter seem to be objective, they are a reconstruction mediated by Miss Giddens's recollection, given that the bulk of the film is a flashback.[53] Despite the problem of having to use solid ghosts, in the sense that they are actors physically in front of the camera, it might be argued that the filmic technique could still be an analogue of the novel, in which the story is told by the governess, upon whom no reliance can be put, except that there are instances when events occur on screen in Miss Giddens's absence.

The extended flashback warns the viewer of the subjectivity of the events that follow, although as no standard device for signaling it is used, such as the scene dissolving "wavily," or the use of a verbal or musical intimation, the degree to which what happens subsequently can be considered some form of reverie is debatable—certainly Stuart Y. McDougal puts it strongly when he says that "...the film constitutes the governess's recollections of all that has happened, told at the instant of Miles's death."[54] He mentions that the visions become increasingly subjective while filmed in a more objective manner, for example the over-the-shoulder-shot at the lake,[55] and this point is strengthened by uncertainty over the status of the events following the initial voice-over, not knowing whether they continue the perspective established by the focus on the owner of the hands, or whether they are to be seen as an objective representation.

Andrew Higson examines the film in the context of the Gothic and suggests that the genre had seen a movement from external horror to internally generated fear between publication of the novel and release of the film.[56] The issue is not as clear-cut as this suggests. There has been a debate about the objectivity of the ghosts in the novel since Edmund Wilson's influential paper[57] with no clear progression from a consensus that the ghosts are veridical to one that the governess is hallucinating. Secondly, there is still a large constituency of consumers of the Gothic ready to believe that depiction of ghosts represents veridicality rather than psychological disturbance. The attempt to determine what is happening here mirrors the investigator's task when examining an alleged haunting. Sightings may be misperceptions or hallucinations. Ghosts could be present, in which case the extent of their influence would have to be assessed over and above any exaggerations by the witness. The children could be naturally precocious but grieving for their parents and acting up as a consequence, playing on Miss Giddens's inexperience (their bereavement and neglect by their uncle has received little attention in the literature. Also, the uncle tends to be taken at face value by critics, although if the film is told by an unreliable narrator, his manner as much as events at Bly could be colored by Miss Giddens's imagination). The secrecy and whispering that Miss Giddens finds so disturbing could be two children trying to cope with only each other on whom to fall back.

Alternatively, their grief could have opened them up psychically to ghosts, and they could either be in some form of benign communication or a more sinister possession could be at work. The difficulty of teasing out causes can be seen in Flora's act of submerging her tortoise. It could either be naive or sadistic; if the latter, either conducted under the influence of Quint or for some other reason; and finally, if influenced by Quint, either from when he was alive, learned from his brutal ways, or actively after his death. Miles's expulsion for allegedly contaminating and corrupting other pupils presents similar difficulties.

Assuming that fraud and error have been ruled out as far as possible, something has to be left that seems significant but eludes definition. Even the film's title provides no clues. The children may be innocents corrupted by ghosts, or indeed innocent of all charges laid by Miss Giddens, or Miss Giddens may be an innocent out of her depth, seeing conspiracy where none exists, reading too much into an innocent situation. If the non-supernatural explanation is accepted, then as Neil Sinyard puts it, the film is a nice reversal of *The Curse of the Cat People* (1944), with adults who see visions and children "who exasperatedly dispute them."[58]

The evidence in the film swings either way at different times. When for example the governess is standing by the lake and sees Miss Jessel, but Mrs. Grose and Flora apparently do not, it could be that the ghosts are the product of an overwrought imagination, or just perhaps that Miss Jessel was there but could only be selectively perceived. It is these unmotivated shifts in point of view that Higson sees as characteristic of the uncertainties of the fantastic.[59] But when Miss Jessel sits crying at the schoolroom desk, the ambiguity breaks down because she leaves a tear behind (Kael too mentions the tear as one item that cannot be contained within a psychological manifestation, but spoils the insight by calling it "that little pearl of ambiguity" when it is the opposite[60]). Even this, James W. Palmer valiantly thinks, could be seen as hallucinatory.[61]

It is true that Miss Giddens tells Mrs. Grose that Miss Jessel had spoken to her in the schoolroom, which is wrong, and this could cast doubt on the entire experience, but there is a difference between the unreliability of a report and the experience of the tear on the desk — the two are not equivalent. In any case, Miss Giddens could have meant communication loosely, something not requiring speech, telling her what she needed, or wanted, to know. Seeing Miss Jessel could be a hallucination, but the water on the desk is concrete compared to the unreality and strangeness of Quint and Miss Jessel in their various manifestations. If the tear is an hallucination the way is open for a reduction ad absurdum in which the whole of Bly has to be regarded as a solipsistic experience, at which point the question of Miss Jessel's status becomes irrelevant.

It is never resolved who calls out "Flora" as Miss Giddens arrives, but the uncertainty sets the scene for a supernatural interpretation. That the ghosts are real becomes the default position, although we only have Miss Giddens's word for their evil intentions. In the first encounter with Flora she is reflected in the lake, a ghostly image in a medium that will later link her to Miss Jessel at the summer house. Reflective surfaces become an important motif in the film — they are associated with the ghosts, but also hint that Miss Giddens has depths that a casual glance might not see.

A proneness to fantasizing is insinuated even before Miss Giddens gets to Bly, when she is asked by the uncle whether she has an imagination. The stereotype of the clergyman's daughter is also brought into play, carrying connotations of spinsterish unworldliness.[62] But those critics who have proposed that Miss Giddens is hallucinating have not considered to any extent what might be involved in such a psychological aberration. Seeing things that are not there would not happen in isolation, but in conjunction with other symptoms. Stress could be caused by fear that the children are consorting with evil spirits, or are even possessed, and frustration at not being able to make others see. She exhibits none of the mental illness that might be associated with hallucinations. Both Butler and Robert Murphy contrast Miss Giddens's plight with that of the protagonist of *Repulsion* (1965),[63] who suffers hallucinations and ends in complete mental collapse. Miss Giddens looks too controlled, if not *in* control, and not at all neurotic, unlike say Eleanor in *The Haunting*.

Miss Giddens's surroundings extend the ambiguity, implying at various times that she is a victim of circumstances, at others that she is the locus of unhealthy impulses. Nature in general is portrayed as unpleasant, carrying as it does the seeds of decay even when at its most vibrant — petals falling when Miss Giddens touches them suggesting a kind of reverse Midas touch, a spider eating a butterfly, a beetle appearing from the statue, beauty concealing the unsavory. During the pony-riding scene, the trees wave menacingly — Don G. Smith thinks that they applaud Miles, alluding to a paranormal phenomenon.[64] The tranquil lakeside is the setting for a ghost sighting. The butterfly could be a metaphor for Miss Giddens, or the emphasis on nature's dark side could suggest a world without compassion, with Quint's stalking of Miss Giddens as characteristic of a natural process.

Increasing our sense of her unreliability as a narrator, Miss Giddens gradually becomes identified with both ghosts: with Quint in the morning room when Mrs. Grose sees her standing outside the window where Miss Giddens has just seen him; and with Miss Jessel in the schoolroom, where she sits down in the late governess's position, and then by the black dress, mimicking Miss Jessel's, which she wears in the latter part of the film. It could be that she is in some way "standing in" for them, but the motivation is not made clear, only the implication that she is being sucked into somebody else's narrative. Alternatively identification could imply that they do not exist independently of her.

The self-consciously Freudian elements in the film, inclining to a subjective interpretation, are at times so subtle that they are easily missed: the phallic tower upon which the figure that could be that of Quint is glimpsed, the pond into which Miss Giddens drops her scissors, the flower petals that fall at her touch, the beetle crawling from the orifice of the statue, these can be seen as nods to a psychological view of Miss Giddens's experiences, but they do not allow an easy either/or approach to determining the precise nature of what the audience sees, whether the ghosts exist outside Miss Giddens's imagination. By presenting the ghosts, in however stylized a fashion, to try to suggest that they might be hallucinations, the ambiguity of the novel has to be compromised. Clayton attempts to redress the balance by inserting the scene in which Miss Giddens finds Quint's picture. She now has a cue when seeing him, and it could be that, as does happen in eyewitness testimony, experience is distorted to conform to the preconception. Certainly her sightings become clearer after seeing the picture.

Steve Seidman[65] lists a range of cues that could lead to a verdict of hallucination, such as Quint's picture and subsequent sighting; his laugh is heard to be harsh after Mrs. Grose describes it that way; after being told of Miss Jessel's grief she hears sobbing; whispering after being told of whispering. In other words, she is not obtaining information paranormally but is building up an image from things she is told and from inferences based upon the children's behavior. But of course these phenomena could be regarded as the ghosts playing with Miss Giddens, perhaps to make her think she was losing her mind. In particular, if she were fantasy-prone, why is Quint's image not more detailed after Miss Giddens sees his picture? The evidence for objectivity is weaker because Miss Giddens has been cued, but it is not invalidated.

If Miss Giddens is insane, as Miles pronounces her, then it is unlikely that he can see Quint during the final confrontation. His "Quint — you devil" refers either to Quint or to Miss Giddens, but as he is addressing Miss Giddens it is more likely that it is to her. If to Quint, it would be more natural to say "Quint — the devil." This might mean that Quint is not present and that Miss Giddens is hallucinating. When Miles tells her "You never fooled us. We always knew," "we" could be referring to Flora or Quint, or both, though calling Miss Giddens a "dirty-minded hag" hints that she is wrong to assume Quint's presence, and that Miles has confessed.[66] While feeling that the film captures the novel's ambiguity, Alain J. Silver suggests that Miss Giddens's inexperience with sex and with the authority thrust upon her could have produced hallucinations, as she confuses Quint with a statue while in a state of heightened emotion in the final scene.[67] The ghosts as product of a stress reaction is a weak argument, and does not account for sightings of the ghosts when calm, such as when she sees Quint through the window; unless Miss Giddens is thought to be in a permanent state of hysteria, when the objection becomes why she does not see them more often.

Hints that Quint and Jessel exist as ghosts are given obliquely by the behavior of Miss Giddens's co-residents. The death-related song that opens the film and Miles's later poem, by when it would seem clear that Quint is "my lord," strengthen the feeling that we are watching a ghost film rather than the story of a woman on the edge of a nervous breakdown. Mrs. Grose exhibits an initial nervousness on meeting Miss Giddens, and there is a moment of confusion when she seems to be talking about Quint while Miss Giddens is referring to the uncle.

Flora too perhaps has Quint in mind when she asks if she would walk the earth when dead if she were bad, and says when an animal is crying outside that Mrs. Grose has told her that they must pretend not to hear it (a non-supernatural explanation for this could be that when Quint and Jessel were alive and conducting their relationship, Mrs. Grose was determined to ignore it and/or protect the children by encouraging them to do the same; this is a house of secrets). When Flora looks into the garden from her bedroom before Miles's return it seems that she has seen somebody out there. Miss Giddens climbs up the tower to find Miles rather than Quint, and it is conceivable that it was Miles whom she saw against the light. Miles says that he has been alone save for his "greedy friends," referring to the pigeons, but carrying the implication that he has greedy friends other than the birds.

If genuine, the selective appearance of the ghosts raises a number of questions: why are they seen only by Miss Giddens, assuming that the others cannot see them? Do they think that the new governess is presuming on their authority? Is Mrs. Grose, as suggested by her name, not refined enough to see them? If so, is the price of refinement a neurotic breakdown? When Mrs. Grose, Miss Giddens and Flora are at the lake and Miss Giddens sees Miss Jessel, Flora could be lying when she says that she can see nothing, and that Mrs. Grose is indeed the only one unable to see the apparitions. This might amount to a class-based selectivity.

Some though not all of the film's contemporary reviews mention the possibility that Miss Giddens hallucinates, but the lurid advertising material accompanying its release[68] seems sure the ghosts are objective, with two intertwined "spirits" answering the strapline's question: "Do They Ever Return to Possess the Living?" A feature on the film in *the Daily Cinema*[69] has a photograph of Deborah Kerr standing in front of a poster proclaiming, next to a close-up of her, "Dare You Face as She Did—The Evil That Possessed the Innocents?" so it is doubtful whether contemporary audiences were primed to see the film as an exercise in ambiguity.[70] The frontispiece of Gary J. Svehla and Susan Svehla's *Cinematic Hauntings* reproduces another poster of Kerr with the words "Did she really see those evil spirits ... *or was she really the love-starved spinster 'the innocents' said she was*" (italics in original). The even-handedness is undercut by the outline of a couple kissing, which might cue a ghost interpretation. The advertising undermines Dyson's assertion that the film was not sold as a horror film,[71] but he is keen to designate it a borderline horror, as the possible subjectivity of Miss Giddens's experiences could classify it "as a psychological drama that uses horror film techniques to advance its narrative,"[72] a severe restriction on what constitutes a horror film. The marketing campaign was perhaps trying to tap into the success generated by *Psycho* (1960)[73] and a review in *The Daily Cinema* suggests that the film would benefit from a *Homicidal*-style "frightbreak."[74]

The likelihood of possession is one that has been raised to explain the influence of Quint and Miss Jessel in novel and film. Some of the film's press material explicitly refers to it: "PSYCHOGENETICS: This unusual term, referring to the dead possessing the mind and body of the living, given by Jack Clayton ... for what occurs in the film...."[75] In similar if less lurid vein, Sinyard, in examining the way in which strangeness and cruelty intrude into otherwise attractive children, describes Flora standing at the end of Miss Giddens's bed "like an incubus."[76] This implies that Quint and Jessel are attempting to manipulate Miss Giddens through the children. But possession and influence are not the same, and there is no evidence that the children are possessed. Their sinister ways could be the result of unwholesome intercourse with the spirits and need not presuppose that the spirits actually took control of the children by inhabiting their bodies. It is possible that as well as ghosts being on the premises, the children have some kind of ESP ability, given Flora's foreknowledge of Miles's early arrival from school.

The film maintains the novel's ambiguity in the sense of a lack of clarity in the presentation, to the extent that many deductions by critics go beyond the information given. For example, Smith considers it clear that when Miles tells Miss Giddens that he likes to lie awake in bed and she responds that it is a bad habit, she is thinking of masturbation.[77] It is equally, if not more, likely that she considers tiredness during the day from insufficient sleep to be a bad thing. It is also a little strong to call her a "pederast."[78] Neither is there evidence for Peter Cowie's suggestion[79] that Miss Giddens is subconsciously attracted to the spirit of Quint, a feeling that comes to a climax when she realizes that Miles's passionate goodnight kiss could be Quint's. The children could have picked up "unnatural" knowledge through associating with the adults when alive, so that they are not possessed but act as if they might be. It is as likely that Miles can see Miss Giddens's repression, and plays on it, as that Quint's spirit still lingers to torment her. The children are clearly manipulative like their uncle (who uses the vocabulary of courtship to woo Miss Giddens to the post), making one wonder whether they needed to be taught by Quint.

Palmer points out the clash of subjective versus third person camera shots in Miss Giddens's encounters with Miss Jessel, the first showing Miss Jessel from Miss Giddens's point of view, but with both of them in the frame in the second and third, undermining what might have been the supposition that Miss Jessel was an hallucination.[80] He feels that even if the

4. Ghost Films 167

camera position seems to be objective, an atmosphere can be created in which techniques such as lighting, framing, shot duration and so on can be utilized to evoke subjectivity. These draw the viewer in such a way that the character's state of mind can be shared. Despite the lack of firm conventions within the film for distinguishing objective from subjective, Palmer thinks that the ghosts are intended to be veridical in both novel and film, although it is a sign of the success of both in balancing the two states that he can advance no firm reasons for his conclusion. Recchia, following Palmer, sees the interjection of objective shots of Miss Giddens and her surroundings, for example the climax when Quint appears, as still able to represent her subjectivity, on the grounds that

> since the story is a subjective account to begin with, any objective shot within it would still be an accurate account of reality as the governess interprets it, whether it be actually shown from the governess's physical point of view or not.[81]

This disposes of the problem of the ghosts' objectivity even though they are clearly visible, but presents its own difficulty: that there are shots when Miss Giddens is absent from the scene, so it is difficult to see how they could represent her viewpoint.

Sounds are often artificially loud on the soundtrack, but although they signal something abnormal in the state of Bly, they do not specify what it is. The fact that sounds in the garden stop prior to Miss Giddens's sighting of Quint/Miles on the tower could either be the aural equivalent of a point of view shot, the sighting being subjective, or it could be, in Palmer's expression, "the prescient response of the external world to the supernatural."[82] Another explanation for the silence is a finding by Andrew MacKenzie in his study of retrocognition. He has noted how silence and stillness are characteristic of reports of timeslips,[83] so perhaps rather than Quint's being a ghost on the tower in the present, Miss Giddens was transported back to when Quint was alive.[84] If so, something paranormal was certainly happening at Bly, but the subjectivity/objectivity issue would remain for non-timeslip periods.

When Flora asks Miss Giddens whether one would walk around on earth if bad, given that her prayer says that one only goes to Heaven if good, the idea is set up that she could have Quint and Miss Jessel in mind. The idea of remaining earthbound if evil is a conventional one, although the culpability of Miss Jessel, who seems to have been corrupted by Quint, is questionable. This forms part of a theme of personal accountability and the unforeseen consequences of actions. Miss Giddens takes on responsibility for combating what she sees as malevolent entities, while surrendering it with regard to Miles's expulsion from school, which she ignores and rationalizes away, with disastrous consequences. Mrs. Grose refuses to acknowledge any problems, though her inaction also has negative consequences. Miss Jessel has apparently been seduced by Quint, not appreciating that the results could follow her beyond the grave. Miles and Flora perhaps consort with evil spirits, not knowing or caring about their souls. Even the uncle abrogates his responsibility for his wards, which might be seen as callous given their bereavement and carrying potentially harmful psychological effects.

On balance, there is more is going on at Bly than the destructive hysteria of a repressed governess, even if it is never clear precisely what that something is. The ghost explanation is the most probable, but is not essential. Smith argues that both are necessary, that they complement each other rather than being mutually exclusive.[85] This is too easy, surrendering the need to analyze the dynamics of the situation and how they interact with Miss Giddens's narrator. Ultimately the status of the ghosts might not matter except that the question involves the degree of responsibility that Miss Giddens bears for Miles's death. If they are subjective, and Miss Giddens is delusional, Miles's death is pointless and she bears the blame. If they are objective and the children possessed, while her actions might be seen as erroneous—she never says how forcing Miles to acknowledge Quint would help—she deserves some credit for her sincerity and courage, though a conclusion that leaves Miles dead cannot be counted "a major victory over the forces of evil."[86]

The Haunting (1963)

SYNOPSIS: Psychical researcher Dr. Markway gathers a group to investigate Hill House, which has a history of supernatural phenomena (a resumé of these is provided in an initial voice-over): Theo and Eleanor, both of whom have had direct experience of the paranormal, and Luke, nephew and heir of the present owner. Eleanor is neurotic and introverted, having spent most of her adult life nursing her invalid mother, who has only recently died. Theo on the other hand is outgoing and confident, at ease with her sexuality. Hill House is an amazing place, built in such a cunning way that it is easy to get lost in its maze of rooms and passages. It is somehow alive. On the first night Eleanor and Theo are in bed when they are awakened by a booming sound, and the following day writing in the hall, referring to Eleanor, is discovered. Markway finds a cold spot, a classic poltergeist symptom, outside the nursery and determines that this is the heart of the house. During the second night, the women hear loud voices, although the words cannot be made out. Frightened, Eleanor holds what she thinks is Theo's hand, but when the light is switched on she is shocked to discover Theo on the other side of the room. Eleanor has had a crush on Markway and is devastated when his skeptical wife, Grace, arrives. Determined not to succumb to what she sees as nonsense, Grace insists on sleeping in the nursery. That night, the original four sleep in the control room, but the booming begins and the door buckles alarmingly. When they reach the nursery, Grace has disappeared. Eleanor is drawn to the library and climbs its dangerous spiral staircase. Markway follows to rescue her, but as he begins to lead her down, a face appears at the trapdoor above her. Realizing the influence the house has over her, Markway decides that Eleanor must leave, but she wants to stay, feeling that she has found home at last. As she is driving away, she sees a running figure in white — later revealed to be Grace — and she crashes into a tree, killing herself. Markway says that it is safe to reenter the house as it has what it wants.

The Haunting, directed by Robert Wise in 1963, is an adaptation of Shirley Jackson's 1959 novel, *The Haunting of Hill House*. Despite having a contemporary setting, the film is firmly in the Gothic "old dark house" tradition. Dyson, who devotes a chapter of *Bright Darkness* to it, considers it to be "the best ghost movie ever produced."[87] Wise began his directorial career with Val Lewton, who was noted for his emphasis on suggestion rather than the graphic depiction of horror. Similarly, *The Haunting* does not show monsters, but hints at a presence stalking the house, mainly by the use of sound and a quasi–Expressionist style. Using infra-red film for contrast and wide-angled lenses so that parallel lines appear to converge, combined with unusual angles, he emphasizes the eccentricity of the architecture; the work of Charles Addams is mentioned in several contemporary reviews. Misty dissolves add to the unreality of the mise-en-scène, as does the unsettling music.[88]

The house becomes a major character rather than merely the setting for the film. The chiaroscuro suggests a brooding mystery into which the characters have stumbled, and over which they have no control. Shots of objects in the house take on the point of view of the house itself, identifying the roaming camera with some unseen entity stalking the building.[89] Language is used particularly effectively to generate ambiguity, and when pronouns are used it is often difficult to tell to whom they apply. Images and dialogue combine to tease the viewer in the attempt to interpret the film's meaning. Even the title of the film is a kind of ectoplasmic smoke before it forms the words.

The story begins with a facetious voice-over by Markway, the chief investigator, giving an impressionistic rendering of the house's character, after which he narrates the flashback to the house's history. He equates hauntings with evil old houses, which he avers constitute an undiscovered country waiting to be explored, the reference clearly a link with death. Even at this stage there is tension between the camera telling the audience "as it is" and Markway's anecdotalizing voice-over, the tension between the two highlighting a major problem of investigating spontaneous phenomena. The house, Markway says, was born bad, although he contradicts this when he states that the evil began the night the original owner's daughter, Abigail, died. He mentions the ingredients of Hill House with a relish that proves to be naive — scandal, murder, insanity and suicide — prefiguring later disquiet about his competence. These attributes make it perfect for his purpose, which is to investigate the house and its supposed ghosts. He has invited a group of individuals to join him, but only two, Eleanor and Theodora (known by the more unisex name Theo), have accepted. The party is completed by Luke, the owner's nephew, who is there to keep an eye on his inheritance. He is the resident skeptic, trying to explain away the phenomena until he too is convinced by the evidence.

The house is an analogue of the warped sensibility of its original owner. It had been built ninety years before by Hugh Crain, but his wife had been killed the day they moved in — her carriage had crashed against a tree by the side of the drive moments before she would have set eyes on the place. Hugh lived in the house with Abigail,[90] and married again, but his second wife also died there in mysterious circumstances. We see her close a door at the top of the stairs, which promptly opens itself again as she walks away (doors, with their metaphysical connotations, become a recurring motif throughout the film). She looks and her eyes widen in terror, although we do not see what she sees, then backs away and tumbles down the stairs. At the bottom, we have an upside-down shot of the hall — her point of view, although she is dead, a disturbing image suggesting the continuation of personality after death. The voice-over resumes by telling us that Crain later moved to Europe, where he dies, leaving Abigail alone.

It is hinted that the deaths of his wives had sent Crain insane, but the house was already built to his eccentric plan, so perhaps he had a predisposition to mental instability. There are no square angles, which means that the topography is unpredictable and it is easy to get lost, perhaps spiritually as well as physically. Also, none of the doors will stay open. Abigail lived alone save for a paid companion, and the transition of the child into an old woman is achieved by careful dissolves. The companion ignored Abigail's cries in her last hours, and local gossip had it that the old lady had been banging in vain on the wall for the companion, who was dallying on the veranda with a man, putting pleasure before her job. The companion inherited the house but lived on her own, eventually committing suicide by hanging herself from the railings at the top of the spiral staircase in the library. This could have been an act of remorse, or perhaps something in the house forced her. She does it in style, carrying the rope up on a silver tray. We see her feet fall into the shot, after which the camera races down the stairs, suggesting a presence that had been with her.

After this lengthy prologue we cut to Eleanor at home with her sister and brother-in-law, the clean lines of a modern apartment contrasting with the heavily ornate style of Hill House. Childish music is playing, but it is not clear if it is diegetic or not. Eventually Eleanor turns off the radio after what is obviously a rare flash of defiance, but not before she is associated with immaturity. Her sister manipulates her guilt over the death two months before of their mother, still raw for Eleanor, and treats her like a child, as the mother, who used her like a servant, must have done. Eleanor has been invited to Hill House and wants to go, but the sister refuses to allow her, obliging Eleanor to steal the car that is half hers. Her first-ever act of rebellion ironically leads to her death. Indeed, Eleanor driving out of the underground parking garage onto the Boston street is reminiscent of Marion in *Psycho* (1960) driving away from her familiar life, and both have a fateful appointment at a 'spooky' location.

There is a parallel between Eleanor and Abigail. Eleanor had been ground down by a demanding mother (in the absence of a father) as Crain's daughter would have been by a strong-willed father (in the absence of her mother), until Eleanor is neurotic and unloved, and Abigail lonely. Both remained unmarried, and it is clear that Eleanor has no experience of men, despite being in her thirties.[91] She blames herself for ignoring her mother on her last night, just as Abigail was ignored by her companion. Normally she would have taken her mother's medicine in, but that night she was tired and miserable. Her sister plays on this to retain control, taking the mother's place and even referring to Eleanor as "young lady."

Perhaps this parallel is what attracts the house to Eleanor. Of all in the group, the house concentrates on her, her personality is gradually absorbed, yet she is flattered that she is its object of attention. She feels it is alive, and likens herself to a small creature swallowed whole by a monster that can feel her movements inside it (at which point she puts up her hands to her mouth like a mouse). She is willingly seduced, because although the house may be destructive, at least it takes an interest. Significantly, the nervous blink that Eleanor's niece torments her about is totally forgotten at Hill House. A supposed eye defect, symbolizing a lack of perception as well as a neurotic symptom of repression, is unnecessary in the liberating atmosphere of her new environment.

Driving to Hill House, Eleanor fantasizes about having her own home, rather than sleeping on a couch in her sister's living room. Before even seeing Hill House she longs to belong. On arrival she feels disgust, but once she is convinced that her desire to belong has been reciprocated by the house, she is adamant that she will not leave. She meets the caretaker, Dudley, and his wife. Mrs. Dudley has a set speech not designed to put visitors at ease, her determination to finish it, however inappropriate the circumstances, hinting at some form of dissociation from reality. The couple are rather menacing, the fact that Mr. Dudley is played by Valentine Dyall, the BBC's *Man in Black*,[92] adding a sinister dimension. It is unclear whether the house has made them strange, perhaps as a defense mechanism, or if they were attracted to it by a morbid predisposition. Going up the stairs, Eleanor is startled by a bust of a young girl, which looks like the figure of a child later identified both with Abigail in the conservatory and perhaps with herself. The place is overfurnished but comfortable looking, like Hammer period film sets. Charlene Bunnell, enthusiastic to portray *The Haunting* and *The Shining* as key films in the transition of the Gothic tradition into film, refers to the inside of the Hill House as "dark and dank,"[93] but there is no evidence for dankness.

At the age of ten Eleanor had been the focus of a poltergeist incident, although she denies this vehemently when questioned by Markway.[94] According to him the evidence for the poltergeist had been good, although Eleanor says that it was the neighbors, as if afraid that she might be the locus of an unexplained power. At one point Theo defines a poltergeist as a "playful ghost" and Markway does not mention RSPK (Recurrent Spontaneous Psychokinesis, presupposing a living human agency). Unless Markway considered Eleanor to possess PK, there would not have been much reason for her presence, although RSPK is unlikely to account for the strength of the activity, nor the history of the house, suggesting as it overwhelmingly does a discarnate presence.

David J. Hogan, on the other hand, considers Nelson Gidding's script to make it clear that the events are caused by Eleanor rather than a ghost.[95] According to Gidding himself, while Wise had treated it as a straightforward ghost story, Gidding had come to the conclusion while writing the screenplay that the story was actually about a mental institution, with Eleanor as the patient, Markway the physician, Theo another patient, Mrs. Markway the head nurse and Luke a male nurse. The noises are inside Eleanor's head and are caused by medication, other phenomena are the result of ECT. When this theory was put to Jackson, she had accepted that it was an ingenious interpretation, but was not what she had intended.[96]

Eleanor is passive, masochistic, and lacks a strong self-identity. She is narcissistic — her most commonly used word is "I" — and she consistently attempts to turn the conversation in her direction. Theo snipes at her, suggesting that she does things because she craves attention. Much of the narrative is composed of her internal monologues as voice overs. She considers herself to be on a spiritual journey, failing to realize that the house is spiritually bankrupt. She acts the victim, seemingly doomed from the start. Even as she and Theo tour the passages on their first evening Theo remarks that the house is calling to Eleanor, who gradually loses her sense of self until she cannot tear herself away.

Theo has been chosen because of her ESP abilities, and she does show sensitivity to her environment. It is impossible to disentangle whether she is psychic or extremely perceptive. She is able to tell when phenomena will stop by how cold she feels, but gets as lost as Eleanor on their first night. Markway says that she had guessed correctly 19 out of 20 cards in tests at Duke University. Presumably he is referring to J. B. Rhine's Zener card experiments at Duke, in which runs were of 25 cards, not 20.[97] In either case a single run would not tell one much. Theo does beat Luke five times in a row at gin rummy, despite his attempts to cheat. Her laboratory success contrasts with Eleanor's uncontrolled, if true, spontaneous exploits. Theo represents control and manipulation, Eleanor loss of control and denial. Theo's character is self-assured, "beatnik" and Greenwich Village in appearance, though with a vulnerable side.[98] She does not supply a surname, and has a penchant for theatrical poses. She is breezy, not taking Markway seriously, and solicitous towards Eleanor, but can be antagonistic, passing this off as teasing when Eleanor overreacts. She seems to be jealous of Eleanor's closeness to Markway, for example getting irritable when Markway compliments Eleanor for realizing that a lot of small wrong angles add up to a big one. She is nasty when she says that *she* does not think that Eleanor killed her mother, the implication being that somebody else, perhaps her sister, even Eleanor herself, thinks that she did.

Eleanor calls her "unnatural," on account of her sexuality, although it is in fact Eleanor who is unnatural in her morbidity, whereas Theo is healthily secure. Perhaps there is some ambivalence, though. Asked what she is afraid of, Theo replies that she is afraid of knowing what she really wants, clearly a reference to her sexuality. Holland claims that the lesbianism was added to the film,[99] but there are a number of references to a friend in the novel with no gender specified, which is itself suggestive. Wise has said that he cut a scene that made her lesbianism too obvious, so that the audience could decide for itself.[100] This does not prevent Phil Hardy from decrying this element, arguing that the film presents Theo's lesbianism as unnatural and paralleling Eleanor's hyper-sensitivity to the paranormal, both becoming part of an attack on women and maternalism throughout the film.[101]

We meet Markway as he is trying to persuade Hill House's owner to allow him to lease it for a few weeks. He is an anthropologist rather than a parapsychologist, but later explains that his background suits him for this type of work. He distinguishes between "ghoulish" and "ghostly" on the first evening, defining ghoulish as a feeling of horror accompanied by a drop in temperature and ghostly as something visible. By this criterion, the events at Hill House are definitely ghoulish, as nothing is seen, whereas a temperature drop accompanies events, at least for Theo, and they establish that there is a cold spot outside the nursery. Markway has not approached trained parapsychologists, instead he has invited people who have had psychic experiences. His rationale is that they might help to stimulate phenomena, but he does not consider that they might be biased. Perhaps he only wants people likely to have less scientific knowledge than he has. Theo and Eleanor have had no training that is mentioned, and Markway treats them as a conduit rather than as colleagues. He is surprised that neither has checked the history of Hill House but is pleased, stating that innocence of its history will make them receptive. For him ignorance is a virtue. Of the six who originally agreed to come, four fail to arrive (perhaps they researched the house). Skeptical Luke is there for selfish reasons, not the pursuit of knowledge. Markway tries to get him to open his eyes, to the extent that by the end of the film he wants the house to be destroyed.

Markway brings no equipment save questionnaires for the assistants to fill in each evening — not even as events occur. By this period cameras, still and ciné, and tape recorders were standard in investigations of this scale, with other paraphernalia such as tape measures, talcum powder, sugar, string and candles used as conditions warranted.[102] Also, despite talk of carrying out experiments, Markway does not specify what they will be. He says that his purpose is to *prove* the existence of the supernatural, so he is clearly being unscientific.[103] He refers to the Borley case, which even by 1959 had been unfavorably scrutinized, though not with universal agreement.[104] Borley may have been an influence on Jackson, and therefore on the film, because Borley Rectory and Hill House share in common cold spots and wall writing.[105]

The major incident that Markway experiences before the last night is a harp playing that he characterizes as preternatural, although he knows as little about its cause as he does about anything else that occurs. We never see a presence but its influence pervades the house. It toys with the team, but Markway the expert especially, by excluding him from the bulk of the events. When he tells Eleanor and Theo that the doors shut of their own accord he attempts to demonstrate but the door stays open as if to contradict him. Later when they look, it is shut. He does not seem to be in control, and his competence is also questioned when he walks into a broom cupboard despite having studied a map. When he and Luke are lured outside by barking and Eleanor and Theo are terrorized, he hears nothing going on inside. He points out that the phenomena cannot hurt Eleanor and Theo, only their own fear, but this cannot be very convincing after what they have experienced. On their last night, it is hard to believe that a force powerful enough to cause doors to bulge would have difficulty opening them.

During the first night Eleanor is awakened by a booming noise, perhaps the house trying to communicate, or perhaps its pulse, promoting the idea that it is a living organism. She sleepily thinks that it is her mother, and knocks on her wall, as Abigail had allegedly knocked in vain for her career. Theo jokes that it must be "earth tremors," and as if in response it gets louder. The noise changes, becomes more echoey. Scraping sounds can be heard and the booming returns. Eleanor bangs on the door and it stops momentarily, then begins again. The handle turns, and shots of ornaments convey an impression that the presence is inside as well as outside the room. Female laughter or crying can be heard. The temperature drops (although the perception of a drop in temperature could be caused by shock). The appearance of Markway and Luke after their wild dog chase defuses the tension for both Eleanor and Theo, and the audience.

At breakfast, Markway says that Eleanor's excitement at the events is a sign that she is falling under the spell of the house, to which Eleanor coquettishly implies that Markway himself could be the cause of her excitement. When Luke finds chalky writing in the hall, saying "Help Eleanor Come Home," Theo suggests that Eleanor likes to be the center of attention and perhaps even wrote it herself, which upsets Eleanor, and shows how high-strung she is. Nobody mentions that the height of the writing makes it unlikely that Eleanor, or indeed Theo, was responsible. The party visit the conservatory and discuss the sculpture there, ostensibly of St. Francis curing the lepers. Luke thinks that the group is symbolic of the house's past residents, and Theo mention that the "companion" looks like Eleanor. Theo herself would be "Abigail," and Markway would be "Crain," Luke being relegated to the dog. So in addition to the earlier parallel between Eleanor and Abigail, another is set up between Eleanor and the companion, who both neglected their duties. Theo suggests that Eleanor ask if 'Crain,' now associated with Markway, would like to dance. There is a shifting series of identifications between past and present occupants of Hill House that cannot be pinned down given the absence of a definite explanation of the phenomena and their cause.

Tension between Theo and heterosexual Luke flares, and Markway orders them out of the conservatory before, as he puts it, somebody gets hurt. Eleanor is unable to enter the library, symbol of learning and self-knowledge. She smells a strange odor, though nobody else can, which reminds her of her mother. The others go in, but Luke finds that the staircase is dangerous. Eleanor goes onto the balcony and leans back, looking at the tower. She talks in voice over of somebody climbing out, and the reverse shot of her could be the point of view of the house or one of its residents. She is losing her balance, literally and metaphorically. Markway catches her, only for Theo to discover them in what appears to be a compromising position. Markway is worried at Eleanor's unreliability, and Theo prophetically remarks to Eleanor "You look like death." Markway discovers a cold spot in the hall by the nursery that he says would not register on a thermometer, not that he ever uses one. This he calls the "heart of Hill House," for Theo it is the "doorway to a tomb." That night Theo sleeps in Eleanor's room for mutual security. Hogan implausibly comments that "the similarity of the names Eleanor and Theodora suggests that the women represent opposite sides of a single sexual persona,"[106] one dominant and healthy, the other timid and unhealthy. If the names were similar, it would more likely imply a loss of difference between the two rather than the strong contrast they exhibit.

Their beds have been pushed together. In the dark, Eleanor hears a male voice whose words cannot be made out, but it sounds like a preacher declaiming, and is perhaps Crain. A female voice can also be heard indistinctly. The distorted sounds complement the geographical distortions of the house. The female voice is crying and screaming, and Eleanor becomes angry at what she thinks is ill treatment of a child, as if it were really happening. She thinks that she is holding Theo's hand, but when she switches on her light she discovers that Theo is on the other side of the room, although how she got there is as unclear as what was going on outside the room. She realizes that rather than Theo's hand, she was grasping Something Else, some kind of simulacrum of Theo's hand, though clearly not revolting, Eleanor's complaint being that it was holding her hand too tightly.

For Eleanor, the journey to Hill House has been an escape, and now she declares that "journeys end in lovers' meetings." Is she referring to Markway or the house? Repeatedly Eleanor talks of "he," and it is not clear if she is referring to Markway or Crain. Theo becomes increasingly hostile, talking of the story Eleanor had made up about her non-existent flat, obviously a fabrication, and of Eleanor's desire for Markway. She teases Eleanor about Markway, provoking Eleanor to attack Theo's lesbianism as "Nature's mistake." She has been slow to catch on, as she had earlier asked Theo if she were married.

Markway's skeptical wife Grace arrives, saying that a reporter has heard what he is doing, and angry that her husband is, as she sees it, wasting his talents. The pair are distant emotionally and Markway is perhaps henpecked, which sits uneasily with his suave manner as an investigator. Eleanor is crushed to discover that Markway is married, and rather nastily suggests that Grace sleep in the nursery. They had not been able to open it previously as they did not have the key, but now it stands ajar. Grace wants to see if the phenomena are genuine and brushes Markway's protests aside. The cold spot she decides is a draft. Like Luke earlier she airily dismisses the phenomena until forced to confront their reality.

Markway decides that the original four should sleep in the control room downstairs. Eleanor is literally foregrounded in the shot, and we hear her voice-over clearly, but Markway's and Theo's voices only faintly, stressing her self-absorption. This is one example of the frequent back-projection used with Eleanor, the cumulative effect of which is to make her stand out from her background, suggesting alienation, being out of kilter with her environment. That night Markway, Eleanor and Theo are sleeping, and Luke is supposed to be on guard upstairs, but he comes down for a drink. Suddenly the door slams shut as if the entity has found the opportunity it was waiting for. All four hear the booming outside the door and see it buckling. Markway wants to go to Grace, in case she does something foolish, not understanding the power of Hill House. Luke initially prevents him, and when he reaches the nursery, Grace has disappeared. Eleanor's isolation is emphasized by having the other three fade out as she walks forward.

Eleanor runs off down the corridors, distorting lenses mirroring her state of mind. In the conservatory she talks to the statue of the figure they have dubbed Crain, and tells him "We killed her, you and I, Hugh Crain." It is not clear who "her" is, or even whether it is the same for both. Eleanor could have her own mother in mind; she could be referring to Grace, making herself complicit in the disappearance by suggesting that Grace sleep in the nursery; to Crain's second wife, stressing her own identification with Abigail, if Abigail had been responsible for the second Mrs. Crain's fall down the stairs; or Eleanor could be identifying with the companion who neglected Abigail and was seen as responsible for her physical death, just as Crain was responsible for stifling her spirit.

Eleanor feels that she is being absorbed by the house. Drawn to the library, she climbs the spiral staircase, the camera's tracking up mirroring the race down after the companion's death, and linking them both. The others arrive, and comment that the smell has gone and it is no longer cold. Markway climbs up the staircase after Eleanor, who is calm, with all traces of nervousness gone. The lack of atmosphere and her sudden self-possession provide some kind of psychic resolution. She shrinks back from Markway, and it seems that she is thinking of hurling herself off the balcony, but Markway grabs her. As she is being rescued, she hears a noise, looks up and sees a face staring out of a hatch that turns out to be Grace, although the identity is not immediately apparent — we just see a wildly staring disheveled face, and given all the talk of the companion's having committed suicide at that spot, it could be taken for her ghost. Markway does not see the face as he is leading Eleanor away, and as soon as Eleanor looks up, the face retreats and the hatch closes.

After bringing her down, Markway decides over her protests that she has to be sent away. Eleanor feels that Grace has taken her place, which is unfair. She is desperate to stay, and states of the house: "It's alive" (!). Markway says that he should have sent her away earlier, something of an understatement. Eleanor is reluctant to go, and spins out her leave-taking, to the extent of making the humiliating confession that she has only her sister's couch to return to. In the background we see leaves swirling, and Theo pulls her coat about her, conveying the possibility that the entity is present.

Driving away, Eleanor crashes into the same tree at which Crain's first wife died. Perhaps she wants to die so that she can be absorbed by the house, but she also sees a figure in white who is later found to be Grace, running parallel with the drive in her gown, and is possibly distracted. Grace does appear to be wraith-like as she runs through the trees. The crash, from Eleanor's point of view, is unclear; she sees Grace, then crashes, but she might have been swerving already. Alternatively, perhaps the steering wheel is being influenced and Eleanor is fighting it because she does not want to die. She asks "why don't they stop me?" But is she referring to Markway's party? They can't help her given her speed. Or is she referring to the "residents" of Hill House, and if so, why should they want to stop her dying and joining them? The survivors too are not sure what happened. After Grace emerges, disheveled, from the grounds, Theo says that Eleanor lost control because she saw her. Grace, another skeptic humbled, says that Eleanor saw her only at the last instant, and Luke concurs, saying that she seemed to aim at the tree. Markway goes back into the house over his wife's protests, but he claims that it is safe, as the house, for the time being, has what it wants.

The book has a famously circular structure, and the film emulates this, except that the concluding voice-over is the dead Eleanor's, suggesting that she has been absorbed — Markway's original voice-over "Whatever walks" becomes "We who walk." This is not altogether a negative outcome, because Eleanor has achieved what she wanted, and fantasized about on the journey to Hill House, a home, and with it unconditional acceptance. The other major difference between the beginning and end is that Markway's opening uses the past tense and Eleanor's uses the present tense (Bunnell confuses the issue by quoting the book, implying that it is the same as the film[107]). For Eleanor, time is static, her future assured in a way it could not be before. This play with duration is reinforced by the structure of the film. In chronological terms the action takes place over two days but it appears to be longer on screen, leading to an unsettling effect.

A major theme is what is natural and unnatural, and whether such qualities are innate. When Markway discusses the house with its owner, they disagree as to the aetiology of the phenomena. For the owner, the house was born bad, and evil is part of its nature, ineradicable. Markway shifts his position, or else is imprecise in his rhetoric. He argues that the place is sick and deranged, the inference being that it is capable of treatment, perhaps considering Abigail to be the cause, despite his initial voice-over stating that the house was born bad. The debate is one of nature versus nurture, but it is impossible to tell who is right, although by the end the implication is that the house is incapable of being healed, once more showing Markway to be misguided.

No conclusions are drawn about the nature of the phenomena, despite the film's unequivocal title. Luke humorously mentions the local mayor's theories, such as underground water (G. W. Lambert's hypothesis which was popular in the 1950s[108]) and sunspots. Markway had said that psychic phenomena are subject to laws, but the occupants would not know what they were until they were transgressed. By the end, the investigators are still no wiser as to their constituents. Naturalistic explanations are dismissed as shallow and not worthy of consideration. Possibly there is a gaggle of ghosts present, the "We who walk here," and voices that might belong to identifiable individuals, such as Hugh Crain and Abigail, are heard. No ghosts are seen, and if they are present it is a mixed case because of the poltergeist elements.

There are alternative interpretations. Silver and Ursini offer mass hallucination,[109] but more seriously, the house possibly stores some kind of residue of hatred and is acting as a battery that needs damaged individuals to feed it. If purely a poltergeist, it could be caused by Eleanor (RSPK), a hypothesis also posited by Silver and Ursini. Sexual repression (there is little doubt that Eleanor is a virgin) might be fuelling the situation. A discarnate entity could be responsible, though again there is the problem of identity. Theo might be the focus: feeling cold could imply that her energy is being used, and her barely concealed hostility to Eleanor hints at seething emotions underneath her sophisticated exterior. However, RSPK is unlikely because of the complexity of the events and the seeming display of intelligence (teasing the "expert" for example). Questions, such as were the events caused by Crain or Abigail, would Eleanor have survived if she had been a stronger person, how much energy might be required to feed the house, how was that energy husbanded in the absence of tenants, does the house draw on Theo's hostility towards Eleanor, does Eleanor commit suicide or is she somehow forced to drive at the tree, are left unanswered. The house remains an enigma.

The Shining (1980)

SYNOPSIS: Jack Torrance, an aspiring writer struggling with an alcohol problem, is hired as caretaker of the remote Overlook hotel during its winter closure. At the interview he is told that the previous caretaker, Grady, murdered his wife and daughters. Jack moves there with his wife Wendy and son Danny. During their tour of the kitchen, Hallorann, the cook, and Danny share a moment of ESP, the "shining," and Danny is warned not to enter room 237. As the weather worsens, Jack finds it increasingly hard to write, and his behavior becomes unreasonable. Danny meets Grady's daughters who invite him to play with them, forever and ever. He also enters room 237, and when Wendy finds him in shock, she accuses Jack of assaulting him, though Danny later says an old woman hurt him. Jack spends time in the bar, where Lloyd, the ghostly bartender, talks to him. When he goes to room 237 at Wendy's behest, he finds a young woman in the bath, but when he embraces her he sees she has transformed into a rotting corpse. Despite this, he tells Wendy that he found nothing in the room. Danny is becoming increasingly detached, and Wendy wants to take him away for treatment, at which Jack, now under the hotel's influence, becomes angry. He destroys the radio and immobilizes the snowmobile. Grady tells Jack that Danny is trying to signal to Hallorann in Florida, and that he must deal with his family. Jack attacks Wendy, but she knocks him out and locks him in a storage area. Hallorann receives Danny's message and sets out for Colorado. Grady releases Jack, who breaks into the family flat with an axe. Hallorann arrives, but Jack kills him. Danny escapes from the hotel and hides in the maze, backtracking so that Jack becomes lost. Wendy and Danny leave in Hallorann's snowmobile while Jack freezes to death. A final shot tracks in on a photograph of a 4th of July ball from 1921, with Jack in the center.

The Shining (1980), based on Stephen King's 1977 novel, can be interpreted as dealing with the interrelationships between ESP (of an undefined type that appears to include clairvoyance, telepathy, precognition and retrocognition),[110] the malign influence of a haunted hotel, and the psychological breakdown of a father and the adverse effect on his family. Its iconic status is indicated by its use in *Twister* (1996) as the film playing at the drive-in which is destroyed by a tornado.[111] Most literature on the film has dealt with the family dynamics, which Hogan sees as the primary strength of the novel,[112] although the ghosts have been afforded a certain amount of scrutiny.

Determining the film's meaning has proved problematic for critics, particularly with regard to the performances of Jack Nicholson and Shelley Duvall. A number of them found they were disappointed that the film did not live up to its promise to be the scariest horror film ever made. James Hala suggests that the conventions are undermined at the points at which the audience should be frightened, for example during Jack's attack on his family.[113] Greg Smith, examining the difficulties faced by the film's first critics, argues that the film is "unnerving precisely because of the tension produced by the conflict among the horror film conventions...."[114] Perhaps this *pavor interruptus* can be seen as akin to a Brechtian alienation device, distancing the audience from the horror so that they are prevented from submerging themselves within the action, and Smith draws attention to the way in which the (specifically U.S.) audience is confronted with unappetizing aspects of itself—concerning sex, class, and particularly race—by director Stanley Kubrick.

In the face of narrative confusions and psychological incoherence, a number of commentators have seen the Overlook as a symbol of the United States, that its

> ghosts are real, capable of driving men mad, and that the most dangerous ghosts of all are the myths of success ("The American Dream") and of the authoritarian father.[115]

One method of trying to tie together the incoherences is to see the film in terms of levels or subtexts. For example, Smith identifies three subtexts, revolving around politics, sexuality and the family.[116] Similarly, Leibowitz and Jeffress identify three levels to the film, each with its own temporal, though overlapping, segment—the fantasy, the family and the shining levels. Leibowitz and Jeffress see the three levels tied together by room 237: Jack meets the nude/hag there (fantasy level); he is exhorted by Wendy to visit it after Danny's experience (family); and Danny fears the room, and had been warned about it by Halloran (shining).[117]

An aspect not considered by Leibowitz and Jeffress is that the three levels could intersect if the phenomena were created by the Shining ability, events reactivated by a combination of undetermined varieties of ESP and PK.[118] They locate the ghosts on the fantasy level, but there are two problems with this categorization. The first is that they are pigeonholing the ghosts a priori when the supernatural provides the underpinning structure for all three levels, as the allegedly paranormal events power the narrative. The family breakdown is accelerated by Jack's discussions with the management, as well as his slide into madness and obsession,[119] and Danny's encounters with the girls and in room 237. The second is that Grady's freeing Jack takes the ghosts to a more concrete plane than fantasy. The fantasy level interpenetrates the other two, and cannot be separated. Christopher Hoile argues that the ghosts are natural to Jack and Danny but uncanny to the viewer because Kubrick has made them substantial and linked them to a specific historical period.[120] This is the general difficulty of estimating the degree of identification between viewer and character, but there is no evidence to suggest that Jack and Danny, and particularly Wendy when she finally sees the phenomena at first hand, find the ghosts anything but uncanny.

Much of the criticism of the film has concentrated on teasing out metaphors in the film. David A. Cook sees the film as "less about ghosts and demonic possession than it is about the murderous system of economic exploitation..."[121] and Titterington also divines a social element, the coldness epitomizing modern life, the hotel a metaphor of the United States and of Hollywood.[122] Peter Nicholls, rather than seeing the Overlook as a metaphor for America, instead sees it as a "metaphor for the inside of Jack's skull,"[123] bringing the focus down to individual psychopathology. This reductionist view implies an extreme approach that sees the film as Jack's solipsistic fantasy.[124]

Stephen Snyder also sees the film in terms of a metaphor concerning the United States, in this case the attitude to leisure with its empty consumerism and antipathy to work — to the extent that insofar as Jack spurns activity he "is, to a considerable degree, a ghost himself."[125] Larry W. Caldwell and Samuel J. Umland too examine the play metaphor in *The Shining*,[126] and decide that the film is parodic and self-reflexive, which undermines any serious intent and cuts off meaningful discussion. In support of their contention, it is true that the paranormal elements do not cohere, comprising rather a catalogue of separate incidents with more or less connectivity to typical real cases. The viewer struggles to make a meaningful pattern in terms of categories such as psychic ability and haunted house narratives, but the film slides free of any one overarching explication. This is far from saying, as Caldwell and Umland propose, that the play metaphor "obviates the film's aesthetic force and therefore undermines any "serious" intent."[127] The play metaphor is clearly present, and its meaning elusive, but playfulness does not equate to meaninglessness.

If the film is seen in symbolic terms then the precise status of the ghosts and other supernatural phenomena is irrelevant, as they are simply carriers for a meaning external to themselves. Liebowitz and Jeffress also see the film as a metaphor for the United States, the hotel standing for its emptiness and moral bankruptcy, "initially seductive but once embraced it shows itself rotting and destructive — like the mysterious woman in room 237."[128] Smith draws attention to the film's examination of racism — the treatment of the Indians whose land was expropriated for the hotel, a literal erasure of a culture from the land, Hallorann's position, subservient but with hidden depths, Grady's snobbish accent, despite having been only the caretaker, and dismissal of Hallorann as a "nigger," thereby showing Jack that if he wants to serve the management, he will have to lose his liberal sensibility.[129]

It is conceivable that the events are to be seen as either subjective *or* objective, or the film could be showing both subjective and objective phenomena but failing to cue the audience as to which is which. Where the two are incompatible, their clash could be regarded as a post-modernist game. William Paul sees this confusion beginning with Jack's visit to the bar,[130] where it is not clear whether Lloyd exists. A more subtle instance of this obfuscation is the "redrum" scene. Danny repeats the seemingly meaningless word over and over, before "murder," which he is saying backwards, is written on the door, which means that he must have had a shining of it reversed. But why did he see it backwards clairvoyantly rather than the right way round? To see it reversed, he would also have seen it in the mirror, that is, his shining would have adopted the audience's point of view. Another example is the girls in the corridor. They could be evoked by Danny's shining, be a reconstruction of his imagination, perhaps in concert with his ESP, or could be veridical apparitions. If this elision of objective and subjective is intended, *The Shining* would be similar to *Jacob's Ladder*, which again does not have markers to distinguish subjective, and therefore potentially unreliable, states.

Michel Ciment, however, draws attention to the dissimilarity between the everyday scenes with camera movement, particularly the use of the

Steadicam, and the static form of the paranormal scenes,[131] which provide a demarcation. It is feasible that Jack could be hallucinating within a haunting context. James F. Smith sees the shift from the haunted hotel aspect to Jack's psychosis, fuelled by or creating his self-obsession, as excluding the motif of love so important to the novel:[132] "Where Stephen King wrote a novel about evil possession, Kubrick shot a film about psychological disintegration."[133]

The "torrents" of blood (possibly a visual pun) pouring from the lift pose a problem for the interpretation of events as either veridical or as clairvoyant apperceptions. The fantastic manner of the flood, which leaves no trace, can only be seen as an authorial interjection. Perhaps it represents the blood of the hotel's victims, including the Indians, hitherto pent up but now released by the presence of the Torrances. Indian motifs are ever-visible, signifying their presence, their genocide a backdrop to the desire to kill that characterizes the hotel.[134] The film can be seen as a revenge tragedy, past misdeeds haunting the present, though Kubrick, by omitting much of the historical detail in King's novel, softened this aspect. Bunnell sees the blood as the very life essence of the vampiric hotel, emphasizing that it is a living entity in its own right,[135] Hoile as the primitive breaking through the supposedly more advanced.[136]

The Overlook becomes sinister once the other workers have left. Until that point, on closing day, it is bustling and friendly. Fear thrives on isolation, which is when the phenomena begin. Once the Torrances are alone with little outside stimulation, social or mental, a condition conducive to cabin fever, they enter a receptive frame of mind. Sensory deprivation is a recognized technique to induce paranormal processes, and in a sense this is what happens to the three living occupants. With so little to occupy themselves other than monotonous routine, their thought processes turn inwards. The fact that Room 237 is made up suggests that during the season it is used for guests, with no untoward occurrences. The ghosts may be veridical, but it takes a certain state of mind to see them.[137]

There may even be an interaction between psi and the phenomena. Jack possesses a modicum, as indicated by his view of Wendy and Danny in the maze,[138] and he becomes more responsive through his link with the management. Danny and Hallorann have 'natural ability," though not good enough in the latter's case to enable him to see Jack hiding behind a pillar,[139] and both see things only there for those who have "eyes" to see. Wendy would be expected to be sensitive, if conforming to the gender stereotype, but she is not. Her comment that the hotel will be like a ghostship after the staff have left is more accurate than she appreciates. She is denied visions until the climax, when the emotional tension, often cited as a significant factor in RSPK cases, enables her to cross the threshold necessary for awareness. That Danny and Jack both see the inhabitants so clearly for such a long period before Wendy is evidence that Jack too possesses the shining, although to what extent is not made clear. If the ghosts are acting on a subjective level, it is also interesting that Jack is told by Grady that Danny is attempting to contact Hallorann telepathically. Perhaps Jack is aware psychically that the distress call has gone out, but the more plausible explanation is that the entities are objective, and have the power to monitor Danny's "calls."

The ghosts cannot be analyzed in isolation from the dynamics of the family, and particularly the role of psi or psychic ability. Danny's and Hallorann's ESP is underexplained in the context of the haunting, as is the amount possibly possessed by Jack and Wendy[140]; Snyder argues that Wendy only sees the ghosts once she has been stripped of cultural illusions,[141] but unlike her husband she is not hypnotized by them. This hints that the ghosts would have been accessible to anybody, including the Overlook's regular staff, but that seems unlikely. Kubrick appreciated that he had to make the ESP imperfect,[142] and because of King's neologism he was able to move away from the public and scientific connotations of the better-known descriptions. The term *Shining* itself may have been drawn by King from John Steinbeck's "play novelette" *Burning Bright* in which it is used, at the very end, in the sense of a noble quality inherent in all humans, despite their manifest imperfections: "With all our horrors and our faults, somewhere in us there is a shining. That is the most important of all facts. There is a shining."[143]

Hala suggests that the much-criticized acting styles can be explained by assuming that events are seen from Danny's point of view, a perception formed by media images, such as Roadrunner cartoons, which are frequently violent.[144] This would explain the cartoonish behavior, although the action is clearly not always seen from Danny's point of view, so that the audience would have to be co-opted to stand in for him during his absences. It also throws into doubt the precise status of the paranormal events, even when Jack or Wendy is present, as they too could be distorted by his preconceptions, as his parents are. Some could even be created by Danny's shining ability.

Hoile quotes Kael's question as to whether the tensions within the family create the ghosts, or whether the latter are the catalyst that enables the tensions to destroy the family, and concludes that the processes are intertwined rather than one being dependant on the other.[145] The role of psychic ability and hauntings intersect in the film, but their relationship begs more questions than it answers, such as whether psychic abilities are necessary and sufficient to create the phenomena, and whether Grady alive possessed them. In turn, are these abilities common, and if so, why does Wendy, whom one would suppose to be sensitive to the needs of her son, not have them to a greater extent?

John Brown delineates two approaches, the psychological (*Turn of the Screw* model) and the metaphorical.[146] He sees *The Shining* as colliding these two normally discrete approaches in a deconstructive post-modern collage that alienated both viewers and critics when it was released—"supernatural realism" as Mark J. Madigan puts it.[147] The hypothesis that the events are products of Jack's imagination, tenable at first, cannot survive his release from the store.[148] (Grixti interprets the hesitation caused by this uncertainty in more traditional Todorovian terms.[149]) In turn it is bizarre that "impersonal forces of evil" cannot manage to arrange satisfactorily to kill Wendy and Danny, and do not intervene when Jack fails dismally.[150] As a result of this collision, criticism is rendered fruitless as interpretations contradict each other, and themselves. This meta-theoretical treatment is interesting, although as with all such approaches, it sees itself as immune to the relativistic difficulties that it identifies as undermining all previous attempts at exposition.

But Brown is too dismissive of the ghosts as veridical rather than as vehicles for metaphor. The two approaches do not collide; the ghosts cannot be hallucinatory, because of the release from the store (the information supplied by Grady has to be set aside, as it could have been obtained by Jack using ESP), but there is nothing to undermine the theory that they do exist, perhaps powered by negative emotions. That they lack plausibility, and do not participate fully in the narrative, is no argument against their existence. There is no reason why supernatural beings should be amenable to human reason, which is not the same as their fulfilling a part in a post-modern program. The beautiful woman turns into a hag possibly because the hotel is toying with Jack, showing him that it can fool him with an illusion, mocking him, in much the same way that a woman turns into a rotting corpse in *Ghost Story* (1981) in order to terrorize those responsible for her death and their children.

Yet the ghosts' being products of Jack's imagination is suggested by the fact that when Wendy finds Jack at the bar he is alone, whereas before he had been talking to Lloyd and drinking, despite the alcohol's having been removed at the end of the season. Mayersberg points out that alcoholics see things that are not there.[151] Or Jack could have entered a timeslip, particularly when the party is taking place in the Gold Room, and is in their era, rather than in an echo of the party occurring in Jack's. Given the feeling that the Overlook is a static place, however, this is not likely.

The anachronistic lavatory also does not fit a consistent image of a 1920s hotel. It is still possible that the phenomena are latent and that Jack is somehow generating the psychic energy necessary to power them, as they do get stronger in proportion to his decline.

Grady's assertion that Jack has always been the caretaker is supported by the photograph seen in the tracking shot at the end of the film. It would appear that Jack, if of course it *is* Jack, had been on the staff in 1921 (and he had had a sense of déjà vu about the building, just as Craig has about the house in *Dead of Night*). Support could be provided by the presence of the ghostly guests in the ballroom. If Jack is able to conjure up images from the "real" past as opposed to an imagined one, the 1920s ambience could tie in with his presence in 1921. Leibowitz and Jeffress see the picture as functioning on both literal and symbolic levels, the former with Jack as a member of the group, hinting at a previous existence at the Overlook, the latter with him as a member of the élite in a hotel that symbolizes the country as a whole.[152] Kubrick told Ciment that the photograph hints that Jack has been reincarnated, and Titterington agrees.[153] Romney also refers to "incarnations," but with his present-day self a shadow of his 1921 self.[154] But there is a contradiction between Grady's allegation and Jack's position in the picture. If Jack occupies such a lowly position in the hotel hierarchy, not even meriting a place in "the management," how is it that he has such a prominent position in the photograph? With his tuxedo on, and standing at the front, he certainly does not look like a caretaker.[155]

For Richard Combs, events at the Overlook are powered by Jack's emotional negativity that supplies the psychic force to enable the past to be replayed.[156] This idea accords with negative energies' being used to power the sinister elements of a house, as in *The Haunting*, but more particularly *The Legend of Hell House*. As Jack deteriorates, phenomena increase in their intensity. The issue of cause and effect is raised,[157] because it is possible that the hotel brought out latent insanity in Jack. Several issues, muted in the final cut of the film though still evident,[158] such as Jack's proneness to violence and a drinking problem, indicate that his surroundings are eliciting tendencies in him; Stephen J. Spignesi goes further and contends that Jack's instability is evident from his first moment on screen.[159]

Kubrick claims that he wanted to use uncertainty over the ghosts' reality to slide unnoticed into the supernatural element,[160] but if they are solid, even speaking and interacting with the environment, the default position is going to be that they are independent. However the supernatural events have hitherto been viewed, Grady's releasing Jack undermines the possibility that they might have been projections of his imagination, perhaps powered by Danny's, and Hallorann's, telepathic abilities. Jack possibly opens the door using PK, but this is less likely than an external agency. If the hotel does have an intrinsic power, the question remains as to why, after Jack has failed to dispose of his domestic difficulties to the extent that Grady has to release him, the hotel allows Jack to fail again while doing nothing to help. This is evidence against the interpretation that the ghosts are veridical, but we are never told the extent of the building's powers. A seeming arbitrariness could be the result of adherence to rules that the viewer cannot fathom, which may be a weak riposte, but the evidence does point to the reality of the phenomena.

The uncertainty over Grady's first name suggests an undifferentiation of the supernatural beings, of whatever kind, which would make Thomas Allen Nelson's characterization of the Overlook as "like some impersonal and Kafkaesque corporate state"[161] highly apposite. Either the apparitions could be part of a single entity, the nature of which is undetermined, its status and origin obscure, and for which surface details are immaterial, or the tangible management that employ Jack is so uncaring that they cannot even remember their employees' names (it is possible that Grady's name mentioned in the interview with Jack is a continuity error, but because of Kubrick's perfectionist reputation, it is always assumed that the discrepancy is part of a deeper mystery). There is a hint that the superficial trappings used to present themselves/itself to the world are unimportant. At the same time the deep cause remains inscrutable. Perhaps the film is not a ghost story at all, but rather deals with demon possession. Or perhaps the recurrent Indian motifs prefigure those of *Poltergeist* (1982) in which the drama arises from the failure of the developers to move an Indian graveyard when building the estate.[162] On another level, Jack's declaration that he would sell his soul for a glass of beer playfully suggests a pact with Satan (emphasized by Lloyd's sinister face) and that he is cheap.

The film has a continuing motif of doublings running through it, both physical and conceptual, some of which have been picked out by Nelson (1982) and that Hoile (1984) sees as rooted in a reading of Freud and Bruno Bettelheim, and, it should be added, also in Gothic literature. There are similarities here to the use of mirroring in *Dead of Night*. Examples are the "twin" girls;[163] Grady's two names and two jobs; the two Jacks, the modern one and the 1921 one; conscious versus subconscious processes; the hotel as maze, noted by Wendy on her initial tour when commenting on the kitchen, and the real one outside[164]; the maze and the model of it in the lobby; the young/old woman in room 237; both Jack and the twin girls saying "forever and ever and ever"; Danny and Hallorann's shining;

Jack and Hallorann as father figures; and the shots of reflections in mirrors, such as Jack's breakfast in bed, half of which is shot in the mirror, and the "redrum" scene.[165]

In the interpretation in which the hotel is symbolic of the United States, this doubling could be said to represent the fractured psyche that characterizes the country, culture versus philistinism, past versus future, an emphasis on family in a country where social mobility renders these fragile. It might also be said to encompass light versus dark, life versus death. Perhaps in this sense the haunting is not the theme of the film as much as the struggle of life against its opposite, so that post-mortem existence is merely one more state counterposed to another.

Kim Newman sees *The Shining* as building on previous film hauntings, particularly *The Haunting*, in which Eleanor finds a home she has never had before, at the cost of her life.[166] That is a partial interpretation, as Hill House gets what it wants ("for now") whereas the Overlook, if it wants Wendy and especially Danny, gets only second best, its faithful but disappointing servant. As in *The Haunting* and *The Fall of the House of Usher*, the haunted house is a metaphor for a haunted mind. Rhodes argues that Jack's "quest" is not a complete failure as his death allows him to merge with the hotel,[167] but although he may be satisfied with the outcome, the hotel's attitude is more inscrutable. When Lloyd informs Jack that his money is no good, Jack takes it in a positive light (free drinks), but perhaps Lloyd means it in the sense that Jack's is not the currency they want. Perhaps Jack has too high an opinion of himself, as suggested by the shot of him standing over the model of the maze, king of all he surveys, and later when he makes his study in the huge hall, sitting behind the table like a mediaeval monarch. Being frozen to death (frozen out) would show him his true place in the organization.

The film creates a tension between the haunted house narrative, though one without its traditional trappings, and the slasher-psycho narrative, to the extent that Morris Dickstein criticizes the film for de-emphasizing the former.[168] Instead, "*The Shining* becomes the first horror film which blames it all on writer's block, beyond which it simply relies on madness, as so many cheap horror films do...." This verdict may be harsh, because Wendy surely qualifies for inclusion in Carol J. Clover's category of *Last Girl*,[169] despite Danny's rather than her being responsible for Jack's demise. Even the failure of Hallorann to effect a relief can be seen in a wider slasher context:

> By 1980, however, the male rescuer is either dismissably marginal or dispensed with altogether, not a few films have him rush to the rescue only to be hacked to bits, leaving the Final Girl to save herself after all.[170]

As with *The Haunting*, the hotel picks on the emotionally vulnerable. Bunnell sees both buildings in terms of wicked personalities: "The [Overlook] hotel grows more malignantly evil every day, for like Hill House, it is the embodiment of evil itself."[171] She sees the characters within the hotel as living a purgatorial existence, but no such firm interpretation can be put on the occupants. Purgatory carries connotations of punishment, whereas the Overlook is an amoral world of hedonism.

The reference to cabin fever and the Donner Party of 1846–7 is prescient, as physical cannibalism is translated into spiritual cannibalism. It could also be seen to anticipate the madness to come — the members of the Torrance party being spiritually devoured — but what is significant about the Donner ordeal is that women and children fared relatively well, as they had family structures to support them, while single men, outside the family support network, coped less well.[172] Similarly Wendy and Danny survive because they remain bonded as a family unit, while the isolated male, with no assistance from the forces at the hotel, dies.

Frank Manchel tries to amend the usual focus on Wendy and Danny by pointing out that Jack, outside the safety of the family, is as much a victim as they are, and dies — a casualty of the hotel's insistence on the preservation of traditional sex roles[173] — while they escape.[174] While stressing that he is not condoning child abuse or violence towards women, Manchel comments that his family's failure to try to understand his problems "contributes significantly to Jack's embracing the 'warmth' of ghosts." Support for this view is perhaps the scene in which Wendy comforts Jack after hearing about his dream of dismembering her and Danny, but then leaves him when she discovers that Danny has been attacked in room 237. Jack sits watching the two, and in his unbalanced state could be feeling excluded, that he does not count compared to Danny, the space between him and the others in the huge hall representing the emotional gulf between them.

The timelessness dimension is an aspect of the film that Kael noticed, referring to "the timelessness of evil."[175] On a first viewing the intertitles supplying days and then hours seem arbitrary, that time in this hermetically sealed universe is meaningless. But, by following an ever-more restrictive pattern (like heading for the center of a maze), moving from a non-specific date, a month after closing day, through days to hours, the intertitles suggest increasing claustrophobia and an ever-closer climax. Kael may be right in talking of timelessness, but it might entail ennui, so that the Overlook's controlling entities, as at Hill House, may be playing to pass the time, to alleviate the burden of a perpetual existence that is a kind of death in life.

Jacob's Ladder (1990)

SYNOPSIS: Jacob Singer, a soldier in Vietnam, is caught in an event in the jungle in which his platoon finds itself seemingly under attack, and in the confusion Jacob is bayonetted in the stomach. Several years later, he is employed as a postal worker, despite an academic background. Divorced from his wife Sarah, their son Gabe accidentally killed, he lives with a colleague, Jezzie. He is haunted by strange nightmares that seem to originate in his army experiences, and New York increasingly takes on a hellish appearance, the horror alleviated only by visits to his chiropractor, Louis. To add to his confusion, he also experiences an alternative reality from time to time in which he still lives with Sarah and Gabe is alive. A fellow veteran tells him that he too has had terrible experiences since returning from Vietnam, which he thinks stemmed from an experiment in which they were guinea pigs. His story is given credence when he is killed in a car bomb. Jacob meets others who were with him in the army, and they too admit to having suffered in the same way. They agree to launch a group action, and they find a lawyer, but he backs out, saying that they never saw active service. Jacob cannot rally his comrades to continue. He meets a chemist, Michael, who tells him that he had been coerced by the CIA into developing a drug, "The Ladder," which would make whoever took it uninhibitedly violent, but when it was administered to Jacob's platoon in a trial, they had attacked each other; he had been stabbed by a fellow American, not an enemy. Louis tells him gently that he did not survive the ordeal, and that the misery is caused by his attachment to life — it will disappear as soon as he lets go. He returns to the flat he shared with Sarah, where he meets Gabe, who escorts him up into the light. In Vietnam, the doctors acknowledge that Jacob fought hard to cling to life.

David J. Skal suggests that the cultural effects of war can linger on for decades after the cessation of hostilities.[176] Thus many contemporary horror films carry the imprint of the Vietnam War, and Skal gives *Jacob's Ladder* (1990) as an example of a film that brought horror and Vietnam together successfully. It also appears to be one of those, like *Carnival of Souls* (1962), in which the protagonist is dead while the events of the film take place, but, along with the audience, realizes this only at the end, in this instance when Jacob's deceased son Gabe comes to help his father to realize that he is being held back by refusal to acknowledge the truth. The message is that the Afterlife is a state of mind, either good or bad, as thinking makes it so. Jacob's refusal to let go means that he inhabits a nether region in which New York takes on the characteristics of Hell. The film is the struggle of a dying man to stay alive, and the necessity to renounce earthly concerns to find eternal peace.

This is a singular vision on screenwriter Bruce Joel Rubin's part, because it implies that one's deeds are irrelevant to one's eventual fate. There is a similarity to *Ghost*, in that not letting go hinders spiritual progression, but unlike that film, in which good souls go upwards and the bad are collected by demons, how one lives has no bearing on the direction. Hell in *Jacob's Ladder* is a personal state, and as soon as the dead let go, the way upwards is open, so that presumably the most evil are still allowed into a state of grace as soon as they have acknowledged their deaths, as opposed to their sins. If Jacob's chiropractor Louis is trying to help Jacob to reconcile himself to death, he does so covertly, rather than simply telling him what he has to do. In this existentialist universe the decision has to be made by oneself.

Rubin also scripted *Brainstorm*, another film on life after death, but there the angels were Douglas Trumbull's idea rather than Rubin's, who was more interested in points of contact between world religions than in promoting a particular theology.[177] *Jacob's Ladder*'s Afterlife is unlike that found in major world religions. It is an eclectic conception, because overlaid on the Christian imagery is an essentially Buddhist philosophy in which the material is an illusion, and spiritual progression depends upon the sloughing off of the sense of self.[178] He talks of his attitude to death in terms of "an unraveling of ego,"[179] so Jacob could be progressing to some form of Nirvana. The transition is certainly dependant on renunciation, but ironically he is guided to his personal salvation by the strength of his tie with Gabe, and the Biblical names in general give the narrative a specifically Old Testament feel, in line with the Jewishness that Rubin stressed but director Adrian Lyne downplayed.[180]

Newman calls *Jacob's Ladder* "effectively a blunt remake" of *Carnival of Souls*,[181] but it does more than trace the problems a person has when death has occurred without it's being realized. In the most straightforward sense, Mary in *Carnival of Souls*, although she is dead throughout that film without knowing it, is not revealed to be so until the denouement. That is a twist, as before it she appears to be alive, albeit subject to increasingly bizarre experiences. Jacob, though, is seen to be badly wounded at the beginning but is pronounced dead only at the end, and in the meantime switches between different realities, giving events the character of an unusually complex near death experience rather than the depiction of a trip to the hereafter.

Jacob's Ladder more clearly bears comparison with *Occurrence at Owl Creek Bridge*.[182] Like Bierce's story, it plays with the idea that a long subjective period can occur within a short space of time.[183] Jacob's New York existence could be the product of his imagination, a life review made up of memories mixed with desires and fears. This concatenation makes a delineation of the narrative difficult because it is never clear if the events at any one point are flashforwards or flashbacks, subjective or objective. Competing interpretations are permissible, and the audience is forced to share the protagonist's confusion. The authorial overview is collapsed so that there is no privileged information to help decipher the narrative.

As the narrative progresses, the past of Vietnam and the present of New York have roughly equal status, and it is difficult to know which is the hallucination and which the reality. The balancing of the two worlds, the possibility that everything is occurring inside Jacob's head, or that he is inhabiting a real world, albeit a nightmarish one he is increasingly unable to comprehend, bear comparison with *AMOLAD*. The straight cuts in the editing give neither priority over the other. The first transition from Vietnam to New York involves Jacob's waking up on a subway train, suggesting he was dreaming because of the convention that when a character wakes up, what went before was a depiction of that person's imagination. This assumption has to be balanced against the increasingly bizarre events in New York in which eventually even mundane elements can appear to be sinister — when he says that he was robbed by Father Christmas it sounds ludicrous, although he is telling the truth.[184]

Until the denouement appears to tip the balance, it seems possible that Jacob is suffering flashbacks typical of post-traumatic stress disorder rather than a fantasy while in his death throes. The experiences with demons and his kidnapping could be attributed to a combination of the after-effects of the drug and government action to maintain the secrecy of the Ladder chemical warfare scheme.[185] The only person other than Louis to tell him he is dead is the surgeon in the nightmarish hospital, which given the immediacy of the situation, is likely to be rejected. Newman sees Michael's explanation of the Ladder experiment as a red herring[186] but it provides a rationale for the weirdness of New York, and a counterweight to the death reverie interpretation. Even the ending, which seems to clarify the issue (death reverie), could conceivably be part of the trauma-induced flashback; if he has nightmares about being wounded in the war, he could also have them about dying there.

His New York life as a hallucination experienced while dying in the jungle, however, begs the question of how Jacob could know the apparently veridical information on BZ that Michael gives him. If New York is a death reverie, then Michael's information is part of it, and there is no substance to his allegations, it is a product of Jacob's imagination. But the ladder's reality means that the New York life is real as well, throwing into doubt the final image of Jacob dead in the field hospital. The announcement at the end of the film, that BZ was used in Vietnam by the U.S. government, appears to strengthen the reality of Jacob's life in New York moments after we have seen him die in Vietnam.

Strengthening the death-reverie-in-Vietnam theory is Jacob's physical discomfort, events in his pseudo–New York life mirroring what is occurring in Vietnam. He suffers a high temperature, which could account for the sight of his girlfriend Jezzie having a snake wrapped around her, although the flickering lights in the disco, if real, could have triggered an epileptic fit. The trouble with his back could be attributed to a similar cause, physiological symptoms in Vietnam being superimposed on his New York fantasy. The light in Louis's office doubles that above the operating table in the hospital in Vietnam where Jacob dies, both representing efforts to help him, but also links to the hospital where he is tortured, which has a similar lamp.

Apart from the supernatural elements in New York that suggest that these scenes are non-realistic, but which can be explained by the Ladder drug, there are other discrepancies that raise the possibility that Jacob is giving himself a post–Vietnam life in his refusal to accept death. For example, his son Gabe is supposed to have died before he went to Vietnam, yet in his life with Jezzie from the Post Office he has kept a letter from Gabe among his war memorabilia that says that he wants his father to come home. Jacob is also supposed to have a Ph.D. but when he is examining his certificates we only see a master's diploma — there is another certificate behind it that may be the discharge certificate he is looking at in the next shot. When Jacob is kidnapped in gangster cliché fashion, he incredibly manages to fight his three assailants until he falls out of the car.

Undercutting the simple flashback/flashforward dichotomy is the introduction of a third reality, in which Jacob is still married and his life with Jezzie is regarded as a nightmare. This world is not as fully delineated as the other two, and can be more easily dismissed as fantasy, partly because the life with Jezzie is so firmly established by this stage, despite the fantastic elements it incorporates. The fact that in this third life Gabe is still alive, and the family has a comfortable home, gives it the air of fantasy lacking in the seediness of Jacob's post-divorce life as a postman. It still though undermines the viewer's confidence in Vietnam as a flashback from Jacob's life with Jezzie. If the scenes of married life are a dream, nothing else in the film can be trusted.

Yet another possibility is that, as occurred with the main character in *Carnival of Souls*, Jacob died in Vietnam but does not realize it, so that the world he is in is everyday reality, nightmarish to him alone. He continues to persist in this increasingly alien environment until rescued by his son.

To be in this type of limbo it would not be necessary to have ghostly attributes, and those he interacts with could have been entirely oblivious to his condition. Michael's Ladder explanation could be true, and so could Louis's speech about demons tormenting him. This approach is congruent with the death reverie theory, but it is also possible, although less dramatically satisfying, that rather than the struggle occurring in Vietnam, it is occurring in New York.

An objection to the near-death experience interpretation for Jacob's flash forwards is that NDEs are usually reported as being benign experiences with a well-documented structure. It is surprising that a dying person would have to endure such negative imagery, particularly if NDEs are viewed as wish fulfilments. However, there is a literature on 'Hellish' NDEs and Kenneth Ring, in a discussion of them in which he proposes a typology and reasons for their occurrence, cites *Jacob's Ladder* as a good example of one particular type.[187] He sees negative NDEs as inversions of positive ones, in which the individual finds it difficult to let go of his or her ego, creating fear and leading to the negative experience. Once the struggle ceases, it becomes positive, and a sense of peace is felt. The hellish experience that Jacob suffers can be seen as an extreme form of the negative type that does not necessarily switch to being a positive experience. Ring's view has been scrutinized by Christopher Bache, who makes the point that surveys have estimated the incidence of negative NDEs at between 1 and 22% of the total.[188] As an NDE, Jacob's type of experience would not be that rare.

Whatever its ontological status, New York's nightmare world possesses a sexual undercurrent, emphasizing the perverted environment of which Jacob is a victim. Lyne cites Francis Bacon as an influence on the film and reports that he wanted the look to be "all human-based — sort of *thalidomidey*—fleshy, horns from the bone, a tail that looks a little like a *shlong*...."[189] During Jacob's first unsettling experience on the subway, he sees a phallic-looking tail under the tramp. Jezzie looks as if she could be having sex during the party, and the snake that coils through her legs takes on the character of an enormous penis. Jacob is seen in intimate situations with both Sarah and Jezzie, but these are rare positive moments, sex the rest of the time taking on an unpleasant aspect. The stress on sexuality does not help us to prioritize one reality over the other because it could either represent Jacob's yearning for life filtered through his death agony, or be an aspect of his breakdown induced by the Ladder.

The film is shot through with Biblical references, from the characters' names to the film title itself, each with a symbolic weight suggesting a transcendental religious experience, but eluding a simple mapping of the modern person onto the Biblical prototype. Together they strengthen the death reverie scenario if Jacob has embraced the consolation of religion, for which a dying person might wish. The effect is to reinforce Jacob's New York life as a meditation on the Afterlife. In Genesis 28:16, Jacob has a vision of a ladder stretching between Heaven and Earth, with angels ascending and descending it. He is as confused as his modern namesake, thinking "Surely the Lord is in this place; and I knew it not," just as Jacob Singer is able to go to Heaven, but does not appreciate what he has to do to get there. In the film, the Ladder has an extra dimension. As well as linking Earth and Heaven, the ladder also goes down into a personal Hell. The choice Jacob Singer is faced with, to let go and travel upwards, or to cling to an illusion and travel downwards, mirrors a psychological struggle, one reaching either down into the dark forces of the personality, isolated and alone, or up to the warmth of companionship represented by Louis and Gabe.

Of the major characters, Gabe and Michael the chemist are the closest to their portrayal in the Bible, though even here the correspondences are loose. Archangel Gabriel is a messenger, as Gabe acts as a catalyst to enable his father to realise what he needs to do. The present-day Michael, in his way also a messenger, bringing news about what happened in Vietnam, is paralleled by "the great prince who standeth for the children of thy people" (Daniel 12:1), and who gives a long prophecy to Daniel, perhaps reflecting modern Michael's role in explicating the plot for Jacob and the audience. Other characters seem to bear no relationship to the Biblical ones, name choices an arbitrary tease, a challenge to find significance where there is none: Sarah, wife of Abraham, has difficulty conceiving to the extent that she persuades Abraham to have a child with their slave, as opposed to Jacob Singer's fecund wife Sarah, who has had three children.

Elijah is Jehovah's champion, challenging the priests of Baal but running away when threatened by Jezebel, finally disappearing from Elisha's view in a "chariot of fire" that has been seen by later commentators as evidence for ancient visitations by aliens,[190] and which adds to the supernatural resonances of the name. There seems to be no connection to Jacob's son Eli, whose most significant act is to give his father the photographs that Sarah was going to discard, and that Jezzie later throws into the incinerator. In the "hanging on" scenario these pictures can be seen as either a help to Jacob to move on by showing him the dead Gabe, or a hindrance by reinforcing the joys of living, reminding him of the good times.

Jezebel, a high priestess of Baal who seduced her husband Ahab from the worship of Jehovah, was unremittingly wicked, unlike the more complicated Jezzie, who does not like "Church names,"[191] and demonstrates a split in her character, being kind and caring one moment, but impatient and hostile another (she dances with the snake at the party, which precipitates the medical crisis, and is present when Jacob is trapped in the hospital, preparing the syringe). Her predominant color is black, and in this she contrasts with the lightness of Gabe. She both helps and hinders Jacob: she destroys his pictures in the furnace, suggesting a hellish destination for the memories that tie us down, an act that might be expected to help Jacob by freeing him from earthly ties. Yet she pulls Jacob back from the brink of death when this could have been his chance to let go, and asks him not to meet Michael, a meeting that prepares him for his eventual reconciliation with the beyond.

Most odd is Louis. He is likened by Jacob to an angel, but his name is similar to Lucifer. Fortunately Louis is a positive character in Jacob's life, giving the key speech to Jacob that because he is fighting death, the angels that would be helping him if he were to let go are perceived as demons tormenting him. The exception of course is Louis himself — his sincerity is never in doubt. He possesses the attributes of an angel, giving advice, rescuing Jacob from the hospital, and acting as a channel between Jacob and Sarah. He wears white, and has a bright light like an angelic halo over his shoulder as he works. Even his job operates on two planes, straightening Jacob out both physically and spiritually. It does not require Jacob to mention that Louis looks like an angel for those qualities to be perceived. His precise status, however, is unclear. Fry sees him as a New Age spokesperson,[192] and his attitude towards angels and demons, seeing them as equivalent, is unorthodox from a Christian perspective. His reality is reinforced by his quoting Meister Eckhart, whom Jacob says he has not read. Unless one appeals to cryptomnesia, or Jacob is lying for some reason, it would seem that Louis exists independently of Jacob's mind.

In addition to the homogeneity of the names' biblical character, the final scenes, culminating in Gabe's escorting his father "into the light," lean heavily on the side of the film as death reverie rather than psychotic breakdown brought on by exposure to hallucinogenic substances. The taxi driver asking where home is, the doorman saying "Dr. Singer — It's been a long time," suggest resolution, peacefulness after struggle, and an acknowledgement that Michael's information has curtailed the need to know that held him back.

The fact that he goes to the apartment he shared with Sarah rather than the one he lived in with Jezzie gives his life with Sarah a greater weight than it had enjoyed previously in the film. Yet while exuding peace and domesticity, the place is unsettling. It looks hastily vacated, the television on but displaying snow — filmic shorthand implying that it has been on a long time — dirty plates on the table, and exercise books and mathematical equipment suggestive of school homework abandoned. This is not the earthly apartment he has come home to, but a mental replica. Desires abandoned, and inner peace found, Jacob can move to a higher spiritual plane. The relative paucity of detail compared to life with Jezzie could symbolize the letting go, or it could be a sign that Jacob's brain, in its terminal stage, does not have the capacity to generate a more complex environment.

The end of the film seems to indicate that the New York life, with both Jezzie and Sarah, is a wish fulfilment conjured up during Jacob's death struggle. The Vietnam surgeons agree that he fought to stay alive. Any contradictions or bizarreness in New York can be accounted for in terms of a dying brain attempting to create a stable model and only partially succeeding. But a pre-mortem experience, however close the percipient to death, is no guarantee that a post-mortem state would be the same, though the possibility exists that there would be a continuity. The pre/post-mortem continuity issue was addressed in *Flatliners*, but part of the problem in *Jacob's Ladder* is that there is no way of knowing whether Jacob was exhibiting a flat EEG while having the hallucinations: brain activity indicates a near-death experience, a flat line supports the reality of the Afterlife. Given the unsophisticated resuscitation technology available in a field hospital, that we go to New York immediately after he has been bayoneted, and that he is declared dead on an operating table in Vietnam, he must have lived for some time after being wounded. One cannot be certain that Jacob really enters the light after brain activity ceases. All possibilities might die with him, but the optimism of the scene with Gabe gives hope that Jacob does go up his personal ladder.

5

Conclusion

> The repeated reënactments of the two-hundred-year-old murder are spooky, beautiful, and passionate; they're a poet's distillation of the mechanical nature of movies.[1]

Pauline Kael's verdict on *High Spirits* (1988) highlights the parallel between film and life after death, the medium's ability to preserve a moment beyond the lives of its subjects, thereby providing an ersatz Afterlife. It has been a recurring motif among commentators. As early as the Lumière show of 22nd March 1895, one of the two reporters present wrote:

> With this new invention, death will be no longer absolute, final. The people we have seen on the screen will be with us, moving and alive after their deaths.[2]

Thomas Edison, writing the same year in the preface to W. K. L. Dickson's *History of the Kinetograph*, saw his attempts to synchronize film with phonographic sound resulting in "grand opera to be given at the Metropolitan Opera House at New York ... with artists and musicians long since dead."[3] In 1896, Maxim Gorky, having visited Lumière's Cinematograph, was concerned that cinema provided a pale imitation of life (literally), "a life without color and without sound ... the life of ghosts."[4] Graham Greene amplified this feeling that the preservation of life on film is simultaneously the preservation of life after death in a 1937 radio talk:

> One really begins to feel that the cinema has got a history when it's so full of ghosts. Miss Jean Harlow walking and speaking after death. ... Past and future are hopelessly intermingled. The man is moving on the screen and at the same time he is dead....[5]

Greene hints at a *frisson* that seeing a dead person moving on screen should give, knowing that he is both there and not-there.[6] Yet this type of ghostliness the viewer does not find disturbing. A film featuring a dead actor playing a ghost does not lend itself to irony, because the overriding sensation is of an ever-present *now*. Past becomes present for the film's duration, life transcends death, and immortality is achieved.[7]

More recently, Denis Gifford claimed a necromantic function for cinema as "the only medium truly to revive the dead,"[8] and Hermann Hecht echoed the theme that, "in one sense, we are always looking at ghosts! ... a reproduction and imitation of reality."[9] He is right in a sense, but a distinction must be made between a case in which no personality element is involved (as when a picture is projected on a screen, and perhaps in certain "Stone Tape"[10] types of haunting, characterized as energy traces imprinted in the fabric of a building) and that of ghosts which can be inferred to exhibit personality. Peter Wollen uses psychical research terminology in an even looser metaphorical sense, talking of the audience's being "haunted" by characters.[11] By the time he talks of cinema's being "an art of ghosts," it seems flabby rhetoric.[12]

Film might have a phenomenological similarity with apparitions as some form of duplicate without consciousness impressed upon the surroundings, but if that constituted the post-mortem state, then one could not agree with the journalist at the 1895 screening that death is no longer final, if by that he meant continuation of awareness. Mark Sanderson is perhaps acknowledging the double meaning in the word "presence": "And what are movie stars— who are said to have presence — if not professional ghosts?"[13]

Film lends itself to paradox: the gaze becomes reflexive as the viewer is aware that the gaze's recipient is an impossible object, tangible and intangible. Marina Warner argues that photographs exist in a liminal state "at the frontier of materiality and immateriality," perhaps corresponding "to the mysterious, ungraspable frontier between body and spirit,"[14] and this is extendible to cinema. Like the ghost, it is neither living nor dead, but instead occupies some intermediate terrain. Warner points out that the Greek *skia*, or shadow, was also used for shade or ghost.[15] She uses the term *Skiagraphy* in the conventional sense of painting with shadow, but it could as easily refer to painting with death, and the title of Jean-Louis Schefer's 1985 paper, *Thanatography, Skiagraphy*, foregrounds the link.[16]

Stephen Neale refers to the parallel between the unreality of the image seen on the screen and the unreality of ghosts in quoting Christian Metz's discussion of perception: "... the perceived is not really an object, it is its shade, its phantom, its double...."[17] Having a spirit depart from the body

5. Conclusion

in the form of a double exposure arising from the corpse and walking away neatly avoids the difficulty of establishing the ghost's provenance.[18] The idea of film's capturing the essence of the photographed subject and preserving it in a kind of Afterlife, irrespective of the manner of consumption, is still with us, despite the development of ever-more-sophisticated technology. Erik Barnouw refers to current modes of image transmission as a "magic industry," summoning up "ghosts of yesterday ... electron apparitions as ephemeral as images projected on smoke."[19] He is right that there is a sense of continuity in ghost shows stronger than technological discontinuities.

In one way, though, reception of the supernatural has changed. Whereas now film is not seen in the context of magic, for earlier viewers the image always had a magical significance. One might argue that Méliès was the originator of film fantasy, the Lumières that of some form of realism, but the first consumers did not see the dichotomy. The 1978 Brighton conference on early film threw up the problem of a teleological reading of film reception, and it has been a theme in the subsequent exploration of the term "primitive" when applied to cinema. For early viewers, possible versus impossible would have been a meaningless distinction, one that would have arisen with the hegemony of realism.

Ghosts' non-representational codes elide the differentiation. The ghost film has license to draw attention to technique that contravenes the continuity style. In *Wonder Man* (1945) the sight of a ghost standing inside a pedestal elicits the comment, "What is this, trick photography?" (photography that helped to win an Oscar). In the same year Jack Benny at the conclusion of *The Horn Blows at Midnight* muses "if you ever saw it in the movies you'd never believe it," and in 1946 Conductor 71 in *A Matter of Life and Death* complains of being starved of Technicolor in Heaven. Tyler talks of the "phoneyness" of "Hollywood artifice," by which he means the unconvincing mise-en-scène of many allegedly realist films.[20] The problem of determining how fantastic is a particular film, is made complicated when realism itself is problematic, lacking an unambiguous demarcation with fantasy.

Ghost films can be seen to be subject to "the interplay of difference and repetition."[21] Waller is mainly discussing vampire narratives, but the same principles apply to ghost films. Vampires enjoy unparalleled brand recognition whereas the ghost is heterogeneous because its attributes are less formalized. The latter stands above history and cannot be reduced to crude metaphors, as for example the economic and sexual ones that Franco Moretti finds in Dracula and Frankenstein.[22] There is no single iconic ghostly figure in the sense that there is an archetypal iconic vampire or mummy. Ghosts are more flexible than their supernatural neighbors, being threatening or friendly, helpful or obstructive, comic or pathetic (or a mixture). The variety of depictions illustrates the lack of a consistent image. These form a palimpsest capable of continual renewal. The ghost straddles too wide a spectrum and is ultimately pressed into service in too many causes to be confined by a single shape and style. As Peter Jackson says of *The Frighteners* (1996):

> ...with ghost movies there are no rules. You don't have to stick to cinematic conventions like you do with vampires or werewolves. You can do anything you want with ghosts because no one really know what they are or how they operate.[23]

The relationship of the living and dead can be seen as the negotiation of a boundary.[24] Boundaries can be opaque, but they can also be permeable, like that between living and dead, and the dead themselves can range from the incorporeal to those who are indistinguishable from the living.[25] Permeable membranes are also associated with erogenous zones. That death and sexuality are connected is suggested by the demon lover. The lamia of classical literature has characteristics typical of many sexually predatory cinematic ghosts. The question arises why one side should trespass on the other. It could represent a dread of the other, the unknown intruding into the safe and quotidian, showing how we can be repelled and fascinated at the same time. The films present an approach/avoidance conflict; we hate it but we cannot look away. The ghost film packages up elements of transgression and melancholy, our desire for a better life to come, our fear of nothingness, or even a worry that we will be called to account for earthly sins.

Perhaps it is this that causes the occasional metamorphosis of the ghost into a figure of fun — an escape valve for what would otherwise be too horrible to contemplate. Some periods show a preponderance of horror comedies, perhaps coinciding with economic depression or used as a means to subvert censorship, as Andy Boot suggests,[26] but it is a constant strand. The humor frequently revolves around an old dark house, with the activity due to the agency of a living individual (although the criminal activity of the living can be intertwined with phenomena caused by ghosts). Possible threats of censorship against the excesses of horror was a problem that comedy could help to assuage, but fundamentally these spoofs show confusion towards death by weakening the intensity of the response.

Fictional ghosts can be seen as a kind of dress rehearsal. That brings into question their frequent negativity, as one would expect a wish fulfilment to be positive. James B. Twitchell splits horror's attraction into three components:[27] it allows society's fears and taboos to be explored in safety; it lets repressed urges escape in fantasy; and it acts as a manual of human sexuality. In fulfilling these functions it deepens our understanding of the human condition. Afterlife films allow exploration of worries concerning death.

Twitchell's third aspect, the inculcation of sexual mores, is less relevant to these films than to those dealing with vampires, zombies, the Frankenstein creature, werewolves and so on, because whereas in those sexual activity has negative consequences, that in ghost films is ambiguous. The erotic aspect expands the possibilities of sexual conduct. For every film in which a revenant seeks revenge on a faithless lover, there is another in which human and spirit conjoin willingly. Cinematic ghosts frequently wish to continue to engage in sexual activity, or the living might seek some form of attachment, particularly when death has not impaired the alluring quality of the deceased. This amounts to a projection of necrophiliac desire. Unacceptable sexual attraction for a corpse can be channelled into the more worthy hope for another's survival. If ghosts are a race apart, then congress with them must be seen in terms of miscegenation. It is significant that interracial sex between living and dead is unknown (not that it is particularly common among the living on film) — perhaps a taboo too far.

That ghosts stand as an emblem of memory can be seen from a comparison of two scenes, formally similar but containing different clusters of meanings. In *All Quiet on the Western Front* (1930), dead German soldiers are superimposed over a cemetery as they march away upwards, looking back. At the climax of *Goodbye Mr. Chips* (1939), pupils who have attended the school during Chips's tenure walk past in a grand roll call, condensing his memories as he lies dying. Like the soldiers, the boys are shown in double exposure, as if ghosts. They may or may not be dead (they are drawn from a career that has spanned half a century, and included the Great War), but they are seen as they were when pupils, existing in an eternal *Now* in Chips's memory. The camera acts as that memory, in which recollections return in ghostly form. In *All Quiet on the Western Front* the scene suggests a fantasy summation, though it could be veridical. The schoolboys' parade on the other hand has never existed in that form but is a synthesis of Chips's memories. In both cases the camera stands in as spectator to concretize an idealized state, in one nobody's point of view, in the other an individual's.

There is also an oft-cited relationship between films and dreams. Dreams often provide film characters the opportunity to lapse into an altered state of consciousness that can provide a carrier for ghosts to appear. The frequent appearance of ghosts in dreams to provide information or advice, or even merely to offer comfort, obfuscates the issue of their reality. Like dreams, ghosts can be illogical, obeying laws different from those of the physical world. The opening shot of *Rebecca* (1940) makes the link clear, when the unseen narrator talks of her dream, in which she revisits Manderley and is able to go through the gate "like a spirit."

Christie argues that the maturation of film around 1908, with its increasing realism, created a change in the treatment of dreams.[28] Whereas before they had been coterminous with the narrative, "dreams made visible," now "the supernatural and the subjective" were delineated as being outside the narrative, possessing a different status. This is true to an extent, as cinema moved away from roots it had in stage magic, but throughout the medium's history certain films have attempted to blur the distinction between objective and subjective, playing on film's inability to penetrate the surface of character,[29] instead relying on viewer inference, which can be manipulated. Hence *Jacob's Ladder* (1990) confuses the viewer's expectations of what constitutes a subjective state, so that hesitation is experienced in the attempt to ascertain whether the film depicts reality or an internal monologue analogous to a dream state. In that sense, Christie would be obliged to argue that Lyne's film is closer in style to Méliès than to almost everything else being produced today, which is clearly not the case; emphasis on narrative and realism does not exclude the subjective and supernatural.

It could be argued that horror allows the viewer to cathect excessive emotions, of both fear and horror, and transpose them into a celebration of life, not a desire to surrender it. Horror films, as their literary ancestors did, liberate the consumer from restricted norms, social and aesthetic. They allow "what if" questions to be explored in the safety of the imagination. These can be both positive and negative, but simply asking the question hints at a continuing desire for separation, not its loss. The potential vacuum of death creates a void into which are projected images of continuing life as a consolation. We may not be able to conceive the absence of being, but we can imagine some extension of our present lives, loved ones translated not in the condition in which they died, but some idealized state, a wish fulfilment in which disease and infirmity are discarded. Decrepitude sloughed off, the ghost will enjoy full vigor, with complete mental and physical faculties.[30] Or we can see the personality in analogical terms, as a shade or reflection of the earthly self. In *Witchboard III: The Possession* (1995), the spirit of a possessed man takes the form of images in mirrors and shiny surfaces.[31]

5. Conclusion

The cinematic ghost hints at a theological conservatism: if one supernatural being, the ghost, can exist, then there is no reason why another, God, should not. This is particularly the case when Heaven is shown, or references made to "Him." Of course there is no logical necessity why the continuation of life after death should imply a theistic framework, and an atheist could consider the evidence for survival to be strong in the same way that a Christian would, without recourse to faith. Yet in cinema ghosts are usually seen in terms of a higher spiritual dimension, frequently because they are fated to retain an earthbound state until the completion of a task or the redemption of a sin. An apparition explained in terms of physics could be encompassed within a framework that would not require a religious component. Those films in which continuation of awareness is maintained by scientific as opposed to naturalistic means are less likely to indicate a wider moral universe predicated on the existence of a Divine Being.

The Afterlife, when it is represented at all, is seen most frequently in ghost films in Christian terms, but the *Star Wars* films present a pantheistic *Force* that is a mystical but non-denominational theological framework that allows individuals to develop exceptional psi abilities and also to survive the body's dissolution. Both Obi-Wan Kenobi and Yoda are still able to give Luke advice after death, if death is the appropriate word for what is more akin to a translation to a higher plane in much the same form that Spiritualists conceive human spirits moving upwards after death, having the ability to communicate with those living beings with enough sensitivity to receive the messages.[32]

The desire for immortality can be seen as a significant factor in the propagation of the ghost story, but bound up with the longing for continuation is an impulse centring on rebirth into a higher plane, a transcendental experience (which Constance Markey ties in with a Nietzschean reading of such films as *Somewhere in Time*, *Altered States* and *Star Trek II*[33]). By this criterion, if some form of consciousness is able to survive by the power of will, she/he/it could be regarded as a type of superman or superwoman. That does depend on the laws governing the Afterlife. Some effort of will may be required, or being "reborn" may be as undemanding of the will as being born into this life.

These films deal to a large extent with ethical issues, not only in the demonic-inspired ones, but in more straightforward ghost tales as well. There is the additional problem of free will, particularly evident in films in which the ghost is obliged to atone for an earthly misdeed. They can act as a focus for irrationality, a challenge to our complacency. They also raise the issue of optimism. Horror films tend to arouse feelings of negativity, and even when victory over a supernatural adversary is assured, it is usually more with a feeling of relief than of hopefulness. Kubrick, though, has said in a semi-syllogism that:

> ghost stories appeal to our craving for immortality. If you can be afraid of a ghost, then you have to believe that a ghost may exist. And if a ghost exists then oblivion might not be the end.[34]

The ghost story is "a promise of immortality"[35] to Kubrick. It should be added that he did not believe in Hell, so was able to focus on the benefits of an Afterlife rather than its possible disadvantages. The cinematic ghost continues a fascination with the supernatural that has lasted for thousands of years. It might be argued that it is a form of attempted escapism reflecting dysfunctional fears. James McClenon, though, sees "the capacity to experience anomalous events"[36] as evolutionarily beneficial, with those social groups unable to have these experiences at a disadvantage. In Darwinian terms, its continuation suggests that it had some function that enabled its possessors to survive. From this perspective, supernatural films perform a positive psychological function by maintaining mental well-being.

A film may conclude with the words "The End," but to be consistent ghost films should add a question mark. Their endless capacity for renewal suggests that films pertaining to the Afterlife, touching as they do on a fundamental issue, will be of continuing interest. They will mutate as cinema evolves, just as film took advantage of other media involving ghosts. Perhaps one day some kind of Star Trek–style holodeck will be programmable with the results of personality profiles, so that individuals may enjoy vicarious immortality. The original consciousness would be absent, making them no more than 3-D home movies; but just as people stare at photographs and films of loved ones who have died, hoping thereby to link with them once more, so the simulacrum would function as a comforting link. Whatever form they take, as the pressbook for *The Haunting* (1963) proclaims, "Ghosts are not a dead subject,"[37] and they never will be for as long as we speculate on the mysteries of human existence.

Filmography

Silents

Title	Director	Date	Country
Alcofrisbas, The Master Magician	Méliès	1903	France
The Apparition	Méliès	1903	France
At the Villa Rose	Elvey	1920	GB
Au Secours	Gance	1923	France
The Avenging Conscience	Griffith	1914	USA
The Avenging Hand	Calvert	1915	GB
The Bells	Young	1926	USA
The Bewitched Inn	Méliès	1897	France
The Bewitched Traveller	Hepworth	1904	GB
Beyond	Taylor	1921	USA
The Cabinet Trick of the Davenport Brothers	Méliès	1902	France
The Cave of the Demons	Méliès	1898	France
The Conquering Power	Ingram	1921	USA
The Corsican Brothers	Smith	1898	GB
The Devil in a Convent	Méliès	1899	France
Dr. Mabuse the Gambler	Lang	1922	Germany
Dr. Trimball's Verdict	Hepworth	1913	GB
Earthbound	Hunter	1920	USA
The Fairy of the Black Rocks	Pathé	1905	France
Feet of Clay	DeMille	1924	USA
The Gambler's Wife	Smith	1899	GB
The Ghost	Biograph	1911	USA
The Ghost of the Moulin Rouge	Clair	1924	France
The Ghost of Old Morro	Ridgely	1917	USA
The Ghost Train	Biograph	1900	USA
Ghosts	Plumb	1912	GB
The Greatest Question	Griffith	1917	USA
The Guyra Ghost Mystery	Cosgrove	1921	Australia
The Haunted Castle	Méliès	1896	France

Title	Director	Date	Country
The Haunted Curiosity Shop	Paul	1907	GB
The Haunted Hotel	Blackton	1907	USA
The Haunted Scene Painter	Booth	1904	GB
How It Feels to Be Run Over	Hepworth	1900	GB
The Infernal Cauldron	Méliès	1903	France
The Inn Where No Man Rests	Méliès	1903	France
Intolerance	Griffith	1916	USA
J'Accuse	Gance	1919	France
The Kid	Chaplin	1921	USA
The Knight of the Snows	Méliès	1912	France
The Magic Sword	Booth	1907	GB
The Man That Might Have Been	Humphrey	1914	USA
The Man without a Soul	Tucker	1916	GB
Mare Nostrum	Ingram	1926	USA
Maria Martin, or the Murder in the Red Barn	Winslow	1902	GB
The Market of Souls	Ince	1919	USA
Mary Jane's Mishap	Smith	1903	GB
The Medium Exposed	Martin	1906	GB
The Mermaid	Goncharov	1910	Russia
The Miser's Doom	Booth	1899	GB
A Mystic Reincarnation	Biograph	1902	USA
The Mystic Swing	Edison	1900	USA
Neptune's Daughters	Biograph	1900	USA
A Novice at X-Rays	Méliès	1897	France
One Glorious Day	Cruze	1922	USA
One Too Exciting Night	Hepworth	1912	GB
The Palace of the Arabian Nights	Méliès	1905	France
Paradise Lost	Biograph	1911	USA
Passion of a Woman Teacher	Mizoguchi	1926	Japan
Peter Ibbetson	Fitzmaurice	1921	USA
The Phantom Carriage	Sjostrom	1920	Sweden
The Phantom Honeymoon	Dawley	1919	GB/USA
Photographing a Ghost	Smith	1898	GB
The Reincarnation of Karma	Vitagraph	1912	USA
The Sea's Shadow	Stark	1912	Germany
Smilin' Through	Franklin	1922	USA
The Spirit of the Conqueror	Unknown	1914	USA
Spiritisme Abracadabrant	Méliès	1900	France
A Spiritualist Photographer	Méliès	1903	France
A Spiritualistic Meeting	Méliès	1906	France
Strange Adventures of a New York Drummer	Edison	1899	USA
Tired Death	Lang	1921	Germany
The Treasure of Arne	Stiller	1919	Sweden
Uncle Josh in a Spooky Hotel	Edison	1900	USA
Unseen Hands	Jacard	1924	USA
The Vanishing Lady	Méliès	1896	France
A Visit to the Spiritualist	Vitagraph	1899	USA
The Werewolf	McRae	1913	USA
Whimsical Illusions	Méliès	1910	France
The Witch	Méliès	1906	France

Without a Soul	Young	1916	USA
Won Through a Medium	Biograph	1911	USA
X-Rays	Smith	1897	GB

English language

The Adding Machine	Epstein	1969	GB
Alice	Allen	1990	USA
Alison's Birthday	Coughlan	1979	Australia
All of Me	Reiner	1984	USA
All Quiet on the Western Front	Milestone	1930	USA
All That Money Can Buy	Dieterle	1941	USA
Almost an Angel	Cornell	1990	USA
Always	Spielberg	1989	USA
An American Werewolf in London	Landis	1981	GB
An American Werewolf in Paris	Waller	1997	GB/USA/ Netherlands/ Lux/France
The Amityville Horror (+ sequels)	Rosenberg	1979	USA
And Now the Screaming Starts	Baker	1973	GB
And You Thought Your Parents Were Weird	Cookson	1992	USA
The Angel Levine	Kadar	1970	USA
Angel on My Shoulder	Mayo	1946	USA
Angels	Dear	1994	USA
Angels in the Outfield	Brown	1951	USA
The Asphyx	Newbrook	1972	GB
The Awakening	Newell	1980	GB
Back from the Dead	Warren	1957	USA
Barnacle Bill	Frend	1958	GB
Beetlejuice	Burton	1988	USA
The Bespoke Overcoat	Clayton	1956	GB
Betsy's Wedding	Alda	1990	USA
Between Two Worlds	Blatt	1944	USA
Beyond Bedlam	Jean	1993	GB
Beyond Evil	Freed	1980	USA
Beyond Tomorrow	Sutherland	1940	USA
Bill and Ted's Bogus Journey	Hewitt	1991	USA
The Bishop's Wife	Koster	1947	USA
Blackbeard's Ghost	Stevenson	1967	USA
Black Rainbow	Hodges	1989	GB
Blithe Spirit	Lean	1945	GB
Blood from the Mummy's Tomb	Holt	1971	GB
Blood Screams	Gebhard	1986	USA
Blood Sisters	Findlay	1986	USA
Blue in the Face	Wang/Auster	1995	USA
The Boogeyman	Lommel	1980	USA
Boogeyman 2	Lommel	1982	USA
Brainstorm	Trumbull	1983	USA
Brainwaves	Lommel	1983	USA
The Breakthrough	Haggard	1993	USA
Burnt Offerings	Curtis	1976	USA
Candyman	Rose	1992	USA

Title	Director	Date	Country
Can't Be Heaven	Friedman	1998	USA
The Canterville Ghost	Dassin	1944	USA
Careful	Maddin	1992	Canada
Carnival of Souls	Harvey	1962	USA
Carousel	King	1956	USA
Casper	Silberling	1995	USA
Chances Are	Ardolino	1989	USA
The Changeling	Medak	1979	Canada
Charlie and the Angel	McEveety	1973	USA
Charlie's Ghost Story	Edwards	1994	USA
A Christmas Carol	Various	Various	Various
Citizen Cohn	Pierson	1992	USA
The Club	Spencer	1994	Canada
The Cockeyed Miracle	Simon	1946	USA
The Cold Room	Dearden	1984	GB
Cold Sweat	Harvey	1993	Canada
The Corpse	Ritelis	1969	GB
Creepshow	Romero	1982	USA
The Crow	Proyas	1994	USA
Crucible of Terror	Hooker	1971	GB
The Curse of the Cat People	Wise/Fritsch	1944	USA
Dad, the Angel and Me	Wallace	1995	USA
Daemon	Finbow	1986	GB
Dark Places	Sharp	1972	GB
Date with an Angel	McLoughlin	1987	USA
Dead Again	Branagh	1991	USA
The Dead Can't Lie	Fionvielle	1988	USA
Deadly Advice	Fletcher	1993	GB
Dead Man Walking	Robbins	1995	USA
Dead of Night	Cavalcanti et al.	1945	GB
Death Ship	Rakoff	1980	GB/Canada
Death Takes a Holiday	Leisen	1933	USA
Defending Your Life	Brooks	1991	USA
The Devil Commands	Dmytryk	1941	USA
The Devil and Max Devlin	Hills	1981	USA
The Devil Rides Out	Fisher	1968	GB
Dr. Terror's House of Horrors	Francis	1964	GB
Don't Look Now	Roeg	1973	GB/Italy
Don't Take It to Heart	Dell	1944	GB
Dragonheart	Cohen	1996	USA
Earthbound	Pichel	1940	USA
Elvis and the Colonel	Graham	1993	USA
Emily's Ghost	Finbow	1991	GB
The Empire Strikes Back	Kershner	1983	USA
Encounter with the Unknown	Thomason	1975	USA
The Entity	Furie	1982	USA
The Evil	Trikonis	1978	USA
The Extraordinary Seaman	Frankenheimer	1969	USA
The Fall of the House of Usher	Corman	1960	USA
Family Plot	Hitchcock	1976	USA
Field of Dreams	Robinson	1989	USA
The First Power	Resnikoff	1990	USA

Flatliners	Schumacher	1990	USA
Fluke	Carlei	1995	USA
The Flying Deuces	Sutherland	1939	USA
The Fog	Carpenter	1979	USA
Forever Darling	Hall	1956	USA
The Forgotten One	Badger	1990	USA
For Heaven's Sake	Seaton	1950	USA
Frankenstein Created Woman	Fisher	1967	GB
The Frighteners	Jackson	1996	NZ/USA
Frozen Ghost	Young	1945	USA
Full Circle	Loncraine	1976	GB/Canada
Gabriel over the White House	LaCava	1933	USA
Ghost	Zucker	1990	USA
The Ghost Breakers	Marshall	1940	USA
Ghost Catchers	Cline	1944	USA
Ghost Chase	Emmerich	1987	W. Germany
Ghost Chasers	Beaudine	1951	USA
Ghost Dad	Poitier	1990	USA
Ghost Fever	Smithee/Madden	1985	USA
The Ghost of Frankenstein	Kenton	1942	USA
The Ghost Goes West	Clair	1935	GB
The Ghost Goes Wild	Grubbs	1947	USA
The Ghost and the Guest	Nigh	1943	USA
Ghost in the Invisible Bikini	Weis	1966	USA
The Ghost in the Machine	Talalay	1993	USA
The Ghost and Mrs. Muir	Mankiewicz	1947	USA
The Ghost Ship	Sewell	1952	GB
Ghost Story	Weeks	1974	GB
Ghost Story	Irvin	1981	USA
The Ghost Talks	Seiler	1929	USA
Ghost Town	Governor	1988	USA
The Ghost Walks	Strayer	1934	USA
Ghost Writer	Hall	1989	USA
Ghostbusters	Reitman	1984	USA
Ghostbusters II	Reitman	1989	USA
Ghostriders	Stewart	1988	USA
The Ghosts of Berkeley Square	Sewell	1947	GB
Ghosts Can't Do It	Derek	1989	USA
Ghosts of Hanley House	Sherrill	1968	USA
The Gift of Love	Negulesco	1958	USA
Gildersleeve's Ghost	Douglas	1940	USA
Grave Secrets	Borchers	1989	USA
A Guy Named Joe	Fleming	1943	USA
The Halfway House	Dearden	1944	GB
Happy Land	Pichel	1943	USA
Haunted	Gilbert	1995	GB/USA
The Haunted Palace	Corman	1963	USA
The Haunting	Wise	1963	USA
The Haunting of Lisa	McBrearty	1995	USA
The Haunting of M	Thomas	1979	USA
The Headless Ghost	Scott	1959	GB
The Hearse	Bowers	1980	USA
Heart Condition	Perriott	1990	USA
Heart and Souls	Underwood	1993	USA

Title	Director	Date	Country
Heaven Can Wait	Lubitsch	1943	USA
Heaven Can Wait	Beatty/Henry	1978	USA
Heaven Only Knows	Rogell	1947	USA
Heavenly Days	Estabrook	1944	USA
The Heavenly Kid	Medoway	1985	USA
Hello Mary Lou, Prom Night 2	Pittman	1987	Canada
Here Comes Mr. Jordan	Hall	1941	USA
Hideaway	Leonard	1995	USA
High Plains Drifter	Eastwood	1973	USA
High Spirits	Jordan	1988	USA
Highway to Hell	de Jong	1992	USA
Hocus Pocus	Ortega	1993	USA
The Horn Blows at Midnight	Walsh	1945	USA
The Horror Show	Isaac	1989	USA
The Horror Star	Vane	1981	USA
House	Miner	1985	USA
House of Darkness	Mitchell	1947	GB
House of Mystery	Sewell	1961	GB
The House of the Spirits	August	1994	Denmark/ Germany/ Portugal
The House Where Evil Dwells	Connor	1982	USA
The Hudsucker Proxy	Coen	1994	USA
Immortal Sins	Hachvel	1991	USA/Spain
The Innocents	Clayton	1961	GB
Intersection	Rydell	1994	USA
The Iron Mask	Dwan	1929	USA
It Happened Tomorrow	Clair	1944	USA
It's a Wonderful Life	Capra	1946	USA
Jack the Ripper Quartette	MacDonald	1958	GB
Jacob's Ladder	Lyne	1990	USA
J. D.'s Revenge	Marks	1976	USA
Jeffrey	Ashley	1995	USA
Kiss of the Beast	Band	1990	USA
Kiss Me Goodbye	Mulligan	1982	USA
Lady in White	LaLoggia	1988	USA
Last Gasp	McGinnis	1994	USA
The Last Winter	Johnston	1990	Canada
Latin Quarter	Sewell	1945	GB
The Lawnmower Man	Leonard	1992	USA
The Legend of Cryin' Ryan	Shapiro/St.Claire	1998	USA
The Legend of Hell House	Hough	1972	GB
The Legend of Lylah Clare	Aldrich	1968	USA
Lifeforce	Hooper	1985	GB
A Life Less Ordinary	Boyle	1997	GB
Liliom	Borzage	1930	USA
Little Buddha	Bertolucci	1994	France/GB
Little Ghost	Shayne	1996	USA
London Belongs to Me	Gilliat	1948	GB
Lovesick	Brickman	1983	USA
Made in Heaven	Rudolph	1987	USA
The Man in the Trunk	St. Clair	1942	USA

The Manitou	Girdler	1977	USA
Map of the Human Heart	Ward	1993	USA
Mark of the Devil	Guest	1984	GB
A Matter of Life and Death	Powell	1946	GB
Maxie	Aaron	1985	USA
The Medium	Sewell	1934	GB
The Medium	Menotti	1951	USA
Meet Joe Black	Brest	1998	USA
The Mephisto Waltz	Wendkos	1971	USA
Michael	Ephron	1996	USA
The Milagro Beanfield War	Redford	1988	USA
Miracle in the Rain	Mate	1956	USA
Miracles for Sale	Browning	1939	USA
Mr. Wrong	Preston	1984	New Zealand
Ms. Scrooge	Karty	1997	USA
My Friend Walter	Millar	1992	GB
My Ghost Dog	Putch	1997	USA
Mystery Train	Jarmusch	1989	USA
Necronomicon	Gans	1993	USA
The Nesting	Weston	1981	USA
Netherworld	Schmoeller	1991	USA
The Newlydeads	Merhi	1987	USA
Night of the Demon	Tourneur	1957	GB
Night of the Ghouls	Wood	1959	USA
Nightmare before Christmas	Selick	1993	USA
A Nightmare on Elm Street (+ sequels)	Craven	1984	USA
Nomads	McTiernan	1986	USA
Nurse Sherri	Adamson	1977	USA
On a Clear Day You Can See Forever	Minnelli	1970	USA
One Dark Night	McLoughlin	1982	USA
The Oracle	Findlay	1986	USA
Orgy of the Dead	Wood	1956	USA
The Other	Mulligan	1972	USA
Our Town	Wood	1940	USA
Out of the Darkness	Krish	1985	GB
Outward Bound	Milton	1930	USA
Pale Rider	Eastwood	1985	USA
Pandora and the Flying Dutchman	Lewin	1950	GB
Paris, France	Ciccoritti	1993	Canada
The Passion of Darkly Noon	Ridley	1996	USA
Pet Semetary	Lambert	1989	USA
Peter Ibbetson	Hathaway	1935	USA
Phantasm (+ sequel)	Coscarelli	1979	USA
The Phantom Speaks	English	1945	USA
The Phantom Thief	Lederman	1946	USA
Phantoms	Band	1990	USA
Photographing Fairies	Willing	1997	GB
A Place of One's Own	Knowles	1945	GB
Poltergeist (+ sequels)	Hooper	1982	USA
Portrait of Jennie	Dieterle	1948	USA
The Possession of Joel Delaney	Hussein	1971	USA
The Preacher's Wife	Marshall	1996	USA
Prelude to a Kiss	Rene	1994	USA

Title	Director	Date	Country
Prison	Harlin	1987	USA
Prom Night 3: The Last Kiss	Oliver	1989	USA
The Prophecy	Widen	1994	USA
Psychomania	Sharp	1972	GB
The Queen of Spades	Dickinson	1948	GB
Re-Animator	Gordon	1985	USA
The Reincarnation of Peter Proud	Thompson	1974	GB
The Remarkable Andrew	Heisler	1942	USA
Resurrection	Petrie	1980	USA
Retribution	Magar	1987	USA
Return to Glennascaul	Edwards	1951	Ireland
Return of Peter Grimm	Nicholls	1935	USA
The Revenge of the Blood Beast	Reeves	1965	Italy/GB
Ruby	Harrington	1977	USA
Scared Stiff	Marshall	1953	USA
The Scoundrel	Hecht/MacArthur	1935	USA
The Screaming Skull	Nichols	1958	USA
Scrooge	Hurst	1951	GB
Scrooged	Donner	1988	USA
Séance on a Wet Afternoon	Forbes	1964	GB
The Search for Bridey Murphy	Langley	1956	USA
The Sender	Christian	1982	US/GB
The Sentinel	Winner	1976	USA
Shadow Dancing	Furey	1988	USA
She's Back	Kincaid	1989	USA
The Shining	Kubrick	1980	GB
The Shocker	Craven	1989	USA
Siesta	Lambert	1987	USA
Silent Tongue	Shepherd	1993	USA
The Sixth Man	Miller	1997	USA
Slaughterhouse Rock	Logothetis	1987	USA
The Sleeping Car	Curtis	1990	USA
Sleepless in Seattle	Ephron	1993	USA
Smilin' Through	Franklin	1932	USA
Smilin' Through	Borzage	1941	USA
Something Evil	Spielberg	1971	USA
Somewhere in Time	Swarc	1980	USA
Spellbound	Harlow	1941	GB
The Spirit Is Willing	Castle	1966	USA
Spook Chasers	Blair	1957	USA
Strangler of the Swamp	Wisbar	1945	USA
Sunset Boulevard	Wilder	1950	USA
Supernatural	Halperin	1933	USA
The Supernaturals	Mastroianni	1986	USA
The Survivor	Hemmings	1981	Australia
Switch	Edwards	1991	USA
The Tale of Hoffman	Powell	1951	GB
Tales from the Crypt	Francis	1972	GB
Tales of Terror	Corman	1962	USA
The Terror	Corman	1963	USA
That's the Spirit	Lamont	1945	USA

Things to Do in Denver When You're Dead	Fleder	1995	USA
Thirteen Ghosts	Castle	1960	USA
The Thirteenth Chair	Browing	1929	USA
The Thirteenth Chair	Seitz	1937	USA
Those Dear Departed	Robinson	1987	Australia
The Three Godfathers	Ford	1948	USA
Thunder Rock	Boulting	1942	GB
The Time of Their Lives	Barton	1946	USA
To Dance with the White Dog	Jordan	1993	USA
To Die For	Litten	1993	GB
The Tomb of Ligeia	Corman	1963	USA
Topper	McLeod	1937	USA
Topper Returns	Del Ruth	1941	USA
Topper Takes a Trip	McLeod	1938	USA
Tormented	Gordon	1960	USA
Tower of London	Corman	1962	USA
True Romance	Scott	1993	USA
Truly, Madly, Deeply	Minghella	1990	GB
Twice Dead	Dragin	1988	USA
Twice Told Tales	Salkow	1963	USA
Two of a Kind	Herzfeld	1983	USA
Two Thousand Maniacs	Lewis	1964	USA
Underground	Kusturica	1995	Fr/Ger/Hum
The Uninvited	Allen	1944	USA
Vault of Horror	Baker	1973	GB
The Veil	Strock	1958	USA
The Venetian Ghost	Barber	1988	GB
Wayne's World 2	Surjik	1993	USA
Wings of Fame	Votocek	1990	Netherlands
Wired	Peerce	1989	USA
Witchboard	Tenney	1986	USA
Witchboard III: The Possession	Svatek	1995	USA
Witchtrap	Tenney	1989	USA
What Dreams May Come	Ward	1998	USA
The Wizard of Oz	Fleming	1939	USA
Wonder Man	Humberstone	1945	USA
The Wraith	Marvin	1986	USA
You'll Find Out	Butler	1940	USA
You Never Can Tell	Breslow	1951	USA
Younger and Younger	Adlon	1993	USA
Zero Patience	Greyson	1993	Canada
Ziegfeld Follies	Minnelli	1945	USA
Zone 39	Tatoulis	1997	Australia

Foreign language

Ai no borei	Oshima	1978	Japan
Cathy's Curse	Matalon	1976	France/Canada
Celine and Julie Go Boating	Rivette	1974	France
Dona Flor and Her Two Husbands	Bareto	1976	Brazil
The Dybbuk	Waszynski	1937	Poland
Fanny and Alexander	Bergman	1982	Sweden

Title	Director	Date	Country
Faraway, So Close!	Wenders	1993	Germany
J'Accuse	Gance	1938	France
Liliom	Lang	1930	France
No End	Kieslowski	1988	Poland
Rashomon	Kurosawa	1950	Japan
The Seventh Seal	Bergman	1956	Sweden
Solaris	Tarkovsky	1972	USSR
The Tenant	Polanski	1976	France
Ugetsu Monagatari	Mizoguchi	1953	Japan
Wings of Desire	Wenders	1987	West Germany

Chapter Notes

Introduction

1. Evans, 1996, p. 46.
2. Bernstein, 1956, filmed the same year.
3. Sequels gradually gave up any pretense to a factual basis. Jay Anson's 1977 purportedly non-fiction original was subjected to unfavorable scrutiny from the beginning (see for example Auerbach, 1986, for an overview of the case).
4. For information on the Enfield case see Playfair, 1980.
5. McClenon, 1994.
6. The ESP "test" at the beginning of *Ghostbusters* (1984) is a humorous exception.
7. King, 1993, p. 291.
8. Grixti, 1989.
9. McClenon, 1994.
10. Finucane, 1982, and Inglis, 1992, survey early accounts of alleged paranormal phenomena, including ghosts.
11. Dolar, 1992, p. 7.
12. Castle, 1995, p. 168.
13. *Ibid.*, pp. 175–77.
14. For an examination of this transition in attitudes to death, see Ariès (1977/81).
15. Boot, 1996, p. 5.
16. Fowkes, 1998, p. 28, mentions Diane Waggoner's distinction between "scary ghost stories" and "ghost fantasies," subdividing the latter into "comic" and "nostalgic fantasy" ghosts, continuing that comic and nostalgic elements can be combined in a single film.
17. Tudor, 1989, p. 6.
18. *Ibid.* p. 20.
19. Newman, 1988b, p. 228. He also maintains, 1996, p. 11, that comedy is horror's "closest kin," making genre evaluations even more complex.
20. Dyson, 1997, p. xiv. His reference to these films as "a glimpse of another world" (ibid.) is something that characterizes any film — even home movies after an interval — and indicates how difficult demarcation can be.
21. Ledwon, 1993, p. 261.
22. Derry, 1977.
23. Briggs, 1977, p. 12.
24. Fowkes, 1998, p. 26, cannot decide whether ghost films are a genre or merely a subgenre. Noël Carroll's analysis of horror places ghosts and haunted houses as separate subgenres (1990, p. 98).
25. Parish, 1994, pp. x–xi. The other useful film guide, with a section on ghosts, is Senn and Johns, 1992.
26. Hienger, 1979, pp. 147–48.
27. An example of one that could be is *The Legend of Hell House* (1972) which Nicholls, 1973, p. 201, describes as having a S.F. slant because of the psychic energy-absorbing machine, even though its operation remains obscure. Another example is the *Phantasm* series (1979 et seq.), where corpses are reanimated and sent to another dimension.
28. For an inquiry into the nature of "Art-horror" see Carroll, 1990.
29. The fact that a noun used to describe a ghost — spook — can also be used as a verb

to characterise their effect indicates ghost films' affinity with horror.

30. Wood, 1984, p. 174. Carroll, 1990, p. 221, footnote 42, feels that in general society ignores rather than represses "the kinds of conceptual possibilities represented by horrific creatures."

31. The only book devoted to a large quantity of recent ghost films (Fowkes, 1998) — the thesis of which is that ghost films are masochistic fantasies "in which the desire to switch genders is part of a desire to achieve sexual sameness" (p. 11) — is muddied by its psychoanalytical excursions.

32. Salt, 1992, pp. 11–14.

33. Chorvinsky, 1989, p. 136.

34. The distinction between the fantastic and the *plausible*, insofar as the latter can be determined by prior experience, as opposed to a distinction between the fantastic and "the real," or "realism," is important.

35. Donald, 1989, p. 10.

36. Ray, 1995, p. 118.

37. Notably France, of course. When Trewey gave a press show in Manchester on 16 May 1896, it was referred to as a "séance" (Brown, 1996, p. 68).

38. Coates, 1984, p. 121. It is stretching the analogy to claim that "celluloid is like flat and divisible ectoplasm."

39. Denman, 1994, p. 11.

40. Virilio, 1984, p. 29.

41. There is an extensive popular literature in horror-oriented magazines, and a limited number of ghost films are analyzed in the collection edited by Svehla and Svehla (1996).

42. Leatherdale, 1985, p. 17.

43. For more on the werewolf/vampire nexus see Woodward, 1979, pp. 147–55.

44. Including two adaptations of *Richard III*, *Tower of London* (1939 and 1962).

45. An earlier example is *The Man without a Soul* (1916) in which a man brought back from the dead lacks moral sense (Low, 1950, pp. 176–77).

46. The reverse case is supplied by *Always* (1989) in which characters can hear Pete's voice seeming to come from inside their heads, although the voice is not internally generated.

47. There is the problem of accounting for the other witnesses.

48. *The Veil* and *Jack the Ripper Quartette* (both 1958) comprise episodes from made-for-TV series that were not sold, so were bolted together for theatrical release.

Chapter 1

1. Musser, 1990, p. 2. As Ceram, 1965, p. 17, points out, forms such as magic lantern shadow plays, automata and marionette theaters did not contribute to the technological development of cinema, but as he shows, cinema was their successor on a cultural level.

2. Fell, 1987, p. 39; Harding and Popple, 1996, pp. 1–3, also locate early cinema in its wider cultural context.

3. Christie, 1994b, p. 111.

4. Haill, 1986.

5. Wirth, 1979; Moxey, 1989; and Bauman, 1992, p. 96, provide an overview of the Reformation macabre tradition.

6. Kurtz, 1934/75, p. 209.

7. Kurtz, 1934/75, p. 189. *The Seventh Seal* (1956) brings together the figure of Death and the Black Death that swept Europe in the middle of the fourteenth century, and which probably contributed to the development of the Danse Macabre.

8. Reprinted in Liesegang, 1926/1986, p. 12 and Ceram, 1965, illustration 22.

9. Stafford, 1994, pp. 92, 232.

10. Reprinted in Dawes, 1979, p. 85.

11. Anon., 1990, pp. 45–46.

12. Liesegang, 1926/1986, pp. 36, 37; he gives the date of the Choreutoscope's construction as possibly 1866 (Ceram, 1965, gives 1866 in the text accompanying his illustrations of both the slide and the mechanism, the case of which is decorated with a skeleton as well). Liesegang, p. 37, notes that an 1884 patent by W. C. Hughes for a larger version of Beale's invention (the "Giant Choreutoscope") was sometimes called the "Phantoscope" — not to be confused with a projector of the same name patented by Francis Jenkins in 1894 (Liesegang, p. 59).

13. Huygens had earlier used the skeleton removing his skull in his sketches for magic lantern slides in the 1650s (Robinson, 1996, p. 33).

14. Grove, 1997, p. 142, downplaying the realization early in its history that photography was capable of extending powers of

Notes—Chapter 1

perception (in 1861 von Reichenbach was attempting to photograph invisible radiations known as "Od-light" (Stenger, 1958, p. 221)); Grove examines X-rays, often called the "New Photography," in the context of psychical research and ghost literature.

15. Hopkins, 1897, pp. 96–99.
16. Kurtz, 1934/75, p. 242.
17. Méliès's ghost films are examined in chapter four.
18. Hammond, 1974, p. 41.
19. Bragg, 1993, p. 62.
20. Skal, 1993, p. 231.
21. King, 1981.
22. Hecht, 1984.
23. *Ibid*. Part 1, p. 2.
24. Anon., 1851/1973, p. 71.
25. Pearsall, 1972, p. 91, likewise dismisses the possibility of magic lanterns being used to produce mysterious lights at Victorian séances.
26. Christopher, 1975.
27. Though when Goethe's *Faust* was given its first private showing in 1819, Phantasmagoria effects were used to show the Earth Spirit (Hecht, 1984, Part 2, p. 6).
28. Hecht, 1984, Part 1, p. 5.
29. *Ibid*. Part 1, p. 5.
30. *Ibid*. Part 1, p. 3.
31. Hecht, 1993, p. 13. Hecht's bibliography is a useful compilation of items showing how frequent was the display of ghosts and the supernatural.
32. Hepworth, 1894, pp. 1–4.
33. Brewster, 1832.
34. Lange-Fuchs, 1987, pp. 2–3.
35. Although thirteenth-century Roger Bacon was sometimes given that credit, he wrote on mirror projection; Lange-Fuchs, 1987, p. 5.
36. Either to Thomas Walgenstein, an acquaintance of Huygens's (Liesegang, 1926/1986, p. 11) or to Huygens himself (Hecht, 1984, Part 2, p. 6).
37. Anon., 1851, p. 54.
38. Liesegang, 1926/1986, p. 12.
39. Hecht, 1984, Part 2, p. 4.
40. Anon., 1825, p. 229.
41. Hecht, 1984, Part 2, p. 4.
42. Isherwood, 1986, pp. 251–52.
43. See Hecht, 1993, pp. 51–52.
44. Heard, 1996b, p. 26, brackets Schröpfer with Cagliostro, but although Cagliostro did evoke phantoms, his career is shrouded in such mystery that there is no way to know how his effects were achieved.
45. Thompson, 1994.
46. Hecht, 1984, Part 2, p. 3. Liesegang, 1926/1986, p. 17, states that the usual fasting period was a more reasonable twenty-four hours.
47. Liesegang, 1926/1986, p. 17.
48. Stafford, 1994, p. 57, illustrates a 1772 engraving of Guyot's device (from *Nouvelles récréations*).
49. Barber, 1989, p. 78.
50. Musser, 1990, p. 19.
51. Barnouw, 1981, p. 24.
52. Reproduced in Liesegang, 1926/1986, p. 18.
53. Referred to by Coe, 1981, pp. 13–14 and McGrath, 1996, p. 15.
54. Christopher, 1975, pp. 50–51.
55. Christopher, 1962, p. 41.
56. Christopher, 1975, p. 52.
57. Hecht, 1984, Part 2, p. 4.
58. Castle, 1988, p. 39. In February 1802 a Phantasmagoria showman had been sent to Bridewell for allowing children in (Heard, 1996b, p. 30). Musser, 1990, p. 28, reproduces a broadside for Robertson *fils*'s 1825–26 exhibition
59. Heard, 1996b, p. 27, argues that Philidor's shows were intended as an exposé, but like those of Philidor's colleagues, there was probably an air of ambiguity about them.
60. Oehler, 1811; Barnouw, 1984, p. 43.
61. It is appropriate that Robertson and Méliès are both buried in Paris's Père Lachaise cemetery, though perhaps not that Robertson has a grand tomb on a main thoroughfare, while Méliès's modest grave is tucked away from a side path.
62. Anon., 1990, p. 23.
63. Hopkins, 1897, p. 7.
64. Anon., 1863.
65. Clarens, 1967, p. 80.
66. Wollen, 1997, p. 16.
67. Musser, 1990, p. 23.
68. Robinson, 1986, p. 4.
69. Hecht, 1993, p. 59. Heard, 1996b, p. 29, notes that wrangles over infringements of Phantasmagoria patents anticipate similar problems in the early days of cinema.
70. Reminiscent of early cinema audiences' alleged fear of approaching trains.

71. Robinson, 1990, p. 7.
72. Varey, 1955, p. 91, quoting Thomas Young (1807).
73. Hopkins, 1897, p. 7.
74. Dawes, 1979, p. 85.
75. Varey, 1955, p. 91.
76. Robinson, 1986, pp. 9–10.
77. Rosenfeld, 1981, p. 163.
78. *Ibid.*
79. Musser, 1990, p. 25; advertisement — relying *very* heavily on de Philipsthal's text (see above) — dated 4 November 1803.
80. Hecht, 1984, Part 2, p. 5.
81. Robinson, 1986, p. 13. Liesegang, 1926/1986, p. 20, shows an 1895 drawing of two projectors being used at the Royal Polytechnic (albeit for front projection), the picture a skeleton in a graveyard.
82. Liesegang, 1926/1986, p. 18. Heard, 1996b, p. 30, mentions this influence, and also that early-nineteenth-century slides for home use were often produced in the Phantasmagoria style, with a colored image surrounded by black.
83. The first page of Vol. 1, No. 1 (September 1874) is reprinted in Liesegang, 1926/1986, p. 23.
84. Dawes, 1979, p. 85. Ceram, 1965, illustration 28, reprints an 1845 engraving showing what has to be an artist's impression of Robertson's set-up, with back-projected phantom and winged skulls, but a conventional magic lantern. Ceram thought that changes of image size were accomplished by "lenses and concave reflectors" (text accompanying illustrations 33 and 34).
85. Hecht, 1984, Part 2, p. 6; 1993, p. 270.
86. Musser, 1990, p. 19.
87. Hepworth, 1951, pp. 17–18.
88. Picknett, 1990, p. 44.
89. Butler, 1995, p. 416.
90. Butler, 1995, p. 417.
91. Castle, 1988, p. 43.
92. *Ibid.* p. 45.
93. *Ibid.* p. 52. There is a tendency on the part of academics who are not psychical researchers to underestimate the extent to which the general population regard ghosts as real, as opposed to imaginary constructs.
94. *Ibid.* 1988, p. 42.
95. Sandell, 1995, p. 1.

96. Brown, 1863/1993, p. 7.
97. A strongly sceptical Brown ascribes ghosts to the mechanics of visual perception and the ease with which the mind can be fooled, as evidenced by this collection of visual illusions.
98. Nickell, 1994. Thoughtography is largely associated with Ted Serios, who claims to project mental images onto Polaroid film.
99. A reversal of this process — apparently materializing images of individuals not visible to the naked eye — is in *Nomads* (1986) in which photographs taken of people subsequently discovered to be dead are found not to contain their images when developed.
100. The method of influencing film without using a camera at all has a variety of names in the literature — early practitioners referred to it as skotography, chemicography, and confusingly, radiography (Fodor, n.d., p. 314). More recently the term scotography has been used (Jule Eisenbud, 1977, p. 415).
101. Gettings, 1978. The first book on spirit photography, by the credulous Georgiana Houghton, was published in 1882, the year the SPR was founded.
102. Edmunds, n.d., p. 3, and Pearsall, 1972, p. 120, state that it was 1862.
103. Gernsheim, 1988, p. 67.
104. Pearsall, 1972, p. 120, refers to a claim by Richard Boursnell to have found extras in 1851.
105. Edmunds gives a partial (but, he says, representative) list of possible methods of fraudulently creating such pictures: Edmunds, n.d., pp. 12–14.
106. Fodor, n.d., p. 313.
107. Pearsall, 1972, p. 120.
108. Gettings, 1978, p. 144.
109. Edmunds, n.d., p. 9.
110. Permutt, 1983, p. 128.
111. Chanan, 1980, pp. 283–84; Chanan, 1996, pp. 118–19.
112. Quoted by Chanan, 1980, p. 284, and Chanan, 1996, p. 119.
113. Eisenbud, 1977, p. 416. Unfortunately these pictures were often fuzzy, and he does not take account of the will to believe. There is also the issue of determining how rigorous controls were — conjurors routinely accomplish the seemingly impos-

sible. Hyslop (1915) argues that some psychic photographs could be produced as a result of hysteria, meaning that the method of production is identical to that used in fraud, but because of a dissociative state the intention to deceive is absent.

114. The First World War in particular brought a resurgence that petered out in the 1930s, and ghost pictures of varying quality still frequently appear in newspapers and magazines.

115. Gettings, 1978, p. 144. Blackwell was surely exaggerating the extent of photographic knowledge at that time.

116. Bazin, 1967, vol. 1, p. 10; of course this is only true insofar as the identity of the portrait's subject is known, either to friends and relatives, or where the subject is famous.

117. Bazin, 1967, vol. 1, p. 10.

118. Castle, 1988, p. 59; a similar theme, illustrated in Castle, 1995, p. 182, is Dicksee's painting *A Reverie*, also mid-nineteenth century; a widower, listening to his daughter play the piano, dreams of his wife, who is manifested at the far left of the scene. Here, given the title, the subjective nature of the wraith is made explicit. Hyslop, 1915, pp. 149–150, mentions the possibility that extras could be images of telepathic communication from discarnate to living.

119. The early use of inserts (achieved by use of double exposure, film insert or a second stage behind the main action) is discussed in chapter three.

120. Booth, 1965, p. 81.

121. *Ibid.*, p. 84.

122. *Ibid.*, p. 83.The 1941 and 1961 film versions do not have the ghost element, but Smith's 1898 one did; all three retain the original title.

123. Anderson, n.d..

124. Haill, 1986, p. 66.

125. Both have been filmed a number of times, though the former has proved the more enduring by far.

126. Kendrick, 1991, p. 157.

127. Originally known as the *Ætheroscope*; Altick, 1978, p. 504.

128. David Price, 1985, p. 117.

129. Layton, 1977.

130. Pepper, 1890, p. 25.

131. *Ibid.* pp. 22–23.

132. An illustration appears in Dircks, 1863, pp. 46–47. McGrath, 1996, p. 22, asserts that Brewster's desire for "phantasms of the most perfect delineation," later to be attained by Hollywood, "was achieved to some extent in the Dircksian Phantasmagoria...." She fails to mention Pepper at all.

133. Dawes, 1979, p. 89.

134. Barnouw, 1981, p. 28.

135. Pepper, 1890, frontispiece.

136. Hepworth, 1951, p. 112.

137. Summarized in Hecht, 1993, p. 266.

138. Dawes, 1979, p. 89.

139. Hopkins, 1897, pp. 55–60; Leahy, 1982, p. 45.

140. Pepper, 1890, p. 29.

141. *Ibid.* Later acts included more conventional ghosts, including two that would become cinematic staples— Scrooge and Marley's Ghost and *Hamlet*'s ghost (Pepper, 1890, p. 30).

142. Dircks, 1863, pp. 65–70.

143. Dircks, 1863, pp. 41–42.

144. Barnouw, 1981, p. 28.

145. Hecht's catalogue entry, 1993, p. 141, adds in parentheses "Ghost at the Britannia," which is not in the original. This production is also referred to in an article quoted by Pepper, 1890, p. 23, who calls it *The Widow and Orphans— Faith, Hope, and Charity*, presumably the same play Albert Lane Cranford describes below.

146. Anon., 1863, p. 423.

147. Price, 1985, p. 118.

148. Cranford, n.d. [c.1936].

149. Hecht, 1993, p. 311; ironic given the vehemence with which Pepper treats the subject (1890, p. 28).

150. Heard, 1995.

151. *Ibid.*, p. 12. An appendix to Harding and Popple's 1996 compilation by Vanessa Toulmin, on fairground exhibitors who switched to the Bioscope, indicates how many had been ghost-show proprietors. A 1909 article reprinted in the same volume hints at the fortuitous introduction of cinema: "...everyone will remember how effectively the old fashioned "ghost show" has been superseded by "living pictures" which came into vogue at a time when the showman was at a standstill for novelties" (p. 198).

152. Hepworth, 1951, pp. 112–13 (Hepworth, who was hired to shoot material for

the London show, calls it "Stereoplastics"); Heard, 1996a, p. v.

153. Hecht, 1993, p. 378.
154. Virilio, 1984, p. 30.
155. Heard, 1995, p. 12; 1996a, pp. i, iii–iv; the slow death of Pepper's Ghost is shown by Heard's statement (1996a, p. v) that patents based on the illusion were being filed in the United States as late as 1927, and that at the time of writing a variant, combined with laser disc technology, could be seen in Las Vegas.
156. Barber, 1989, pp. 84–85.
157. Hecht, 1993, p. 58.
158. Usai, 1994, p. 14; Bottomore, 1996, pp. 136–39, outlines how the sophistication of the magic lantern caused lanternists — Cecil Hepworth among them — to downplay the prognosis for moving pictures.

Chapter 2

1. Dawes, 1979, p. 83.
2. Barber, 1989, p. 85.
3. Vardac, 1949, p. 91.
4. *Ibid.*, p. 179.
5. Gunning, 1990.
6. Musser, 1990, p. 2.
7. Bowser, 1982, pp. 6–7. She warns that the 1902 figure may be slightly inflated as it includes Biograph films copyrighted in that year but for which production dates were not available at the time of writing.
8. An extract from a 1912 book by Frederick Talbot reprinted in Harding and Popple (1996, pp. 97–99) notes the decline of "'trick film' fever" thanks to the market's being "inundated with so-called magic pictures, of which the majority were inane or conventional," so that "the public appetite became satiated."
9. Many of the films described here are now lost, and descriptions rely heavily on Hammond, 1974, and especially Frazer, 1979.
10. A poster advertising Ira Davenport's February 1879 "Farewell Tour" (Anon., 1879) describes a "séance," a guest at which had been Dion Boucicault, writer of *The Corsican Brothers*, a play adapted from the story by Dumas *père* (1845).
11. Hammond, 1974, p. 36.
12. Hammond, 1974, pp. 22–23.
13. Frazer, 1979, p. 121; Clarens, 1967, p. 8.
14. Frazer, 1979, p. 121.
15. Hammond, 1974, p. 30. The Lumières produced a number of fictional films (numbers 2001–2023) which they termed "phantasmagorical views" (Gaudreault, 1996, pp. 75–76) — one at least of which, No. 2001 (*Le Château Hanté*), could have been made by Méliès. While noting this, Gaudreault points out that others have no supernatural elements whatsoever.
16. Frazer, 1979, p. 63.
17. Hardy, 1985, p. 16, claims this to be the first vampire film and Dyson, 1997, p. 1, the first example of the supernatural horror film — a heavy freight for such a modest film to bear.
18. Robertson, 1991, p. 115.
19. Low and Manvell, 1949, p. 19; Gifford, 1973a, p. 16.
20. Sadoul, 1947, p. 11.
21. Hammond, 1974, p. 56.
22. Kovács, 1983.
23. Hammond, 1974, p. 16.
24. The French title refers to the picture rather than the "photographer" — in fact Méliès is a conjuror, not a photographer in the film — but the meaning is equivalent. Niver, 1968, p. 32, draws attention to the white background and splice.
25. Frazer, 1979, p. 159; the original appeared in Paris, 1961, p. 63.
26. Fischer, 1979, examines the cavalier treatment of women by Méliès.
27. Brakhage, 1972, p. 20.
28. As can be seen in Adair, 1995, p. 10.
29. The screen also goes black momentarily when *The Ghosts of Berkeley Square* (1947) accidentally kill themselves.
30. Gifford, 1973a, p. 195.
31. Frazer, 1979, p. 63.
32. Niver, 1968, p. 13, refers to *Uncle Josh's Nightmare*, and points out that it and the 1899 film are practically the same, though the sets are different.
33. Niver, 1968, pp. 63–64.
34. "Phantom" in the title of sundry Victorian melodramas played a similar role; Booth, 1965, p. 85.
35. Salt, 1982, p. 282.
36. Shipman, 1982, Vol. 1, p. 23.
37. See Gauld, 1968 and Herbert & McKernan, 1996, p. 135, for further details. Ep-

person, 1997, p. 142 ff, disposes of the notion that Smith was implicated in the mysterious death of the SPR's Hon. Secretary Edmund Gurney, whose assistant Smith was, in 1888.

38. Low and Manvell, 1949, p. 19; Gifford, 1973a, p. 16; Chanan, 1996, p. 117.
39. Salt, 1992, p. 35.
40. Low and Manvell, 1949, pp. 78–79; Christie, 1994b, p. 117, Chanan, 1980, p. 286, and 1996, pp. 117–18, include a description of the film from Smith's catalogue.
41. This film is described in an article by Victor W. Cook on Smith in *Chamber's Journal*, 30th June 1900, but referred to as *A Guardian Angel*; there is also a description of how filmic ghosts are produced [i.e. by double exposure]. Cook continues, "but Mr. Smith has introduced several cunning little devices in spirit-raising that he preserved a discreet silence about" before going on to say that Smith had shown his spirit productions to an appreciative royal family (Cook's article is reprinted in Harding and Popple, 1996, pp. 94–96).
42. Bowser, 1982, p. 6.
43. *Ibid.*, p. 11.
44. Gifford, 1973b.
45. Gifford, 1973a, p. 22.
46. Barnouw, 1981, p. 89.
47. As late as 1912 Hay Plumb could make a comedy for Hepworth, *Ghosts*, in which men dress as ghosts to scare each other. Two years later Elwin Neame made Hepworth another comedy with the same title in which a girl investigating a haunted house finds that the "ghost" is another researcher. From these descriptions in Gifford, 1973b, both films sound retarded for the period.
48. Gifford, 1973a, p. 192. This melodrama was also filmed in 1908, 1913, 1928, and most notably in 1935 (although the last, best-known, one eliminates the supernatural element); these are all British.
49. Bowser, 1973, p. 318.
50. Christie, 1994b, p. 129.
51. Usai et al., 1989, pp. 113, 114.
52. Ralston, 1872, pp. 139–46.
53. Parish, 1994, pp. 317–18.
54. Hardy, 1985, p. 18, suggests that *The Avenging Conscience* might be the horror cinema's first masterpiece.

55. Kael, 1993, pp. 40–41; Wagenknecht and Slide, 1975, p. 44.
56. Quoted in Clarens, 1967, p. 43.
57. Pearson, 1992, pp. 111–13.
58. Pearson, 1992, p. 113.
59. Low, 1950, pp. 176–77.
60. Parish, 1994, pp. 132–33.
61. Briggs, 1977, p. 23.
62. This gag was used again in Buster Keaton's 1922 *The Electric House* in which a maid becomes entangled in a sheet and is thought to be a ghost.
63. Wagenknecht and Slide, 1975, p. 137.
64. Allen, 1993, p. 86, sees the link between mother and son in terms of a "Doctrine of Sympathy," which he defines as "an explanation for the existence of emotional bonds between those connected by blood which are so intense that they 'psychically unite' people even when they are physically separated."
65. Wagenknecht and Slide, 1975, p. 136.
66. Kramer and Welsh, 1978, p. 66.
67. Shipman, 1982, Vol. 1, p. 42.
68. Parish, 1994, p. 271.
69. Quoted in Parish, 1994, p. 241.
70. Eisner, 1952/73.
71. Turim, 1989, p. 97.
72. Remade as *La Charrette Fantôme* (1939) by Duvivier in France, and as *Körkarlen* (1958) — also an alternative title for the original — by Mattson in Sweden.
73. Kurtz, 1934/75, pp. 210–11.
74. Turim, 1989, p. 96.
75. Shipman, 1982, p. 64.
76. Bergman was strongly influenced by Sjöström and used him as an actor in *Wild Strawberries*. The published script includes a tribute given by Bergman after Sjöström's death in 1960.
77. Parish, 1994, p. 84.
78. *Ibid.*
79. The 1940 remake is a more straightforward revenge film, with a ghost assisting his wife to capture his murderer. Hence justice is served in place of the rather amoral conclusion of the original.
80. Reade, 1970, p. 132; Robertson, 1991, p. 87. A brief account of the Guyra poltergeist case is provided by Healy and Cropper, 1998.
81. Parish, 1994, pp. 27–28.
82. Carey, 1970.

83. Quoted in Parish, 1994, p. 263.
84. Parish, 1994, p. 90.
85. *Ibid.*, p. 354.
86. Earlier versions of *The Bells* had appeared in 1913, 1914 (twice) and 1918, and there were further remakes in 1931 and, as *The Burgomeister*, in 1935. The lost 1931 version is described in Eyles and Meeker, 1992, pp. 35–36.
87. The 1939 version concludes with the four musketeers riding horses towards the camera in double exposure which has a more emblematic feel than the earlier film.
88. This makes Dyson's assertion (1997, p. 158) concerning *The Uninvited* (1944) that Paramount "were on new ground attempting to produce a sophisticated supernatural entertainment" a galling one, possibly caused by his starting his selective history of "the supernatural horror film" in 1931.

Chapter 3

1. See for example Tyrrell, 1953.
2. "Veridical"/"objective" and "hallucinatory"/"subjective" will be used interchangeably.
3. But *not The Halfway House* (1944) and *A Place of One's Own* (1945), contrary to what Murphy, 1992, p. 195, states.
4. General Extrasensory Perception, a term encompassing telepathy and clairvoyance, which does not necessitate communication with discarnate entities.
5. Fowkes, 1998, p. 12, argues that the comedy ghost film emblematizes problems of gender. The male ghost, unable to affect its surroundings, represents a masochistic fantasy. The spectator is in the same position, meaning that "The framework of comedy combined with the device of the film ghost prove to be uniquely suited to a masochistic conception of narrative film pleasure" (p. 13). Unfortunately for the elegance of this parallel, male film ghosts frequently have more effect than Fowkes credits.
6. Sanderson, 1996, p. 59.
7. For example see McClenon, 1994, p. 39.
8. Tudor, 1989, p. 37.
9. A good example is *The Devil Commands* (1941), discussed below.
10. Tudor, 1989, p. 93.
11. Quoted by Fowkes, 1998, p. 19.
12. Parish, 1994, pp. 308–09. His remarks are in a discussion of the versions of *Smilin' Through* (filmed in 1922, 1932 and 1941).
13. Senn and Johns, 1992.
14. They do not acknowledge that the trend was started by the success of 1935's *The Ghost Goes West*.
15. Dyson, 1997, pp. 160–161, while admitting that much of *The Uninvited* is too cosy to be frightening to a modern audience, notes the influence of the ghost's depiction on those films that Industrial Light and Magic were producing in the 1980s. He argues (p. 184) that the real terror of the atom bomb caused a decade-long hiatus in the supernatural horror film. While he overstates the case, it is true that the early 1950s were not rich in paranormal elements, with the exception largely of lighter-toned films and, significantly, *Rashomon* (1950) and *Ugetsu Monogatari* (1953). Nineteen fifty-six saw a surge in supernatural production, largely influenced by the Bridey Murphy reincarnation case. Equally wrong is Fowkes, 1998, p. 18, who contends that there were few Afterlife films between the late 1940s and 1978's *Heaven Can Wait*.
16. Remarkably, the 40 percent figure is reasonably accurate if confined to English-language sound films.
17. Fowkes, 1998, p. 139.
18. Fowkes, 1998, pp. 151–52.
19. Lyttle, 1990, p. 17.
20. Grafe, 1995, p. 33.
21. Halliwell, 1986, p. 269.
22. Reprinted in Parish, 1994, p. 25. The title of *A Matter of Life and Death* (1946) was changed to the more anodyne *Stairway to Heaven* in the United States.
23. Harper, 1994, p. 105; she also says (p. 119) that *A Place of One's Own* (1945) was the only Gainsborough film up to *Jassy* (1947) not to be successful, adding (p. 134) that this was due partly to the miscasting of James Mason and a lack of interest in the occult.
24. Kobal, 1973, p. 97. *Outward Bound* could be added to the list.
25. Kobal, 1973, p. 99.

26. Rhodes, 1996a, p. 226.

27. BBFC, 1998 (personal communication); the anonymous writer continues by saying that as the film was never resubmitted it remains unclassified, and that as the records no longer exist it cannot be determined how the criteria for rejection were applied to other titles in a similar vein. Strictly speaking, *Outward Bound*'s television outings would appear to be illegal.

28. Landy, 1991, pp. 389–90. She does not discuss possible reasons for these taboos; the use of "cultural" rather than "social" suggests a weltanschauung that is deep-rooted, and therefore with a longer history than the period since 1914, as opposed to a shorter-term psychic shock caused by war.

29. Tudor, 1989, p. 8. This discussion can only touch on the complexities of Tudor's analysis.

30. *Ibid.* p. 75.

31. *Ibid.*

32. References to "ghosts in real life" in this discussion are not intended to assume their objective reality. "Alleged" is always implicit.

33. Mulvey, 1975.

34. At the other extreme, Fowkes, 1998, p. 95, points out that Mr. Jordan in *Heaven Can Wait* (1978) often enters a scene by the camera panning to reveal his presence. This makes his mode of entry enigmatic, and also, it could be added, economical for the producers.

35. Bauman, 1992, p. 15; italics in original.

36. The use of a shaft of light as a metaphor is of course most closely associated with Jesus, "The Light of the World."

37. Descending stairs suggests a Hellish destination, but in this instance the implication is that they are journeying to a neutral Underworld.

38. See for example Tyrrell, 1953, p. 42 ff.

39. All played by Alec Guinness, calling to mind *Kind Hearts and Coronets* (1949).

40. *Hatchet for a Honeymoon* (1969) plays a variation on the point-of-view problem, since the murderer is the only person who *cannot* see his dead wife— everybody else can, assuming that she is still alive.

41. Moberly and Jourdain, 1955, p. 46; italics in original.

42. Wolfenstein and Leites, 1950/70, p. 240.

43. Wolfenstein and Leites, 1950/70, p. 241.

44. Fisher, 1997, p. 75, mentions McDougall's "finding" that a patient who had just died lost ¾ oz.

45. Stenger, 1958, p. 222. Underwood, 1993, pp. 64–65, describes Hippolyte Baraduc's photographs of his dead son, and later his wife, at the moment of death. The former image showed "a formless mass of broken white cloud or mist," the latter "three luminous globes" that in another picture taken soon afterwards had combined into one.

46. The spectrum of ghostly types undermines Fowkes's point that "ghost films engage in a denial of the physical body" (1998, p. 12). Only transparent/ineffectual ones do, and there are plenty of physical ones.

47. Nicholls, 1984, p. 185, has pointed out that the ghost's characterisation is confused, at times sad and lost, at others malevolent, and this inconsistency can also be traced back to plot requirements. Kael, 1993, p. 588, criticizes *Poltergeist* for lacking coherence in its effects, and it is difficult to connect the initial playfulness of the piled-up chairs with the gruesomeness of the finale.

48. Ingmar Bergman's *Summer Interlude* (1951) provides a precursor to Casper's visual style. Henryk and Marie fantasize about the death of Henryk's aunt, who has cancer and has already described herself as "a ghost." Marie begins drawing, and the drawing becomes an animated cartoon of the aunt. Henryk "kills" her, whereupon she turns into a Casper-type figure and flies about.

49. Quoted in Sellar et al., 1987, p. 132.

50. A version was also made in 1926.

51. A ghost seeking justice for a third party is less common than seeking it for themselves. Another example, with a Solidarnosc agenda, is Krzysztof Kieslowski's *No End* (1988) in which a lawyer's ghost helps a striker who is being prosecuted.

52. Harper, 1994, p. 178, argues that the film "lacks a coherent narrative structure," but the penance theme is straightforward, even if the punishment is harsh for a foolhardy act of patriotism for which they were the only ones to suffer. There was a mid-Victorian haunting at 50 Berkeley Square (Pearsall, 1972, pp. 155–56) but in the film the house is number 7.

53. Finucane, 1982, p. 43.

54. Just before she appears, with bullet holes, he talks about being "spooked" by his last job.

55. A cliché derived from *Les Diaboliques* (1955) and seen in *Carnival of Souls* (1962), *The Changeling* (1979), *The Shining* (1980) and *Fatal Attraction* (1987).

56. Fox, 1979, p. 39.

57. Directed by Phil Alden Robinson, who also wrote *All of Me*.

58. The non-specific origin of the voice is a problem for the narrative. Hill, 1992, p. 306, asserts that it is Ray's own voice, bringing a blessing to himself as well as to others, but this leaves open how he could have known what he had to do, and why the information is not more precise. It would be as plausible to attribute the voice to God, giving Ray a cryptic test. Probably the most fantastic element to the film is the assumption that, despite hearing voices that lead him to carry out bizarre acts, Ray is eccentric rather than psychotic.

59. Cooper, 1995; Kirtz, 1995.

60. Cooper, 1995, pp. 163, 164.

61. Like much in the film that is left unexplained, where the players have been and where they go when not on the field is unclear.

62. Counts, 1989, p. 4.

63. Awbonnie in *Silent Tongue* (1993) is in a similar predicament but is not as sanguine as Kat's mother.

64. Seaweed has a niche as a symbol of drowning, featuring in *Tormented* (1960), *The Fog* (1979) and the third story in the *Creepshow* (1982) anthology.

65. Coward was pleased with the role: "I thought I was very good in the parts I was dead" (Hoare, 1995, p. 107).

66. They are saved by Max's selflessness, whereas, within the terms of the film, there is no reason why they should escape. The reverse of Max's trajectory is provided in the 1943 *Heaven Can Wait*. A man who considers himself to have been a rake applies for admission to Hell but his 'sins' are so modest that he is dispatched to The Other Place.

67. The 1992 Disney remake of *The Canterville Ghost* overcomes the discrepancy between misdeed and punishment by having Sir Simon killed by his wife's relatives for having driven her to suicide by his erroneous accusation of infidelity.

68. Keyser, 1981, p. 127, wrongly claims that the 1951 version is the first to do so. *Ms. Scrooge* (1997) is an elderly black woman, making the difficult childhood obligatory.

69. Kael, 1991, p. 38.

70. Rowell, 1993, p. 18.

71. Keyser, 1981, p. 126.

72. According to Ray, 1995, p. 206, L. B. Mayer's favorite film.

73. Barr, 1993, p. 186.

74. Like the Irish diplomat in *The Halfway House*, who similarly realizes that neutrality is untenable.

75. See Aldgate and Richards, 1994, for the production history of *Thunder Rock*. The intensity of the debate with the captain suggests objectivity.

76. Flying with a ghost is also seen in *Casper* (1995).

77. Well known as a second-hand book center, where suitable reading would not be difficult to find.

78. Wolfenstein and Leites, 1950/70, p. 234.

79. The following year, one of *The Ghosts of Berkeley Square* walks through the other, but each retains his own attire.

80. Parish, 1994, p. 321.

81. Smith, 1996, p. 101. Hardy, 1983, p. 338, refers to the stranger as "literally a reincarnation" gaining revenge on those "responsible for his death in a previous life."

82. Smith, 1996, p. 110.

83. *Ibid*. p109. As he points out, this is unlikely as the stranger would not have the detailed knowledge revealed in the flashbacks.

84. *Ibid*. p. 107.

85. Tyler, 1971, p. 104. Thornton Wilder is reported to have been happy with the changed ending, feeling that his point had been made (Marilynn Wilson, 1981, p. 1836), but it is noteworthy that the play was

first performed in 1938, and the film appeared in a much-changed world.

86. Cary Grant had a scheduling problem (see Druxman for the production background to the series). Within the terms of the narrative this selectivity is hardly fair on Mrs. Kerby.

87. Less frequently does the ghost of a natural parent help out (as opposed to merely offering advice). An example is *The Sender* (1982), in which a young man able to transmit his nightmares to others is assisted by his dead mother.

88. If we disbelieve the sisters, this is not a ghost film as there is no independent evidence for the child's survival; the film is discussed more fully below.

89. Peter Straub wrote this and the novel upon which *Ghost Story* (1981) was based. Both have protagonists struggling to come to terms with guilt for past actions.

90. Simone Simon was reported not to have cared for the role on the grounds that she had little to do; Bodeen, 1971, p. 56.

91. Telotte, 1985, p. 123.

92. Irena's possible subjectivity had also been noted by Clarens, 1967, p. 114, and Butler, 1979, p. 52. Tom Milne, 1971, p. 55, argues that Irena is created from Amy's idealized image. The possible *construction* of a ghost after seeing a dead person's photograph is also found in *The Innocents*. In Paige's reading (1997, p. 295), Amy and Irena form a "sisterhood" against Oliver's patriarchal tyranny, though Paige argues that despite the evidence Irena is subjective. Notwithstanding his regard for Val Lewton, Dyson (1997, p. 183) dismisses the film in a single sentence, with Irena "the figment of a lonely child's imagination," allowing him to argue that Lewton's RKO films after *I Walked with a Zombie* (1943) are not supernatural. He characterizes it as "a delicate study of child psychology, rather than a horror film" (p. 230) as if the two were mutually exclusive.

93. Butler, 1967, p. 52; Nicholls, 1984, p. 187. As *Cat People* hinges on Irena's possible transformation into a cat when sexually aroused, she could hardly be Amy's mother, though Oliver links them together through "sickliness," as if Irena were her mother. Newman, 1999, p. 22, notes Bodeen's "standard sequel approaches" in *Curse*; as a result Amy "is almost Cat Woman's daughter."

94. Sinyard, 1992, p. 61.

95. This appears to be what Thompson, 1993, p. 95, note 10, is also saying.

96. Milne, 1971, p. 55; Hardy, 1985, pp. 84–85, fails to attribute the material he took from this article. Newman, 1999, p. 22, concurs that Irena goes because Amy no longer needs her.

97. Monogamy is not essential, and there is no reason why pre-mortem relationships should continue as if without interruption—in *The Terror* (1963) a soldier in love with a woman later realizes that she is the ghost of a local nobleman's wife. As the husband is still alive, issues of loyalty are foregrounded.

98. Arnold et al., 1997, p. 49.

99. In *Ghost Story* (1981) the ghost passes for alive and it is only when she presents a rotting persona that her supernatural nature is clear.

100. Senn and Johns, 1992, p. 271, mention that the sexual activity with a ghost in this film is a screen first.

101. Both directed by Sidney Franklin. It was remade as a semi-musical by Frank Borzage in 1941. Borzage had himself acted in a fake haunted castle film, *Wee Lady Betty* (1917).

102. As was 1922's Norma Talmadge in the Moonyean role.

103. Grafe, 1995, p. 25.

104. Fowkes, 1998, also raises the possibility that the Captain is subjective, the product of a would-be liberated woman facing the difficulties of a patriarchal society, and wishing for a more masculine replacement for her ineffectual husband who has died (p. 149). If Captain Gregg is a product of Lucy's subconscious, he cannot be said to have "ghost-written," as Fowkes puts it (p. 150), *Blood and Swash*.

105. Grafe, 1995, p. 47.

106. *Ibid.*, p. 48.

107. Jordan, 1989, p. x.

108. Fowkes, 1998, sees *Always, Truly, Madly, Deeply, Kiss Me Goodbye* and *Ghost* as masochistic—"the ghosts each engage in a masochistic contract with a woman to ensure their own pain and ineffectuality" (p. 36)—which misses the point. Masochism suggests perverse self-gratifi-

cation, the opposite of what these ghosts, except Jolly in *Kiss Me Goodbye*, do, which is to help the one left behind to move on. They behave selflessly after an initial period of struggle and actually empower loved ones paralyzed by bereavement.

109. See for example Brode, 1995, pp. 190, 193.

110. The latter is a remake of *Dona Flor and Her Two Husbands* (1976).

111. See for example Drek, 1990; Francke, 1991; Stilwell, 1997.

112. Fowkes, 1998, p. 25, ignores these when she describes ghost and "out-of-body transformation" films as fantasies, then continues "But the fantasies also tend to operate in the context of heterosexual romance."

113. He had drunk from the Fountain of Youth and never died—he was not reincarnated, as many reviewers thought.

114. Joe Fisher, 1990, pp. 255–56.

115. Twitchell, 1985, p. 141.

116. Neale, 1980, links them to castration anxieties.

117. In a slightly different category is Awbonnie in *Silent Tongue* (1993) who, although an unpleasant ghost, is earthbound due to love of her husband. Jenkins, 1982, p. 42, notes a reversal of the post–Halloween horror in *Ghost Story*—instead of female teenagers in jeopardy, the targets for aggression are old men. The *Variety* reviewer (credited as "Har.") asks why she should have held off for half a century before wreaking her revenge, allowing the four to lead prosperous lives (*Variety*, 16 December 1981). Perhaps there is no need to haunt people if their guilt is doing the job.

118. An example is *Ai no borei* (1978) in which a woman and her lover murder her husband, who haunts them. The template for this type of triangle is Santo Kyoden's *A Weird Story of Revenge in the Swamp of Asaka* (1803).

119. There are exceptions: the ghost in *Ghost Chase* (1987) occupies a clock, then a large puppet that it is able to animate; in *The Other* (1972), either a child is possessed by the spirit of his dead evil twin, or the trauma has caused mental instability. Nicholls, 1984, p. 207, feels that the choice is between possession and schizophrenia (presumably meant in the sense of split personality) whereas Hogan, 1986, p. 27, sees the influence of the dead brother as an example of his return as a demonic presence.

120. Possession frequently has a sexual element that can amount to rape. *Nurse Sherri* (1977) is forced to kill by her host (who wants revenge on doctors involved in the operation during which he died), as in *Supernatural* (1933) (here possession is denoted by heavier makeup). In *Nurse Sherri*, though, the dead spirit rapes his victim as well. In *The Entity* (1982) the possession seems to occur for no other reason than the invader's sexual gratification.

121. If it is possession, the mechanism is unclear—parading as other individuals is not sufficient motivation for the spirit of a person imitated to occupy the imitator.

122. Derry, 1977, p. 98.

123. See Perry, 1996.

124. Based on a play by Shloimeh Ansky, also filmed in 1969.

125. Other musicians whose ghosts have featured on film are Jim Morrison in *Wayne's World 2* (1993), encouraging Wayne to do something with his life, and John Lennon, who literally phones in his performance in *Paris, France* (1994). In *Wired* (1989) the ghost of John Belushi is taken on a tour of his past life by an angel masquerading as a taxi driver. The tour acquires the characteristics of Purgatory, but no improvement in Belushi's character occurs.

126. *Elvis and the Colonel* (1993) concedes that he died on the stated date, but still has his ghost as narrator of the story of his relationship with Colonel Parker.

127. This usage is obviously different from Gilbert Ryle's, but more appropriate, as Ryle was using the term "ghost" by analogy (See *The Concept of Mind*, 1949).

128. The method used to eliminate the ghost, although technological, does not bear a great deal of scrutiny. A virus introduced into the mainframe clogs its memory and prevents the spirit from roaming freely, until he is forced into a particle accelerator and destroyed.

129. The latter is analyzed in the next chapter. Vietnam has been a backdrop to few ghost films, another example being *House* (1985), in which a veteran is haunted

by the ghost of an army colleague who blames him for his death.

130. A similar scene occurs in *Nomads* (1986). A character has an unnerving but coherent experience, then wakes up in his car with such a start that he smashes his head against the windshield. Like *Carnival of Souls*, its status is not clear. The experient thinks that he has had a nightmare, but looks in his rear view mirror and sees one of the revenants that have been persecuting him.

131. "House" is used loosely to cover all types of dwelling — even the railway carriage in *The Sleeping Car* (1990).

132. London, 1975, p. 82.

133. Millbank, 1994, points out the same division in Gothic literature.

134. That there can be a sexual component is shown by films with brothels inhabited by ghosts of prostitutes, such as *The Nesting* (1981) and *Blood Sisters* (1986).

135. Carroll, 1990, p. 98.

136. A similar story line in *Ghost Story* (1974), in which Talbot witnesses a scene from forty years before, does not end happily for the house guests.

137. King, 1993, p. 315.

138. *Ibid.*, p. 296.

139. The French title, *Fantôme à Vendre*, makes Murdoch's status as commodity, linked to the castle's sale, more apparent. By the time of *High Spirits* (1988) the tide had turned, and Peter Plunkett is fighting to save the family home from being sold and moved to the United States — Jordan cites *The Ghost Goes West*, *Topper* and *Blithe Spirit* as influences (Jones, 1989, p. 18).

140. *High Spirits* is a descendant of this tradition, with mobile bed, as in *The Dream of a Rarebit Fiend* (1906). The film is truer to many modern alleged hauntings than its horror forebears. The convention is for them to drive visitors away, whereas in reality it is common for hotels and pubs to announce hauntings as hooks for business, just as Castle Plunkett is marketed as a tourist attraction.

141. Cabana, 1995, p. 22; McCarty, 1995, p. 13.

142. Cabana, 1995, p. 23.

143. Clarens, 1967, p. 56.

144. They do this by means of loud music, a technique advocated, tongue in cheek, by Baker and Nickell, 1992, pp. 142–44, to "de-ghost" premises.

145. Newman, 1988a, p. 159.

146. Derry, 1977, p. 22.

147. Nelson, 1982, p. 230.

148. This is a rare example of action transposed from the United States to England rather than vice versa. The source novel, Richard Matheson's *Hell House*, is set in Maine.

149. The mental medium, Florence, is played by Pamela Franklin, who was Flora in *The Innocents*.

150. The implication of building over a burial ground in *Poltergeist* is that disaffected Indians are responsible, but the issue is muddied by the Other Dimension; in the two sequels nineteenth-century Preacher Kane is shown to be behind events (the daughter Carol Anne is also psychic, so perhaps the phenomena need to be met half way).

151. Anson, 1977. He also worked on the screenplay of *The Exorcist*. There is a large literature on the Amityville hoax; see for example Auerbach, 1986; Harris, 1986; Stein, 1993.

152. King, 1993, pp. 168–70.

153. The cemetery in *Pet Sematary* (1989) that brings corpses back to life is also the site of an Indian burial ground.

154. Brophy, 1986, p. 7, claims that the horror is situated "in a social-realist frame."

155. The mirror as locus of ghostly malevolence is also found in *Dead of Night* (1945), *The Boogyman* (1980) and its sequel *Boogyman 2* (1982), and *Mark of the Devil* (1984).

156. Newman, 1988a, p. 166.

157. Casper wants to be friends but still terrifies almost everybody he meets.

158. Varnado, 1987, p. 87.

159. MacKenzie, 1982, pp. 27–28, gives two examples of apparitions of the living who appear not to have realized that they had been in two places at once.

160. Hardy, 1985, p. 30, wrongly states that the 1922 version was the first.

161. Dyson, 1997, p. 78.

162. Such organizations often have names that are variants on "The Society for Psychical Research."

163. The film is based upon an investigation conducted in Culver City in the

1970s; Marianne Stone, 1996. She concludes that the cause was RSPK, not an entity.

164. Pirie, 1973, p. 125.

165. *Ibid.*, p. 126.

166. Much of the narrative is told in flashback to Krasner, who plays a listening role similar to that of van Straaten, both played by Frederick Valk, in *Dead of Night* the same year.

167. The disguising of a corpse as a sculpture was later used in *A Bucket of Blood* (1959).

168. This film is usually lumped in with four other films by Sewell, *The Medium*, *Latin Quarter*, *Ghost Ship*, and *House of Mystery* (see for example Boot, 1996, p. 14), but it is quite different in tone to the last three at least — all it has in common with them is the ghostly theme.

169. For example Ghostbusters UK (formerly Grimsby Ghostbusters), who use a converted hearse.

170. *The Changeling* is an exception to this often arbitrary mixing of ghost and poltergeist phenomena. The banging heard on a regular basis is an "echo" of the child banging on the bath as he is drowned by his father.

171. Biograph Bulletins, 1908–12, p. 351.

172. The opposite occurs in *The Medium* (1951). An ostensibly fake medium cannot countenance the possibility that she has been subject to a paranormal event when she feels a hand touch her throat during a séance, leading to mental collapse.

173. The point is not crucial to the plot. Gifford (1973b) lists further versions in 1930 and 1939 and is explicit that in all three the medium is fraudulent.

174. The film's first audiences would have been familiar with the trial of medium Helen Duncan in 1944.

175. Browning had made the 1930 version of *The Thirteenth Chair* (remade in 1937), in which a fake medium uses a séance to unmask a murderer.

176. Another depiction of Spiritualism in a detective story is the Charlie Chan *Black Magic* (1944).

177. As a result he is possessed and the evil spirit has to be exorcised, reflecting the established Church's hostility towards Spiritualism. Landy, 1991, pp. 400–01, provides a description of the plot.

178. Or are they? Kinder and Houston, 1987, p. 58, argue that these images are taken from Heather's vision during the sequence in the restaurant ladies' room which John integrates in a belated realization that he too is psychic; this is unlikely, as the film concentrates on John, and the audience would more readily take his point of view than Heather's.

179. Palmer and Riley, 1995, pp. 18–19, come to the same conclusion.

180. The extent of John's abilities is left unclear. When Izod (1992, p. 78) says that his words "I know this place" demonstrate second sight as he had not seen it before, Izod is forgetting that John could have walked that way earlier, Venice being fairly small. Even if he does ignore his talents, death is a harsh punishment.

181. Wilson, 1999, p. 284.

182. In his concern for his wife, he forgets the vision's significance (Feinman, 1978, p. 93); it is unclear why he should be sensitive to his daughter's fate but not his own. Kinder and Houston (1987, p. 55) discuss fate and free will (what is the point of a warning if one cannot change the outcome?), "pulp metaphysics" according to Nicholls, 1984, p. 143. Estrin, 1990, p. 261, also emphasizes the issue of the accidental forestalling preparedness, but not the implication that precognition would render the story redundant. The level of ESP varies according to plot requirements.

183. Gifford, 1974, p. 10.

184. Cold reading involves the medium's obtaining information in such a way that the client is not aware of having provided it, so that when it is fed back, it will appear to have been paranormally derived (see Baker and Nickell, 1992, p. 171); also, snippets are often exaggerated in the client's mind after the session. There are other ways to glean information, such as through newspapers—Milne, 1973, p. 238, mentions this in connection with Heather's knowledge of Christine.

185. Admittedly the statement refers to Christine, and in any case, convinced that life continues after death, perhaps Heather is unconcerned that John will die and sees no reason to be sad about it.

186. Sanderson, 1996, p. 61.

187. For example Gifford, 1974, p. 10;

Kael, 1977, p. 233; Donaldson, 1981, p. 663; Lavery, 1982, p. 53; and Palmer and Riley, 1995, p. 16, all see a parallel between John's job, fitting mosaics into a pattern, and the film's hunting for clues that help to make sense of a seemingly arbitrary universe. Gomez's discussion of the importance of interpretation in Roeg's work (1981, p. 47) also touches on this issue.

188. Gomez, 1981, pp. 48–49. Feinman, 1978, p. 87, asserts that despite not knowing what they are laughing about, the implication is "that they represent danger and evil for Laura and John."

189. In the similarly themed *Witchtrap* (1989), psychical researchers investigating a haunted house are killed by the ghost of the house's previous owner, a Satanist.

190. It so happens that the medium is the maid rather than Madam Arcati.

191. See for example Blackmore, 1993, for a discussion of the issues.

192. As the main character in *Intersection* (1994) is dying, he experiences flashbacks that become progressively shorter and fragmented, with decreasing realizm, perhaps to show the effects of anoxia.

193. Where this differs from the ghosts of the living discussed above is in the absence of a witness. There is no evidence that Arvik is objectively in two places at once. We are inside his head looking out.

194. There is no reason to believe that the image is anything other than a hallucination, crystallizing regret.

195. Written by Bruce Joel Rubin, who went on to script *Ghost* (1990) and *Jacob's Ladder* (1990).

196. Milne, 1983, p. 328.

197. Brosnan, 1991, p. 349.

198. Brosnan, 1991, p. 349.

199. Stockton, 1982, p. 12. In a discussion about inducing visions of the departed under laboratory conditions, Moody, 1994, p. xi, mentions *Flatliners*, adding "no one in his or her right mind would attempt such a stunt."

200. Death in *Dr. Terror's House of Horrors* (1964) is indistinguishable from his fellow travellers (although he is called Dr. Schreck, i.e. death) until the end of the film, when they realize who he is, and that they are dead.

201. Kurtz, 1934/75, p. 209 ff.

202. This is not typical. Death does not usually cajole.

203. Fittingly, he disguises himself as an aristocrat. The remake of *Death Takes a Holiday*, *Meet Joe Black* (1998), a title evoking the everyman nature of *Meet John Doe* (1941), moves away from traditional depictions of Death by assigning the main role to Brad Pitt who passes himself off as a tax investigator.

204. Bergman, 1995, p. 236.

205. Sarris, 1975, p. 89.

206. Peary, 1983, p. 142, quoting *Bergman on Bergman*, published in 1970.

207. Ward, 1998, p. 18.

208. Crick, 1996, p. 162, asks why mother and daughter could wander but not meet until the climax, and why they leave when the murderer is not dead, undermining the idea that their reunion is made possible by achieving justice.

209. Draco the Dragon in *Dragonheart* (1996) goes one better and after death *becomes* a star.

210. See MacGregor, 1992, pp. 77–79, for a fuller discussion.

211. Judgment need not be in a celestial context: that in *Orgy of the Dead* (1956), with Criswell listening to the tales of the dead in a graveyard, has more the quality of a Stanley Spencer-style resurrection.

212. Heaven is like graduate school, where entities are trained for their future lives on earth. In this and in *Defending Your Life*, the romance that drives the narrative is initiated there.

213. A point made by Wilson, 1991, p. 66.

214. MacGregor, 1992, p. 145.

215. Bureaucracy is shown in *A Matter of Life and Death* (1946) and is alluded to in *Blithe Spirit* (1945).

216. Tyler, 1971, p. 104, sees the Afterlife in *Between Two Worlds* as Protestant, whereas of course the Examiner may merely take a form appropriate to that batch of passengers.

217. Not *Guidebook*, as Newman, 1988b, p. 228, indicates, nor *Guide to the Newly Deceased*, as favored by Senn and Johns, 1992, p. 261.

218. She is saved, and transported to Heaven, by Chris's decision to stay with her

in Hell, an emphasis on love also found in *A Matter of Life and Death* (1946).

219. Campbell, 1949/68.

220. According to Rhodes, 1996a, p. 214, Vane wrote the play while acting in a London stage version of *The Thirteenth Chair*. As significant as the change of name of the two versions is the reason for the attempted suicide of the main characters, from an extramarital affair in the first to an inability to obtain exit visas in the second, indicating the changed mores of the respective periods

221. Strick, 1976, pp. 139–140.

222. Virilio, 1984, p. 62.

223. That the setting is of minor importance is shown by the remake of *Lifeboat* (1944) as *Lifepod* (1993), transferring the action from a boat to a spaceship.

224. One instance when advice is not in the recipient's interest is in *A Matter of Life and Death* (1946); Conductor 71, to all intents an angel, tries to inveigle Peter up the stairs to Heaven.

225. *Made in Heaven* (1987) also features fluffy wings.

226. Athanael in *The Horn Blows at Midnight* also falls from the top of a building, into a giant coffee cup that is part of an advertisement for the product that influenced his dream.

227. A variant is *Mr. Destiny* (1990), where an angelic bartender shows a man what his life would have been like had a key event been different; although he had been miserable about the outcome the whole of his adult life, he discovers that it was far better than the one he had desired.

228. This is the British title; the American one is the same as the 1951 version, a change probably predicated on presumed British ignorance of what an outfield is, forgetting that cricket also has an outfield and that British audiences might therefore be familiar with the term.

229. In the original an angel strikes a deal with the manager of the Pittsburgh Pirates that his team will be given assistance in return for the manager's desisting from profanities, a quaint notion by 1994.

230. The aristocratic young ghost in *Little Ghost* (1996) can also transform into sparkles, an effect that owes more to computer generated imagery than to psychical research.

231. A similar theme is provided by the basketball film *The Sixth Man* (1997), where rather than an angel, help is provided by a dead player, visible only to his brother, although he is able to interact with matter and morph his shape. As in the baseball films, he does not assist in the final game. Angels enjoy U.S. sports—in *Angels in the Endzone* (1997), an angel helps a high-school football team.

232. This film is a marginal exception to the Hollywood rule that whereas single mothers can be divorcées, single fathers must be widowers, in that the parents had divorced prior to the mother's death, hence the father's inept parenting skills when he takes charge of his daughter.

233. That they threaten the couple to bring them together, not realizing that they are already falling in love, suggests a lack of insight.

234. Wenders's *Wings of Desire* (1987) and *Faraway, So Close!* (1993), the former remade as *City of Angels* (1998), also feature angels who become mortal and find love, suggesting that the spiritual is not an adequate substitute for the full range of human activity. Unusually in angel films, they can hear the thoughts of mortals.

Chapter 4

1. Hutchings, 1993, p. 26.
2. Barr, 1993, p. 55.
3. Perry, 1994, p. 86.
4. Moberly and Jourdain, 1911/55. Perry, 1994, p. 86, highlights the segment's ambiguity when he calls it "a simple haunting" and a few sentences later says that "It seems that she has stepped into the previous century."
5. Jancovich, 1992, p. 79.
6. *Ibid.*, pp. 79–81.
7. Hutchings, 1993, p. 27.
8. Frederick Valk, who plays van Straaten, plays a similar role as Dr. Krasner in the same year's *Latin Quarter*.
9. Barr, in notes to 1st edition, 1977, p. 187; the comment was removed from the second edition (1993).
10. Clarens, 1967, p. 117.
11. Timelessness is signalled in the first story by the cessation of the clock during

Notes—Chapter 4

Hugh's precognitive experience, echoed in *AMOLAD* the following year. Silence is discussed in *The Innocents* below. In the *Dead of Night* story the track towards the curtains could be construed as hinting that there is a mystery 'beyond the veil'.

12. Harris, 1986, pp. 102–09, gives an account, with a still showing Miles Malleson on the hearse.
13. Hutchings, 1993, pp. 31, 35.
14. Dyson, 1997, p. 172, links the crying to that heard in *The Haunting* (1963). The psychoanalytic "method" reaches its nadir when Dyson argues that Sally, having repulsed the host, chooses non-sexual contact with the child, cuddling him before putting him to bed—"...unclear of the story's intention we are left only with a rather unpleasant smell of necrophilia." (p. 173) He has said that the contact is non-sexual, so how could it whiff of necrophilia? It is the kind of comforting embrace that Sally later elicits from the host's mother when she in turn is distressed.
15. And Creed, 1989, p. 68.
16. Another example that undermines Hutchings's hypothesis is *Full Circle* (1976). Julia attempts unsuccessfully to perform a tracheotomy on her daughter, cutting her throat in the process. She is subsequently haunted not by her daughter but by the ghost of an evil girl who while alive had murdered a boy. The girl eventually kills Julia, by cutting her throat.
17. Taylor, 1989. Ivan Butler, 1979, p. 64, alludes to the case in his analysis of the film
18. Hutchings, 1993, p. 32.
19. Joan's lack of taste in choosing such an item has not been remarked on, although the contrast between its ornateness and the flat's crisp modernity has—for example Barr, 1993, p. 56, sees the dark reality of the mirror pushing up into the ordered shallowness of Peter's life.
20. Dyson, 1997, p. 174.
21. Landy, 1991, p. 390, and Dyson, 1997, p. 175, draw attention to the Gainsborough parallel.
22. Kael, 1968, p. 255.
23. The reverse of the same year's *Blithe Spirit*, in which one man ends up with two women.
24. Butler, 1979, pp. 64–65, and Dyson, 1997, p. 178, make a similar point.
25. Agee, 1967, p. 213; first published 17 August 1946.
26. Dyson, 1997, p. 177.
27. Pirie, 1973, p. 23; Hutchings, 1993, p. 35. Similarly Kawin, 1990, p. 52: "...in the movie, the dreamer ... kills the psychiatrist and then is pursued by characters from the inner stories until they get him and he wakes up...."
28. Butler, 1979, p. 65.
29. Barr, 1977, p. 59.
30. Gough-Yates, 1971.
31. Harper and Porter, 1989, p. 188.
32. Powell, 1986, p. 496.
33. The audience at the first Royal Command performance at the Empire Theater was greeted with the marquee slogan "Was it a dream or did it really happen?" as part of the display, emphasizing the ambiguity.
34. Harper and Porter, 1989, p. 186.
35. Ellis, 1978. Christie, 1994a, p. 59, also refers to these twin discourses.
36. Salt, 1992, p. 181.
37. Presumably François Philidor's *L'-Analyze du jeu des Échecs* (1749).
38. Hanson, 1990, p. 562.
39. Christie, 1994a, p. 58, rightly calls this gesture "a final, compressed poetic image."
40. Powell, 1986, p. 487.
41. *The Lay of the Last Minstrel*, Canto III, Verse II.
42. Ellis, 1978, p. 103; Harper, 1994, p. 107, also refers to Durgnat's view, as well as the Robsons, who saw the film as a metaphor for a Nazi New Order, and Nicholas Pronay, who she says characterised the film as a celebration of "an untidy individualism."
43. Ibid., p. 29.
44. Warman, 1946, p. 42.
45. Barr, 1986, p. 19. Christie, 1994a, p. 59, also draws attention to the "focus on the process of representation."
46. Harper, 1994, p. 108, feels that the shot from inside the eye grants the audience access to Peter's subjectivity, and with it his knowledge of Western culture ("the whole of culture and human history" goes too far).
47. Hutchings, 1993, p. 30.
48. Director Jack Clayton had previously directed the unambiguous ghost short *The

Bespoke Overcoat (1956), a loose adaptation of Gogol's story.
49. Silver and Ursini, 1994, pp. 122–23.
50. Kael, 1966, p. 164.
51. Haggerty, 1989, pp. 153–54.
52. See Palmer, 1977, pp. 209–13, and Higson, 1994, for a discussion of point of view in the film.
53. Edward Recchia, 1987, p. 30; Higson, 1994, p. 206, argues that it is not clear that it is a flashback.
54. McDougal, 1985, p. 148; this time-dilation would place this film with *An Occurrence at Owl Creek Bridge* and *Jacob's Ladder*. It is generally assumed, following the novel, that Miles is dead although this is not completely certain — he could have fainted. However, Miss Giddens's initial voice-over suggests that he is dead, and a faint would not have the same dramatic impact.
55. McDougal, 1985, p. 152.
56. Higson, 1994, p. 205; he quotes Jackson, 1981, p. 24, in support, but the model also follows Tudor's (1989) analysis of horror tracing movement from external to internal threats.
57. Wilson, 1934/1960. There were earlier analyzes along similar lines; see Heller, 1989, pp. 10–11.
58. Sinyard, 1992, p. 66.
59. Higson, 1994, p. 208.
60. Kael, 1966, p. 166.
61. Palmer, 1977, p. 198.
62. Boot, 1996, p. 156, considers her "a sexually vibrant young woman."
63. Butler, 1979, p. 66; Murphy, 1992, p. 79.
64. Smith, 1996, p. 135.
65. Seidman, 1979, p. 204.
66. Derry, 1977, p. 99, links *The Innocents* to another film in which a disturbed boy is forced to say a name in order to free himself from a malign influence — *The Other* (1972), and mentions Rumpelstiltskin as the archetypal story in which saying a name leads to power over it.
67. Silver, 1981, pp. 153–54.
68. See for example *Motion Picture Herald*, Vol. 225 No. 13, p. 4, and *Film Daily*, Vol. 119 No. 113, p. 8.
69. 27 November 1961, p. 8.
70. This approach is similar to that accorded to *AMOLAD* — reality or dream? — at its premiere.

71. Dyson, 1997, p. 213.
72. *Ibid.*, p. 215
73. Smith (1996, p. 127) also mentions William Castle's schlock tactics as an influence on 20th Century–Fox's promotion of this film, although exploitation techniques in support of a highbrow ghost film can be seen as early as Griffith's *The Greatest Question* (1919).
74. 24 November 1961, p. 8. *Homicidal* (1961) was another Castle production.
75. Quoted by Smith, 1996, p. 128. The term psychogenetics used in this way is unknown to psychical research; it refers to the ways in which the behavior of an organism is influenced by its genetic make-up.
76. Sinyard, 1992, p. 64. He means a succubus.
77. *Ibid.*, p. 134.
78. Smith, 1996, p. 145.
79. Cowie, 1962, p. 36.
80. Palmer, 1977, p. 212.
81. Recchia, 1987, p. 34.
82. Palmer, 1977, p. 211. Allen, 1977, sees the alternatives as either "heightened perception" or "neurotic hypersensitivity" (quoted in Beja, 1979, p. 224), but heightened perception could be included as a symptom of hypersensitivity, so the two are not strictly bipolar, although he clearly intends the two to stand for objective and subjective interpretations respectively.
83. MacKenzie, 1997, p. 130.
84. The use of silence in *Carnival of Souls* (1962), when Mary finds that she cannot be seen by the people around her, shows her to be out of kilter with reality.
85. Smith, 1996, p. 145.
86. Murphy, 1992, p. 195.
87. Dyson, 1997, p. 228.
88. Dyson (1997, p. 231 ff) identifies five aspects of the cinematography that give the film its visual power: fluid use of the camera, disruption of spatial orientation, unsettling editing style, image composition and use of sound. This approach could owe something to his period as editor for Orson Welles.
89. The French title for the film is *La Maison du Diable*, an unsubtle ploy that undermines Wise's manifest intentions, and harks back, though with even less justification, to Méliès's 1896 *Le Manoir du Diable*.

Notes—Chapter 4

90. Contrary to Clarens's assertion that he did not; Clarens, 1967, pp. 152–53.

91. At one point Luke refers to Theo and Eleanor as "little Miss ESP" and "Bridey Murphy" respectively. This could be a veiled suggestion that Eleanor is the reincarnation of Abigail.

92. Dyall was The Man in Black on the radio program *Appointment with Fear* from 1943–55, made a film appearance in the role in 1949, and had also appeared in several ghost-related films: *Latin Quarter* (1945), *The Ghost of Rashmon Hall* (1947) and *The Queen of Spades* (1948). He was a resurrected warlock in *City of the Dead* (1960).

93. Bunnell, 1984, p. 89. Where the films are similar is in the inability of the viewer to be able to formulate an image of the buildings' overall topography, although in *The Haunting* this reflects the architecture, so that the viewer's confusion mirrors the occupants'.

94. Clarens, 1967, p. 153, assumes that she and Theo are both mediums.

95. Hogan, 1986, p. 85.

96. Leemann, 1995, pp. xii–xiii (foreword by Gidding).

97. Rhine, 1937/50, pp. 49–50.

98. Senn, 1996, p. 81, calls her "the terrified adult/child, who not only cowers before the unknown but becomes instantly petulant whenever she fails to get her own way."

99. Holland, 1981, p. 1000.

100. Hartnoll, 1974, p. 54.

101. Hardy, 1985, p. 154.

102. Cornell, 1996.

103. This approach can be contrasted with that of Barrett (a nod to psychical researcher William Barrett?) in *The Legend of Hell House* (1972), who is interested in what processes could underlie paranormal phenomena, rather than merely trying to prove that they exist.

104. For example by Dingwall, Goldney and Hall, 1956.

105. Upton Sinclair was supposed to have written a scenario for a film on Borley (Tabori, 1950/74, p. 241), which was never produced.

106. Hogan, 1986, p. 85.

107. Bunnell, 1984, p. 92.

108. See for example Haynes, 1982, pp. 106–08.

109. Silver and Ursini, 1994, p. 144.

110. See Grixti, 1989, p. 61, for a short discussion on what shining might comprize. Both Mayersberg, 1980/1, p. 57, and Titterington, 1981, p. 119, note the shining's ability to see forwards and backwards in time, and talk of it in terms of a metaphor for cinema itself.

111. *Twister*'s tag line is *The Dark Side of Nature*, echoing Catherine Crowe's *The Night-Side of Nature*, 1848.

112. Hogan, 1986, p. 50.

113. Hala, 1990, p. 206.

114. Smith, 1997, p. 300; he also includes the farcical elements as adding to this unsettling mixture (p. 301).

115. Leibowitz and Jeffress, 1981, p. 47.

116. Smith, 1997, p. 301.

117. Leibowitz and Jeffress, 1981, p. 49.

118. Diane Johnson, who co-wrote the script with Kubrick, refers to an 'additive' theory in a 1978 interview, where she talks about ghosts being real, imaginary, or being real but needing psychic ability on the part of the percipient (she, presumably incorrectly, refers to the *ghosts* as having "psychic powers") to manifest; quoted in Rhodes, 1996b, pp. 269–70.

119. Smith, 1997, p. 303, argues that Jack may not be mad but merely feigning to turn work into play, though he does not say why Jack would go to such extreme measures for fun, and this method is not particularly productive.

120. Hoile, 1984, p. 7.

121. Cook, 1984, p. 2 (Romney, 1999, pp. 10–11, does interpret the film in terms of possession, both of the characters and of the audience). Smith, 1997, p. 301, sees the economic emphasis as evidence of a Marxist influence on Cook's part. Titterington, 1981, p. 118, and Smith, 1997, p. 305, also draw attention to the film's use of red, white and blue, which works at a subliminal level.

122. Titterington, 1981, pp. 119, 120.

123. Nicholls, 1984, p. 93.

124. Titterington, 1980/1, p. 120, referring to *Repulsion*, asks whether the events could be in Jack's mind.

125. Snyder, 1982, p. 12.

126. Caldwell and Umland, 1986.

127. *Ibid.*, p. 111.

128. Liebowitz and Jeffress, p. 46.

129. Smith, 1997, pp. 301–02. Smith as-

sumes that Kubrick's attitude to Hallorann is positive, not allowing for the possibility that, in portraying his Florida room as tacky, Kubrick is laughing at him. Smith also argues (p. 305) that Jack has not considered that Grady might have been offered the same inducements, but ended up as permanent butler. Grady's role is not clear, but he is more than simply a butler, acting as spokesperson for the management.

130. Paul, 1994, p. 349.
131. Ciment, 1983, p. 190.
132. Smith, 1990, p. 182.
133. Smith, 1990, p. 188.
134. It is appropriate that Danny saves himself by using an Indian trick, backtracking and erasing his footprints in the snow.
135. Bunnell, 1984, p. 97.
136. Hoile, 1984, p. 8.
137. Romney, 1999, p. 11, wonders whether Jack sees the woman at all — she could be Danny's "metaphor for the urgency of events." Jack's telling Wendy that he has seen nothing is poor evidence for this. Paul, 1994, p. 349, also suggests that Jack's experience is possibly Danny's communication to Dick Hallorann, confusing fantasy and reality for the audience.
138. Jack fails to learn from his scrutiny, while Danny's explorations save his life. Paul, 1994, pp. 339, 341, in his examination of Jack and Danny's relationship in the aptly titled chapter *The Revenge of Oedipus* points out the inverse parallel between Danny's movement outwards and Jack's retreat into himself.
139. Danny's shining also fails when Jack is on the rampage. Danny escapes outside but re-enters the hotel when Hallorann is on the way. Hallorann can "pick up" Danny in Florida but Danny cannot pick up Hallorann down the road.
140. The tennis ball that rolls across the floor in front of Danny appears to be the one that Jack had earlier been bouncing against the wall, linking him with the phenomena. Repetitive bouncing, and later typing, point to a sterile mind. A mysterious bouncing ball, with no obvious thrower, had previously been seen in *Kill, Baby, Kill* (1966) and *The Changeling* (1979).
141. Snyder, 1982, p. 11.
142. Ciment, 1983, p. 188.

143. Steinbeck, 1970, p. 94; emphasis in original.
144. Hala, 1990, p. 208 ff. Smith, 1997, p. 303, makes a similar connection between cartoon and other media images and the cartoonish nature of the violence.
145. Hoile, 1984, p. 5.
146. Brown, 1992. Mayersberg, 1980/1, p. 54, had earlier likened the film to an updated James story, the narrative either a figment of Jack's imagination or re-enactments or memories of the past.
147. Madigan, 1990, p. 195.
148. Ciment, 1983, p. 181, quotes Kubrick making this observation. Madigan, 1990, pp. 194–5, refers to Ciment, but omits the page number, instead eliding the point with a quotation by Kubrick on p. 187.
149. Grixti, 1989, p. 62 ff.
150. Brown, 1992, p. 115.
151. Mayersberg, 1980/1, p. 56. Would DT-induced hallucinations be this coherent?
152. Leibowitz and Jeffress, 1981, p. 50.
153. Ciment, 1983, p. 194; Titterington, 1981, p. 120.
154. Romney, 1999, p. 9. However he later (p. 11) muses that if Jack is the in-house entertainer for the resident ghosts, then his appearance at the center of the photograph could be seen as a reward (perhaps consolation would be a better term) after his defeat. One still wonders how a "big night back in 1921" could be "everlasting" (*ibid.*) — it seems anchored in the time continuum rather than outside it.
155. Smith, 1997, p. 305, refers to Jack's position in the photograph as "token," whereas he is center stage.
156. Combs, 1980.
157. Unless we assume that the two conditions are merely correlated.
158. A list of cuts, amounting to almost thirty minutes, accompanies Combs's review. One of these is a scene with a doctor in which Wendy reveals Jack's dislocation of Danny's shoulder in a drunken rage, plus Jack's pledge never to touch alcohol again.
159. Spignesi, 1991, p. 568.
160. Ciment, 1983, p. 181.
161. Nelson, 1982, p. 200.
162. The reference to the graveyard hints at revenge for the desecration, but as Smith,

1997, p. 301, points out, all the ghosts that are seen are white. It is possible that Indians provide the controlling intelligence. (The ethnicity of the ghosts could be a reason why Hallorann was not recruited by the hotel.)

163. They are clearly not twins but it is a convenient shorthand that has been adopted in the literature. They bear a passing resemblance to, and may have been partly inspired by, Diane Arbus's 1967 photograph *Identical Twins, Roselle, New Jersey*.

164. Rhodes, 1996b, pp. 272–73, discusses the maze/labyrinth motif, seeing it as a symbol of life and exploration, both externally and of the self. Even bearing in mind its inclusion on the pragmatic grounds that the hedge animals in King's novel were impossible to recreate convincingly, the maze could be seen as symbolizing a pointless activity that Danny transcends but to which Jack falls prey.

165. Smith, 1997, p. 300, also sees Kubrick's use of mirrors as reflecting its (American) audience's unpleasantnesses, what is going on in the film paralleling what happens beyond the screen in everyday life.

166. Newman, 1988a, p. 166.

167. Rhodes, 1996b, p. 277.

168. Dickstein, 1984, pp. 75–76.

169. Clover, 1989.

170. Clover, 1989, p. 124. Admittedly he does inadvertently save Wendy and Danny by distracting Jack during his climactic attack on the bathroom door.

171. Bunnell, 1984, p. 95.

172. See Shipman, 1991, for a discussion of the Donner Party's survival rates.

173. One result of Jack's incapacity is that Wendy does the job for which he was hired, maintaining the hotel.

174. Manchel, 1995, p. 76.

175. Kael, 1993, p. 674. This co-existence of discrete time periods can also be seen in *Portrait of Jennie* (1948).

176. Skal, 1993, p. 386.

177. Teitelbaum, 1991, p. 50.

178. Carrol Fry (Fry et al., 1998) also sees the film as a New Age vision of Christianity, containing an element of Eastern mysticism.

179. Teitelbaum, 1991, p. 50.

180. *Ibid.*, In a linked article, Leayman, 1991, p. 52, mentions the script's "Old Testament sternness and psychological insight that impart an epic, magisterial quality that director Adrian Lyne's film fails to capture."

181. Newman, 1991, p. 50.

182. Bierce, 1892. Newman obliquely refers to Bierce, as do Fry and Craig — Craig's contribution is partly entitled "An Occurrence on Jacob's Ladder"—more explicitly (Fry et al., 1998).

183. Similarly, Boorman (1998, p. 5), says of Lee Marvin's character, Walker, in *Point Blank* (1967), "He exists on two planes: a realistic one, and one where the whole film is being imagined by him in the moment of his death. He could just as easily be a ghost or a shadow." Thomson (1998, pp. 14–17) also raises the possibility that the story is Walker's dying fantasy.

184. Later the subway, with a sign saying "Hell," takes on symbolic emphasis. Fry argues that this sign, stating that help is available for drug users, is a reference to the help available from Louis and Michael. Judith Mayne, 1993, pp. 150–51, mentions the subway in the same year's *Ghost* linking the two (earthly) worlds, the upscale area of Sam and Molly and the down-at-heel neighborhood of the murderer Willie and of Oda Mae, the journeys on which provide Sam with the information he needs to operate among the living.

185. The element of a covert, unaccountable, government using individuals as guinea pigs would later find expression in *The X-Files*. Ken Jurkiewicz (Fry et al., 1998, p. 232) characterizes *Jacob's Ladder*, along with similar "wish-fulfilment melodramas" such as *Ghost*, *Always*, and *Flatliners*, as a New Age response to social problems that seem overwhelming, the lesson being that nothing can be done to alleviate conditions in this life. In this reading, Jacob stands in for the alienated urban resident. Far from bringing comfort, Jurkiewicz sees these films contributing to problems of modern life by increasing the sense of helplessness.

186. Newman, 1991, p. 50.

187. Ring, 1994, pp. 12–13. His article is part of a debate within the same issue of *Journal of Near-Death Studies* in which

other researchers of frightening NDEs respond, with a commentary on their papers by Ring.
188. Bache, 1994, p. 33.
189. Teitelbaum, 1990, p. 5.
190. See for example Thomas, 1965, pp. 46–56: *Elijah, Pioneer of Petrol*.
191. The word "church," along with her Hispanic appearance, mark her as probably Roman Catholic rather than Jewish, adding further theological confusion.
192. Fry (Fry et al., 1998, p. 225).

Chapter 5

1. Kael, 1991, p. 45.
2. Shipman, 1982, Vol. 1, p. 18.
3. In Dickson and Dickson, 1895.
4. Skal, 1993, p. 31. The original appeared in *Nizhegorodski listok*, 4 July 1896; the translation quoted by Skal first appeared in *New Theater*, March 1937, p. 11. Harding and Popple, 1996, pp. 5–6, provide another version that has "It is not life but its shadow, it is not motion but its soundless spectre." The excerpt in Christie, 1994b, p. 124, however, substitutes "movement" for "ghosts" or "spectre," removing any paranormal implication.
5. Parkinson, 1993, p. 511. Coates, 1984, p. 121, echoes this when he talks of "the living ghost of the screen image"; see Briggs, 1977, pp. 111 ff, for a discussion on the ghost story as a means of communicating with the past.
6. Perez (1998) alludes rather dialectically to this paradoxical being/not-being in the title of his book *The Material Ghost*, the term being used metaphorically. Todorov, 1977, p. 155, has only half the story when he refers to the ghost as "absence par excellence."
7. Gorky saw a downside when he continued his 1896 review "It seems as if these people have died and their shadows have been condemned to play cards in silence unto eternity" (Harding and Popple, 1996, p. 5), which is in line with the idea that hauntings are a replay, without consciousness, of past actions.
8. Gifford, 1973a, p. 208; similarly Lyttle, 1990, p. 17: "…what is that imagination of life projected onto the screen except a spectre made from light and the audience's imagination?"
9. Hecht, 1984, Part 1, p. 2.
10. Coined by Nigel Kneale for the title of his 1972 television script.
11. Wollen, 1997, p. 18.
12. Dead stars' comeback thanks to digital technology adds another dimension to notions of their survival of death.
13. Sanderson, 1996, p. 70.
14. Warner, 1995, p. 41.
15. *Ibid.*, p. 45. Tyler, 1971, p. 92, also refers to "the soul as shadow and reflection." Perhaps it follows that black and white is a more natural vehicle for ghost films than color; Coates, 1984, p. 124, refers to "the spectral poignancy of black and white," which color lacks.
16. Bologna and Tomlinson termed part of their Phantasmagoria show "skiagraphic," but this element was largely non-occult (Musser, 1990, pp. 25–26).
17. Neale, 1980, p. 32.
18. The soul-as-double could explain the use of mirrors or reflective surfaces as a motif in ghost films; if spirits are analogous to reflections, then if one can exist though immaterial, perhaps the other can also.
19. Barnouw, 1981, p. 105.
20. Tyler, 1971, p. 87.
21. Waller, 1986, p. 8.
22. Moretti, 1982.
23. Braund, 1997, p. 130.
24. Carroll, 1990, pp. 31–32, links boundary crossing of a culture's conceptual scheme to impurity, and disgust. The ghost is a "fusion figure," along with such other creatures as vampires, mummies, zombies, blurring the distinction between living and dead (p. 43).
25. *Don't Look Now* (1973) constantly draws attention to boundaries with motifs such as water, mirrors and windows, concretizing the intangible.
26. Boot, 1996, p. 45.
27. Twitchell, 1985, p. 65.
28. Christie, 1994b, p. 128.
29. Leaving aside voice-overs.
30. *Can't Be Heaven* (1998) looks for a moment as if it will ignore this convention; grandmother dies and is reunited with her lover, who died young many years before and whose ghost has maintained his youth-

ful vigor. They kiss, but the inter-generational romance implication is dispelled when she is transformed into the young woman she was when they were originally together.

31. The mirror has a venerable place in the occult as a means of communication with the dead. See Moody, 1993, for a discussion of mirror gazing.

32. See Auerbach, 1997, for an overview of psi in the first Star Wars trilogy.

33. Markey, 1982.

34. Nelson, 1982, pp. 197–98.

35. Ciment, 1983, p. 181. Rhodes, 1996b, p. 261, begins his chapter on *The Shining* with this quotation and one on the same theme by Stephen King, recalling a conversation King had had with Kubrick.

36. McClenon, 1994, p. 35.

37. Quoted in Senn, 1996, p. 98.

Bibliography

Adair, Gilbert. *Flickers: An Illustrated Celebration of 100 Years of Cinema*. London, Faber and Faber, 1995.
Agee, James. *Agee on Film* Vol. 1. New York: Grosset and Dunlap, 1967.
Aldgate, Anthony, and Jeffrey Richards. *Britain Can Take It: The British Cinema in the Second World War*, 2nd ed. Edinburgh: Edinburgh University Press, 1994 (1st ed. 1986).
Allen, Jeanne Thomas. "*Turn of the Screw* and *The Innocents:* Two Types of Ambiguity." In *The Classic American Novel and the Movies*, edited by Gerald Peary, and Roger Shatzkin. New York: Ungar, 1977.
Allen, Michael. "Narrative Structure and Spatial Articulation in D. W. Griffith's Feature Films After Intolerance." Unpublished Ph.D. thesis, University of East Anglia, 1993 (published as *Family Secrets: The Feature Films of D. W. Griffith*. London: British Film Institute, 1999).
Altick, Richard D. *The Shows of London*. London: Belknap, 1978.
Anderson, David. "The Corsican Effect." Unpublished MS. Miscellaneous file "Set Design — Technical") (n.d). Theater Museum Library (London).
Anson, Jay. *The Amityville Horror: A True Story*. Englewood Cliffs, N.J.: Prentice-Hall, 1977.
Ariès, Philippe. *The Hour of Our Death*. English translation New York: Alfred A. Knopf, 1981. (First published as *L'Homme devant la mort*, 1977.)
Arnold, Ken, Brian Hurwitz, Francis McKee and Ruth Richardson. *Doctor Death: Medicine at the End of Life* (Catalogue to accompany an exhibition at the Wellcome Institute for the History of Medicine). London: Wellcome Trust, 1997.
The Astrologer of the Nineteenth Century. London: William Charlton Wright, 1825.
Auerbach, Loyd. *ESP, Hauntings and Poltergeists: A Parapsychologist's Handbook*. New York: Warner, 1986.
Auerbach, Loyd. "Psi and the Jedi." *Fate*, February 1997.
Bache, Christopher. "A Perinatal Interpretation of Frightening Near-Death Experiences: A Dialogue with Kenneth Ring." *Journal of Near-Death Studies*, Vol. 13, No. 1 (Fall 1994).
Baker, Robert A., and Joe Nickell. *Missing Pieces: How to Investigate Ghosts, UFOs, Psychics and Other Mysteries*. Buffalo, N.Y.: Prometheus, 1992.
Barber, X. Theodore. "Phantasmagorial Wonders: The Magic Lantern Ghost Show in Nineteenth-Century America." *Film History*, Vol. 3, No. 2 (1989).

Barnouw, Erik. "The Fantasms of Andrew Oehler." *Quarterly Review of Film Studies*, Vol. 9, No. 1 (Winter 1984).
_____. *The Magician and the Cinema*. Oxford: Oxford University Press, 1981.
Barr, Charles, ed. *All Our Yesterdays: 90 Years of British Cinema*. London: British Film Institute, 1986.
_____. *Ealing Studios*, 2nd ed. London: Studio Vista, 1993.
Bauman, Zygmunt. *Mortality, Immortality and Other Life Strategies*. Cambridge: Polity, 1992.
Bazin, André. *What Is Cinema?* 2 vols. Berkeley: University of California Press, 1967.
Beja, Morris. *Film and Literature, An Introduction*. New York: Longman, 1979.
Bergman, Ingmar. *Images: My Life in Film*. London: Faber and Faber, 1995.
Bernstein, Morey. *The Search for Bridey Murphy*. London: Hutchinson, 1956.
Bettelheim, Bruno. *The Uses of Enchantment: The Meanings and Importance of Fairy Tales*. London: Thames & Hudson, 1976.
Bierce, Ambrose. "An Occurrence at Owl Creek Bridge." In *The Midst of Life*. London: Chatto & Windus, 1892.
Blackmore, Susan. *Dying to Live: Near Death Experiences*. Amherst, N.Y.: Prometheus, 1993.
Bodeen, DeWitt. "Writing Curse of the Cat People." *Focus on Film*, No. 7 (1971).
Boorman, John. "Hero, drunkard, film star, friend." *The Guardian, Friday Review*, 5 June 1998.
Boot, Andy. *Fragments of Fear: An Illustrated History of British Horror Films*. London: Creation, 1996.
Booth, Michael R. *English Melodrama*. London: Herbert Jenkins, 1965.
Bottomore, Stephen. "'Nine Days' Wonder': Early Cinema and Its Sceptics." In *Cinema: The Beginnings and the Future*, ed. by Christopher Williams. London: University of Westminster, 1996.
Bowser, Eileen. Introduction to *Biograph Bulletins 1908–1912*. New York: Octagon Books, 1973.
_____. "Preparation for Brighton: The American Contribution." In *Cinema 1900–1906: An Analytical Study*, ed. by Roger Holman. Brussels: FIAF, 1982.
Bragg, Melvyn. *The Seventh Seal (Det Sjunde Inseglet)*. London: British Film Institute, 1993.
Brakhage, Stan. *The Brakhage Lectures: Georges Méliès, David Wark Griffith, Carl Theodore Dreyer, Sergei Eisenstein*. Chicago: Good Lion, 1972.
Brandon, Ruth. *The Life and Many Deaths of Harry Houdini*. London: Secker and Warburg, 1993.
Braund, Simon. "'You Can Do Anything You Want With Ghosts....'" *Empire*, No. 98 (August 1997). (Sidebar to review of *The Frighteners*).
Brewster, David. *Letters on Natural Magic Addressed to Sir Walter Scott, Bart*. London: John Murray, 1832.
Briggs, Julia. *Night Visitors: The Rise and Fall of the English Ghost Story*. London: Faber, 1977.
Brode, Douglas. *The Films of Steven Spielberg*. Secaucus, N.J.: Citadel, 1995.
Brophy, Phillip. "Horrality: The Textuality of Contemporary Horror Films." *Screen*, Vol. 27, No. 1 (January/February 1986).
Brosnan, John. *The Horror People*. London: Macdonald & James, 1976.
_____. *The Primal Screen*. London: Orbit, 1991.
Brown, John. "The Impossible Object: Reflections on the Shining." In *Cinema and Fiction: New Modes of Adapting, 1950–1990*, ed. by John Orr and Colin Nicholson. Edinburgh: Edinburgh University Press, 1992.

Brown, J. H. *Spectropia or Surprising Spectral Illusions Showing Ghosts Everywhere and of Any Colour*. London: Griffith and Farran, 1863. (Facsimile reprint of 2nd ed.; Whitstable: Pryor Publications, 1993.)
Brown, Richard. "Marketing the Cinématographe in Britain." In *Cinema: The Beginnings and the Future*, ed. by Christopher Williams. London: University of Westminster, 1996.
Bunnell, Charlene. "The Gothic: A Literary Genre's Transition to Film." In *Planks of Reason: Essays on the Horror Film*, ed. by Barry Keith Grant. Metuchen, N.J.: Scarecrow Press, 1984.
Butler, Alison. "The Last Vision/Machine." *Screen*, Vol. 36, No. 4 (Winter 1995).
Butler, Ivan. *Horror in the Cinema*, 3rd ed. rev. New York: A. S. Barnes; London: Thomas Yoseloff, 1979. (1st ed., *An Illustrated History of the Horror Film*, 1967.)
Cabana, Raymond G. "Roland West." In *The Fearmakers: The Screen's Directorial Masters of Suspense and Terror*, ed. by John McCarty. London: Virgin, 1995.
Caldwell, Larry W., and Samuel J. Umland. "'Come and Play with Us': The Play Metaphor in Kubrick's *Shining*." *Literature/Film Quarterly*, Vol. 14, No. 2 (1986).
Campbell, Joseph. *The Hero with a Thousand Faces*, 2nd ed. Princeton, N.J.: Princeton University Press, 1968,
Carey, Gary. *Lost Films*. New York: Museum of Modern Art, 1970.
Carroll, Noël. *The Philosophy of Horror, or Paradoxes of the Heart*. New York: Routledge, 1990.
Castle, Terry. *The Female Thermometer: Eighteenth-Century Culture and the Invention of the Uncanny*. New York: Oxford University Press, 1995.
_____. "Phantasmagoria: Spectral Technology and the Metaphorics of Modern Reverie." *Critical Inquiry*, Vol. 15 (Autumn 1988). (Reprinted in *The Female Thermometer* (1995) as "Phantasmagoria and the Metaphorics of Modern Reverie)."
Ceram, C. W. *Archaeology of the Cinema*. London: Thames and Hudson, 1965.
Chanan, Michael. *The Dream That Kicks: The Prehistory and Early Years of Cinema in Britain*. London: Routledge and Kegan Paul, 1980.
_____. "The Treats of Trickery." In *Cinema: The Beginnings and the Future*, ed. by Christopher Williams. London: University of Westminster, 1996.
Chorvinsky, Mark. "Yeti and the Cinema." In *Tom Slick and the Search for the Yeti*, ed. by Loren Coleman. London: Faber and Faber, 1989.
Christie, Ian. *Arrows of Desire: The Films of Michael Powell and Emeric Pressburger*. London: Faber and Faber, 1994 [cited as 1994a]. (First pub. 1985.)
_____. *The Last Machine: Early Cinema and the Birth of the Modern World*. London: British Film Institute, 1994 [cited as 1994b].
_____, (ed.) *Powell, Pressburger and Others*. London: British Film Institute, 1978.
Christopher, Milbourne. *The Illustrated History of Magic*. London: Robert Hale, 1975.
_____. *Panorama of Magic*. New York: Dover, 1962.
Ciment, Michel. *Kubrick*. London: Collins, 1983.
Clarens, Carlos. *An Illustrated History of the Horror Movie*. New York: Paragon, 1967. (Published in the United Kingdom as *An Illustrated History of the Horror Film*, Capricorn, 1967.)
Clover, Carol J. "Her Body, Himself: Gender in the Slasher Film." In *Fantasy and the Cinema*, ed. by James Donald. London: British Film Institute, 1989.
Coates, Paul. "The Story of the Lost Reflection." *New Left Review*, No. 143 (January/February 1984).
Coe, Brian. *The History of Movie Photography*. London: Ash and Grant, 1981.
Combs, Richard. "*The Shining*." *Monthly Film Bulletin*, Vol. 47, No. 562 (November 1980).

Cook, David A. "American Horror: *The Shining.*" *Literature/Film Quarterly*, Vol. 12, No. 1 (1984).
Cooper, Caroline M. "*Field of Dreams:* A Favorite of President Clinton — But a Typical Reaganite Film?" *Literature/Film Quarterly*, Vol. 23, No. 3 (1995).
Cornell, A. D. Personal communication on investigation techniques in early 1960s (1996).
Counts, Kyle. "Conjurer of Dreams." *Cinefantastique*, Vol. 20, Nos. 1/2 (November 1989).
Cowie, Peter. "Clayton's Progress." *Motion*, No. 3 (Spring 1962).
Cranford, Alfred Lane. Letter on *Pepper's Ghost* to unidentified newspaper. Miscellaneous file "Set Design — Technical" (n.d., c.1936). Theater Museum Library (London).
Creed, Barbara. "From Here to Modernity: Feminism and Postmodernism." *Screen*, Vol. 28, No. 2 (Spring 1987).
_____. "Horror and the Monstrous-Feminine: An Imaginary Abjection." In *Fantasy and the Cinema*, ed. by James Donald. London: British Film Institute, 1989.
Crick, Robert A. "*Lady in White.*" In *Cinematic Hauntings*, ed. by Gary J. Svehla and Susan Svehla. Baltimore, Md: Midnight Marquee, 1996.
Crowe, Catherine. *The Night-Side of Nature: Or, Ghosts and Ghost-Seers.* Wellingborough: Aquarian, 1986 (1st ed. 1848).
Dawes, Adwin A. *The Great Illusionists.* Secaucus, N.J.: Chartwell, 1979.
Denman, Chip. "Sitting in the Dark: Tinseltown's Fascination with Spiritualism." *The Skeptic*, Vol. 8, No. 4 (1994).
Derry, Charles. *Dark Dreams: A Psychological History of the Modern Horror Film.* New York: Barnes/Yoseloff, 1977.
Dickson, W.K. L., and Antonia Dickson. *History of the Kinetograph, Kinetoscope and kinetophonograph.* New York: Albert Bunn, 1895.
Dickstein, Morris. "The Aesthetics of Fright." In *Planks of Reason: Essays on the Horror Film*, ed. by Barry Keith Grant. London: Scarecrow Press, 1984.
Dingwall, Eric J., Kathleen M. Goldney, and Trevor H. Hall. *The Haunting of Borley Rectory: A Critical Survey of the Evidence.* London: Proceedings of the Society for Psychical Research, Vol. 51 (Part 186), 1956.
Dircks, Henry. *The Ghost! As Produced in the Spectre Drama: Popularly Illustrating the Marvellous Optical Illusions Obtained by the Apparatus Called the Dircksian Phantasmagoria.* London: Spon, 1863.
Dolar, Mladen. "'I Shall Be with You on Your Wedding Night': Lacan and the Uncanny." *October*, No. 58 (1992).
Donald, James, ed. *Fantasy and the Cinema.* London: British Film Institute, 1989.
Donaldson, Leslie. "*Don't Look Now.*" In *Magill's Survey of Cinema: English Language Films*, ed. by Frank N. Magill. Second series, Vol. 2. Englewood Cliffs, N.J.: Salem Press, 1981.
Drek. "Cello." *Variety*, 19 November 1990 (reprinted in *Variety's Film Reviews*, Vol. 21, 1989–1990. New Providence, N.J.: R. R. Bowker).
Druxman, Michael B. *One Good Film Deserves Another.* South Brunswick, N.J. and New York: A. S. Barnes; London: Thomas Yoseloff, 1977.
Dyer, Peter John. "All Manner of Fantasies." *Films and Filming*, Vol. 4, No. 9 (June 1958).
Dyson, Jeremy. *Bright Darkness: The Lost Art of the Supernatural Horror Film.* London: Cassell, 1997.
Edison Films Catalogue. West Orange, N.J., 1902.
Edmunds, Simeon. "*Spirit*" *Photography.* London: Society for Psychical Research, n.d. [1965].

Eisenbud, Jule. "Paranormal Photography." In *Handbook of Parapsychology*, ed. by Benjamin B. Wolman. Jefferson, N.C.: McFarland, 1977.
Eisner, Lotte H. *The Haunted Screen: Expressionism in the German Cinema and the Influence of Max Reinhardt*. London: Secker & Warburg, 1973. (Rev. ed. first published in French, 1952; further rev. ed. 1965.)
Ellis, John. "Watching Death at Work." In *Powell, Pressburger and Others*, ed. by Ian Christie. London: British Film Institute, 1978.
Epperson, Gordon. *The Mind of Edmund Gurney*. London: Associated University Presses, 1997.
Estrin, Mark W. "*Don't Look Now*." In *International Dictionary of Films and Filmmakers, Vol. 1: Films*, ed. by Nicholas Thomas. Chicago: St. James Press, 1990.
Evans, Henry Ridgely. *The Old and the New Magic*. Chicago: Open Court, 1906.
Evans, William. "Science and Reason in Film and Television." *Skeptical Enquirer*, Vol. 20, No. 1 (January/February 1996).
Eyles, Allen, and David Meeker, eds. *Missing Believed Lost: The Great British Film Search*. London: British Film Institute, 1992.
"Farewell Tour!" (poster) 23 February 1879. Harry Price Library, University of London.
Feinman, Neil. *Nicolas Roeg*. Boston, Mass.: Twayne (Twayne's Theatrical Series), 1978.
_____. "Primordial Film Forms." In *A History of Films*. New York: Holt, Rinehart and Winston, 1979. Reprinted in *Space, Frame, Narrative: Early Cinema*, ed. by Thomas Elsaesser. London: British Film Institute, 1990.
Fell, John L. "Cellulose Nitrate Roots: Popular Entertainments and the Birth of Film Narrative." In *Before Hollywood: Turn of the Century American Film*. New York: Hudson Hills, 1987.
Finucane, R. C. *Appearances of the Dead: A Cultural History of Ghosts*. London: Junction, 1982.
Fischer, Lucy. "*The Lady Vanishes*." *Film Quarterly* (Fall 1979).
Fisher, Joe. *Hungry Ghosts: An Investigation into Channelling and the Spirit World*. London: Grafton, 1990.
Fisher, Len. "In the Realm of Intangibles." *New Scientist*, Vol. 156, No. 2113/2114 (20/27 December 1997).
Fodor, Nandor. *Encyclopaedia of Psychic Science*. London: Arthurs Press, n.d. [Preface dated 1933].
Fowkes, Katherine A. *Giving Up the Ghost: Spirits, Ghosts, and Angels in Mainstream Comedy Films*. Detroit: Wayne State University Press, 1998.
Francke, Lizzie. "*Truly, Madly, Deeply*." *Sight and Sound*, Vol. 1 (New Series), Issue 6 (October 1991).
Frazer, John. *Artificially Arranged Scenes: The Films of Georges Méliès*. Boston, Mass.: G. K. Hall, 1979.
Fry, Carrol, Robert Craig, and Ken Jurkiewicz. "Three Viewers Viewing: A Viewer-Response Symposium on *Jacob's Ladder*." *Literature/Film Quarterly*, Vol. 26, No. 3 (1998).
Gaudreault, André. "Evidence of Editing in the Lumière Films." In *Cinema: The Beginnings and the Future*, ed. by Christopher Williams. London: University of Westminster, 1996.
Gauld, Alan. *The Founders of Psychical Research*. London: Routledge and Kegan Paul, 1968.
Gernsheim, Helmut. *The Rise of Photography 1850–1880: The Age of Collodion*. Vol. 3 of *The History of Photography*. London: Thames & Hudson, 1988.

Gettings, Fred. *Ghosts in Photographs: The Extraordinary Story of Spirit Photography.* New York: Harmony, 1978.
Gifford, Denis. *The British Film Catalogue 1895–1970: A Guide to Entertainment Films.* New York: McGraw-Hill, 1973 [cited as 1973b].
_____. *A Pictorial History of Horror Movies.* London: Hamlyn, 1973 [cited as 1973a].
Gifford, James. "Don't Look Now." *Photon*, No. 25 (1974).
Gilson, Paul. "Georges Méliès, Inventeur." *La Revue du Cinema*, 1st Series, No. 4 (15 October 1929).
Goldston, Will. *A Magician's Swan Song.* London: John Long, n.d.
Gomez, Joseph. "Another Look at Nicolas Roeg." *Film Criticism*, Vol. 6, No. 1 (Fall 1981).
Gough-Yates, Kevin. *Michael Powell: In Collaboration with Emeric Pressburger.* London: National Film Theater, 1971.
Grafe, Frieda. *The Ghost and Mrs. Muir.* London: British Film Institute, 1995.
Grant, Barry Keith, ed. *Planks of Reason: Essays on the Horror Film.* London, Scarecrow Press, 1984. (First pub. in *American Nightmare: Essays on the Horror Film*, ed. by Andrew Britton, et al. Toronto: Festival of Festivals, 1979.)
Grixti, Joseph. *Terrors of Uncertainty: The Cultural Contexts of Horror Fiction.* London: Routledge, 1989.
Grove, Allen W. "Röntgen's Ghosts: Photography, X-Rays, and the Victorian Imagination." *Literature and Medicine*, Vol. 16, No. 2 (Fall 1997).
Gunning, Tom. "The Cinema of Attractions: Early Film, Its Spectator and the Avant-Garde. In *Space, Frame, Narrative: Early Cinema*, ed. by Thomas Elsaesser. London: British Film Institute, 1990.
Haggerty, George E. *Gothic Fiction/Gothic Form.* University Park, Pa.: Pennsylvania State University Press, 1989.
Haill, Catherine. "'Spirits and Ghosts That Glide by Night.'" *The Scottish Opera Yearbook 1985/86* (1986).
Hala, James. "Kubrick's *The Shining*: The Specters and the Critics." In *The Shining Reader*, ed. by Anthony Magistrale. Mercer Island, Wa.: Starmont, 1990 (Starmont Studies in Literary Criticism No. 30).
Halliwell, Leslie. *Halliwell's Harvest: A Further Choice of Entertainment Movies from the Golden Age.* London: Grafton, 1986.
Hammond, Paul. *Marvellous Méliès.* London: Gordon Fraser, 1974.
Hampton, Benjamin B. *History of the American Film Industry: From Its Beginnings to 1931.* New York: Covici Friede, 1931; reprint, Dover, 1970.
Hanson, Patricia King. "A Matter of Life and Death (Stairway to Heaven)." In *International Dictionary of Films and Filmmakers, Vol. 1: Films*, ed. by Nicholas Thomas. Chicago: St. James Press, 1990.
Har. "Ghost Story." *Variety*, 16 December 1981. (Reprinted in *Variety's Film Reviews, 1981–1982*, Vol. 17, ed. R. R. Bowker, 1984.)
Harding, Colin, and Simon Popple. *In the Kingdom of Shadows: A Companion to Early Cinema.* London: Cygnus Arts, 1996.
Hardy, Phil, ed. *The Aurum Encyclopedia of Horror.* London: Aurum, 1985.
_____. *The Encyclopedia of Western Movies.* London: Octopus, 1983.
Harper, Sue. *Picturing the Past: The Rise and Fall of the British Costume Film.* London: British Film Institute, 1994.
_____, and Vincent Porter. "*A Matter of Life and Death*—The view from Moscow." *Historical Journal of Film, Radio and Television*, Vol. 9, No. 2 (1989).
Harris, Melvin. *Sorry, You've Been Duped!* London: Weidenfeld and Nicholson, 1986.
Hart, Hornell, and associated collaborators in the International Project for Research

on ESP Projection. "Six Theories about Apparitions." *Proceedings of the Society for Psychical Research*, Vol. 50, Part 185 (May 1956).
Hartnoll, G. "Robert Wise to Date." *Focus on Film*, No. 19 (Autumn 1974). Includes filmography by Allen Eyles.
"Haunted Hoxton." *All the Year Round* ("Conducted by Charles Dickens"), Vol. 9, No. 218 (27 June 1863).
Haynes, Renée. *The Society for Psychical Research 1882–1982: A History*. London: MacDonald, 1982.
Healy, Tony, and Paul Cropper. "Stone Me!" *Fortean Times*, No. 116 (November 1998).
Heard, Mervyn. "Giving Up the Ghost." Transcript of talk given at "Celebrating 1895," a conference held at the National Museum of Photography, Film and Television, Bradford (1995).
_____. Introduction to *The True History of Pepper's Ghost*. Reprint, The Projection Box, London, 1996 [cited as 1996a].
_____. *The Magic Lantern's Wild Years*. In *Cinema: The Beginnings and the Future*, ed. by Christopher Williams. London: University of Westminster, 1996 [cited as 1996b].
Hecht, Hermann. "The History of Projecting Phantoms, Ghosts and Apparitions, Part 1." *New Magic Lantern Journal*, Vol. 3, No. 1 (February 1984); Part 2, Vol. 3, No. 2 (December 1984).
_____. *Pre-Cinema History: An Encyclopaedia and Annotated Bibliography of the Moving Image Before 1896*, edited by Ann Hecht. London: Bowker-Saur and British Film Institute, 1993.
Heller, Terry. *"The Turn of the Screw": Bewildered Vision*. Boston: Twayne, 1989.
Hienger, Jörg. "The Uncanny and Science Fiction." *Science-Fiction Studies*, Vol. 6, Part 2 (July 1979).
Hepworth, Cecil M. *Came the Dawn: Memories of a Film Pioneer*. London, Phoenix House, 1951.
Hepworth, T. C. *The Book of the Lantern: Being a Practical Guide to the Working of the Optical (or Magic) Lantern*. 5th ed. London: Hazell, Watson and Viney, 1894 (1st ed. 1889).
Herbert, Stephen, and Luke McKernan, eds. *Who's Who of Victorian Cinema*. London: British Film Institute, 1996.
Higson, Andrew. "Gothic Fantasy as Art Cinema: The Secret of Female Desire in *The Innocents*." In *Gothick Origins and Innovations*, edited by Allan Loyd Smith and Victor Sage. Amsterdam: Rodopi, 1994.
Hill, Geoffrey. *Illuminating Shadows: The Mythic Power of Film*. Boston: Shambhala, 1992.
Hoare, Philip. "Noel Coward: The Last Gentleman Player." *Premiere*, Vol. 3, No. 11 (December 1995).
Hogan, David J. *Dark Romance: Sex and Death in the Horror Film*. Jefferson, N.C.: McFarland, 1986.
Hoile, Christopher. "American Horror: *The Shining*." *Literature/Film Quarterly*, Vol. 12, No. 1 (1984).
Holland, Larry Lee. "*The Haunting*." In *Magill's Survey of Cinema: English Language Films*, ed. by Frank N. Magill, Second series, Vol. 3. Englewood Cliffs, N.J.: Salem Press, 1981.
Hopkins, Albert A. *Magic: Stage Illusions and Scientific Diversions Including Trick Photography*. London, Sampson Low, Marston & Co., 1897. Reprinted as *Magic; Stage Illusions, Special Effects and Trick Photography*, New York: Dover, 1976.
Houghton, Georgiana. *Chronicles of the Photographs of Spiritual Beings and Phenomena Invisible to the Material Eye*. London: E. W. Allen, 1882.

Hutchings, Peter Ward. *The British Horror Film: An Investigation of British Horror Production in Its National Context*. Unpublished Ph.D. thesis, University of East Anglia, 1989.
_____. *Hammer and Beyond: The British Horror Film*. Manchester: Manchester University Press, 1993.
Hyslop, James H. "Photographing the Invisible (A review)." *Journal of the American Society for Psychical Research*, Vol. 9 (1915).
Inglis, Brian. *Natural and Supernatural: A History of the Paranormal from Earliest Times to 1914*. Rev. ed. Bridport: Dorset, Prism, 1992.
_____. *Science and Parascience: A History of the Paranormal 1914–1939*. London: Hodder and Stoughton, 1984.
Isherwood, Robert M. *Farce and Fantasy: Popular Entertainment in Eighteenth-Century Paris*. Oxford: Oxford University Press, 1986.
Izod, John. *The Films of Nicolas Roeg*. London: Macmillan, 1992.
Jackson, Rosemary. *Fantasy: The Literature of Subversion*. London: Methuen, 1981.
Jackson, Shirley. *The Haunting of Hill House*. New York: Viking, 1959.
James, Henry. *The Turn of the Screw*. London: Penguin, 1984; first pub. 1898.
Jancovich, Mark. *Horror*. London: Batsford, 1992.
Jenkins, Steve. "*Ghost Story*." *Monthly Film Bulletin*, Vol. 49, No. 578 (March 1982).
Jones, Alan. "*High Spirits*." *Cinefantastique*, Vol. 19, Nos. 1/2 (January 1989).
Jordan, Neil. *High Spirits*. London: Faber and Faber, 1989.
Kael, Pauline. *5001 Nights at the Movies: Shorter Reviews from the Silents to the '90s*. Expanded ed. London: Boyars, 1993.
_____. *I Lost It at the Movies*. London: Jonathan Cape, 1966.
_____. *Kiss Kiss Bang Bang*. Boston, Mass.: Little, Brown, 1968.
_____. *Movie Love: Complete Reviews 1988–1991*. New York: Penguin, 1991.
_____. *Reeling*. London: Marion Boyars, 1977.
Kawin, Bruce. "A Connoisseur's Guide to Literature and Film," by Leonard Wolf [Review]. *Film Quarterly*, Vol. 43, No. 4 (Summer 1990).
Kendrick, Walter. *The Thrill of Fear: 250 Years of Scary Entertainment*. New York: Grove Press, 1991.
Keyser, Lester J. "A Scrooge for all Seasons." In *The English Novel and the Movies*, ed. by Michael Klein and Gillian Parker. New York: Frederick Ungar, 1981.
Kinder, Marsha, and Beverle Houston. "Seeing Is Believing: *The Exorcist* and *Don't Look Now*." In *American Horrors: Essays on the Modern American Horror Film*, ed. by Gregory A. Waller. Chicago: University of Illinois, 1987.
King, Stephen. *Danse Macabre*. London: Warner, 1993 (first pub. 1981).
_____. *The Shining*. London: New English Library, 1977.
Kirtz, Mary K. "Shoeless Joe Transfigured on a Field of Dreams." *Literature/Film Quarterly*, Vol. 23, No. 1 (1995).
Kobal, John. "Love After Death." Chapter 3 in *Romance and the Cinema*. London: Studio Vista, 1973.
Kovács, Katherine Singer. *George Méliès and the Féerie*. In *Film Before Griffith*, ed. by John L. Fell. Berkeley: University of California, 1983.
Kramer, Steven Philip, and James Michael Welsh. *Abel Gance*. Boston, Mass.: Twayne, 1978.
Kurtz, Léonard P. *The Dance of Death and the Macabre Spirit in European Literature*. Geneva: Slatkine Reprints, 1975 (first pub. New York, 1934).
Landy, Marcia. *British Genres: Cinema and Society, 1930–1960*. Princeton, N.J.: Princeton University Press, 1991.
Lange-Fuchs, Hauke. *Magic Lantern Bibliography*. No place of publication given: The Magic Lantern Society of Great Britain, 1987 (Research Project No. 1).

Lanterne Magique et Fantasmagorie. Paris, Musée National des Techniques, 1990.
Lavery, David. "The Horror Film and the Horror of Film." *Film Criticism*, Vol. 7, No. 1 (Fall 1982).
Layton, David. "A Victorian Showman of Science." (Founding Fathers of Science Education 4) *New Scientist*, Vol. 75 (1 September 1977).
Leahy, Kevin. "Tavern of the Dead." *Popular Archaeology*, October 1982.
Leatherdale, Clive. *Dracula: The Novel and the Legend*. N.p.: Leisure Circle, 1985.
Leayman, Charles D. "*Jacob's Ladder*: The Film Is But a Ghost of the Potential of Rubin's Famed Script." *Cinefantastique*, Vol. 21, No. 5 (April 1991).
Ledwon, Lenora. "*Twin Peaks* and the Television Gothic." *Literature/ Film Quarterly*, Vol. 21, No. 4 (1993).
Leibowitz, Flo, and Lynn Jeffress. "The Shining." *Film Quarterly*, Vol. 34, No. 3 (Spring 1981).
Leemann, Sergio. *Robert Wise on His Films: From Editing Room to Director's Chair*. With a foreword by Nelson Gidding. Los Angeles: Silman-James, 1995.
Liesegang, Franz Paul. *Dates and Sources: A Contribution to the History of the Art of Projection and to Cinematography*. Edited by Hermann Hecht. London: Magic Lantern Society of Great Britain, 1986 (first pub. 1926).
London, Rose. *Cinema of Mystery*. London: Lorrimer, 1975.
Low, Rachael. *The History of the British Film 1914–1918*. London: George Allen and Unwin, 1950.
_____, and Roger Manvell. *The History of the British Film*. Vol. 1, 1896–1906. London: George Allen & Unwin, 1949.
Lyttle, John. "Raising the Spirits of the Age: Films About Ghosts Are Suddenly in Fashion." *Independent*, 4 October 1990.
MacGregor, Geddes. *Images of Afterlife: Beliefs from Antiquity to Modern Times*. New York: Paragon House, 1992.
MacKenzie, Andrew. *Adventures in Time: Encounters with the Past*. London: Athlone, 1997.
_____. *Hauntings and Apparitions*. London: Heinemann 1982.
Madigan, Mark J. "'Orders from the House': Kubrick's *The Shining* and Kafka's 'The Metamorphosis.'" In "*The Shining Reader*, ed. by Anthony Magistrale. Mercer Island, Wa.: Starmont, 1990 (Starmont Studies in Literary Criticism No. 30).
The Magic Lantern: How to Buy and How to Use It, and How to Raise a Ghost ("by A Mere Phantom"). London: Houlston, 1880 (1st ed. 1865).
Magill, Frank N., ed. *Magill's Survey of Cinema: English Language Films*. Englewood Cliffs, N.J.: Salem Press, 1981.
Magistrale, Anthony, ed. "*The Shining*" *Reader*. Mercer Island, Wa.: Starmont, 1990 (Starmont Studies in Literary Criticism No. 30).
Manchel, Frank. "What About Jack? Another Perspective on Family Relationships in Stanley Kubrick's *The Shining*." *Literature/Film Quarterly*, Vol. 23, No. 1 (1995).
Margrave, Seton. *Successful Film Writing: As Illustrated by "The Ghost Goes West*." London: Methuen, 1936.
Markey, Constance. "Birth and Rebirth in Current Fantasy Films." *Film Criticism*, Vol. 7, No. 1 (Fall 1982) ("Horror and Fantasy" issue).
Mayersberg, Paul. "The Overlook Hotel." *Sight and Sound*, Vol. 50, No. 1 (Winter 1980/81).
Mayne, Judith. *Cinema and Spectatorship*. London: Routledge, 1993.
McCarty, John (ed.) *The Fearmakers: The Screen's Directorial Masters of Suspense and Terror*. London: Virgin, 1995 (1st ed. 1994).

McClenon, James. *Wondrous Events: Foundations of Religious Belief*. Philadelphia: University of Pennsylvania Press, 1994.
McDougal, Stuart Y. *Made into Movies: From Literature to Film*. New York: Holt, Rinehart and Winston, 1985.
McGrath, Roberta. "Natural Magic and Science Fiction: Instruction, Amusement and the Popular Show, 1795–1895." In *Cinema: The Beginnings and the Future*, ed. by Christopher Williams. London: University of Westminster, 1996.
Millbank, Alison. "I Could a Tale Unfold." In *Romantic Literature from 1790 to 1830*, ed. by G. Ward. London: Bloomsbury, 1994.
Milne, Tom. "*Brainstorm*." *Monthly Film Bulletin*, Vol. 50, No. 599 (December 1983).
_____. "*The Curse of the Cat People*." *Focus on Film*, No. 7 (1971).
_____. "*Don't Look Now*." *Sight and Sound*, Vol. 42, No. 4 (Autumn 1973).
Moberly, C. A. E., and E. F. Jourdain. *An Adventure*. 5th ed. London: Macmillan, 1955 (1st ed. Macmillan, 1911).
Moody, Raymond A. *Life after Life*. New York: Bantam, 1976 (1st ed. 1975).
_____, with Paul Perry. *Reunions: Visionary Encounters with Departed Loved Ones*. London: Little, Brown, 1994 (1st ed. 1993).
Moretti, Franco. "The Dialectic of Fear." *New Left Review*, No. 136 (November/December 1982).
Moxey, Keith P. F. *Peasants, Warriors and Wives: Popular Imagery in the Reformation*. Chicago: University of Chicago Press, 1989.
Mulvey, Laura. "Visual Pleasure and Narrative Cinema." *Screen*, Vol. 16, No. 3 (Autumn 1975).
Murphy, Robert. *Sixties British Cinema*. London: British Film Institute, 1992.
Musser, Charles. *History of the American Cinema*. Vol. 1, *The Emergence of Cinema: The American Screen to 1907*. New York: Scribner's, 1990.
Neale, Stephen. *Genre*. London: British Film Institute, 1980.
Nelson, Thomas Allen. *Kubrick: Inside a Film Artist's Maze*. Bloomington: Indiana University Press, 1982.
Newman, Kim. "*Beetlejuice*." *Monthly Film Bulletin*, Vol. 55, No. 655 (August 1988) [cited as 1988b].
_____. "Bring Back the Cat." *Sight and Sound*, Vol. 9 (New Series), Issue 11 (November 1999).
_____. "'Jacob's Ladder.'" *Sight and Sound*, Vol. 1 (New Series), Issue 6 (October 1991).
_____. *Nightmare Movies: A Critical History of the Horror Film, 1968–88*. London: Bloomsbury, 1988 [cited as 1988a].
_____, ed. *The British Film Institute Companion to Horror*. London: British Film Institute, 1996.
Nicholls, Peter. *Fantastic Cinema: An Illustrated Survey*. London: Ebury Press, 1984.
Nickell, Joe. *Camera Clues: A Handbook for Photographic Investigation*. Lexington: University Press of Kentucky, 1994.
Niver, Kemp R., ed. *Biograph Bulletins 1896–1908*. Los Angeles: Locare Research Group, 1971.
_____. *The First Twenty Years: A Segment of Film History*. Los Angeles: Locare Research Group, 1968.
Oehler, Andrew. *The Life, Adventures, and Unparalleled Sufferings of Andrew Oehler*. Trenton, N.J.: Oehler, 1811.
"Outward Bound." 21 July 1998 (Personal Communication from British Board of Film Classification).
Paige, Linda Rohrer. "The Transformation of Woman: The 'Curse' of the Cat Woman

in Val Lewton/Jacques Tourneur's *Cat People, Its Sequel, and Remake*." *Literature/Film Quarterly*, Vol. 25, No. 4 (1997).
Palmer, James W. "Cinematic Ambiguity: James's *The Turn of the Screw* and Clayton's *The Innocents*." *Film/Literature Quarterly*, Vol. 5, No. 3 (1977).
Palmer, James, and Michael Riley. "Seeing, Believing, and 'Knowing' in Narrative Film: *Don't Look Now* Revisited." *Literature/Film Quarterly*, Vol. 23, No. 1 (1995).
Parish, James Robert. *Ghosts and Angels in Hollywood Films*. Jefferson, N.C., McFarland, 1994.
Parkinson, David, ed. *The Graham Greene Film Reader: Mornings in the Dark*. Manchester: Carcanet, 1993.
Paul, William. *Laughing Screaming: Modern Hollywood Horror and Comedy*. New York: Columbia University Press, 1994.
Pearsall, Ronald. *The Table-Rappers*. London: Michael Joseph, 1972.
Pearson, Roberta E. *Eloquent Gestures: The Transformation of Performance Style in the Griffith Biograph Films*. Berkeley: University of California Press, 1992.
Peary, Danny. *Cult Movies 2: 50 More of the Classics, the Sleepers, the Weird, and the Wonderful*. New York: Dell, 1983.
Pepper, John Henry. *The True History of the Ghost and All About Metempsychosis* ("By Professor Pepper"). London: Cassell, 1890. Reprinted as *The True History of Pepper's Ghost*. Facsimile Series No. 2, The Projection Box, London, 1996.
Permutt, Cyril. *Beyond the Spectrum: A Survey of Supernormal Photography*. Cambridge: Patrick Stephens, 1983.
Perez, Gilberto. *The Material Ghost: Films and Their Medium*. Baltimore: The Johns Hopkins University Press, 1998.
Perry, George. *Forever Ealing: A Celebration of the Great British Film Studio*. Rev. ed. London: Pavilion, 1994 (1st ed. 1981).
Perry, Michael, ed. *Deliverance: Psychic Disturbance and Occult Involvement*. 2nd ed. London: SPCK, 1996 (1st ed. 1987).
Picknett, Lynn. *The Encyclopaedia of the Paranormal: A Complete Guide to the Unexplained*. London: Macmillan, 1990.
Pirie, David. *A Heritage of Horror: The English Gothic Cinema 1946–1972*. London: Gordon Fraser, 1973.
Playfair, Guy Lyon. *This House Is Haunted: An Investigation of the Enfield Poltergeist*. London: Souvenir, 1980.
Powell, M. *A Life in Movies: An Autobiography*. London: Heinemann, 1986.
Prawer, S. S. *Caligari's Children: The Film as Tale of Terror*. Oxford: Oxford University Press, 1980.
Price, David. *Magic: A Pictorial History of Conjurors in the Theater*. New York: Cornwall, 1985.
Price, Harry. *The Most Haunted House in England*. London: Longmans, Green, 1940. Reprinted by Time-Life, 1990.
Ralston, W. R. S. *The Songs of the Russian People: As Illustrative of Slavonic Mythology and Russian Social Life*. London: Ellis and Green, 1872.
Ray, Robert B. *The Avant-Garde Finds Andy Hardy*. London: Harvard University Press, 1995.
Reade, Eric. *Australian Silent Films: A Pictorial History of Silent Films from 1896 to 1929*. Melbourne: Lansdowne Press, 1970.
Rebello, Stephen. "Jack Clayton's *The Innocents*." *Cinefantastique*, Vol. 13, No. 5 (June/July 1983).
Recchia, Edward. "An Eye for an I: Adapting Henry James's *The Turn of the Screw* to the Screen." *Literature/Film Quarterly*, Vol. 15, No. 1 (1978).

Rhine, J. B. *New Frontiers of the Mind*. Harmondsworth, Middlesex: Penguin, 1950 (1st ed. 1937).
Rhodes, Gary Don. "*Outward Bound*." In *Cinematic Hauntings*, ed. by Gary J. Svehla and Susan Svehla. Baltimore, Md: Midnight Marquee, 1996 [cited as 1996a].
_____. "*The Shining*." In *Cinematic Hauntings*, ed. by Gary J. Svehla, and Susan Svehla. Baltimore, Md.: Midnight Marquee, 1996 [cited as 1996b].
Ring, Kenneth. "Solving the Riddle of Frightening Near-Death Experiences: Some Testable Hypotheses and a Perspective Based on *A Course in Miracles*." *Journal of Near-Death Studies*, Vol. 13, No. 1 (Fall 1994).
Robertson, Patrick. *The Guinness Book of Movie Facts and Feats*. (4th ed.) London: Guinness Publishing, 1991.
Robinson, David. "Introduction — Shows and Slides." In *Magic Images: The Art of Hand-Painted and Photographic Lantern Slides*, ed. by D. Crompton, D. Henry, and S. Herbert. London: Magic Lantern Society of Great Britain, 1990.
_____. Realising the Vision: 300 Years of Cinematography. In *Cinema: The Beginnings and the Future*, ed. by Christopher Williams. London: University of Westminster, 1996.
_____. "Robinson on Robertson." *The New Magic Lantern Journal*, Vol. 4, Nos. 1–3 ("The Ten Year Book") (April 1986).
Romney, Jonathan. "Resident Phantoms." *Sight and Sound*, Vol. 9 (New Series), Issue 9 (September 1999).
Rosenfeld, Sybil. *Georgian Scene Painters and Scene Painting*. Cambridge: Cambridge University Press, 1981.
Rowell, Geoffrey. "Dickens and the Construction of Christmas." *History Today*, December 1993.
Sadoul, Georges. *An Index to the Creative Work of Georges Méliès (1896–1912)*. London; August 1947. (Special supplement to *Sight and Sound*.)
Salt, Barry. "The Evolution of the Film Form up to 1906." In *Cinema 1900–1906: An Analytical Study*, ed. by Roger Holman. Brussels: FIAF, 1982.
_____. *Film Style and Technology: History and Analysis*. London: Starword, 1992.
Sammon, Paul M. *Splatterpunks: Extreme Horror*. London: Xanadu, 1990.
Sandell, Roger. "Still Seeking Satan." *Magonia*, No. 51 (February 1995). Reprinted in *The Skeptic*, Vol. 9, No. 1 (1995).
Sanderson, Mark. "*Don't Look Now*." London: British Film Institute, 1996.
Sarris, Andrew. "*The Seventh Seal*." In *Focus on "The Seventh Seal*," ed. by Brigitta Steene Englewood Cliffs, N.J.: Prentice Hall, 1972.
Schefer, Jean-Louis. "Thanatography, Skiagraphy." *Word & Image*, Vol. 1, No. 2 (April–June 1985). Extract from *Espèce de chose mélancolie*.
Seidman, Steve. "*The Innocents*: Point of View as an Aspect of the Cinefantastic System." In *Film Reader 4*, ed. by Blaine Allen, et al. Evanston, Ill.: Northwestern University, 1979.
Sellar, Maurice, Lou Jones, Robert Sidaway, and Ashley Sidaway. "Things That Go Bump in the Night." In *Best of British: A Celebration of Rank Film Classics*. London, Sphere, 1987.
Senn, Bryan. "*The Haunting*." In *Cinematic Hauntings*, ed. by Gary J. Svehla and Susan Svehla. Baltimore, Md.: Midnight Marquee, 1996.
_____, and John Johns. *Fantastic Cinema Subject Guide: A Topical Index to 2,500 Horror, Science Fiction, and Fantasy Films*. Jefferson, N.C.: McFarland, 1992.
Shay, Estelle. "Quick Cuts: Digital Soul Searching." *Cinefex*, No. 56 (November 1993).
Shipman, David. *The Story of Cinema*. (2 vols.) London: Hodder and Stoughton, 1982.
Shipman, Pat. "Life and Death on the Wagon Trail." *New Scientist*, 27 July 1991.
Silver, Alain J. "*The Innocents*." In *Magill's Survey of Cinema: English Language Films*,

ed. by Frank N. Magill. Second series, Vol. 3. Englewood Cliffs, N.J.: Salem Press, 1981.

_____, and James Ursini. *More Things Than Are Dreamt Of: Masterpieces of Supernatural Horror — From Mary Shelley to Stephen King — In Literature and Film*. New York: Limelight, 1994.

Sinclair, Upton. *Mental Radio: Does It Work, and How?* London: T. Werner Laurie, 1930.

Sinyard, Neil. *Children in the Movies*. London: B. T. Batsford, 1992.

Skal, David J. *The Monster Show: A Cultural History of Horror*. London: Plexus, 1993.

Smith, David H. "*High Plains Drifter.*" In *Cinematic Hauntings*, ed. by Gary J. Svehla and Susan Svehla. Baltimore, Md.: Midnight Marquee, 1996.

Smith, Don G. "*The Innocents.*" In *Cinematic Hauntings*, ed by Gary J. Svehla and Susan Svehla. Baltimore, Md.: Midnight Marquee, 1996.

Smith, Greg. "'Real Horrorshow': The Juxtaposition of Subtext, Satire, and Audience Implication in Stanley Kubrick's *The Shining*." *Film/Literature Quarterly*, Vol. 25, No. 4 (1997).

Smith, James F. "Kubrick's or King's — Whose Shining Is It?" In *The Shining Reader*, Anthony Magistrale. Mercer Island, Washington, Starmont, 1990 (Starmont Studies in Literary Criticism No. 30).

Snyder, Stephen. "Family Life and Leisure Culture in *The Shining*." *Film Criticism*, Vol. VII, No. 1 (Fall 1982).

Spignesi, Stephen J. *The Shape Under the Sheet: The Complete Stephen King Encyclopedia*. Ann Arbor, Mich.: Popular Culture, Ink, 1991.

Stafford, Barbara Maria. *Artful Science: Enlightenment Entertainment and the Eclipse of Visual Education*. Cambridge, Mass.: MIT Press, 1994.

Stein, Gordon. *Encyclopedia of Hoaxes*. Detroit: Gale Research, 1993.

Steinbeck, John. *Burning Bright*. London: Pan, 1970 (1st ed. 1951).

Stenger, Erich. *The March of Photography*. London: Focal Press, 1958.

Stilwell, Robynn. "Symbol, Narrative and the Musics of *Truly, Madly, Deeply*." *Screen*, Vol. 38, No. 1 (Spring 1997).

Stockton, Jerry. Letter on near death experiences. *Omni* Vol. 4, No. 8 (1982).

Stone, Marianne. "*The Entity* Revisited." *Fate*, June 1996.

Strick, Philip. *Science Fiction Movies*. London: Octopus, 1976.

Sullivan, Jack, ed. *The Penguin Encyclopedia of Horror and the Supernatural*. Harmondsworth: Viking, 1986.

Svehla, Gary J., and Susan Svehla, eds. *Cinematic Hauntings*. Baltimore, Md: Midnight Marquee, 1996.

Tabori, Paul. *Harry Price: The Biography of a Ghost-Hunter*. London: Sphere, 1974 (1st ed. 1950).

Taylor, Bernard. *Cruelly Murdered: Constance Kent and the Killing at Road Hill House*. (2nd ed.) London: Grafton, 1989.

_____. "*Jacob's Ladder.*" Cinefantastique, Vol. 21, No. 3 (December 1990).

Teitelbaum, Sheldon. "Bruce Joel Rubin: Movie Metaphysician." *Cinefantastique*, Vol. 21, No. 5 (April 1991).

Telotte, J. P. *Dreams of Darkness: Fantasy and the Films of Val Lewton*. Urbana and Chicago: University of Illinois Press, 1985.

Thalbourne, Michael A. *A Glossary of Terms Used in Parapsychology*. London: Heinemann, 1982.

Thomas, Paul. *Flying Saucers Through the Ages*. London: Tandem, 1965. (First published in French as *Les Extraterrestres*, 1962.)

Thomson, David. "As I Lay Dying." *Sight and Sound*, Vol. 8 (New Series), Issue 6 (June 1998).

Thompson, John O. "Cat Personae." In *Cinema and the Realms of Enchantment: Lectures, Seminars and Essays by Marina Warner and Others*, ed. by Duncan Petrie. London: British Film Institute, 1993.
Thompson, Paul B. "Summoning the Chevalier." *Fate*, June 1994.
Titterington, P. L. "Kubrick and *The Shining*." *Sight and Sound*, Vol. 50, No. 2 (Spring 1981).
Todorov, Tzvetan. *The Fantastic: A Structural Approach to a Literary Genre*. Ithaca: Cornell University Press, 1973.
Tudor, Andrew. *Monsters and Mad Scientists: A Cultural History of the Horror Movie*. Oxford: Blackwell, 1989.
Turim, Maureen. *Flashbacks in Film: Memory and History*. New York and London: Routledge, 1989.
Twitchell, James B. *Dreadful Pleasures: An Anatomy of Modern Horror*. Oxford: Oxford University Press, 1985.
Tyler, Parker. "Supernaturalism at Home." Chapter 4 in *Magic and Myths of the Movies*. London: Secker & Warburg, 1971.
Tyrrell, G. N. M. *Apparitions*. Rev. ed. London Society for Psychical Research, 1953 (1st ed. 1943).
Underwood, Peter. *Ghosts and How to See Them*. London: Anaya, 1993.
Usai, Paolo Cherchi. *Burning Passions: An Introduction to the Study of Silent Cinema*. (First pub. 1991; English translation London: British Film Institute, 1994.)
Usai, Paolo Cherchi, Lorenzo Codelli, Carlo Montanaro, and David Robinson, eds. *Silent Witnesses: Russian Films 1908–1919*. London: British Film Institute, 1989.
Vardac, A. Nicholas. *Stage to Screen: Theatrical Method from Garrick to Griffith*. Cambridge, Mass.: Harvard University Press, 1949.
Varey, J. E. "Robertson's Phantasmagoria in Madrid, 1821." *Theater Notebook*, Part 1: Vol. 9 (October 1954–July 1955); Part 2: Vol. 11 (October 1956–July 1957).
Varnado, S. L. *Haunted Presence: The Numinous in Gothic Fiction*. Tuscaloosa: University of Alabama Press, 1987.
Virilio, Paul. *War and Cinema: The Logistics of Perception*. (First pub. in 1984; English translation London. Verso, 1989.)
Wagenknecht, Edward, and Anthony Slide. *The Films of D. W. Griffith*. New York: Crown, 1975.
Waller, Gregory A. *The Living and the Undead: From Stoker's "Dracula" to Romero's "Dawn of the Dead."* Urbana: University of Illinois Press, 1986.
_____, ed. *American Horrors: Essays on the Modern American Horror Film*. Chicago: University of Illinois, 1987.
Ward, Vincent. "Never Say Die" [Comments accompanying articles by Kim Newman and Edward Lawrenson]. *Sight and Sound*, Vol. 8 (New Series), Issue 12 (December 1998).
Warman, Erich. *"A Matter of Life and Death": The Book of the Film*. London: World Film Publications, 1946.
Warner, Marina. "Stealing Souls and Catching Shadows." *Tate*, Issue 6 (Summer 1995).
Williams, Christopher, ed., *Cinema: The Beginnings and the Future; Essays Marking the Centenary of the First Film Show Projected to a Paying Audience in Britain*. London: University of Westminster, 1996.
Wilson, David. "Wings of Fame." *Sight and Sound*, Vol. 1 (New Series), Issue 1(May 1991).
Wilson, Edmund. "The Ambiguity of Henry James." In Edna Kenton. *A Casebook on Henry James's The Turn of the Screw*, ed. by Frank N. Magill. New York: Crowell, 1960 (first pub. 1934).

Wilson, Kristi. "Time, Space and Vision: Nicolas Roeg's *Don't Look Now*." *Screen*, Vol. 30, No. 3 (Autumn 1999).
Wilson, Marilynn. *Our Town*. In *Magill's Survey of Cinema: English Language Films*, ed. by Frank N. Magill, Second series, Vol. 4. Englewood Cliffs, N.J.: Salem Press, 1981.
Wirth, Jean. *La Jeune Fille et la Mort: Recherches sur les Thèmes Macabres dans l'art Germanique de la Renaissance*. Geneva: Droz, 1979.
Wolfenstein, Martha, and Nathan Leites. *Movies: A Psychological Study*. New York: Atheneum, 1950.
Wollen, Peter. "Compulsion." *Sight and Sound*, Vol. 7, Issue 4 (New Series) (April 1997).
Wolman, Benjamin B. *Handbook of Parapsychology*. Jefferson, N.C.: McFarland, 1977.
The Wonders of Light and Shadow. London: Society for Promoting Christian Knowledge, 1851. Reprinted by Arno Press, New York, 1973.
Wood, Robin. "An Introduction to the American Horror Film." In *Planks of Reason: Essays on the Horror Film*, ed. by Barry Keith Grant. London: Scarecrow Press, 1984.
Woodward, Ian. *The Werewolf Delusion*. New York: Paddington Press, 1979.

Index

Adair, Gilbert 222
Addams, Charles 169
The Adding Machine (1969) 135
An Adventure (1911) 66
Agee, James 150
Ai no borei (1978) 228
Alcofrisbas, The Master Magician (1903) 38
Aldgate, Anthony 226
Alice (1990) 62, 81–82
All of Me (1984) 99
All Quiet on the Western Front (1930) 203
All That Money Can Buy (1941) 62
Allen, Jeanne Thomas 234
Allen, Michael 223
Altered States (1980) 8, 205
Altick, Richard D. 221
Always (1989) 93, 134, 135, 218, 227, 237
Amityville (series) 51, 108, 109
The Amityville Horror (1977) 51
The Amityville Horror (1979) 2, 61, 97, 113
And Now the Screaming Starts (1973) 76
And You Thought Your Parents Were Weird (1992) 102, 117, 133, 221
Anderson, David 221
The Angel Levine (1970) 140–141
angels 88, 128, 136–141, 196, 197
Angels (1994) 139
Angels in the Endzone (1997) 232

Angels in the Outfield (1951) 139
Ansky, Shloimeh 228
Anson, Jay 229
The Apparition (1903) 38
Appointment with Fear (1943–1955) (radio series) 235
Arbus, Diane 237
Ariès, Philippe 217
Arnold, Ken 227
The Asphyx (1972) 67
Astaire, Fred 127
At the Villa Rose (1920) 60, 118
Au Secours! (1923) 106
Auerbach, Loyd 217, 229, 239
The Avenging Conscience (1914) 44–46, 50
An Awfully Big Adventure (1994) 126

Bache, Christopher 195
Back from the Dead (1957) 99, 100
Bacon, Francis 195
Bacon, Roger 219
Baker, Robert A. 229, 230
Baraduc, Hippolyte 225
Barber, X. Theodore 18, 19, 33, 34
Barnacle Bill (1958) 65
Barnes, John 21
Barnouw, Erik 19, 30, 31, 43, 201, 219
Barr, Charles 79, 143, 145, 147, 158, 233
Barrett, William 235
The Bat (1920) 105
Bauman, Zigmunt 62, 218
Bazin, André 28

257

Beetlejuice (1988) 62, 71, 101, 107, 108, 126, 135
Beja, Morris 234
The Bells (1871) 29, 53
The Bells (1926) 53
Benny, Jack 201
Bergman, Ingmar 50, 225
Bernstein, Morey 217
The Bespoke Overcoat (1956) 234
Betsy's Wedding (1990) 79
Bettelheim, Bruno 188
Between Two Worlds (1944) 52, 53, 59, 80–81, 126, 135, 136
The Bewitched Inn (1897) 37
The Bewitched Traveller (1904) 41
Beyond (1921) 51
Beyond Bedlam (1993) 64, 68
Beyond Evil (1980) 100
Beyond Tomorrow (1940) 135–136
The Bible 137, 140, 192, 195–197
Bierce, Ambrose 192
Bill and Ted's Bogus Journey (1991) 132
Biograph 41, 42, 43, 117, 137, 222
Bioscope 221
The Bishop's Wife (1947) 139
Bitzer, Billy 42
Black Magic (1944) 230
Black Rainbow (1989) 124
Blackbeard's Ghost (1967) 75
Blackmore, Susan 231
Blackton, Stuart 40
Blithe Spirit (1945) 89, 117, 122, 229, 231, 233
Blood Sisters (1986) 229
Blue in the Face (1995) 79
Bodeen, DeWitt 227
The Boogyman (1980) 229
Boogyman 2 (1982) 229
Boorman, John 237
Boot, Andy 202, 217, 230, 234
Booth, Michael R. 28, 222
Booth, W. R. 41, 42, 76
Borley rectory 174
Borzage, Frank 227
Bottomore, Stephen 222
Boucicault, Dion 29, 42, 222
Bowery Boys 122–123
Bowser, Eileen 35–36, 223
Bragg, Melvin 219
Brainstorm (1983) 67, 127–128, 129, 137, 192

Brainwaves (1983) 102
Brakhage, Stan 39
Braund, Simon 238
The Breakthrough (1993) 67
Brewster, David 16, 19, 26
Bridey Murphy 224
Briggs, Julia 4, 46, 238
Brighton Conference, 1978 201
British Board of Film Censorship 60
Brode, Douglas 228
Brophy, Phillip 229
Brosnan, John 129, 231
Brown, J. H. 24
Brown, John 186
Brown, Richard 218
Browning, Tod 119
A Bucket of Blood (1959) 230
Buddhism 192
Bulwer-Lytton, Edward 31
Bunnell, Charlene 172, 179, 184, 190
The Burgomeister (1935) 224
Butler, Alison 24
Butler, Ivan 89, 150–151, 163, 227, 233

Cabana, Raymond G. 229
Caberet du Néant 30
Cabin in the Sky 4
The Cabinet Trick of the Davenport Brothers (1902) 36
Caldwell, Larry W. 182, 183
camera obscura 15
Campbell, Joseph 136
Candyman (1992) 71
Can't Be Heaven (1998) 238
The Canterville Ghost (1944) 62, 76, 87, 92
The Canterville Ghost (1992) 226
Carey, Gary 223
Carnival of Souls (1962) 103, 104, 124, 126, 135, 191, 194, 226, 234
Carousel (1956) 75
Carrie (1976) 70
Carroll, Noël 104–105, 217, 218, 238
Casino (1995) 63
Casper (1995) 68, 74, 88, 117, 226
Castle, Terry 3, 24, 28, 219
Castle, William 58, 105, 107, 234
The Cat and the Canary (1922) 105
The Cat and the Canary (1927) 106
The Cat and the Canary (1939) 111
Cat People (1942) 89

Index

Cathy's Curse (1976) 100
The Cave of the Demons (1898) 38
Céline et Julie vont en Bateau (1974) 105
Cellar, Maurice 225
Ceram, C. W. 218, 220
Chan, Charlie 230
Chanan, Michael 220, 223
Chances Are (1989) 134
The Changeling (1979) 68, 104, 110, 117, 121–122, 226, 230, 236
Chaplin, Charlie 137
Charlie and the Angel (1973) 139
Charlie's Ghost Story (1994) 71, 88
La Charrette Phantôme (1939) 223
Le Château Hanté (1897) 222
Childe, Henry Langdon 22
Child's Play (series) 100
Chiller 9
choreutoscope 23
Christie, Ian 11, 204, 223, 233, 238
A Christmas Carol (1843) 29, 76
A Christmas Carol (various) 76
Christopher, Milbourne 15, 19–20
Ciment, Michel 183–184, 187, 236, 239
Cinematograph 199
Citizen Cohn (1992) 71
City of Angels (1998) 137, 232
City of the Dead (1960) 235
Clair, Réne 52
Clarens, Carlos 37, 106, 145, 219, 223, 227, 235
Clayton, Jack 163, 166, 233
Clover, Carol J. 189
Coates, Paul 6–7, 238
The Cockeyed Miracle (1946) 82
Coe, Brian 219
cold reading 120
Cold Sweat (1993) 71
Combes, Richard 187
consolation for the living 77–78
continuation of personality 4, 9
Coogan, Jackie 137
Cook, David A. 182
Cook, Victor W. 223
Cooper, Caroline M. 73
Corman, Roger 104
Cornell, A. D. 235
The Corpse (1969) 71
The Corsican Brothers 83
The Corsican Brothers (1852) 29

The Corsican Brothers (1898) 38, 42
Counts, Kyle 226
Cowie, Peter 166
Cox, Alex 143, 148
Craig, Robert 237
Cramer, Steven Philip 223
Cranford, Albert Lane 221
Creed, Barbara 147
Creepshow (1982) 78–79, 226
Crick, Robert A. 231
Criswell 231
Cropper, Paul 223
Crowe, Catherine 235
Crucible of Terror (1971) 71
cryptomnesia 91, 197
The Curse of the Cat People (1944) 161

Dad, the Angel and Me (1995) 139
Dance of Death 11, 12, 131
Date with an Angel (1987) 138
Dawes, Adwin A. 22, 30, 34, 218, 220, 221
The Dead Can't Lie (1988) 72, 96
Dead Man Walking (1995) 71
Dead of Night (1945) 58, 60, 100, 142–151, 158, 187, 188, 229, 230
Deadly Advice (1993) 82
Death Takes a Holiday (1933) 131, 132
Defending Your Life (1991) 134, 135, 136
Defoe, Daniel 3
DeMille, Cecil B. 52
demon lover 89
Denman, Chip 7
de Philipsthal, Paul 19
Derry, Charles 4, 106–107, 234
The Devil and Max Devlin (1981) 75
The Devil Commands (1941) 102–103, 224
The Devil in a Convent (1899) 38
Les Diaboliques (1955) 107, 226
Dickens, Charles 29, 31, 50, 76
Dickson, Antonia 238
Dickson, W. K. L. 199
Dickstein, Morris 189
Dingwall, Eric J. 235
Dircks, Henry 30, 31
Dr. Mabuse, der Spieler (1922) 49
Dr. Terror's House of Horrors (1964) 103, 231
Dr. Trimball's Verdict (1913) 40
Dolar, Mladen 3

Dona Flor and Her Two Husbands (1976) 228
Donald, James 218
Donaldson, Leslie 231
Donner party 190, 237
Don't Look Now (1973) 88, 120–121, 125, 238
Don't Take It to Heart (1944) 106
doppelgänger 110
Dracula 201
Dragonheart (1996) 231
The Dream of a Rarebit Fiend (1906) 229
dreams 4, 20, 24, 44–45, 46, 49–50, 65, 90, 92, 96, 103, 134, 138, 143, 144, 190, 193, 194, 203–204, 221, 232, 233, 234
Drek 228
Druxman, Michael B. 227
dualism 61
Duncan, Helen 230
Dunne, J. W. 66
Durgnat, Raymond 156
Duvall, Shelley 181
Duvivier, Julien 223
Dyall, Valentine 172
The Dybbuk (1937) 100
Dyson, Jeremy 4, 111, 148, 150, 165, 169, 224, 227, 233

Ealing Studios 143, 145
Earthbound (1920) 51
Earthbound (1940) 83
Eastwood, Clint 85
EC Comics 14
Eckhart, Meister 197
Edison, Thomas 41, 199
Edison Studios 131
Edmunds, Simeon 26, 220
Eisenbud, Jule 27, 220
Eisner, Lotte H. 6, 49
The Electric House (1922) 223
Ellis, John 154–155, 156, 157, 158
Elvis and the Colonel (1993) 228
Emily's Ghost (1991) 88
Enfield Poltergeist 2
Entente Cordiale (1912) 37
The Entity (1982) 89, 113, 228
epistemology 61
Epperson, Gordon 222–223
Estrin, Mark W. 230

Evans, Williams 1
The Exhibitor's Trade Review 48
The Exorcist (1973) 52, 97, 99, 100, 229
expiation of sins 75
extra sensory perception 88, 91, 102, 121, 124, 173, 181, 184, 185, 186, 188, 224, 230
The Extraordinary Seaman (1969) 69, 76
Eyles, Allen 224

Fairbanks, Douglas, Sr. 53
The Fairy of the Black Rocks (1905) 14
The Fall of the House of Usher (1960) 104, 189
Family Plot (1976) 119
Fanny and Alexanda (1982) 50
Far Away, So Close (1993) 232
Fatal Attraction (1987) 226
Faust and Mephistopheles (1898) 42
Féerie tradition 38–39
Feet of Clay (1924) 52
Feinman, Neil 230
Fell, John L. 11
Field of Dreams (1989) 73
Figure of Death 131–133
Film Blanc 58
film ghosts: aids related 94–95; anatomy of 55–56; attributes of 56–61; continuation without awareness of death 103–104; hungry 95–96; interactions with matter 67–70; of the living 110–111; lovers 89–94; in the machine 101–103; meetings with Elvis 101; of and for children 87–89; possession 97–101, 188; representations of 61–67; those who are unable to rest 70–75; who appear to be phoney but are real 111; who dispense sage advice 78–82; who return because of unfinished business 82–87; who use the living to play out a drama from their own lives 96–97
Finucane, R. C. 217, 226
The First of the Few (1943) 157
First World War 44, 46, 59, 60, 221
Fischer, Lucy 222
Fisher, Joe 228
Fisher, Len 225
Fitzhamon, Lewin 41
Flatliners (1990) 128–129, 130, 198, 237
Fluke (1995) 67, 129

Flying Deuces (1939) 138
Fodor, Nandor 26, 220
The Fog (1979) 72–73, 226
The Fog (1979) 72
For Heaven's Sake (1950) 140
Forever Darling (1956) 139–140
The Forgotten One (1990) 71, 73, 96, 104, 126
Fowkes, Katherine A. 58–59, 217, 224, 225, 227, 228
Francke, Lizzie 228
Frankenstein 201, 203
Frankenstein (1910) 131
Frankenstein (1931) 21
Franklin, Pamela 229
Franklin, Sidney 227
Frazer, John 37, 39, 222
Freud, Sigmund 5–6, 46, 82, 188
The Frighteners (1996) 116–117, 130, 133, 202
Fry, Carrol 197, 237
Full Circle (1976) 88, 233

Gabriel Over the White House (1933) 140
Gainsborough Studios 148
The Gambler's Wife (1899) 42
Gance, Abel 48, 106
Gaudreault, André 222
Gauld, Alan 222
genre issues 3–5
German Expressionism 49
Gernschein, Helmut 26
GESP 56, 66
Gettings, Fred 25, 26, 221
The Ghost (1911) 43
Ghost (1990) 58, 59, 65–66, 69, 93, 95, 98, 117, 135, 138, 192, 227, 231, 237
The Ghost and Mrs Muir (1947) 4, 90–91, 92
The Ghost Breaker (1914) (1922) 111
The Ghost Breakers (1940) 111
The Ghost Catchers (1944) 106
Ghost Chase (1987) 228
Ghost Chasers (1951) 122–123
Ghost Dad (1990) 126
Ghost Fever (1985) 90
The Ghost Goes West (1935) 52, 60, 62, 76, 105, 112, 224
The Ghost Goes Wild (1947) 81
The Ghost in the Invisible Bikini (1966) 75

The Ghost in the Machine (1993) 9, 102
Ghost of a Chance (1987) 136
Ghost of Dragstrip Hollow (1959) 111
The Ghost of Frankenstein (1942) 78
The Ghost of Old Morro (1917) 46
The Ghost of Rashmon Hall (1947) 235
The Ghost of the Moulin Rouge (1924) 52
Ghost Ship (1952) 113–114
Ghost Story (1974) 100, 112, 229
Ghost Story (1981) 73, 96, 186, 227
The Ghost Talks (1929) 54
Ghost Town (1988) 74
Ghost Train (1900) 42
Ghost Writer (1989) 71
Ghostbusters (1984) 112, 116
Ghostbusters II (1989) 116
Ghostbusters UK 230
Ghosts Can't Do It (1990) 100
The Ghosts of Berkeley Square (1947) 68, 70–71, 106, 115–116, 222, 226
Ghosts of Hanley House (1968) 84
Ghostwatch (1992) (TV Series) 2, 51
Gidding, Nelson 172
Gifford, Denis 38, 200, 222, 223, 230
Gifford, James 120
The Gift of Love (1958) 78
Gildersleeve's Ghost (1940) 79
Gish, Lillian 46, 47
Goldney, Kathleen Molly 235
Gomez, Joseph 121, 231
Goodbye Mr. Chips (1939) 203
Gorky, Maxim 199
Gothic 4, 22, 24. 46, 59, 105, 109, 111, 161, 169, 172, 188, 229
Gough-Yates, Kevin 233
Grafe, Frieda 59, 92
Grant, Cary 227
The Greatest Question (1919) 44, 46, 234
Greene, Graham 199–200
Griffith D. W. 43, 44–46, 137, 234
Grixti, Joseph 2, 186, 235
Grove, Allen W. 13
A Guardian Angel (1899) 223
Guinness, Alec 225
Gunning, Tom 35, 36
Gurney, Edmund 223
A Guy Named Joe (1943) 93
The Guyra Ghost Mystery (1921) 51

Haggerty, George E. 160
Haill, Catherine 11, 221
Hala, James 181, 185
The Halfway House (1944) 60, 79, 80, 145, 224, 226
Hall, Trevor H. 235
Halliwell, Leslie 59
Hamer, Robert 143
Hamlet (1913) 65
Hammer Studios 148
Hammond, Paul 14, 36, 38, 219, 222
Hanson, Patricia King 155
Happy Land (1943) 77, 93
Harding, Colin 218, 221, 222, 223, 238
Hardy, Phil 174, 222, 223, 227, 229
Harlow, Jean 199
Harper, Sue 59, 226, 233
Harris, Melvin 229, 233
Harrison's Reports 51, 59
Hartnoll, G. 235
Hatchet for a Honeymoon (1969) 225
Haunted (1995) 107
The Haunted Castle (1896) 38
The Haunted Curiosity Shop (1901) 42
The Haunted Hotel (1907) 40
haunted house 104–110
The Haunted House (1925) 105
Haunted House Films 57
The Haunted Oak (1904) 41
The Haunted Palace (1963) 100
The Haunted Scene Painter (1904) 41
The Haunted Screen (1973) 49
The Haunting (1963) 58, 70, 104, 105, 108, 112, 163, 168–180, 187, 189, 206, 233
The Haunting of Hill House (1959) 169
The Haunting of Lisa (1995) 111
The Haunting of M (1979) 71–72
The Haunting of Seacliffe Inn (1994) 74, 97
Hawthorne, Nathaniel 106
Haynes, Renée 235
The Headless Ghost (1959) 83–84
Healy, Tony 223
Heard, Mervyn 33, 219, 222
Hearn, Lafcadio 23
Heart Condition (1990) 68, 99
Hearts and Souls (1993) 84
Heaven 75, 133–134, 135, 136, 139, 140, 205
Heaven Can Wait (1943) 226

Heaven Can Wait (1978) 84, 100, 134, 224, 225
Heaven Only Knows (1947) 140
Heavenly Days (1944) 81
The Heavenly Kid (1985) 139
Hecht, Hermann 15, 16, 17, 21, 22, 31, 200, 221, 222
Hell 135, 136
Heller, Terry 234
Hello Mary Lou, Prom Night 2 (1987) 109
Hepworth Cecil M. 23, 30, 32, 40, 41, 65, 222
Hepworth, T. C. 16
Herbert, Stephen 222
Here Comes Mr. Jordan (1941) 84, 100, 134
Hideaway (1995) 129–130
Hienger, Jörg 4
High Plains Drifter (1973) 84–85, 90
High Spirits (1988) 71, 92, 112, 199, 229
Higson, Andrew 161, 162, 234
Hill, Geoffrey 226
History of the Kinetograph (1895) 199
Hitchcock, Alfred 21, 107, 144, 149
Hoare, Philip 226
Hoffmann, Ernst 110
Hogan, David J. 172, 181, 228
Hoile, Christopher 182
Holbein, Hans 12, 14
Holland, Larry Lee 173
Home, D.D. 35
Homicidal (1961) 166
Hong Kong 92–93
Hopkins, Albert A. 13, 27, 30–31, 36, 220, 221
The Horn Blows at Midnight (1945) 134, 138, 201, 232
Horror and Fantasy 5–6
The Horror Show (1989) 102
Houdini, Harry 119
House (1985) 228
House of Darkness (1947) 71, 84
House of Mystery (1961) 114–115
The House of the Seven Gables (1851) 106
The House of the Spirits (1994) 78
The House Where Evil Dwells (1982) 97
Houston, Beverle 230
How It feels to Be Run Over (1900) 40
Howard, Leslie 136

The Hudsucker Proxy (1994) 138
The Human Comedy (1943) 93
Hurst, Brian Desmond 77
Hutchings, Peter 143, 144–145, 146, 147, 158–159
Huygens, Christiaan 17, 218, 219
Hyslop, James H. 221

I Walked with a Zombie (1943) 227
I Want You (1951) 58
Illusions Fantasmagoriques (1898) 41
The Illustrated Man (1969) 85–86
incest 96, 100
Industrial Light and Magic 224
The Infernal Cauldron (1903) 38
Inglis, Brian 217
Ingram, Rex 52
The Inn Where No Man Rests (1903) 37
The Innocents (1961) 56, 58, 114, 159–168, 227, 229, 233
Internet 9126
Intersection (1994) 126
Intolerance (1916) 133
The Iron Mask (1929) 53
Irving, Henry 35
Isherwood, Robert M. 17
It Happened Tomorrow (1944) 81
It's a Wonderful Life (1946) 138–139
Izod, John 230

J. D.'s Revenge (1976) 99
J'Accuse (1919), (1938) 48
Jack the Ripper Quartette (1958) 71, 111, 218
Jackson, Peter 202
Jackson, Rosemary 234
Jackson, Shirley 169, 172–173
Jacob's Ladder (1990) 103, 129, 130, 135, 136, 138, 183, 191–198, 204, 231, 234
James, Henry 110, 159
Jancovich, Mark 144
Jassy (1947) 224
Jeffress, Lynn 181–182, 183
Jeffrey (1995) 95
Jenkins, Steve 228
Johns, John 58, 61, 217, 227, 231
Johnson, Diane 235
Jones, Alan 229
Jordan, Neil 92, 229
Jurkiewicz, Ken 237

Kael, Pauline 44, 76, 148, 160, 162, 185, 190, 199, 225, 231
Kawin, Bruce 233
Keaton, Buster 223
Kendrick, Walter 221
Kerr, Deborah 165
Keyser, Lester J. 77, 226
The Kid (1921) 137
Kieslowski, Krzysztof 225
Kill, Baby, Kill (1966) 236
Kind Hearts and Coronets (1949) 225
Kinder, Marsha 230
King, Stephen 2, 14, 105, 181, 184, 185
Kipps (1942) 64–65
Kircher, Athanasius 13, 17
Kirtz, Mary K. 226
Kiss Me Goodbye (1982) 93, 94, 100–101, 227
Kiss of the Best (1990) 68
Kneale, Nigel 238
The Knight of the Snows (1912) 38
Kobal, John 60
Körkarlen (1958) 223
Kovács, Katherine Singer 38
Kubrick, Stanley 181, 182, 184, 185, 187, 188, 206
Kurtz, Léonard P. 12, 231, 233

Lady in White (1988) 69, 87, 133
Lagerlöf, Selma 49–50
Lambert, G. W. 179
Landy, Marcia 60, 230, 233
Lang, Fritz 14, 131
Lange-Fuchs, Hauke 16
Last Action Hero (1993) 132
Last Gasp (1995) 98–99
The Last Winter (1990) 68, 88
Latin Quarter (1945) 59, 113, 119, 232, 235
Laurel and Hardy 138
Lavery, David 231
The Lawnmower Man (1992) 9, 102
Layton, David 221
Leahy, Kevin 221
Leatherdale, Clive 8
Leayman, Charles D. 237
Ledwon, Lenora 4
Leemann, Sergio 235
The Legend of Cryin' Ryan (1998) 88
The Legend of Hell House (1972) 90, 104, 107–108, 112–113, 121, 187, 235

Legend of Lylah Clare (1968) 98
Leites, Nathan 67
Leni, Paul 106
Lewis, Matthew 28
Lewton, Val 227
Liebowitz, Flo 181–182, 183, 187
Liesegang, Franz Paul 13, 17, 218, 219, 220
Life After Life (1975) 124
A Life Less Ordinary (1997) 139
Lifeboat (1994) 232
Lifeforce (1985) 67
Lifepod (1993) 232
Liliom (1930) (1933) 75
Linder, Max 37, 106
Little Ghost (1996) 88, 232
London, Rose 229
London Belongs to Me (1948) 118–119, 122
Love and Death (1975) 132
Lovesick (1983) 82
Low, Rachael 38, 46, 218, 223
Lumière Brothers 37, 199, 201
Lyne, Adrian 204, 237
Lyttle, John 59, 238

MacGregor, Geddes 231
MacKenzie, Andrew 167, 229
Made in Heaven (1987) 126, 133, 134, 232
Madigan, Mark J. 186
Magic (1978) 100
magic lantern 11, 19, 23, 30
The Magic Sword (1907) 42
Malleson, Miles 233
Man Alive (1945) 122
The Man in the Trunk (1942) 69–70, 71
The Man That Might Have Been (1914) 46, 48
The Man Without a Soul (1916) 218
Manchel, Frank 190
Le Manoir du Diable (1896) 234
Manvell, Roger 38, 223
Map of the Human Heart (1993) 125
Mare Nostrum (1926) 52, 126, 131
Maria Martin (1902) 43
Mark of the Devil (1984) 85, 229
The Market of Souls (1919) 48
Markey, Constance 205, 239
Marvin, Lee 237
Mary Jane's Mishap (1903) 42

Mason, A. E. W. 118
Mason, James 139–140
The Masque of Red Death (1960) 133
Matheson, Richard 229
A Matter of Life and Death (1946) 84, 133–134, 137, 144, 149, 151–154, 155–159, 193, 201, 224, 231, 233, 234
Mattson, Arne 223
Maxie (1985) 98
Mayersberg, Paul 6, 186, 235, 236
Mayne, Judith 237
Maytime (1937) 90
McCarty, John 229, 230
McClenon, James 2, 206, 224
McDougal, Stuart Y. 160
McGrath, Roberta 219
McKernan, Luke 222
The Meaning of Life (1983) 132, 136
The Medium (1934) 60, 113
The Medium (1951) 230
The Medium Exposed (1906) 42
mediums 19
mediumship 98, 114, 117–124
Meeker, David 224
Meet Joe Black (1998) 231
Meet John Doe (1941) 231
Meet Mr. Lucifer (1953) 7
Méliès, Georges 12, 14, 24, 28, 35, 36–39, 40, 41, 43, 50, 105, 201, 204, 234
melodrama 29
memories 73
Mental Radio (1930) 102
The Mephisto Waltz (1971) 100
The Mermaid (1910) 43, 52, 53, 65, 126
Messter, Oskar 32, 131
Metropolis (1927) 14, 131
Metz, Christian 150, 200
Michael (1996) 139
A Midsummer Night's Dream 158
The Milagro Beanfield War (1988) 79
Millbank, Alison 229
Milne, Tom 227, 230, 231
Miracle in the Rain (1956) 93
Miracles for Sale (1939) 119
mirror projection 11
mirrors 15
The Miser's Doom (1899) 43
Mr. Destiny (1990) 232
Mizoguchi, Kenji 53
The Monster (1925) 105
Moody, Raymond A. 124, 125, 231, 239

Moretti, Franco 201
The Motorist (1906) 40
Moxie, Keith 218
Ms. Scrooge (1997) 226
Mulvey, Laura 225
mummies 202
Murphy, Robert 163, 224, 234
Musser, Charles 11, 19, 23, 35, 238
My Friend Walter (1992) 88
Mystery Train (1989) 101
A Mystic Reincarnation (1902) 41
The Mystic Swing (1900) 41

Neale, Stephen 200, 228
Neame, Elwin 223
near-death experiences 77, 86, 95, 117, 124–130, 140, 195, 198
Nelson, Thomas Allen 107, 188
Neptune's Daughters (1900) 42
The Nesting (1981) 84, 229
New York Times 51
The Newlydeads (1987) 109
Newman, Kim 4, 89, 106, 109, 189, 192, 231
Nicholls, Peter 89, 182, 217, 225, 227, 228, 230
Nicholson, Jack 181
Nickell, Joe 25, 229
Night of the Demon (1956) 112, 119, 120
Night of the Ghouls (1959) 111
A Nightmare on Elm Street 3: Dream Warriors (1987) 71
The Night-side of Nature (1848) 235
Niven, David 69
Niver, Kemp R. 222
No End (1988) 225
Nomads (1986) 99, 220, 229
A Novice at X-Rays 14
Nurse Sherri (1977) 228

An Occurrence at Owl Creek Bridge (1892) 192
An Occurrence at Owl Creek Bridge (1962) 234
Oehler, Andrew 20
The Omen (1976) 60
Omni magazine 129
On Borrowed Time (1939) 133
One Glorious Day (1922) 51
The Oracle (1986) 117
Orgy of the Dead (1956) 231

The Other (1972) 228, 234
Our Town (1940) 86
out of body experiences 128
Outward Bound (1930) 60, 136, 224

Paige, Linda Rohrer 227
The Palace of the Arabian Nights (1905) 14
Pale Rider (1985) 85
Palmer, James W. 162, 166–167, 230, 234
Paradise Lost (1910) 137
Paramount Studios 224
parapsychologist 108, 112–117
Paris, France (1994) 228
Parish, James Robert 4, 84, 223, 224
Parkinson, David 238
Parrish, James Robert 58
Parsifal (1904) 33
The Passion of a Woman Teacher (1926) 53
The Passion of Darkly Noon (1996) 79
Paul, Robert 14, 40, 41, 42
Paul, William 183, 236
Pearsall, Ronald 219, 220, 226
Pearson, Roberta E. 45
Peary, Danny 231
Pepper, John Henry 23
Pepper's ghost 11, 29–33
Perez, Gilberto 238
Permutt, Cyril 220
Perry, George 144
Perry, Michael 228
Pet Sematary (1989) 229
Peter Ibbetson (1921) (1935) 90
Peter Ibbetson (1935) 62
Phantasm (series) 217
phantasmagoria 11, 18–25, 28, 33, 34
The Phantom (1996) 79
The Phantom Carriage (1920) 131
The Phantom Chariot (1920) 49, 50, 90
The Phantom Honeymoon (1919) 48
Phantom of the Opera (1925) 14, 21
The Phantom Speaks (1945) 99
The Phantom Thief (1946) 118
Phantoms (1990) 68
Philadelphia, Jacob 19–20
Philidor, François 233
Philidor, Paul 20
Philipsthal, Paul de 18, 19
Photographing a Ghost (1898) 42

Photographing Fairies (1997) 65, 67
Picknett, Lynn 220
Pirie, David 147, 150
A Place of One's Own (1945) 68, 99, 224
Playfair, Guy Lyon 217
Plumb, Hay 223
Poe, Edgar Allan 8, 44, 110
Point Blank (1967) 237
point of view 64, 65–66
Poltergeist (1982) 70, 108, 112, 188, 225
Poltergeist 3 (1988) 112
poltergeists 2, 5, 8, 35, 37, 38, 41, 62, 70, 98, 105, 108, 168, 172, 179, 223, 230
Popple, Simon 218, 221, 222, 223, 238
Porter, Edwin S. 33, 42
Porter, Vincent 233
Portrait of Jennie (1948) 66–67, 103–104, 237
possession 51–52, 54, 83, 96, 97–101, 108, 119, 121, 150, 161, 165, 166, 182, 184, 188, 204, 235
Possession of Joel Delaney (1971) 99
Powell, Michael 152, 155, 156
The Preacher's Wife (1996) 139
Presley, Elvis 101
Price, David 221
Prison (1987) 109
Prom Night 3: The Last Kiss (1989) 109
Pronay, Nicholas 233
The Prophecy (1994) 137
Psycho (1960) 107, 144, 149, 166, 171
psychokinesis (PK) 5, 70, 109, 172, 182, 188
Purgatory 133, 134–136

The Queen of Spades (1948) 71, 235

Ralston, W. R. S. 223
Randall and Hopkirk (Deceased) (TV series) 4, 94–95, 117
Rashomon (1950) 119–120, 224
Ray, Robert B. 6, 226
Reade, Eric 223
Rebecca (1940) 204
Recchia, Edward 167, 234
recurrent spontaneous psychokinesis (RSPK) 172, 180, 185, 230
reincarnation 2, 73, 96, 100, 129, 134, 136, 138, 224

The Reincarnation of Peter Proud (1974) 126
The Remarkable Andrew (1942) 82–83
Repulsion (1965) 163, 235
Resurrection (1980) 125
Retribution (1988) 98
The Return of Peter Grimm (1935) 70
Return to Glennascaul (1951) 107
revenge 72, 84–86, 97
Revolt of the Zombies (1936) 104
Rhine, J. B. 173
Rhodes, Gary Don 60, 189, 232, 235, 237
Richards, Jeffrey 226
Riley, Michael 230
Ring, Kenneth 195
Roadrunner cartoons 185
Robertson, Étienne-Gaspard 13, 20–23
Robertson, Patrick 38, 223
Robinson, David 22, 218
Robinson, Phil Alden 226
Roeg, Nicolas 121
Rogers, Will 51
Romney, Jonathan 187, 235, 236
Rooney, Mickey 77
Rosenfeld, Sybil 22
Rowell, Geoffrey 76
Rubin, Bruce Joel 129, 192, 231
Ruby (1977) 98, 126
Ryle, Gilbert 228

Sabom, Michael 129
Sadoul, Georges 36, 38
Salt, Barry 6, 222, 223, 233
Sandell, Roger 24
Sanderson, Mark 57, 121, 200
Sarris, Andrew 132
Scared Stiff (1945) (1953) 111
Schefer, Jean-Louis 200
Schröpfer, Johann 16, 17–18, 20
Scott, Walter 156
Scrooge: or, Marley's Ghost (1901) 42, 76
Scrooged (1988) 76
The Scroundrel (1935) 75
Seance on a Wet Afternoon (1964) 123–124
The Search for Bridey Murphy 2
The Sea's Shadow (1912) 131
Second World War 59–60
Seidman, Steve 164

Seiler, Lewis 54
selective perception 61–62
The Sender (1982) 227
Senn, Bryan 58, 61, 217, 227, 231, 235, 239
Sentimental Journey (1946) 78
The Seventh Seal (1956) 14, 50, 77, 131, 132–133, 218
Sewell, Vernon 113–116
Shadow Dancing (1988) 98
Shallow Grave (1994) 63
She's Back (1989) 86
The Shining (1980) 104, 107, 108, 109, 172, 180–190, 226
Shipman, David 42, 48, 223, 238
Shipman, Pat 237
The Shocker (1989) 102
Siesta (1987) 103
silent cinema 34–54
Silent Tongue (1993) 226, 228
Silver, Alain J. 159, 164, 179, 180
Simon, Simone 227
Sinclair, Upton 102, 235
Sinyard, Neil 85, 161, 166, 227
Sir Arne's Treasure (1919) 49
The Sixth Man (1997) 232
Sjöström, Victor 49, 223
Skal, David J. 14, 191, 238
The Skeleton Dance (1930) 14
skeletons 12–14, 39, 40, 41, 45, 53
Slaughterhouse Rock (1987) 109
The Sleeping Car (1990) 229
Slide, Anthony 47, 223
Smilin' Through (1922) (1932) 90
Smith, Albert E. 40
Smith, David H. 85
Smith, Don G. 163, 166, 168, 234
Smith, G.A. 14, 38, 41–42
Smith, Greg 181, 183, 235, 236, 237
Smith, James F. 184
Snyder, Stephen 182, 185
Society for Psychical Research 42, 114, 223, 229
Solaris (1972) 5, 57
Somewhere in Time (1980) 125, 130, 205
The Sorrows of Satan (1925) 137
soul 67
Spectrescope 31
Spellbound (1941) 119
Spignesi, Stephen J. 187

The Spirit Is Willing (1967) 97
The Spirit of the Conqueror (1914) 44
spirit photography 11, 25–28, 32, 62
A Spiritualist Photographer (1903) 39
Spook Chasers (1957) 111
Stafford, Barbara 218, 219
Star Trek II: The Wrath of Khan (1982) 205
Star Wars (series) 205
Stein, Gordon 229
Steinbeck, John 185
Stenger, Erich 225
Stiller, Mauritz 49
Stilwell, Robynn 228
Stockton, Jerry 231
Stone, Marianne 230
Strange Adventures of a New York Drummer (1899) 41
Strangler of the Swamp (1945) 84
Straub, Peter 227
Strick, Philip 136
The Student of Prague (1913) (1926) (1936) 110
Summer Interlude (1951) 225
Sunset Boulevard (1950) 62–63
Supernatural (1933) 98, 118
The Supernaturals (1986) 73
The Survivor (1981) 103
Svehla, Gary J. 165, 218
Svehla, Susan 165, 218
Switch (1991) 126, 137
symbolic representations 62

Tabori, Paul 235
Talbot, Frederick 222
Tales from the Crypt (1972) 103
The Tales of Hoffman (1951) 133
Tales of Terror (1962) 8, 96
Talmadge, Norma 227
Taylor, Bernard 147
Technicolor 158
technology 101–103, 107–108, 112, 116, 127–129, 198
Teitelbaum, Sheldon 237, 238
telepathy 64, 120
Telotte, J. P. 89
The Terror (1963) 227
That's the Spirit (1945) 75
theatrical ghosts 28–29
Thesiger, Ernest 68

268 Index

Things to Do in Denver When You're Dead (1995) 133
13 Ghosts (1960) 105
The Thirteenth Chair 232
The Thirteenth Chair (1930) (1937) 230
Thomas, Paul 238
Thompson, John O. 227
Thompson, Paul B. 18
Thomson, David 237
The Three Godfathers (1948) 10, 63
Thunder Rock (1942) 81
The Time of Their Lives (1946) 83
timeslips 79
Tired Death (1921) 131–132
Titterington, P.L. 182, 187, 235, 236
To Die For (1993) 94–95, 138
Todorov, Tzvetan 159, 160, 238
The Tomb of Ligeia (1965) 96, 99
Topper (1937) 4, 58, 59, 62, 83, 86, 229
Topper Returns (1941) 69, 86–87
Topper Takes a Trip (1939) 86
Tormented (1960) 86, 226
Toulmin, Vanessa 221
Tower of London (1939) (1962) 218
Trewey, Lucien 218
trick films 35–36, 39, 43, 105
A Trip to Paradise (1921) 75
True Romance (1993) 101
Truly, Madly, Deeply (1990) 93–94, 227
Trumbull, Douglas 128, 192
Tudor, Andrew 3, 5, 57–58, 60–61, 61, 234
Turim, Maureen 49, 50
The Turn of the Screw (1898) 9, 159, 186
Twice Dead (1988) 106
Twice Told Tales (1963) 106
Twister (1996) 181
Twitchell, James B. 95, 203
Two of a Kind (1983) 140
2001 (1968) 128
Two Thousand Maniacs (1964) 73
Tyler, Parker 86, 201, 231, 238
Tyrrell, G. N. M. 224, 225

Ugetsu Monogatari (1953) 224
Umland, Samuel J. 182, 183
Uncle Josh in a Spooky Hotel (1900) 41
Underwood, Peter 225
Undressing Extraordinary (1901) 14

The Uninvited (1944) 58, 63, 98, 105, 224
Universal Soldier (1992) 104
unquiet ghosts 70–75
Unseen Hands (1924) 52
Ursini, James 159, 179, 180
Usai, Paolo Cherchi 33, 223

Valenti, Peter L. 58
Valk, Frederick 230, 232
vampires 2, 3, 5, 8, 9, 46, 58, 72, 92, 201, 202, 203, 218, 222, 238
The Vanishing Lady (1896) 14, 39, 41, 42
Vardac, A. Nicholas 34–35
Varey, J. E. 220
Varnado, S. L. 110
Vault of Horror (1973) 103
The Veil (1958) 110–111, 218
Vertigo (1958) 21
Virilio, Paul 7, 32, 136
virtual reality 127
A Visit to the Spiritualist (1899) 40
Vitagraph 40
vital spark 67

Wagenknecht, Edward 44, 47
Waggoner, Diane 217
Waller, G. A. 201, 238
Ward, Vincent 133
Warlock Moon (1973) 71
Warman, Erich 155, 233
Warner, Marina 200
Wayne's World 2 (1993) 228
Wee Lady Betty (1917) 227
Welles, Orson 234
Welsh, James, Michael 223
werewolves 5, 9, 202, 203, 218
What Dreams May Come (1998) 133, 136
Whimsical Illusions (1910) 39
Wild Strawberries (1957) 50
Wilder, Thornton 86, 226
Williams, Randall 32
Wilson, David 231
Wilson, Edmund 161
Wilson, Kristi 120
Wilson, Marilynn 226
Wings of Desire (1987) 137, 232
Wings of Fame (1990) 134–135
Wired (1989) 228

Wirth, Jean 218
Wise, Robert 169, 173–174
The Witch (1906) 38
Witchboard (1986) 117, 119
Witchboard III: The Possession (1995) 117, 204
witchcraft 75
Witchtrap (1989) 231
Without a Soul (1916) 131
Wizard of Oz (1939) 126–127
Wolfenstein, Martha 66, 67
Wollen, Peter 21, 200
Won Through a Medium (1911) 43, 117–118
Wonder Man (1945) 83, 99, 201
Wood, Robin 5, 144

Woodward, Ian 218
The Wraith (1986) 84

The X-Files (television series) 2, 237
X-rays 13, 121
X-Rays (1897) 14

You'll Never Find Out (1940) 118
Young, Thomas 220

Zecca, Ferdinand 42
Zero Patience (1993) 94
Ziegfeld Follies (1945) 127, 134, 203
zombies 203
Zone 39 (1993) 63

www.ingramcontent.com/pod-product-compliance
Lightning Source LLC
Chambersburg PA
CBHW030613230426
43661CB00053B/1965